W9-BLM-323

COMMUNITY DEVELOPMENT AROUND THE WORLD:
PRACTICE, THEORY, RESEARCH, TRAINING

New social structures, new agencies, and new social movements have had a dramatic impact on community development across the world. In this book, more than forty authors in six countries representing the major regions of the world offer a truly global perspective on the changing nature of the practice and theory of community development.

The collection approaches community development from many different angles, featuring a critical review of the international literature, twenty detailed case studies dealing with key issues, and separate country-by-country studies of education, research, and theory. Despite obvious differences between countries in their economic, political, and socio-cultural contexts of practice, common themes emerge. The book concludes with a new framework theory for use in policy development, program planning, and alternative practice.

Comprehensive and challenging, *Community Development around the World* is essential reading for students, analysts, and practitioners in the field.

HUBERT CAMPFENS is Professor of Community Development and Social Planning in the Faculty of Social Work at Wilfrid Laurier University, Ontario, Canada.

EDITED BY HUBERT CAMPFENS

Community Development around the World: Practice, Theory, Research, Training

UNIVERSITY OF TORONTO PRESS
Toronto Buffalo London

© University of Toronto Press Incorporated 1997
Toronto Buffalo London
Printed in Canada

Reprinted 1999

ISBN 0-8020-0903-4 (cloth)
ISBN 0-8020-7884-2 (paper)

Printed on acid-free paper

Canadian Cataloguing in Publication Data

Main entry under title:
Community development around the world

Includes bibliographical references.
ISBN 0-8020-0903-4 (bound)
ISBN 0-8020-7884-2 (pbk.)

1. Community development – Cross-cultural studies.
I. Campfens, Hubert.

HN49.C6C647 1997   307.1'4   C96-931390-X

University of Toronto Press acknowledges the financial assistance to its
publishing program of the Canada Council and the Ontario Arts Council.

Contents

Preface

The idea of doing a study on community development (CD) involving countries from various regions of the world arose more as an after-thought while I was taking off in January 1993, for the better part of the year, on various technical missions and as a visiting professor to Chile, Israel, the Netherlands, Ghana, Bangladesh, and Nepal. At this point there was no formal proposal and no financial support. The timing to take on such a project – while I was personally touching on each major region of the world in the same year – seemed perfect. I would be long enough in each country to assess the appropriateness and feasibility of its participation, and to form and get to know a national team to collaborate with me on the project.

To ensure cultural authenticity and an in-depth look at these countries' experiences with CD, there had to be a knowledgeable national team in each country to whom I could delegate full responsibility for the various tasks involved. Too often studies of this kind are carried out by outsiders, who base their results on limited field observations and who inject their own cultural perspectives, interests, and time-specific and interpretative biases into their work. My long involvement in international co-operation, particularly in Latin American countries, has made me fully aware of the perils of intellectual imperialism, which is what results when Western practitioners and scholars interpret other people's experience without acknowledging the vastly different cultural realities and perspectives that are at play. The idea of national teams, therefore, became a central feature of the project for me. However, my difficulties in putting this idea into practice on the proposed scale, and in seeing it through, at times appeared insurmountable, and more than once the project almost collapsed.

Regarding the three participating countries of the developed, industrialized North (Canada, the Netherlands, and Israel) we could usually count on the support of the institutions with which the team members were affiliated, and this helped keep the project at a low budget. Most of all, the co-ordinators and I could communicate instantaneously by fax, e-mail, and the Internet. Still, there were obstacles to overcome, such as language differences, which required that Dutch and Hebrew texts be translated into English. This involved considerable time and expense for the respective teams.

The project was far more complicated with respect to the three Third World countries. It was not merely a problem of translating the material from Bengali, Spanish, and local dialects into English. The participating authors had the desired qualifications, experiences, and commitment to produce a high-quality study but lacked institutional support and access to the modern communications technology that is taken for granted in the more affluent nations. To take Ghana as a case in point, the circumstances of the country's study co-ordinator, Fred Abloh, made it necessary for us to correspond through regular mail, which either got lost or took weeks to arrive, with Fred working often in the interior. This slowed down the progress of the project. Also, he did not have access to the facilities necessary to address the research and theory parts of the country's study. Luckily, and with the approval of Fred, I was able to bring on board Steven Ameyaw, a Ghanaian associated with a Canadian university, who had done a great deal of field research for his doctoral thesis on women and development in his country of birth. A grant from the Academic Development Fund of Wilfrid Laurier University covered some of the costs of the study team operating in Ghana.

There were similar obstacles relating to the Bangladesh study. In that country I encountered a number of people in the city of Rajshahi in the Bengal region who had a great deal to contribute to the project because of their experience and critical reflections. But in order to communicate with the Bangladesh team, I had to rely on the Canadian High Commission in Dhakka to act as a go-between. Important to mention here is that the first financial support for this international project came from the Canadian International Development Agency (CIDA), through its regional office in Dhakka. The Bangladesh team and I had presented our grant proposal to that office. The support that they offered made possible the participation of Bangladesh.

As for the Latin American region, I had counted on the participation of Peru because of its considerable history in CD and my own deep involvement with that country during one of the most difficult periods in its history, from 1985 to 1990. Because of continuing political and economic problems, I had to turn to Chile at the eleventh hour. Teresa Quiroz and Diego Palma, who are both well known throughout Latin America for their contribution to research and development practice, and who had returned to Chile in 1989 after many years of exile, agreed to join the study after some arm twisting on my part and the promise of external funding. The Inter-American Development Bank provided a grant supporting the Chilean study.

The Ministry of Human Resources Development of the Government of Canada followed later with a grant to support my own activities as international co-ordinator and general editor. One such activity involved getting the leaders of the various national teams together in Amsterdam in the summer of 1994 so that we could exchange the first drafts of our respective contributions and decide on the outline of the final, comparative chapter. That gathering generated much synergy and excitement as we became fully aware of the uniqueness and distinctiveness of this international project, which was a coming together of vastly different cultures, economic and political realities, and perspectives. As one participant observed at our Amsterdam workshop, the composition of the book's contributors reflects the diversity of the human community we are trying to write about. Our group leaps the bounds of culture, religion, ideology, social status, income, gender, age, sexual orientation, academic discipline, profession, and institutional and community affiliation. What we all share is a belief in and a commitment to advance the cause of community and human development.

For a book such as this, I needed to find a publisher with a strong reputation and reach for international marketing. This search meant entering territory unknown to me, and I soon became aware of the growing complexities of the highly competitive international publishing world, and of the technological breakthroughs that now make possible publication in forms other than the printed word. From the various offers received for publication, I chose University of Toronto Press (my 'alma matter'), not only because it met the criteria mentioned earlier, but also because its executive editor, Virgil Duff, showed genuine interest and provided continuing support from our first point of contact.

The assistance provided by the people working closely with me throughout the production of this book has been truly enormous, as this preface has already made clear. My first thanks go to the co-ordinators of the six national studies. They stood by their promise to deliver their parts in sometimes the most difficult of professional and personal circumstances. Of course I applied a principle that I had learned earlier in my professional life: when you want something of quality to get done, you go after the busiest and most involved people. The co-ordinators in turn brought capable people on board, each of whom shared their experience and expertise, from which we all benefit.

The person I relied on from day to day, to get this whole international production together and in proper form for the publisher, has been Gail Wideman. She went well beyond the call of duty in giving much of her own time to this project. To her I owe my deepest gratitude. Others have also assisted along the way, such as Joseph Katan, who developed with me the original framework for the study; Teresa Quiroz and Profulla Sarker, who joined me in grant proposal writing, and made possible the participation of their respective countries; and several of the national co-ordinators, who helped me formulate my earlier drafts of the intro-duction – specifically, Joseph Katan, André Jacob, Harvey Stalwick, and Cees de Wit. To my son David, a graduate in development planning and international co-operation, goes also a special thanks for his valu-able comments and editing assistance. And then there are the various master's and doctoral students who also have lent their support by reading the entire study and providing comments. These include Norma Profitt, Linda Snyder, Jennifer Proudfoot, Sherilyn McGregor, and Iara Lessa.

It is my partner, Monica Escobar, who introduced me in 1986 to the rich experiences of Latin America shantytown women in organizing and grass roots CD, especially in Lima, Peru, who gave me the inspira-tion for this project and the continuing moral support to carry on. And finally, I am grateful to all those countless people in communities across the globe who contributed to the case studies we offer here through their activities, views, and aspirations for a better future.

Acronyms

General

CD	Community development
CED	Community economic development
CDC	Community development corporations
GATT	General Agreement of Tariffs and Trade
GDP	Gross domestic product
GNP	Gross national product
IMF	International Monetary Fund
NGO	Nongovernmental Organization
UN	United Nations
OD	Organizational development
OECD	Organization for Economic Cooperation and Development
SAP	Structural adjustment program

Canada

BBBF	Better Beginnings, Better Futures
CCVT	Canadian Centre for Victims of Torture
CMHC	Canadian Mortgage and Housing Corporation
ENF	Entre Nous Femmes
ESL	English as a Second Language

Netherlands

EC	European Community
NIZW	National Institute of Care and Welfare
SCD	Social and Cultural Development

Israel
NSC   Neighbourhood steering committee
SCW   Service for Community Work
UO   Ultra-Orthodox

Ghana
ICCES   Integrated Community Centres for Employment Skills
IGP   Income-generating projects
PAMSCAD   Program of Action to Mitigate the Social Cost of
             Adjustment

Bangladesh
BARD   Bangladesh Academy for Rural Development
BRAC   Bangladesh Rural Advancement Committee
CARITAS   International NGO (Roman Catholic, Rome-based)
ESCAP   Economic and Social Commission for Asia and the
             Pacific
FDP   Family Development Program
GB   Grameen Bank
GO   Government organization
IRDP   Integrated Rural Development Program
KSS   Village level co-operation societies
MC   Mothers' centre
RCD   Rural community development
SIP   Slum improvement project
UCD   Urban community development
UNDP   United Nations Development Program
UNICEF   United Nations Children's Fund
TCCA   *Thana* Central Co-operative Association

Chile
CDL   Co-ordination for local development
CEAAL   Latin American Association for Adult Education
CEPAL-ECLA   Economic Commission for Latin America
COREDE   Regional Council for Development
FLASCO   Latin American Faculty of Social Sciences
FOSIS   Solidarity and Social Initiative Fund
MECE   Program for the Improvement of Equity and Quality
             in Education
MINEDUC   Ministry of Education

MIDEPLAN	Ministry of Planning and Co-operation
MINESAL	Ministry of Health
PIIE	Interdisciplinary Program for the Investigation of Education
TILNA	Workshops for Local Integration at the National Level

Part 1

Introduction to the
International Study

HUBERT CAMPFENS

Introduction

During the 1980s and 1990s, countries throughout the world were confronted with the dramatic impact of global restructuring. This has resulted in new tensions at the community and group levels; these tensions, in turn, have influenced the practice and theory of community development (CD). CD is, of course, also defined by the cultural, social, political, and economic realities of the particular countries and communities where it is carried out.

For example, in Bangladesh, which has a traditional rural society rooted in Islam, the central question is how to deal humanely with massive poverty and with a rapidly expanding population that is fast approaching its ecological limits. In Israel, one of the main questions in CD is how to integrate the large numbers of Jewish immigrants – who come from a variety of countries and differ greatly in socio-cultural background – into a modern, prosperous society that is an active welfare state. Also of central importance there is how to maintain political and social stability in a heterogeneous society characterized by splits between various ethnic, social, and religious groups. In the Netherlands some of the main factors at play in CD are the existence of an advanced welfare state, and the highly individualistic and consumer-oriented lifestyle now enjoyed by a growing majority. Some people perceive these factors as contributing to a loss of community and as undermining the long-standing tradition of mutual aid at the interpersonal level that once extended beyond the immediate family and close friends.

At this juncture it is essential to examine the current state of CD practice and theory with the goal of determining the shifting patterns and common themes and pulling them together in a relevant theoretical framework. This is especially important because of the renewed interest in CD found in many parts of the world.

NEW AGENTS OF COMMUNITY DEVELOPMENT

In the 1950s and 1960s, CD was promoted by governments, and by the United Nations (UN) through its affiliated institutions, as part of the following: the independence and decolonization movements in Africa and Asia; attempts to modernize the underdeveloped, largely agricultural societies and 'backward' regions of the developed countries; and the War on Poverty launched by governments in the more affluent nations of the West in the late 1960s.

Relations have since changed between the state and civil society, because of the struggles with global restructuring and changing ideologies; as a result, new actors have appeared on the scene who practice CD in ways that differ greatly from the approaches of earlier decades. One very clear trend is the increasing involvement since the early 1980s of nongovernmental organizations (NGOs), or voluntary sector agencies, in a field previously dominated by programs initiated and administered by governments. It is estimated that in the South alone, NGOs number in the hundreds of thousands. Many of these Southern NGOs have links with the thousands of international NGOs, which are based mainly in the member countries of the Organization for Economic Co-operation and Development (OECD) (CCIC, 1990; Clark, 1991; Campfens, Machan, & Murphy 1992; Edwards & Hulme, 1992). In the North, where they have a long history as part of the voluntary sector, NGOs are attracting greater attention; more and more, in response to governments pulling back the 'safety net' provided by welfare state programs, people are looking for alternative forms of support.

The central question is this: What mission are these NGOs pursuing? According to Korten (1987), there has been a significant growth in 'second generation' NGOs, which emphasize developmental strategies rather than the traditional 'charity' and 'welfare' activities (see also *New Internationalist*, 1992). Some NGOs that belong to a 'third generation,' Korten observes, have adopted a more catalytic role; in coalition with others, they strive to achieve reforms at the regional and national levels that support people-centred and sustainable development at the local level. Other such groups focus mainly on educating the public about development issues, or on acting as advocates for specific groups. In a later publication, (1990, p. 128) Korten identifies 'fourth generation' NGOs that align themselves with social movements (e.g., environmental, human rights, and women's movements) for the purpose of 'mobilizing a movement around a people-centred development vision.'

Another trend witnessed in recent years is the spectacular rise of social and co-operative movements, many of which serve as agents of CD. Among the most numerous of these movements, according to Fuentes and Frank (1989), are the myriad of apparently spontaneous, self-managing local rural and urban organizations that seek to ensure their members' survival through co-operative production, distribution, and consumption. But, as pointed out by Develtere (1994), these 'defensive' social movements do not explain the rise of all those social and co-operative movements that exist to create change, and that are guided by an ideological agenda which challenges the prevailing practices of those institutional systems of the state and civil society that determine the nature of development and the allocation of resources.

These latter movements are often driven by the search for alternatives to the capitalist industrial models, to the state-controlled social programs, and to the centralized, hierarchical, top-down, institutionalized structures of decision-making. The alternatives these groups apply may take the form of redirecting the economy toward the community, the environment, and a sustainable future (Daly & Cobb, 1989; Albert & Hahnel, 1991). Social initiatives are linked to economic ones through the creation of innovative, participatory, community-based organizations that are accessible, that empower residents, that generate income and local job opportunities, and that finance community infrastructure and social services. The general aim of these alternative development models is to support the pattern of social relationships that make up the community while promoting solidarity, fostering self-management, and improving the life chances and well-being of the residents. The growing community economic development (CED) movement in Canada, the United States, and Western Europe is one of the better examples of this trend (Ross & Usher, 1986; MacLeod, 1989; Economic Council of Canada, 1990; Dobson, 1993; Wilkinson, 1994; Perry & Lewis, 1994; Brandt, 1995). The groups that comprise this movement are found to be mediated by community development corporations (CDCs) as social enterprises or profit-seeking ventures; or by co-operatives that are member owned and operated (e.g., worker, food, housing, social capital, health, and child care co-ops); or by various other organizational forms that link their activities to those of others for the general benefit of the community.

Some of these searches for alternative models emphasize economic benefits; others focus on social relations. The desire is to create a more co-operative, people-oriented society based on mutual aid (Melynk, 1986; Quarter, 1992) as an antidote to the highly individualistic, competitive, and alienating environment prevalent in the economically developed nations of the West. In contrast, other social movements may emphasize the political dimension – for example, community empowerment (Albert, 1992; Friedmann, 1992; Shragge, 1993), or the democratization of the development enterprise (Fairbairn, 1990; Clark, 1991).

Many of the current social and co-operative movements carry traces of past movements and intellectual traditions, and arise in the context of a variety of factors and actors that influence their shape (Develtere, 1994). Furthermore, those movements which seek alternative forms of development enter into an antagonistic relationship with those groups which want to maintain control over the instruments of transformation and the 'production of social life.' This is typically the case in statist or industrial societies (Touraine, 1985). For example, current governments may not be very interested in supporting those alternative models of development which challenge the private sector or empower the population to voice its demands and discontents (Shragge, 1993). Consequently, those struggling for economic survival in a rapidly transforming society may prefer to avoid conflict, opting instead for more collaborative approaches (i.e., partnerships) with business and government.

In the current economic and ideological environment, where debt reduction and limiting the state's responsibility in social welfare have become priorities on the political agenda, governments may look more favourably on community initiatives that promote alternative forms of development. This is especially true if the initiatives create employment, generate income, and deliver social services less expensively. This helps governments to achieve their political agendas but also leaves 'political space' for those involved in CED, co-operatives, mutual aid, and related activities. The radical view on these activities takes the position that an educational strategy ought to go hand in hand with the process of meeting the basic socio-economic needs of people; this would lead to a critical understanding of (a) the sources of oppression and exploitation, and (b) the need for creating movements of solidarity.

The emergence of these new agents of CD, with their particular interests and goals, requires a closer examination of the CD field in order to determine the current state of theory and practice. General theories, although useful in their own right, are not very helpful in explaining how CD, as it is practised by these new agents as well as by the more traditional agents, takes place in a particular economic, political, and cultural context. What is needed is a country-and-case focus guided by a conceptual framework.

This book aims at providing a solid understanding of the current state of the art in the field of community development (CD). Six countries are considered, representing the major regions of the world: Canada, the Netherlands, and Israel from the 'developed' industrialized world (the North), and Bangladesh, Ghana, and Chile from the 'developing' or Third World regions (the South).

More specifically, this study is intended to inform policy-makers, program planners, and graduate students about the present state of community development. It cuts across cultural boundaries, sectoral activities and concerns (i.e., economic, social, and environmental), academic and professional disciplines, and organizational levels (i.e., governmental, nongovernmental, and community organizations). Furthermore, it aims to promote an integrative understanding of what is happening with development at the local level, with efforts at mobilizing and nurturing the human community, and with the building of different organizational partnerships to address issues of equity, welfare, and sustainable development.

When undertaking a cross-cultural study of this magnitude, one needs to be particularly mindful of first, differences in the terms used for describing the same phenomena, and second, differences in social and intellectual traditions that have led CD initiatives to emphasize one aspect of development over others. For instance, what might be referred to as CD practice in Ghana, which has one of the longest histories of government-supported CD in the world, would be called 'social promotion' in Latin American countries, which draw on the new social practices of 'popular education,' liberationist theology, and participatory action research. There are those who associate CD with 'locality development' in a social, economic, and/or political sense, so that it includes the building of mutual aid and social support systems, the development of economically self-reliant communities, and the democratization of social relations. For others, CD means community groups becoming 'empowered' to undertake social action in pursuit of social development or social change in the larger society. Clearly, these differences reveal the changes in perception concerning what appropriately constitutes a 'community' and what constitutes 'development.'

Language and terminology are two barriers. A third is that the published case literature and concept papers rarely place experiences or ideas in the broader context of the particular country so that they are intelligible and useful for the international reader. Furthermore, anthologies that survey CD experiences in different countries often lack the conceptual structure that makes real comparison possible for the interested student, for the policy or program planner, or for the practitioner in the field. To illustrate this point, 'A Survey of Contemporary Community Development in Europe' (Van Rees et al., 1991) includes a number of analytically strong concept papers and practice experiences but lacks a solid framework. One needs to separate that which may be considered a universal dimension or characteristic of CD practice from that which is unique to the particular culture or social system.

STUDY FRAMEWORK

To ensure cultural authenticity, the project teams for the six country studies were asked to produce their own studies, with the proviso that they adhere to the following conceptual framework, which consists of five parts:

- Three or four case illustrations of current practice.
- A description of institutions and programs that support CD practice in one form or another.
- A discussion of issues related to education and training for practice.
- A discussion of developments in research.
- A discussion of developments in theory.

A number of questions were formulated with reference to each part of the framework. These served as a suggested outline. This framework was meant to facilitate a comparative analysis that would identify those issues, characteristics, and new trends which are common among the countries studied; and those which are peculiar to the particular economic, social, cultural, and political conditions of each country.

Generally, the study participants held themselves to the framework, moving from case presentation and analysis to a discussion on theory and policy. However, there are some variations in emphasis, which are mainly a function of each country's unique situation, traditions, and creative initiatives. Only the Chile study significantly deviates from the framework, starting off with an examination of state policy on decentralization and local development, and following with a presentation of three case illustrations, and an analysis of the realities of local development. The emphasis on policy analysis reflects the Chilean political reality: civil society there was severely constrained by an authoritarian state for an extended period. In contrast, the Israeli study focuses on community work as an activity, which professionals and citizens engage in to achieve different goals. The Dutch and Ghana teams include a historical overview of CD. Finally, the Canadian study includes a separate section on Quebec because of the special status of that province as a 'distinct society' within the Canadian federation.

As for the cases, they reflect a cross-section of the broad field of CD practice. They emphasize current issues, and population groups that are greatly affected by the forces of change in our contemporary world. For example, the Canadian team focuses, among other cases, on refugees and their relationships with professionals and with the larger community under the auspices of a nongovernmental centre; and on single mothers in their efforts as a group to create a community of affordable housing in the tradition of community economic development. The Dutch include cases about service delivery for the elderly residents of an Amsterdam neighbourhood; about antipoverty measures in communities facing deindustrialization; and about innovative community actions relating to the physical environment. The Israelis examine resolution measures for interethnic conflicts between Jews and Arabs at the local level, and community work in an ultra-Orthodox neighbourhood. The Ghana team evaluates income-generating projects for women, and examines issues relating to the use of local building materials in housing construction and to job skills training for young people. The Bangladesh team focuses on co-operative and integrated development projects for landless peasants and rural women and on actions aimed at urban slum improvement. The Chileans, faced with the aftermath of a seventeen-year dictatorship and the reinstatement of democracy, focus on decentralization and local development, and on new initiatives being taken to alleviate poverty and improve primary health care and education. Most of the practice cases were written by those directly involved, in collaboration with a researcher or the country's project co-ordinator.

As the project's international co-ordinator, I corresponded with the team co-ordinators in the six countries. Each country's team co-ordinator was fully responsible for overseeing and co-ordinating the various tasks involved in producing the country study. Each country study begins by providing appropriate information on the country itself so as to place what follows in proper context. This will, it is hoped, enhance understanding of the issues addressed, for those international readers who are not familiar with the respective countries. Contributors to the country studies were selected by reputation, and are regarded by key informants as recognized authorities in their subject areas. They were selected during an exploratory one-month visit to each of the participating countries, which I undertook in 1993.

BOOK STRUCTURE

In Part II, 'International Review of Community Development Theory and Practice,' I begin with a brief description of the international context. I then discuss the following: alternative responses from the community and state; CD as an evolving concept and form of practice; social values and principles of CD; and intellectual traditions and trends from the past to present that have influenced CD.

I have deliberately stayed clear of presenting in the introductory parts of the book any findings from this multicountry study, as is common practice. Instead I provide a conceptual framework to facilitate the reader's own critical assessment of the six studies that form the main body of the book. To have introduced general findings at this stage would have reduced the significance of the country focus. After all, the distinctive feature of this book's design is that it combines a country focus with a comparative analysis. The findings based on the comparative analysis form the substance of the last part of the book (Part IX) and help to identify the characteristics of the 'New CD.'

Parts III to VIII are the country studies, which are ordered according to their regional association: the first three discuss the Northern, developed regions (Canada, the Netherlands, and Israel), and the last three discuss the Southern, developing regions (Ghana, Bangladesh, and Chile). Each of these six studies follows a similar format: illustrations from practice are followed by reflections on the current state of CD from a research and theoretical or policy perspective.

In Part IX, 'International Framework of CD Theory and Practice,' I analyse the contributions from the individual countries in light of the issues raised in the introduction to the international study, and determine the nature and extent of change in CD. I do this by highlighting a number of contrasts between countries, then identifying specific shifts in CD theory and practice, and then bringing into focus what appear to be some emerging and common themes. The last part concludes with a 'Framework Theory Outline,' which serves as a guideline for issues to be considered in the policy and practice of the new community development. In the Appendix, 'Highlights of Cases Compared,' I provide a brief overview of each case presented.

The references for Part I appear at the end of Part II, at page 40.

Part II

International Review of
Community Development:
Theory and Practice

HUBERT CAMPFENS

International Review of Community Development

While it is useful to place a study of CD in a national context, CD must *inter-*
also be placed in an international context that takes note of the unprec- *nationally*
edented mega-level changes that are affecting communities across the
globe. These changes suggest that we are moving rapidly out of the era
of nation states toward a global society dominated by regional market
economies and growing interdependence.

Concomitant with this trend toward a system of internationalized *v in*
capital, many governments are turning to neoliberal monetarist policies, and this has undermined the politics of social democracy that le-
gitimated the rise of the welfare state in many countries throughout *welfare*
much of this century. Teeple (1995), and other economic and political *state*
analysts like him, have demonstrated in considerable detail how the
world is increasingly being confronted with the bold assertion of corporate property rights at the expense of the basic needs and human rights
of the population at large.

The foundations of this new world order, the 'Pax Americana,' were
laid in 1944 with the Bretton Woods Agreement. This agreement triggered the creation of the International Monetary Fund (IMF), the International Bank for Reconstruction and Development – now called the
World Bank – and the General Agreement on Tariffs and Trade (GATT),
which has since transformed itself into the World Trade Organization.
These new institutions maintained the economic hegemony of the developed nations (especially the United States) over the South; in doing
so, they introduced a new North–South dichotomy that replaced the
former relations, which were based on colonialism. For the Western

world it meant the beginning of a major push toward the monetarization of the social order, in which social relations were to be governed chiefly by money.

Neoconservatism, world trade, and the communications revolution are the forces on the world scene most responsible for the current megachanges. Neoconservatism has been credited – positively by some, negatively by others – with having revived free enterprise and the spirit of voluntarism, at least in some of the more highly industrialized nations of the North, though also in some Third World societies. Besides free trade and a globalization of capital, the neoconservative agenda embraces the following:

- A reconstruction of society, with a sharply reduced role for the state and its bureaucracy in the marketplace and a return to the primacy of the individual over the collective.
- A shift from 'state care' to 'community care' in dealing with human needs and problems. This involves the dismantling and privatization of the welfare state (in health, education, and social service programs), and a renewed emphasis on self-help, neighbourliness, the voluntary sector, and community.
- Tax reform, with a shift from a progressive tax regime that concerns itself with the welfare of the most vulnerable groups in society toward one that favours the business sector. Supposedly, this will generate productive wealth for the creation of jobs.

Margaret Thatcher, who as prime minister of Great Britain in the 1980s was one of the world's most outspoken supporters of the neoconservative agenda, was truly messianic in her desire to reverse one hundred years of what she saw as a dangerous drift toward collectivism. Her views and policies were copied by many other neoconservative governments, most notably those in the United Sates under Ronald Reagan and George Bush. The 1994 U.S. Congressional elections made it clear how relentlessly the 'silent majority' of Americans were moving to the right. For the political right, 'the counter-cultural, redistributionist, bureaucratic welfare state is a disaster' that needs to be replaced with a policy that promotes individualism and traditional family values; that places priority on cutting deficits and balancing the budget; that emphasizes law and order by cracking down on crime, illegal immigrants, and welfare recipients; and that upgrades the military for international interventions. Judging by the opinion polls, the public debate seems to have shifted from a concern with social inequity to one of moral decay ('Americans move to the right,' *The Globe and Mail*, 10 November 1994 A30).

But political leaders like Thatcher and Reagan, and their followers, were not satisfied in burying socialism only at home. They carried their zeal into the international arena, using such powerful agencies as the IMF to restructure other societies to their liking, and disregarding countries' historical, cultural, and economic realities. The IMF, in its negotiations with Third World countries that required new loans to finance their huge debts, now expected those countries to accept structural adjustment programs (SAPs), regardless of social conditions (Walton & Seddon, 1994). In basic terms, this involved cutting off existing subsidies to the poor, reducing the state bureaucracy, raising prices for goods and services while reducing wages for labour, and devaluating the currency. Governments were also expected to change their economic policies so that domestic production and consumption were de-emphasized. They were now expected to focus on exports (a policy referred to as export substitution), the point being for them to increase their foreign currency reserves so that they would be able to pay off their debt.

In a sense, the Third World countries had become instruments for boosting Western capitalism and guinea pigs on which to test neoliberal policies before putting them in place in the developed nations. This was very clear in the case of Chile, which in the 1970s, under a military dictatorship that stayed in power through ruthlessly repressive measures, served as the world's first laboratory for experiments with monetarism and the 'free market.'

The highly acclaimed Uruguayan writer and historian Eduardo Galeano is less than flattering about this neoconservative agenda, with its complement of neoliberal economic policies, when he writes about the new Utopia. Looking north over the wall of power, he finds greed and contempt disguised as destiny:

The Cold War is over. Hours of glory. We've won. The class struggle no longer exists, and to the East there are no longer enemies but allies. The free market and consumer society have won universal consensus, not more than delayed by the historical diversion of the communist mirage. Just as the French Revolution wanted it we are all free, equal and fraternal now. And property owners too. Kingdom of greed, paradise on Earth. Like God and Communism before, capitalism has the highest opinion of itself and no doubt about its own immortality. (Galeano, 1990)

ALTERNATIVE RESPONSES FROM THE COMMUNITY AND THE STATE

The relations between the state and civil society are in the process of being restructured, and what can be perceived as a victory for those who own and run the planet is a disaster for those many people residing in communities caught in the middle. Within this environment of structural change, the question at hand is how communities (often assisted by NGOs) and the state respond to people's basic human needs and day-to-day problems, as viewed from the perspective of CD.

The South
Especially in Latin America, there has been a rapid growth in grass roots organizations that address basic family consumption and income requirements in a general environment of survival. These groups typically address the needs of those who lost the little state support that existed when SAPs were introduced. Many of these groups are run and controlled by impoverished women, who operate communal kitchens, glass-of-milk committees, and income-generating co-operative arrangements. Organizations of this type are usually based on self-help principles and the practice of a radical political discourse that is feminist, antiracist, and liberationist. The community-based groups are often assisted by NGOs, churches, and political parties, all of which offer alternative forms of organization and action. They differ markedly from the more traditional, male-led neighbourhood block organizations found in poor barrios across Latin America; most often, these groups are engaged in meeting 'community needs' related to water supply, sanitation systems, roads, garbage disposal, schools, community and day care centres, community health, neighbourhood vigilance, crime control, and other such infrastructure and service needs (Campfens, 1987, 1990; Barrig, 1990). The 'defensive' grass roots movements led by impoverished women are only one facet of the trend toward social and co-operative movements, many of which are searching for alternative forms of development in their desire to create change from the bottom up.

   The rise of these new, autonomous, self-managing grass roots organizations contrasts sharply with the fate of the state-initiated or administered CD programs that were so prominent across the developing world during the 'development decades' of the 1950s and 1960s. During these decades there was a general mood of idealism and optimism; it was believed that the living standards of the poor in the underdeveloped and 'stagnant' nations of the world, and in the backward regions of the developed nations, could be raised by development aid and by assistance in the form of massive transfers of resources such as capital, technology, and labour (in the form of volunteers). Inspired by the earlier success of the Marshall Plan, which was designed to rebuild the European economies after the devastation of the Second World War and to create markets for American products, U.S. President John F. Kennedy launched the Alliance for Progress in 1961, which pumped billions of dollars into Latin America. Kennedy saw this plan as a way to free millions of people from the bonds of poverty, hunger, and ignorance so that they could enjoy the abundance that modern science and technology can bring. However, many critics, some of whom quickly dubbed Kennedy's plan the 'Alliance Against Progress,' believed that the main purpose was to counteract the influence of Cuba's revolution in South and Central America (for more on this, see the introduction to the Chilean study).

During this period, CD programs were established to mobilize people in their local communities as an integral part of the five-year plans masterminded by national planners and operating under a centralized system of management and resource allocation. This model, adopted in much of South America and other Third World regions, was an unequivocal failure (Karunaratne, 1976; Korten, 1987).

Yet despite their failures, state-initiated and -administered CD programs continued to hold an appeal, especially among governments that, faced with heavy debt loads and limited capital resources, were looking for low-cost alternatives for meeting basic human and community needs. For instance, in Peru in the early 1980s, Belaunde Terry's Acción Popular government – a liberal democratic government that favoured modernizing economic policies – legislated into existence a National System of Popular Co-operation (NSPC). Its goal, as stated in the Act, was 'to guarantee the permanence and realization of the ancestral [meaning Inca] practice of "voluntary" work for the common good' (Government of Peru, 1980). The program was introduced 'as a means by which people and communities, exercising their initiative and disinterested efforts, [will] try to achieve their well-being within the context of a dynamic form of community development, and thereby become fully integrated into the economic and social life of the country thus reaffirming a national identity' (Campfens, 1987, p. 16). This reads like a lofty ideal, which Biddle (1966) would undoubtedly have considered a very 'fuzzy definition' of CD.

When APRA – a social democratic party – assumed power in Peru in July 1985, following a period of mass protests against the SAPs, it introduced some substantive changes to the NSPC, though not to its fundamental goal. This CD program, which continued until the 1990 change in government, reflected many of the same ideas on CD that were found in the earlier official literature coming especially out of the UN (1959, 1960, 1963a, 1963b).

Evidently, the new social and co-operative grass roots movements and the government-administered programs provide two CD experiences that stand in sharp contrast to each other, each being rooted in its respective social and intellectual traditions, one leaning toward state, corporate, and institutional interests, the other toward social and community interests.

The search for new models and social experiments in CD is also evident in other Third World regions. For example, in Bangladesh, a non–welfare state and an essentially rural society, the government opted for a 'co-operative village' based approach on a nationwide scale as a means to achieve integrated rural development (for more on this, see the Bangladesh study). In the early 1970s it adopted the two-tier co-operative system, called the 'Comilla model,' after experiments and 'action research' during the 1960s. Despite its various limitations, a modified version of this system continues to be part of official policy.

NGOs in Bangladesh, instead of emphasizing growth in the agricultural sector to meet the subsistence needs of a rapidly growing population, have pioneered an approach based on co-operative groups that stresses poverty alleviation and integrates a variety of programs, such as literacy, family planning, nutrition, and primary health-care education, with income-generating projects that target women, poor farmers, and landless peasants. As described in the Bangladesh study, the relative success of these efforts has led a number of government ministries to write similar features into their own programming.

The North

Development practitioners, community leaders, and government planners in the developed nations of the North have for their part been seeking to soften the impact on community life of recession, deindustrialization, and economic and social restructuring. They sense the limits of traditional, macrolevel economic-development strategies, and they perceive co-operative forms of community organizing and community economic development (CED) as a practical alternative for strengthening communities socially as well as economically. Taking Canada as an illustration, CED had its beginnings in the co-operative movement of the early twentieth century (MacPherson, 1989). Thus, CED preceded the emergence of the welfare state. Calling attention to movements that predate the welfare state is relevant particularly for those developed nations that currently are moving rapidly toward post–welfare state conditions, in which there will be a diminished role for the state in social welfare and the marketplace. One of those pre–welfare state movements is the Antigonish Co-operative Movement in the Atlantic region of Canada. This movement has been an influential force in co-operative movements in developing nations as well, among fishermen and farmers. It has shown that co-operatives can be vehicles for launching economic organizations for community improvement, and thereby achieve community control over credit provisions, basic purchases, marketing, and social services. An important feature of this movement is that it works within an adult education framework; through group discussions aimed at identifying the causes of economic problems, it empowers people and encourages them to organize for change. Another important feature of this form of co-operativism – one that sets it apart from the more unifunctional co-operatives, which are oriented mainly toward mutual self-help in a particular area of life – is that the needs and interests of the membership coincide with those of the larger community. The experience of the Evangeline co-op in Prince Edward Island is a good contemporary example of this; a multifunctional co-operative structure has been created that links producer, consumer, marketing, financial, housing, and health co-operatives at a second-tier level through a Co-operative Council. This comprehensive approach aims at ensuring that people co-operate in many areas of life for effective communitywide development (Wilkinson, 1994). The Mondragon group of the Basque region of Spain is another CED model that has had great influence internationally in the co-op movement (Wiener & Oakeshott, 1987).

CED in Canada takes a broad-based approach and derives its impetus from within communities. Typically, CED programs strive to overcome social and economic underdevelopment, disadvantage, and marginalization. They often arise as an immediate response to a crisis situation in the community; such a crisis may relate to an industrial plant closure, or economic inactivity, or, for such groups as the homeless, street people, and aboriginal people, simply hopelessness (New Economy Development Group, 1993).

As observed by Quarter (1992), not all co-operatives function as businesses motivated by profit. Many are 'nonprofits' and are organized into share-less corporations that deploy revenues or donations to cover expenses related to a particular service. Some mainly serve a defined membership sharing a mutual interest (these are the more traditional co-operatives); others provide humanitarian and social services to the larger public (these are also known as voluntary associations or community organizations). Most of the latter groups tend to be small and labour-intensive, and depend heavily on community volunteers for their ability to deliver services. Certainly, as governments in 'developed' nations step up their efforts to cut funding for social programs, increasing emphasis will be placed on the voluntary sector and the contributions of these volunteers.

These nonprofits are financed either through members' fees and fees for services, or through fund-raising efforts aimed at a wide variety of sources, including governments, labour unions, churches, foundations, corporations, and individuals. These nonprofits provide various community services to the poor, young people, the elderly, the sick, and the disabled. The services that many nonprofits deliver may not fit the traditional, narrower definitions of CD. However, they do involve activities that draw on community resources, and they often involve citizens – as co-operative members or as volunteers – in the planning, implementation, and evaluation of organizational activities.

Within the social services, health, and housing fields there is considerable experimentation with participatory, community-based, development-oriented approaches as an alternative to 'professional,' client-based services. This trend will be clear in several of the practice cases provided in the Canadian, Dutch, and Israeli studies.

CD AS AN EVOLVING CONCEPT AND FORM OF PRACTICE

From an international perspective, it is clear that CD has been one of the most significant social forces in the process of planned change (Chekki, 1979). This was certainly true for the first development decades of the 1950s and 1960s, when, under the direction of the UN and its affiliated organizations (UNESCO, ILO, FAO, WHO, UNICEF), CD was actively promoted throughout the developing world as part of the nation-building process and as a means of raising standards of living among the poor. However, the basic assumptions upon which approaches to CD and national development were based during this period, as articulated by the UN organizations and their associated 'expert groups,' were soon challenged for their contradictory and culturally biased nature (Galbraith, 1962; Biddle, 1966; Alldred, 1976).

It became apparent that the basic concepts of CD – such as human needs, community, participation, and development – required thorough re-examination. For instance, Alldred (1976) called attention to the complexities and unequal realities of rural and urban communities, and questioned the popular notion of unrestrained, self-reliant development by local communities. He perceived that politically disquieting inequalities emerge as a consequence of different communities pursuing their own development priorities at their own pace and with unequal resource bases to call upon. He argued that to achieve balanced development at the community (local) level, or for that matter at the regional and national levels, some directive planning by central authorities is necessary.

Today, we would advocate a more pluralistic and participatory approach to planning in which state agencies function more in partnership with NGOs and community organizations. The welfare state in developed nations may rightly be criticized in regard to its competence in running social services and dealing with social problems single-handedly, but it still has an important role to play in social development, particularly as a policy maker, standard setter, and principal funder. According to Drucker (1994), nations immersed in the current climate of social transformation need to expand their two-sector notion of society (those two sectors being government and business) to include a third sector. He stresses that this third sector, comprised of NGOs, nonprofit and grass roots organizations, and the multitude of volunteers, should assume a significant share of the responsibility for taking on the social challenges facing modern societies.

Appeals for community mobilization to address issues of economic and social development have often been based on an idealized notion of the community as a 'unitary' concept (i.e., village or city neighbourhood). There is an assumption that democratic consensus will somehow overcome differences and bring the various segments in the community together to form a united front of community action. In a recent publication on community, Godway and Finn (1995) appropriately ask, 'Who is this we?' They then provide a variety of helpful critiques of the standard theorizing about communities and their political and social practices. Others, too, have begun to challenge common beliefs about the nature and requirements of communities – beliefs that have been taken for granted for too long. More specifically, it is pointed out that unitary notions of the community as a 'locality' have tended especially to undervalue the role of conflict and disadvantage within communities (Molyneux, 1985; Campfens, 1990; Wekerly, 1996). The older notions often ignore existing power structures – in which certain groups benefit from the status quo – and the stratification of communities along the lines of social class, ethnicity, gender, sexual orientation, age, religion, and cultural tradition (Nanavatty, 1988; Ng, Walker, & Muller, 1990).

Therefore, within the context of intergroup conflict and competing interests, CD theory and practice may choose to focus on intergroup relations and mediation to achieve a fair and balanced development, as will be discussed in the Israeli country study. It may also assist in organizing marginalized groups and/or minorities to help them gain a measure of power, as will be discussed in the Quebec and housing society cases in the Canadian study.

One of the more significant advances in CD in recent years has related to the growing demand for a form of planned change that empowers marginal groups to participate in community and institutional decision-making processes, either through their own social organizations (which function as pressure or lobbying forces), or as representatives of their own grass roots organizations on communitywide councils (as illustrated in the case on poverty in the Netherlands study). The latter approach combines 'the power' and 'integration' approaches of CD, whereas the former involves competing with many others for limited public resources. Certainly, practices that focus on equity and fairness would contribute to balanced development, social stability, and peace.

Bregha (1970), by placing the issue of conflicting interests in a development context, noted that CD has two different objectives. He pointed to 'development as increase in resources and productivity' as having been the major focus of CD in the developing world, and to 'development as allocation of assets and power' as the major preoccupation of CD practice in the more affluent societies of the industrialized West. Drawing on the writings of C. Wright Mills (1956), Bregha expressed deep concern about the decline of voluntary community associations as genuine instruments of the public in the context of structural transformation in Western societies. With the marginalized in society already politically fragmented, the weakening of voluntary associations can only leave them even more powerless. To counter this, CD must emphasize the development of social organizations among the poor and the minority groups in society.

A similar point regarding the importance of social organization work was made more recently by Michael Cernea (1993), a senior adviser for social policy at the World Bank. Speaking on the subject of sustainability and officially induced development programs, Cernea criticized the singular focus on economic and environmental sustainability, arguing that sustainable development cannot be achieved merely through economic expansion, prudent environmental management, and the accumulation of technological prowess. Rather,

sustainability requires the continuous creation and re-creation of adequate *patterns of social organization* within which technological progress can unfold properly, the use of resources can be managed soundly, and the social actors of development can participate both individually and collectively, sharing in the formulation of goals and benefits of development. (Cernea, 1993, p. 19).

Of course, this type of social organizational work is at the heart of CD practice. It goes beyond motivating local people to participate in government, or in NGO-induced development programs; in doing so, it links official decisions to the will of the 'organized' community.

In short, what Bregha, Cernea and others argue (Gran, 1983; Kothari, 1984) is that effective collaborative relationships must be established between state or institutional agencies and voluntary organizations if balanced, just, and sustainable development is to occur. This in turn requires the presence of self-managing voluntary organizations and a less coercive approach on the part of state agencies and institutions. A number of studies have begun to consider what interactions are required for effective collaborative relationships (Albert, 1992; Belanger, 1995).

The problem for CD is clearly not the obsolescence of its main underlying values and principles, as will be clear in the six country studies presented in this volume. Rather, the question is how to adapt these values and principles to a range of social phenomena, thereby bringing about fundamental changes that will resolve the contradictions inherent in a social system that is caught up in a fast-changing economic and social order.

SOCIAL VALUES AND PRINCIPLES OF CD

In a review of the international literature, a number of common social values and principles that underlie the practice of CD can be identified. These are listed next.

- Co-operative, responsible, and active communities of involved men and women should be nurtured, and mobilized for the purposes of mutual aid, self-help, problem-solving, social integration, and/or social action.
- At all levels of society, down to the very lowest, participation must be enhanced, and the ideal of participatory democracy must be fostered, in order to counter the apathy, frustration, and resentment that often arise from feelings of powerlessness and oppression in the face of unresponsive power structures.
- As much as possible and feasible, CD should rely on the capacity and initiatives of relevant groups and local communities to identify needs, define problems, and plan and execute appropriate courses of action; in this, the goals are to foster confidence in community leadership, to increase competency, and to reduce dependence on state, institutional, and professional interventions.
- Community resources (human, technical, and financial) and, where necessary, resources from outside the community (in the form of partnerships with governments, institutions, and professional groups) should be mobilized and deployed in an appropriate manner in order to ensure balanced, sustainable forms of development.
- Community integration should be promoted in terms of two sets of relations: 'social relations' among diverse groups distinguished by social class or significant differences in economic status, ethnicity, culture, racial identity, religion, gender, age, length of residence, or other such characteristics that may cause tensions or lead to open conflict; and 'structural relations' among those institutions – such as public sector agencies, private sector organizations, not-for-profit or charitable organizations, and community organizations and associations – that take care of social challenges at the community level. Regarding the latter, the aim is to avoid unnecessary competition, lack of co-ordination, and duplication of services.
- Activities, such as circles of solidarity, should be organized that empower marginal or excluded population groups by linking them with the progressive forces in different social sectors and classes in the search for economic, social, and political alternatives.
- Those who are marginalized, excluded, or oppressed should be given the essential tools that will enable them to critically analyse and become conscious of their situation in structural terms, so that they can envisage possibilities for change.

In a particular situation, the emphasis accorded to any of these social values and principles of CD depends greatly on whether the practice involves a social movement, a process of change, or a concrete program. Also, the sponsorship may emanate from an organized citizens' group, a particular profession, an NGO, an institution, or a state agency, or any combination of these; each of these has its own particular and sometimes contradictory interests and priorities. These differences in sponsorship and emphasis make it particularly difficult to offer a general definition of CD that includes all possible practice situations.

INTELLECTUAL TRADITIONS UNDERLYING CD

Simply put, CD is a demonstration of the ideas, values, and ideals of the society in which it is carried out. From a humanitarian perspective, it may be seen as a search for community, mutual aid, social support, and human liberation in an alienating, oppressive, competitive, and individualistic society. In its more pragmatic institutional sense, it may be viewed as a means for mobilizing communities to join state or institutional initiatives that are aimed at alleviating poverty, solving social problems, strengthening families, fostering democracy, and achieving modernization and socio-economic development.

Has CD had its time? Decidedly not! The value of community and the notion of development, which are the two pillars of CD, do not disappear over time because of the failure of certain experiences or programs. However, out of necessity, CD often changes shape to fit its environment. Those who have had a long experience in CD practice know all too well that the process is accompanied by frustration and pain, and that success is never certain. But they also know how challenging, liberating, empowering, and exhilarating CD can be for the participants.

To understand the complex and often contradictory nature of CD today, one must recognize how its practice is rooted in a range of competing intellectual traditions and ideologies that date back to the eighteenth and nineteenth centuries, when Europe and North America were being transformed by industrialization. These traditions range from those preoccupied with societal guidance through the application of scientific knowledge and technical reason (representing a basically conservative ideology), to the more radical intellectual traditions of utopianism, anarchism, and historical materialism.

John Friedmann (1987), who reviewed these intellectual traditions and ideologies from the perspective of the four 'corners' of planning and development (i.e., policy analysis, social reform, social learning, and social mobilization), characterized the conservative position as representing those societal interests and professional disciplines that take existing power relations as a given. The supporters of this position proclaim their political neutrality, express predominantly technical concerns, view their primary mission as to serve the state and society's dominant institutions, and apply their scientific knowledge to the task of reconstructing society through social engineering and centrally directed planning. In other words, in advancing the public interests of the state and major institutions, they place their faith in 'technical reason.'

At the opposite end of the continuum are those intellectual disciplines that look to alternative forms of development based on oppositional or counter movements. Rather than addressing the concerns of the ruling élite, they focus on the people who, as victims of the existing order and members of the underclass, need to be mobilized. This approach is based on the belief that the underclass is fundamentally opposed to the bureaucratic state, to hierarchical relations, and to other such manifestations of alienating power. They place their faith in political and social processes at the grass roots level and within civil society; in doing so, they reject the strong emphasis on rationality and technology that is embodied in the scientific approach to modernization and scientific planning.

Since two planning and development interests – 'social mobilization' and 'social learning' – are of particular concern to the practice of CD, they will be examined more closely here in relation to the two opposing intellectual positions of societal guidance and oppositional movements.

Societal Guidance: Social Mobilization and the Institutionalists
In the early nineteenth century the Frenchman Henri de Saint Simon conceived the idea of 'societal guidance.' In the mid-nineteenth century Simon's compatriot, Auguste Comte, took this idea further with his theory of 'positivism' and notion of the power of 'technical reason,' both of which greatly influenced the emerging bourgeoisie (Hayek, 1955). The ideas of these two men gave the necessary push for the establishment of the industrial order in Western societies; this same order later found its way into the colonies (now developing nations) of the world.

Saint Simon argued that the scientists and engineers must place their knowledge in humanity's service in the same way that physicians apply their knowledge to the human body. Social scientists, being regarded as familiar with society's organic laws, and as having the ability to predict the outcomes of planned interventions, were called upon to reform society, guided by comprehensive plans.

This intellectual tradition found its parallel in economic development doctrines such as Rostow's stages of economic growth (1960). In turn these doctrines were the basis of the modernization and industrialization strategies applied during the 1960s by the UN agencies, the international financial institutions, the corporate sector, and the ruling élites of the developing nations. It was in this context that CD gained international prominence; as a new 'social technology,' CD was called upon to mobilize local communities and to join in national efforts to achieve socio-economic development. It drew on the scientific knowledge of cultural anthropologists, social psychologists, and sociologically oriented systems analysts. It also drew on the professional disciplines of adult education, agricultural extension, and the group-work and community-organization methods of social work.

Besides state agencies, many institutions and NGOs have launched CD, co-operative, and participatory programs that fall within the tradition of societal guidance and social reform. These institutionalists (to use a generic term) are less likely to question existing power relations in society. Their tendency is to focus on the weaknesses in organizations that undermine the effectiveness of program delivery. Community workers may be called upon to promote citizen, client, or community participation; but their focus at such times is on correcting programs. These planners tend to view their own institutions and state agencies as rational and benign actors that are responsive to organized community pressure and lobbying. The search for participation in government or in institutionally initiated programs is perceived by critics as little more than a loyalty ritual for gaining favours and access to essential goods and services (Arnstein, 1969).

However, even those NGO practitioners who acknowledge that co-operation and communalism in the social mobilization tradition are the principal underpinnings of community development in the South and the North have come to acknowledge that it is the state which ultimately determines how much change will be tolerated as a result of such programs (Edwards & Hulme, 1992).

Oppositional Movements: Social Mobilization and Alternative Development
According to John Friedmann (1987), the oppositional movements that
emerged in Europe in the early nineteenth century, which formed the
intellectual basis for the radical social-mobilization practices of modern
times, were a response to the social upheaval wrought by the industrial
revolution and to the inhuman conditions created by early capitalist greed.
The conditions of the 1990s are not dissimilar to those of that time; consider the spread of neoconservatism and anti–welfare statism, the imposi-
tion of SAPs, and the rise of free-market ideology as articulated by Milton
Friedman, a highly influential economist (1984; Friedman et al., 1984).

People in oppositional movements distinguish themselves from the
social reformists and adherents to the societal guidance model in that
they assert the primacy of direct collective action from below. Their
main concerns relate to the moral ordering of human life and to the
political practices of social emancipation and human liberation. The
oppositional movements share two things: a political analysis that calls
attention to the pervasive alienation of human beings under institutions
of capitalism; and a determination to change the established relations of
power to achieve social solidarity. However, they differ in the strategies
they choose. These strategies can be grouped into three categories: 'confrontational politics,' 'politics of disengagement,' and 'politics of free
association and mutual aid.'

Confrontational Politics
The Marxists and neo-Marxists aimed their activities at gaining the up-
per hand in a relentless class struggle, in which the power of the state
was used to create a new economic and social order based on the principles of social justice and equality. They were definitely not antistatists
(especially the Leninists); rather they were against a state that tolerated
or actively supported the exploitation of labour and the alienation of
human beings. In other words, the notions of societal guidance, rational
planning, and technical reason were quite acceptable to them provided
that the levers of the state were controlled by and used in the interests
of the dispossessed.

The more activist forms of CD during the 'wars on poverty' in the
late 1960s and early 1970s, which were often carried out in depressed
urban neighbourhoods of the Western industrialized nations, fell within
this tradition of confrontational politics. There was an increasing demand for more participatory forms of democracy and for an equitable
sharing of the opportunities and goods and services offered by society.

The inspiration for this kind of practice came from Marxist ideas on the social class struggle – albeit in forms less driven by ideology – and from the labour union movement. This tradition is reflected in the writings and organizing techniques of Saul Alinsky (1946, 1971), who was arguably the most effective and influential neighbourhood activist of this era. Alinsky organized the poor to fight for their rights as citizens through direct action. It is important to emphasize, however, that Alinsky's form of radicalism was aimed not at transforming society but rather at getting a better deal for those living at its margins. The same can be said of the strategies adopted by the more recent oppositional movements, which rally around consumption issues and are not interested in fundamentally transforming society. Such groups are essentially pragmatic, and ready to accommodate themselves to the basic nature and function of capitalist societies.

Utopianism and Disengagement

In contrast to the Marxists, the Utopians (along with the social anarchists and co-operativists) rejected the state as the principal vehicle through which to order civil society. Instead, they focused on creating 'alternative communities,' which would demonstrate more humane ways of living that depended on voluntary rather than political action.

Robert Owen, a Welsh businessman, was perhaps the most influential writer in the early Utopian tradition. In 1825, Owen developed a model community for the families of his employees and discovered that his business could make a profit even though he provided good wages and working conditions. Consequently, he began to propagate the notion that capital and labour, acting in enlightened self-interest, could come together in an organic and harmonious whole. Owen's philosophy laid the foundations for socialism, social reform, trade unionism, and the co-operativist movement (de Schweinitz, 1943).

Owen, together with other early Utopians, inspired the communitarian movement, which believed in the perfectibility of life on earth, the importance of brotherhood and sisterhood, the need to live in harmony with nature, and the merging of mind and body. In the nineteenth century this movement created communes and 'intentional communities,' which led to the co-operatives, planned communities, and Israeli kibbutzim of modern times. Other examples of such communities are the Mennonite and Amish religious communities, the Jewish ghettos of eastern Europe, and the secular communes that rose in the wake of the hippie movement (Poplin, 1979). The Chinese communes of the Mao

Zedong era can be regarded as more modern versions of the intentional community.

The early Utopians believed that it was possible to establish self-managing, co-operative communities that were apart from the state, faced minimal intrusion by the rest of society, and operated money-free economies based on the exchange of labour. Supposedly, these communities would give free rein to the passionate nature of human beings (Fourier, 1976); and emphasize human development; and liberate their members from the behavioural restrictions bred by competition, rational calculation, and utilitarian notions.

When these 'purposeful' communities turn into closed societies, they often run the risk of becoming totalitarian and oppressive, thereby crushing individual autonomy, creativity, and social innovation. This danger is particularly present in those modern-day communities that reject any outside assistance in the form of state aid, professional guidance, and nongovernmental assistance. An illustration of this is the experience of the Self-Reliance Movement in the Rangpur region of Bangladesh. After the war of independence in 1971, out of fear that they would become dependent on others, sixty villages made an oath not to accept any assistance from the outside. They held themselves to this oath even throughout the 1974 famine. This movement, which died down in 1975 with political changes in the country, demonstrates how strongly people can desire and believe in self-reliance (International Labour Office, 1987, 1989). More important, however, this example reveals how isolationism, even when intended to emancipate people from the divisive, oppressive, and exploitative forces of capitalism, can sometimes create other forms of oppression.

In contrast to the Utopians, with their isolationist and escapist tendencies, Owen was interested in reorganizing society from within. Above all, he wanted to establish a system of co-operation that would take the place of capitalism. When the rich did not show much interest in his appeals, he turned his attention to the working class, promoting co-operative associations among them and helping to promulgate the socialist philosophy (de Schweinitz, 1943, pp. 172–3). Trade unionists picked up on his notion of mutual benefits, setting up funds to insure workers against sickness, unemployment, and old age. Some of these ideas were later adopted by governments as part of the emerging welfare state.

In the more liberal tradition, Owen also contributed to the modern co-operative movement, through his ideas on co-operation and the return of dividends on purchases. These ideas were embraced by the Rochdale Consumers' Co-operative store in 1844, and set out in the charter of Rochdale's founders. Subsequently, the International Co-operative Alliance (ICA), expanding on the 1844 Rochdale Charter (Melnyk, 1985; Develtere, 1994), set out the following principles: open and voluntary membership; democratic control; limited return on investment; return of surplus to members; co-op education; and co-operation between co-operatives (i.e., a co-op commonwealth). The ICA's principles emphasize private property, a basic tolerance of capitalism, and pragmatic unifunctionalism (Melnyk, 1985). Because of this, the ICA has been criticized for placing too much emphasis on the practical objective of serving its members, and losing sight of the longer-term vision, which is to create a co-operative society (Melnyk, 1985; Wilkinson, 1994).

Voluntary Association, Mutual Aid, and Communitarianism
Many of the modern mutual-aid associations, co-operatives, and communitarian movements – which are frequently supported and promoted by CD practitioners – have their intellectual roots in the writings of social anarchists like Proudhon (1979) and Kropotkin (1989), who strongly rejected all forms of authority, especially that of the state. Their goal was to create alternative, self-governing communities based on the principles of mutual aid and self-help. Also, they believed in seeking social reform through grass roots mobilization. They believed, further, that structural reform could be achieved through peaceful means and co-operation.

For Proudhon, a desirable society is characterized by the following: a revival of the communal traditions of mutualism or fair exchange; a minimalist state; a joining together based on the principle of federation, with lower- and higher-order social groupings; a convergence of the private and public, or the individual and collective; and complete autonomy of each person when entering into voluntary association with others. This conforms with some aspects of contemporary neo-conservatism.

It can be argued (and Kropotkin does argue) that the ethics of mutual aid, as reflected in the communitarian tradition, have sustained societies through the ages – not the self-assertion of the individual (individualism), with everyone for himself or herself in competition with all others (which is the basis of 'survial of the fittest' and free-market ideology); and not the idea of 'the state for all' (state collectivism). The notions of support, mutual aid, and human solidarity were present at the earlier, primitive stages of human life, as Kropotkin demonstrated in his epic historical analysis. These notions were also expressed throughout the clan and tribal periods, and in the agricultural village communities, medieval guilds, and industrial unions of more modern times. The rise of self-help groups, informal mutual support networks, and local economic-development societies in the midst of the highly industrialized, urbanized, and professionalized societies of the West suggests that communitarianism is re-emerging as a fundamental value. In the United States, the communitarian movement is a growing intellectual force that is a reaction to the breakdown of communities, the proliferation of individual rights over community rights, the imbalance between rights and responsibilities, and the unbridled pursuit of individual self-interest (Etzioni, 1993).

Within this tradition, the operative principles of voluntary associations include the following: co-operation, mutual aid and exchange, direct participatory democracy, the practice of consensus in decision-making, and the formation of a federative structure. The federative principle assumes the need for local action groups to form coalitions to facilitate leadership training and to acquire technical, material, and financial resources. Coalitions also help local groups pursue common objectives in the larger society. The special appeal of communitarianism in an alienating modern society lies in its potential to liberate individuals from oppression so that they can recover their essential humanity and practice political community in free association with others.

Titmus argued, within the socialist tradition and in support of welfare statism, that mutual aid and altruism must be learned and fostered because they are not inherent human traits (Mayer, 1985). Kropotkin took an opposite position, arguing that mutual aid is a natural law that has been a major factor in the evolution of all species, including our own. Mutual aid will persist even when it is ignored by human-service professionals or when the state tries to suppress it as a threat to the élite or to the existing institutional order (as has happened often throughout history). Kropotkin believed that it is our consciousness of human solidarity – be it only at the level of instinct – and the fact that we realize our commonality as human beings that pulls us together in the face of life's hardships and vicissitudes.

Instead of taking the law of mutual aid as their point of departure, both the capitalists (advocating unrestricted competition and individualism) and the Marxists (arguing for the class struggle) adopted the Darwinian law of nature. Darwin's theory of evolution, which he based on his observations of 'mutual struggle and contest' and 'survival of the fittest' in the animal world, came to be applied to human society; social life was now seen as based on continual strife between groups and individuals. Marxism and capitalism, two competing ideologies with different political and economic agendas and one single common thread, have had a huge influence on how our societies have organized themselves in the twentieth century (Woodcock, 1989).

The spirit and ethics of mutual aid and the tradition of communitarianism have generally received little attention from either the state and its institutional planners or the mainstream human-service professions, all of which focus predominantly on individual-centred forms of helping. Yet, as Kropotkin puts it, 'Sociability is the greatest advantage in the struggle of life. Those species which willingly or unwillingly abandon it are doomed to decay' (1989: p. xxvii).

SOCIAL LEARNING: KNOWLEDGE AND COMMUNITY ACTION

The intellectual tradition of social learning has contributed greatly to the professional practice of CD; it has done so by examining the contradictions between theory and practice and finding methods to overcome them. Theorists in this tradition have argued that knowledge is derived from experience and validated in practice. Thus, knowledge or theory is not static; rather, it is forever changing, being part of a dialectical cycle in which existing theory is enriched or modified by the lessons drawn from practice, which in turn are applied in the ongoing process of action. Thus, practice and learning are construed as correlative processes.

In other words, social learning that begins and ends in action differs sharply from the policy analysis tradition practised by state and institutional planners, who focus on the processes of rational decision-making, which are more linear and are directed from above and involve the examination of anticipated and unanticipated results.

As Friedmann (1987) claims, social learning is a complex process that involves the action itself; a political strategy, including tactics which aim at overcoming resistance and which draw on a theory of practice that will guide the actor's conduct in specific roles; theories of reality that assist us in understanding the world around us (this includes a theory of history and a theory of the specific situation the social learner is engaged in); and the values that inspire and direct the action. Together, these four elements constitute 'social practice.' These questions remain: In what social, economic, and political context should social learning take place? And who should the learners or actors be?

American Empiricism and the 'Expert'.
The early social-learning tradition was heavily influenced by the pragmatism of John Dewey (1946, 1963), an American philosopher and educator whose scientific epistemology stressed 'learning by doing.' For him, 'experience' meant the absence of any division between subject and object. He concluded that valid knowledge rests on a consensus theory of truth, with the actors continuously exploring the new, leaving behind the old, and relying on the inquiry into facts. It is important to note that for Dewey, the principal actors in resolving the contradictions and problems in society were to be the 'experts' (trained technicians in the modern state), since they were especially equipped to undertake an inquiry into the facts (following scientific principles) and arrive at the 'true' answer to the problem at hand.

This philosophical position contradicted Dewey's other view, involving the 'Great Community,' in which he postulated that such a search for truth was to start in the community among neighbours. He claimed that 'democracy must begin at home, and its home is the neighbourly community ... the local is the ultimate universal' (1946, pp. 213–15). His Great Community Utopia, however, was not likely to be realized as long as the experts and professionals continued to manipulate the neighbours according to their notions of development and their plans. It was not until much later, with the introduction of 'participatory action research' (PAR) – an innovation in social technology originating in Latin America (Fals-Borda, 1986, 1991; Fals-Borda & Rahman, 1991) – that this contradiction began to be addressed more seriously in development practice from an institutional perspective (Sarri & Sarri, 1992; Banks & Wideman, 1995).

Findings on Group Dynamics and Implications for Professional Role Activity
Dewey's writings on social learning were taken up by Kurt Lewin (1948) and his associates, who engaged in a form of 'action research.' The emphasis here was on studying groups and group dynamics, and linking theory to techniques for changing reality. Lewin argued that true learning involves a restructuring of one's relations with the world; this called for a process of re-education. He felt that this could best be done in groups, since groups form the life-space in which most people move about and develop as persons, workers, and citizens. Significantly, re-

searchers in the field of group dynamics found that successful attitudinal and behavioural changes required the group members themselves to go through the experience of being 'acting subjects,' and to collectively act on their environment. In this way, they served as both actors *and* learners. This empirically based finding had major implications for the role orientation of the 'change agent.' Rather than acting as the expert in problem solving, the change agent was advised to function more as an enabler, or guide, or trainer, with relevant groups. A national training laboratory in group dynamics, set up in 1947 in the United States, encouraged groups of learners to develop greater self-awareness and interpersonal skills, with the assistance of a professional trainer who was competent in managing group relations.

Murray Ross, a professor at the University of Toronto's School of Social Work during the early 1950s, picked up on these new insights on social learning and applied them to community work (Ross, 1955). His theoretical formulations on the role of the professional worker became highly influential in the training of community workers around the world. He viewed 'guide' and 'enabler' as primary roles for professional workers in community organization and development. For him, a 'guide' was one who helps a community move effectively in the direction it chooses. The choice of direction must be that of the community; guides contribute by drawing on their expert knowledge of many factors to help the community evaluate alternative courses of action and arrive at decisions.

Ross saw an 'enabler' simply as a person who facilitates the development process. The components of this role include the following: awakening and focusing discontent among people at the community level about economic and social conditions; encouraging associations and organizations to assume responsibility for action; nourishing good interpersonal relations; and emphasizing common objectives. Ross's views on professional roles were later complemented by significant insights derived from experience in more revolutionary settings, such as in grass roots work in Third World communities and in feminist practice, where concerns typically centre on different forms of oppression. In particular, the notion of awakening and focusing discontent has become a central feature of practice with social movements.

Organizational Development and Community Development
As a result of research in group dynamics, a new social technology emerged known as 'organizational development.' Corporate managers

took a great interest in this, particularly in the industrialized world. But as Friedmann points out (1987), the limitations of organizational development (OD) are severe, so it cannot be considered for general application, especially in the fields of public policy and community development. 'OD refuses to face up to differences in people's access to the bases of social power and the basic relations of dominance and dependence that exist in every social system' (Friedmann, 1987, p. 220). Also, OD lacks a major social theory.

OD tools are perhaps of greatest benefit to managers interested in 'downsizing' their operations in a neoconservative environment. This is evident from the legions of consultants who are now being contracted by corporations and other institutions (including NGOs in the international co-operation field) to conduct training workshops, to facilitate strategic-planning processes involving the total staff, and to undertake other such organizational tasks. Clearly, OD has little to do with community-focused development. Such a focus calls for mutual help in the provision of social services; builds local CD organizations; engages in community-level management; reorients institutional practices to facilitate social learning among members of community-based or grass roots organizations; and generally attempts to close the gap between the bureaucracy and the poor (Korten & Alfonso, 1981; Korten & Klaus, 1984). New guides are appearing to correct this weakness in the field of OD, particularly for those organizations interested in aligning themselves more with grass roots social movements and the community (Lakey, Lakey, Napier, & Robinson, 1995).

Theory and Practice in Revolutionary Settings

Mao Zedong's essay 'On Practice' (1968) is generally viewed as one of the most important writings in the social learning tradition. He wrote it in 1937 with a very different social context in mind than that of the developed industrialized world in which Dewey and his followers operated. Also, his comments on the essential unity of theory and practice were aimed at the 'masses,' who were to be the primary learners and actors in the revolutionary social practice.

Regardless of these obvious differences, Mao and Dewey were in fundamental agreement that the source of all valid knowledge is found in the practice of changing reality. Mao, however, was much more specific than Dewey in defining social practice. He insisted that it must be synchronized with the laws of the objective external world, which for him consisted of the realities of material production, the class struggle, and scientific experiment. Dewey failed to bridge the real dualism between subject and object; Mao succeeded.

What set Mao apart from the Marxists was his desire to avoid any form of dogmatism and empiricism in the revolutionary struggle. Since China's historic circumstances were quite different from those of the (now former) Soviet Union, its road to socialism required that Chinese revolutionaries learn from their own practice by examining the Chinese reality. The important lesson to be learned from Mao's thoughts – a lesson that also can be applied to nonrevolutionary contexts – is that the process of mutual adjustment between theory and practice is not only never-ending but also historically, culturally, and situationally specific.

Popular Education and 'Conscientization'

Internationally, popular education is probably best known through the innovative literacy work that Paulo Freire carried out with the peasants of northern Brazil. With his ideas on oppression and 'critical consciousness,' Freire revolutionized social practice. In contrast to 'social animation,' which focuses on what social actors will 'do' in bringing about change in their social reality, conscientization practice concerns itself with what the participants will 'be.' Critical consciousness, as defined by Freire (1970), goes beyond 'magical' consciousness, which is characterized by fatalism and inactivity, and 'naïve' consciousness, in which reality is understood in terms of imposed norms and standards. It implies a search for knowledge: a critical reflection on reality, followed by action that carries an ideological option up to and including the transformation of one's own world, be it a community, a social condition, or something else. The general process, thus understood, contains psychological as well as sociological processes.

During his two-year residency at Harvard University in the late 1960s, Freire laid the foundations of what he would later call 'a political pedagogy.' This pedagogy assumes that alienation and isolation generate a state of dependency and domination by the established powers. It involves a process of demasking, through action and reflection, the oppressive condition of institutional practice, and acquiring the capacity for conscious and creative intervention.

Community practitioners, in applying the principles of popular education, have gone beyond Freire's original concept of critical consciousness or liberation education, which they see as only a preliminary or 'prepolitical' act, and one that must be joined to organizing activities. It is in the process of autonomous organizing that alternative projects of society and culture emerge, as reflected in women-led popular kitchens, and local committees dealing with day care and nutrition, and youth organizations, and human rights groups (Rossel, 1986).

Organization is a crucial factor because it facilitates popular mobilization. In effect, autonomous popular organizations act as counterweights to the dominant forces in society, which tend to manipulate the struggles of grass roots groups to their own ends.

When the principles of popular education are being applied, a new concept of professional practice is required. Within the dynamic of popular autonomous organizations, the practitioner does not intervene from an élitist and discriminatory position, but rather participates in a democratic process. Nor does the practitioner assume a top-down, authoritarian position, but rather a horizontal one that involves a dialogue of mutual learning. In this way the community group is not regarded as a recipient of pedagogical or social labour, but is instead converted into a true subject of the educational procedure and collective organizational expression.

Liberation Theology and the 'Option for the Poor'

The contribution of liberation theology (Gutierrez, 1973; Bonino, 1975; Tamez, 1982), which shares many principles with popular education, can be summarized around the following four themes:

- If there is to be effective action, the poor and oppressed must be listened to, and the world must be seen through their eyes.
- Knowledge of the truth and awareness of conditions is not in itself sufficient to acquire a new vision. Material and cultural conditions must be created that will enable the poor to gain liberty and arrive at truth.
- There will be liberation only when the poor assume their own liberation. The traditional work of charity and assistance to the poor that treats them as objects is not acceptable. The poor must be treated as subjects of their own transformation and participate actively in the formulation and execution of development initiatives.
- The poor, not science or technology, should be regarded as the point of departure in development and liberation. This is not to minimize the importance of science and technology but rather to emphasize the correct priority.

It has been pointed out by liberationist theologians, such as Gutierrez (1983), that we have given too much attention to the abstract libertarian ideas and ideals of the dominant culture in the West. Consequently, we have failed to acknowledge those historical movements of the oppressed that brought about real processes of liberation. Also, the liberties achieved by the rich and scientifically advanced countries often resulted in new forms of domination on the periphery of Western development, in effect recolonizing the Third World (Gutierrez, 1986).

Reconstruction of the Development Expert

Proponents of participatory action research, popular education, and liberation theology have contributed to the deconstruction of the 'development expert.' Their critique has gone beyond arguing in favour of the adoption of small-scale appropriate technology in development projects (see Schumacher, 1973); warning against the danger of the community becoming dependent on outside or foreign experts (Nindi, 1990); and recognizing the need for human or community capacity-building and empowerment.

Their fundamental concern is with the preeminence of Western science and technical reason, and with the present reliance on the modernist framework in defining development. Postmodern feminists, in addition to the above, are concerned about the patriarchal character of the knowledge produced about women and their needs (Ong, 1990, 1993; Parpart, 1993). They join the other critics by calling for a 'development expert' who can be open and listen thoughtfully to others; and who can cut loose from the universalizing theories, conceptual frameworks (dominated by modernist, binary, and patriarchal thought structures of Western culture), and rational discourses on basic needs to allow different voices and experiences to be heard; and who will design policies and practices based on the concrete, spatial, environmental, and cultural contexts in which people live (Esteva, 1987; Escobar, 1992; Alatas, 1993; Parpart, 1995).

As Hobart (1993: 15–16) said so aptly: 'knowing is not an exclusive prerogative of some superior knowing subject.' There are limits to the claim of knowing (Goetz, 1988). The principal challenge is to recognize the complexity of the communication between the 'development expert' and the community, as partners in the development enterprise. Listening and communicating cannot be assumed but must be problematized and worked on (Goetz, 1988; Parpart, 1995).

Not surprisingly, the 'option for the poor' and recent calls for listening to the poor and oppressed have resulted in a growing literature on oral testimonies. There are even guides appearing (Slim & Thompson, 1995) that are designed specifically to help CD workers improve their listening and learning skills so that they will make the knowledge, experience, culture, and priorities of local people central to their work.

The developments highlighted here, with reference to the intellectual traditions and contributions to CD, by necessity were selective. Undoubtedly, there are other factors that may be pointed to as having influenced CD as a form of 'planned change' *from above* within the tradition of societal and institutional guidance; as a form of 'social mobilization' *from below* as part of an alternative development or social movement; or as a form of 'social learning' involving professional practitioners working in partnership with community or community groups.

CONCLUSION

In this introduction I have identified the concepts, forms of practice, values, intellectual traditions, and global transformations that have influenced and formed CD theory and practice over the years. I hope that I have now provided a context and conceptual framework that the reader can use in critically assessing the six country studies presented next.

References

Alatas, S. (1993). On the indigenization of academic discourse. *Alternatives*, 18: 307–38.

Albert, J. (1992). If we don't do it, it won't get done: A case study from Nicaragua. *International Social Work*, 35(2).

Albert, M., & Hahnel, R. (1991). *Looking forward: Participatory economics for the twenty-first century*. Boston: South End Press.

Alinsky, S. (1946). *Reveille for radicals*. Chicago: University of Chicago Press.

– (1971). *Rules for radicals: A pragmatic primer for realistic radicals*. New York: Random House.

Alldred, N. (1976). Some contradictions in community development: The need for a stronger community approach. *Community Development Journal*, 11(2): 134–40.

Americans move to the right [editorial]. (1994, 10 November). *The Globe and Mail*, Toronto. A30.

Arnstein, S.R. (1969). A ladder of citizen participation. *Journal of American Institute of Planners*, 35: 216–24.

Banks, K., & Wideman, G. (1995). *The company of neighbours: Building social support through the use of ethnography*. Paper presented at the Canadian Anthropology and Sociology Meeting, June 1995, Montreal.

Barrig, M. (1990). Women and development in Peru: Old models, new actors. *Community Development Journal*, 25(4): 377–85.

Belanger, J.M. (1995). *The state and community in community participation: A case study*. Doctoral thesis, Wilfrid Laurier University, Waterloo, Ontario.

Biddle, W. (1966). The fuzziness of definition of community development. *Community Development Journal*, 2: 5–12.

Bonino, J. (1975). *Doing theology in a revolutionary situation*. Philadelphia: Fortress.

Brandt, B. (1995). *Whole life economics*. New Society Publishers.

Bregha, F. (1970). Community development in Canada: Problems and strategies. *Community Development Journal*, 5(1): 30–6.

Campfens, H. (1987). *The marginal urban sector: Survival and development initiatives in Lima, Peru*. Research Paper 161. Toronto: University of Toronto, Centre for Urban and Community Studies.

– (1988). Forces shaping the new social work in Latin America. *Canadian Social Work Review*, 5(Winter): 9–28.

– (1990). Issues in organizing impoverished women in Latin America. *Social Development Issues*, 13(1): 20–43.

Campfens, H., Machan, G., & Murphy, M. (1992). *The voluntary sector in international cooperation and community development*. Paper presented at the 25th International Congress of Schools of Social Work, July, Washington, DC.

CCIC (Canadian Council of International Cooperation). (1990). *I.D. profile: A who's who and what's what of international development*. Ottawa: CCIC.

Cernea, M. (1993). Culture and organization: The social sustainability of induced development. *Sustainable Development*, 1(2): 18–29.

Chekki, D. (1979). *Community development: Theory and method of planned change*. New Delhi: Vikas Publishing House.

Clark, T. (1991). *Democratising development: The role of voluntary organizations*. London: Earthscan.

Daly, H., & Cobb, J. (1989). *For the common good: Redirecting the economy toward community, the environment and a sustainable future*. Boston: Beacon Press.

de Schweinitz, K. (1943). *England's road to social security: From the Statute of Laborers in 1349 to the Beveridge Report of 1942*. University of Pennsylvania: University of Pennsylvania Press.

Develtere, P. (1994). *Co-operation and development: With special reference to the experience of the Commonwealth Caribbean*. Leuven, Belgium: ACCO.

Dewey, J. (1946). *The public and its problems: An essay in political inquiry*. Chicago: Gateway Books (original 1927).

– (1963). *Experience and education*. London: Collier Books (original 1938).

Dobson, R. (1993). *Bringing the economy home from the market*. Montreal: Black Rose Books.

Drucker, P. (1994, November). The age of social transformation. *The Atlantic Monthly*.

Economic Council of Canada. (1990). *From the bottom up: The community economic development approach*. Ottawa: Government Publication Centres.

Edwards, M., & Hulme, D. (eds.). (1992). *Making a difference: NGOs and development in a changing world*. London: Earthscan.

Escobar. A. (1992). Imagining a post-development era? Critical thought, development and social movements. *Social Text* 31/32: 20–56.

Esteva, G. (1987). Regenerating people's space. *Alternatives* 12(1): 125–52.

Etzioni, A. (1993). *The spirit of community: The reinvention of America*. New York: Touchstone Books.

Fairbairn, B. (1990). Co-operatives as politics: Membership, citizenship as democracy. In M.E. Fulton (ed.), *Cooperative organizations and Canadian society*. Toronto: University of Toronto Press. 129–40.

Fairbairn, B., Bold, J., Fulton, M., Hammond Ketilson, L., & Ish, D. (1991). *Co-operatives and community development*. Saskatoon: Houghton Boston Printers.

Fals-Borda, O. (1986). *The challenge of social change*. London: Sage Publications.

– (1991). *Knowledge and social movements*. Santa Cruz, CA: Merrill Publishers, University of California.

Fals-Borda, O., and Rahman, A. (1991). *Action and knowledge: Breaking the monopoly with participatory action research*. New York: Apex Press.

Fourier, C. (1976). *Design for utopia: Selected writings of Charles Fourier (1772–1837)*. New York: Schocken.

Freire, P. (1967). *Educaçao como prática da liberdade*. Rio de Janeiro.

– (1970). *Pedagogy of the oppressed*. New York: Herder & Herder (translated from the original Portuguese manuscript of 1968).

Friedman, M. (1984). *Market or plan? An exposition of the case for the market*. London: Centre for Research in Communist Economics.

Friedman, M., Stein, B., Johnson, M., & Keller, G. (1984). *Politics and tyranny: Lessons in the pursuit of freedom*. San Francisco: Pacific Institute for Public Policy Research.

Friedmann, J. (1987). *Planning in the public domain: From knowledge to action*. Princeton, NJ: Princeton University Press.

– (1992). *Empowerment: The politics of alternative development*. Cambridge: Blackwell.

Fuentes, M., & Frank, A.G. (1989). Ten theses on social movements. *World Development*, 17(2): 179–91.

Galbraith, J.K. (1962, September). The poverty of nations. *Atlantic Monthly*.

Galeano, E. (1990). The other wall: The view from the South. *The New Internationalist*, 213: 7.

Godway, Eleanor M., & Finn, Geraldine (eds.). (1995). *Who is this 'we'? Absence of community*. Montreal: Black Rose Books.

Goetz, A. (1988). Feminism and the limits of the claim to know: Contradictions in the feminist approach to women in development. *Millennium* 17(3): 477–96.

Government of Peru. (1980). *Decreto Legislativo No. 1, Sistema Nacional de Cooperación Popular*, November 4.

Gran, G. (1983). *Development by people: Citizen construction of a just world*. New York: Praeger.

Gutierrez, G. (1973). *A theology of liberation*. Maryknoll, NY: Orbis.

– (1983). *The power of the poor in history*. Maryknoll, NY: Orbis.

– (1986). *La verdad los hará libres: Confrontaciones*. Lima: Instituto Bartolomé de las Casas.

Hayek, F. (1955). *The counterrevolution of science: Studies on the abuse of reason*. New York: Free Press.

Hobart, N. (1993). *As I lay laughing: Encountering global knowledge in Bali*. Paper presented at Association of Social Anthropology (ASA). IV Decennial Conference, Oxford, England, 26–31, July.

International Labour Office. (1987). *The animator in participatory rural development: Concept and practice*. Geneva: ILO.

– (1989). *Promoting people's participation and self-reliance*. Proceedings of a regional workshop of trainers, August 21 to September 1, Zimbabwe. Geneva: ILO.

Karunaratne, G. (1976). The failure of the community development programme in India. *Community Development Journal*, 11(2): 95–118.

Korten, D. (1987). Third-generation NGO strategies: A key to people-centered development. [supplement] *World Development*, 15: 145–59.

– (1990). *Getting to the 21st century: Voluntary action and the global agenda*. West Hartford, CT: Kumarian Press.

Korten, D., & Alfonso, F. (eds.). (1981). *Bureaucracy and the poor: Closing the gap*. Singapore: McGraw-Hill.

Korten, D., & Klauss, R. (eds.). (1984). *People-centred development: Contributions toward theory and planning frameworks*. Hartford, CT: Kumarian Press.

Kothari, R. (1984). Party and state in our times: The rise of non-party political formation. *Alternatives*, 9(4): 541–64.

Kropotkin, P. (1989). *Mutual aid: A factor of evolution*. Montreal: Black Rose Books (original 1914).

Lakey, B., Lakey, G., Napier R., & Robinson, J. (1995). *Grassroots and nonprofit leadership: A guide for organizations in changing times*. Philadelphia: New Society Publishers.

Lewin, K. (1948). *Resolving social conflicts: Selected papers on group dynamics.* New York: Harper and Brothers (original 1940).

MacLeod, G. (1989). Worker co-ops and community economic development. In J. Quarter and G. Melynk (eds.), *Partners in enterprise.* Montreal: Black Rose Books.

MacPherson, I. (1989). *Each for all: A history of the co-operative movement in English Canada: 1900–1945.* Toronto: Macmillan.

Mao Zedong. (1968). On Practice. In *Four essays on philosophy.* Peking: Foreign Language Press (original 1937).

Mayer, R. (1985). *Policy and program planning: A developmental perspective.* Toronto: Prentice-Hall Canada.

Melnyk, G. (1985). *The search for community: From utopia to a co-operative society.* Montreal: Black Rose Books.

Mills, C. Wright (1956). *The power élite.* Oxford: Oxford University Press.

Molyneux, M. (1985). Mobilization without emancipation? Women's interests, the state, and revolution in Nicaragua. *Feminist Studies,* 2(2): 227–54.

Nanavatty, M. (1988). The community development movement in South East Asian countries: An Asian perspective. *Community Development Journal,* 23(2): 94–9.

New Economy Development Group (1993). *Community economic development in Canada: A different way of doing things.* Ottawa: Department of Human Resources and Labour Canada.

Ng, R., Walker, G., & Muller, J. (eds.). (1990). *Community organization and the Canadian state.* Toronto: Garamond Press.

NI. (1992). Changing charity: 50 years of Oxfam. *The New Internationalist,* No. 228 (February).

Nindi, B. (1990). Experts, donors, ruling élites and the African poor: Expert planning, policy formulation and implementation – A critique. *Journal of Eastern African Research and Development,* 20: 41–67.

Norwood Evans, E. (1992). Liberation theology, empowerment theory and social work practice with the oppressed. *International Social Work,* 35(2).

Ong, A. (1990). State versus Islam: Malay families, women's bodies, and the body politic in Malaysia. *American Ethnologist* 17(2): 258–76.

– (1993). *Anthropology, China, and modernities: The geo-politics of cultural knowledge.* Paper presented at Association of Social Anthropology (ASA). IV Decennial Conference, Oxford, England, 26–31 July.

Owen, R. (1972). *A new society and other writings (1771–1858).* New York: Dutton.

Parpart, J. (1993). Who is the 'other'? A postmodern feminist critique of women and development theory and practice. *Development and Change,* 24(3): 439–64.

– (1995). Deconstructing the development 'expert': Gender, development and the 'vulnerable groups.' In M. Marchand & J. Parpart (eds.), *Feminism/postmodernism/development*. New York: Routledge. 221–43.

Perry, S., & Lewis, M. (1994). *Reinventing the local economy*. Centre for Community Enterprise.

Poplin, D. (1979). *Communities: A survey of theories and methods of research (2nd Edition)*. New York: Macmillan.

Proudhon, P. (1979). *The principle of federation*. Toronto: University of Toronto Press (original 1863).

Quarter, J. (1992). *Canada's social economy: Co-operatives, non-profits, and other community enterprises*. Toronto: Lorimer.

Ross, D., & Usher, P. (1986). *From the roots up*. Toronto: Lorimer.

Ross, M. (1955). *Community organization: Theory and principles*. New York: Harper & Row. (Re-edited in 1967 with B. Lappin, who added a chapter on integrating principles and practice.)

Rossel, M. (1986). Evolución de la educación popular in America Latina y en el Perú. *Tarea* (15).

Rostow, W. (1960). *The stages of economic growth*. Cambridge: Cambridge University Press.

Sanders, I. (1958). Theories of community development. *Rural Sociology*, 23: 1–12.

– (1970). The concept of community development. In J. Cary (ed.), *Community development as a process*. Columbia: University of Missouri Press.

Sarri, R., & Sarri, C. (1992). Participatory action research in two communities in Bolivia and the United States. *International Social Work*, 35(2): 267–80

Schumacher, E. (1973). *Small is beautiful: Economics if people mattered*. London: Blond & Briggs.

Shragge, E. (1993). *Community economic development: In search for empowerment and alternatives*. Montreal: Black Rose Books.

Slim, H., & Thompson, P. (1995). *Listening for a change: Oral testimony and community development*. Philadelphia: New Society Publishers.

Tamez, E. (1982). *Bible of the oppressed*. Maryknoll, NY: Orbis.

Teeple, G. (1995). *Globalization and the decline of social reform*. Toronto: Garamond Press.

Touraine, A. (1985). An introduction to the study of social movements. *Social Research*, 52(4): 749–87.

United Nations. (1959). *Public administration aspects of community development programs*. New York: UN Technical Assistance Program.

– (1960). *Community development and related services*. New York.

– (1963a). *Report of the ad hoc group of experts on community development*. New York.

– (1963b). *Community development and national development*. New York.

Van Rees et al. (1991). *A survey of contemporary community development in Europe*. The Hague: Gradus Hendriks Stichting.

Walton. J., & Seddon, D. (eds.). (1994). *Free markets and food riots: The politics of global adjustment*. Oxford: Blackwell.

Wekerly, G. (1996). Reframing urban sustainability: Women's movements: Organizing and the local state. In R. Keil, G. Wekerly, & D. Bell (eds.), *Local places in the age of the global city*. Montreal: Black Rose Books. 137–45.

Wiener, H., & Oakeshott, R. (1987). *Worker-owners: Mondragon revisited*. London: Anglo-German.

Wilkinson, P.A. (1994). *Against the tide: Community-initiated development, the Evangeline experience*. Doctoral thesis, University of Toronto.

Woodcock, G. (1989). Introduction to *Mutual aid* by Peter Kropotkin. Montreal: Black Rose Books.

Part III

Canada

Co-ordinated by HARVEY STALWICK and
ANDRÉ JACOB

Canada

1. INTRODUCTION
Harvey Stalwick

Canada's almost 30 million people inhabit the second-largest country in the world. This makes for a density of only 3 persons per square kilometre (compared with 412 in the Netherlands and 869 in Bangladesh). The vastness of Canada's land mass distorts the real picture: almost 75 per cent of Canadians live within 150 kilometres of the American border, and over half are concentrated in an urban corridor running from Quebec City to Windsor, Ontario. Canada is well over three times more urban than the United States: 29 percent of its people live in metropolitan areas over 1 million, compared with 8 percent in the United States. In the 1860s, Canada's first prime minister, John A. Macdonald, expressed the view that the country had 'too much geography.' With less than 25 percent of its people living in rural areas – a figure that is declining – this lament applies in the 1990s as well.

Canada's immense land area is divided into ten provinces and two territories. With over 60 percent of the population in just two of the provinces – Ontario and Quebec – there has been a long history of disputes between the periphery and the centre. The federal presence in provincial affairs has generally been strong under a British-based, Westminster-style, parliamentary system of government. Since the 1960s the provinces have been more assertive in seeking a restructuring of government powers, especially in the areas of taxation and the sharing of federal resources for delivering services and overcoming regional economic disparities.

The emerging reality of Quebec nationalism is of particular interest to the aboriginal people of Canada, who have long expressed their desire for 'First Nation' status and for self-government.

Canada's economic resources are considerable, and it ranks high in global competitiveness. In most economic sectors, including energy and food, it is self-sufficient, and its capacity to generate wealth through exports is high. However, this capacity is belied by rising unemployment and child poverty and by the reduction of transfer payments from the federal government to the provinces. Jobless growth has cast a long shadow over the economy; so has the problem of the soaring federal debt. The attention given to servicing this debt tends to divert attention from the social agenda.

Decentralization, the emergence of regionalism, and the decline of the centre have led to a resurgence of interest in community development (CD). The present shift to local initiatives, nongovernmental organizations, and associative activities contrasts with the emphasis in the 1960s and 1970s on top-down programs, which included federal initiatives such as the Company of Young Canadians (CYC), the Agency for Rural Development (ARDA), Opportunities for Youth (OFY), the Local Initiatives Program (LIP), and the Local Employment Assistance Program (LEAP), and many similar programs that were introduced by provincial governments.

The four Canadian case studies presented here reflect various attempts to think and act at the neighbourhood, local, and regional levels – to bring about change from the bottom up. The Quebec study on conscientization and community practice outlines this process particularly well.

Ethnic diversity in Canada is moving far beyond the two founding nations (the 'two solitudes') of French and English Canada. There are over one hundred different ethnic and cultural communities in the country. In the 1970s the attention long given to official bilingualism and biculturalism (English and French Canada) began to merge with public policies fostering multiculturalism. In 1988 the Multiculturalism Act was passed by the federal government. With the exception of the First Nations (indigenous) peoples, Canada is a nation of immigrants. The social goal that is emerging is not for an assimilationist melting-pot but for a 'mosaic' that builds bridges between cultures in a creative way. However, this vision is not shared by all. As the economy tightens, immigration policies are being challenged and human rights mechanisms to counter racism are being weakened. A major opportunity for CD is to strengthen and celebrate Canada's diversity. In 1988, one-third of all Canadians could trace their ancestry to sources other than the two founding nations. As we enter the next millennium, this one-third will increase to one-half, because of the present high rate immigration from Africa, Asia, and Latin America.

John A. Macdonald also stated in the 1860s that Canada had 'too little history.' The demographic projections and the growing wealth of cultural diversity, combined with present discussions on sovereignty for Quebec, suggest that this lament no longer describes the country.

2. CURRENT PRACTICE

A. The Canadian Centre for Victims of Torture, Toronto: Transforming Relations between Refugees, Professionals, and the Community
Adrienne Chambon, Joan Simalchik, and Mulegeta Abai

INTRODUCTION

CD has traditionally been concerned with geographically based entities; increasingly, however, it is focusing on communities that are based on shared identity or needs rather than physical location. Even so, ethnically diverse populations of victims have not often been considered in this newer way. A community perspective often treats ethnic groups as homogeneous, and focuses restrictively on ethnic leadership and intergroup coalitions. Victims are generally conceptualized along an individualistic paradigm, as this is consistent with the typical arrangements for helping them. The organization of victimized groups is seldom associated with the mobilization of marginal populations; mainly, such organization is done through mutual aid or advocacy activities (Kurtz & Chambon, 1987). Yet there is a need to find ways to empower high-risk groups so as to benefit both the target population and society at large. This case study fills this empirical and conceptual gap in regard to ethnically diverse trauma victims – an area in which Canada has taken a leadership role.

The growing influence of NGOs and of the voluntary sector on community change has now been recognized, particularly in regard to immigrant and ethnically diverse populations. We can anticipate that their involvement in the development of innovative CD strategies will continue to grow (Campfens, 1987, 1990).

The Canadian Centre for Victims of Torture (CCVT) is an excellent CD case to examine because it deals with a vulnerable population in the context of ethno-racial diversity, and because over the past ten years this NGO's philosophy, activities, and organizational structure have evolved well beyond institutional boundaries to foster a unique and comprehensive community initiative. We will demonstrate that the CCVT illustrates a continuity model in CD that incorporates the following: traditional grass roots and leadership development; the more recent notions of empowerment, mutual support groups, and linkages between formal and informal resources; and participation in new social movements, both at the local level (through a gendered view of community partnerships) and at the more global level (through the human rights movement and international initiatives).

A VULNERABLE POPULATION

According to the 1951 UN Convention, to which Canada is a signatory, refugee status covers those persons who, because of persecution or a well-founded fear of persecution for reasons of race, religion, nationality, political opinion, or membership in a particular social group, are unable or unwilling to return to their country of birth or permanent residence. Canada is one of the main host countries; in recent years, convention refugees and those in related situations ('designated class') have represented 15 to 20 percent of its immigrant population. Within Canada, Ontario is the main province of resettlement; within Ontario, Metropolitan Toronto is the main location (Marr, 1992).

Refugees face multiple challenges in coping with the traumatic circumstances of their flight and in adjusting to present circumstances. It is estimated that approximately 30 percent of refugees have survived the devastating experience of torture in its many forms. As described in the Canadian federal report on refugee mental health, 'the goal of torture is to destroy personality, not to extract confessions' (Canadian Task Force on Mental Health, 1988, p. 87). The physical and emotional sequelae of torture are well documented in the mental health literature. The general psychiatric term 'post-traumatic stress syndrome' is used to describe a condition in which the victim endures 'a re-experiencing of the event through painful, intrusive recollection, recurrent dreams or nightmares, feelings of being detached or estranged from others, loss of the ability to become interested in things which ... had [been] previously enjoyed and problems dealing with intimacy' (Allodi & Cogwill, 1982; Canadian Task Force on Mental Health,1988, p. 85; Mollica, 1988). Traumatic re-experiencing occurs not only in the immediate aftermath of torture. For many years, recall of the experience can be triggered by everyday situations ranging from the sight of a common object that was used for the purposes of torture to an interaction reminiscent of an interrogation. More generally, any institutional contact perceived as threatening can bring on the symptoms.

Like other immigrants, refugees face the challenge of resettling, meeting their basic needs, and adjusting to unfamiliar institutional and cultural arrangements (Stein, 1986). Further, refugees from Third World countries suffer from the unanticipated impact of racial discrimination, which makes the host society less than a safe haven (Abai, 1992). These multiple sources of distress are not independent of one another (Allodi, 1991; Chambon, 1989). Earlier trauma makes victims susceptible to all forms of oppression, isolation, or marginalization; it also disrupts their normal coping abilities. Survivors of persecution and torture often experience particular difficulty in vocational and social rehabilitation (Stein, 1986; Canadian Task Force on Mental Health, 1988, p. 88).

Also, victims of torture tend to deny a great deal; this makes them an invisible population. They are extremely reluctant to communicate the horror and degradation of their past experiences; exacerbating this is the lack of awareness, and even disbelief, among the public at large (including professionals) outside the regions where these events are perpetrated (Hossie, 1991, p. 1).

HISTORY AND ACTIVITIES OF THE CCVT

The CCVT was the first centre of its kind in North America, and the second internationally (after the pioneer centre in Copenhagen). Similar centres had been operating in countries under dictatorships, such as Chile, Argentina, and South Africa, but those were hidden from public view. The CCVT was founded by a group of physicians in 1977 under the auspices of Amnesty International to service Metropolitan Toronto; it was incorporated in 1983. Since then, nine other centres for survivors of torture have opened in Canada (Montreal, Vancouver, Winnipeg, London, Hamilton, Edmonton, Calgary, Ottawa, Kitchener, and Victoria). In 1994, they regrouped under a national network. Along with centres elsewhere (e.g., Minneapolis, Chicago, the San Francisco Bay area, and New York), they are part of a growing international network.

According to its own intake figures, since its inception the CCVT has served over 6,000 survivors of torture from many countries on several continents (the national figures indicate 130 source countries for a total yearly intake of 36,608 refugees in 1992, and 24,543 in 1993; see Canada, Immigration and Refugee Board, 1989–94; Marr, 1992.) The five largest groups served by the agency in the 1992–5 period arrived from Somalia, Sri Lanka, Ghana, Iran, and El Salvador. Recently, more refugees have been arriving from the former Yugoslavia. Of the 766 refugees served by the CCVT during 1993 and originating from 65 countries, 286 were women and 485 were men. In 1992, the CCVT served no less than 903 refugees, from 66 countries. In 1991 the figures were 754 from 53 countries. This diversity of backgrounds is a reflection of the widespread use of torture around the world (it is practised in over ninety countries, according to Amnesty International's 1994 report). It is also testimony to the effectiveness of Canada's refugee-asylum policy, although this is currently being tightened. It can be argued that the contribution of refugees to multicultural Metropolitan Toronto has been underestimated.

A PROFILE OF PROGRAMS AND SPONSORS

The CCVT makes available a wide range of resources, including the following: in-house settlement services, social assistance, housing, child care facilities, English-as-second-language (ESL) courses, counselling, crisis intervention, mutual support groups, art therapy, a drop-in program, and a volunteer befriending program. It also refers victims to professional networks of physicians, psychiatrists, and lawyers, mainly for immigration issues; runs public education and community consultation programs geared to outside professionals and communities; and supports international projects.

The CCVT has diversified its sponsorship. It has sought and obtained funding from government, private, nonprofit, and for-profit sectors. Government is the major source of funding (56 percent of expenditures in the 1992–3 fiscal year, 70 percent in 1993–4); primarily this involves federal programs (respectively 45 percent and 60 percent of the total budget). Provincial, municipal, and city governments participate to a much lesser extent. The UN Voluntary Fund is the primary funder in the nonprofit sector, followed by the United Way (a citywide, federated, voluntary fund-raising agency for social development purposes) through its short-term grants to high-risk populations and its donor-designated contributions. A number of private foundations also participate. Finally, some revenues are raised through fund-raising events.

This diversity of funders ensures a broad range of activities. However, financial support is fragile, as most of the sources depend on yearly applications.

A COMMUNITY ORIENTATION

The mission statement of the CCVT (1993) reads as follows:

The Canadian Centre for Victims of Torture is a non-profit, registered charitable organization dedicated to the continuing needs unique to survivors of torture and their families in Canada and abroad, and to increase public awareness in Canada and abroad of torture and its effects upon survivors and their families.

Unlike its early counterparts (the centres in Copenhagen and Minneapolis, which were instituted along a medical/clinical model), from its inception the CCVT adopted an explicit community orientation. This approach was followed later on by the other Canadian centres, thereby affirming a specific Canadian orientation:

While the CCVT was funded by a group of physicians, they did not create a clinic, but a 'centre' intended to be a community focal point and coordinating mechanism. A variety of programming was designed to assist survivors, based on the recognition that torture is primarily a social rather than a medical phenomenon, and therefore requires a social rather than an exclusively medical response. As a result, an integrated service model was developed ... (CCVT Newsletter #6, May 1992, p. 6)

PROFESSIONAL/NONPROFESSIONAL BALANCE

The centre is seen by its executive director as a 'nexus' where branches of the community meet with the mainstream in a supportive way, rather than as a splinter group. Board and staff patterns reflect this orientation.

COMPOSITION OF THE BOARD

The original board members were predominantly white Canadian professionals. A deliberate strategy led to considerable change in the composition of the board and its committees. This was to ensure that survivors from Third World countries were represented, as well as individuals exposed to the refugee situation and institutions. Today, the board includes members from El Salvador, Sri Lanka, Ethiopia, and Iran; there are also African-Canadian and Japanese-Canadian members. Board members tend to have professional training; this maintains a strong presence of lawyers, teachers, accountants, and professionals from the health and mental health sectors.

STAFF

The CCVT relies on three categories of staff: in-house paid staff (20 full-time staff in 1992, down to 13 in 1996, because of decreased revenues); dozens of professionals, who are available through the referral networks; and over 300 volunteers, who assist the in-house programs and staff the volunteer befriending program and the board.

The core staff play a pivotal role in the day-to-day activities of the centre. They include intake workers, counsellors, crisis intervention staff, and volunteer co-ordinators. CCVT staff are not mainstream professionals; however, a large number hold professional degrees from their home country. The same strategy of representation applies as to the board members. The staff are of diverse national backgrounds, and most are refugees. Some are survivors of torture. The similarities between staff and participants help to prevent potentially harmful divisions between experts and clients and the 'disabling' effect of the professionalization of services (Illich, 1977; McKnight, 1977). The participant/staff continuum contributes to responsive and effective assistance and serves as the basis for community ties.

Professional services are available through extensive referral networks. Although such services are crucial to the CCVT's mission, they are housed outside the centre and are peripheral to its day-to-day activities. A balance has been found between the outside professionals and the core staff, whereby the former provide their valued expertise as part of a team, without occupying dominant positions. These professionals are selected for the compatibility of their views with those of the centre and are further socialized through in-service training. It is assumed that mainstream professionals have a lot to learn from the CCVT staff. For this reason the centre provides field placement opportunities for students in social work and medicine.

Volunteers are the 'heart' of the centre. They contribute enormously to the success of the programs. Without their participation many survivors would not be served and some services would not be provided at all. As with the board and staff, the volunteers come from various groups and include a large number of refugees. Volunteers are considered an integral part of the centre's activities and receive extensive orientation and educational training.

NORMALIZATION AND THE INTEGRATED SERVICE APPROACH

The centre's in-house programs provide a continuum of mental health and resettlement resources adapted to the survivors' needs. The CCVT follows an integrated service approach rather than a mental health model. Thus, ESL classes emphasize life skills and adaptation, and instructors are trained by the core staff in how to incorporate the personal experiences of refugees into their teaching. The service continuum reflects a normalizing approach reminiscent of earlier developments (Wolfensberger, 1972). Most important, this approach is congruent with the cultural requirements of these groups, most of whom are unfamiliar with Western psychiatry or counselling. Participants tend to maintain contact with the centre after they begin to resettle. Some take part in festivities, while others join the volunteer network. Often, they renew contact during periods of crisis.

EXTENDING THE COMMUNITY CONCEPT

Several more recent activities of the centre go beyond the notion of a community-oriented organization to encompass CD.

Mutual Support Groups
A group model for working with survivors of torture was developed jointly by the health network and centre staff (Blakeney, da Costa, & Dirie, 1991). Its initial success in the Somali Women's Program in 1990 led to its being adapted to Somali men's groups and to groups in the Iranian, Central and South American, West African, and Bosnian communities. It is a gender-based model that acknowledges the importance of common national and linguistic origins, as well as gender, if open exchanges are to take place. The groups are led by co-facilitators; these include a mental health volunteer and a staff person of the same cultural background as the group members. Their credibility is greatly enhanced by their familiarity with the victims' experience. The group members determine the group's agenda.

Consistent with the centre's approach, the groups address individual and collective psychosocial needs – how to manage crisis situations and trauma; dealing with isolation, racism, family separation, and changing gender roles; and adapting to Canadian society generally – along with material concerns, such as how to arrange social assistance and housing, and find work, and arrange schooling for children. Individual sharing is complemented by an educational component, and empowerment is achieved through mutuality:

Less emphasis is placed on cognitive understanding and insight into partici-pants' problems. More emphasis is placed on group validation of participants' shared experiences; and on participants sharing with each other practical ways of coping. (Blakeney et al., p. 2)

The model preserves cultural continuity for most communities (Miller, 1994; Triandis, 1993):

The self help group model is similar to the broad cultural concept of the [fe-male] network in the extended family. For most of the group members, this network has been completely disrupted by the time of their arrival in Toronto. (Blakeney et al., p. 1)

Broader community integration is achieved through recreational ac-tivities and linkages with ethnospecific associations and neighbourhood community centres, enrolment in which is facilitated. The support groups become the seed for continuing group interaction and cohesiveness:

A strong sense of common purpose and solidarity developed within the group, in spite of past political differences. The amount of group activity outside of regular group hours, and independent of facilitators, increased markedly as the group progressed. Many group members demonstrated significant leadership skills, for example in organizing meetings. (CCVT, Newsletter #7, 1993)

At an advanced stage of the process, several groups have initiated extensive advocacy activities (e.g., around access to housing), thus fur-ther modifying their relationship to the environment:

[This model] is very suitable for the type of women who quickly perceive the injustices they face as newcomers in Canada. They do not merely want to learn about the system, but want to try to change things. (Blakeney et al., p. 1)

A number of participants have expressed an interest in facilitating future groups in their community and have requested additional training in advocacy skills. This suggests that leadership development programs will soon grow in importance.

These groups are the backbone of community partnerships, several of which have been established on the basis of gender affiliation. As an example, the Women Supporting Women project recruits and trains women volunteers from several ethnic communities to help their peers solve problems relating to health, employment, education, self-esteem, and family violence. This program is sponsored by the CCVT, by the women's organization, Women's Health in Women's Hands, by the Davenport Perth Neighbourhood Centre; and by the Department of Public Health.

Community Networks: The Volunteer Befriending Program
Through committed relationships (a minimum of three hours a week for one year), the befriending program rebuilds the refugees' sense of normalcy and belonging. As explained in the centre's Volunteers Guide (CCVT, 1993, p. 8), 'Befriending creates a natural bond of community which is indispensable to the survivor's mental health and well-being.' The same document (p. 1) states the goals of the program as follows:

- To provide support, foster independence, and mitigate the effects of torture so that survivors can gain self confidence, avoid the sense of shame, the sense of failure, and the sense of guilt – the failure of a dream, etc. which are usually common to victims of torture;
- To provide an effective means of cultural exchange in a non-threatening way and in an atmosphere of trust and friendship. To break the isolation, to help them rediscover joy and to bolster their self-esteem that has been inhibited or lost as a result of the torture;
- To assist them to make the transition from victims to active community members; and
- To create a bridge through the ' befrienders' who are part of the community to come to an awareness of the survivor's situation, to create sensitivity to survivors so that the community through the individual will devise strategies for change and empower the community to address both the iinternal and external needs of survivors and help movements within the community that challenge the social, political, and economic inequalities and in the process reinforce the concept of human rights.

Extensive training and educational activities are offered to the volunteers. These emphasize that a 'saviour' attitude must be avoided. Volunteers are trained to establish instead an empowering equal-peer relationship that preserves the survivor's decision-making capacity.

The befriending program benefits both survivors and the community at large. Through the healing powers of friendship and social networks, the program 'enable(s) survivors to make the transition from victim to active community member' (CCVT, 1993, p. 8). It also enables them to re-establish trusting and emotionally supportive relationships (countering the fear, mistrust, and powerlessness resulting from torture), and to participate in community life beyond survivor communities. Finally, it helps them to adapt to the new society by improving their language and cultural skills and smoothing access to community and government resources.

To the befriender, the program opens up new horizons and a rich opportunity to learn about the cultures and experiences of the survivors. In the process, new friendships are established. Also, the program encourages people to reflect on the values of democracy and cultural diversity, and promotes social justice (Abai, 1992). Collectively, the befriending program directs the community to respond appropriately to the plight of survivors of torture, and fosters movements that challenge inequalities, while reinforcing the concept of human rights.

Community Education and Advocacy

A social understanding of torture as government-sponsored repression, and of refugee displacement as an international phenomenon (Zolberg, 1989), has led to thoughtful and systematic activities in community education (Simalchik, 1990, 1991). These activities foster awareness of and responsiveness to individual suffering. They also encourage people to participate in social movements and to support social justice efforts abroad.

From the start, enhancing the community's awareness of the refugees' right to asylum was a critical objective of the CCVT. This component has gained in importance in recent years, and in 1990 it was incorporated into the mission statement (see above) to make it clear that it was just as central as providing direct assistance to survivors and community education. The Salvadoran Jesuit and psychologist Martin-Baro wrote that since the aim of persecution is to isolate individuals and render them ineffective, communities must take responsibility for the effects of socially organized violence. They must come forward in breaking the silence and create 'circles of solidarity' (Simalchik, 1993).

Additional funding now supports a quality newsletter, which disseminates information and position papers. The funds also helped to establish a resource centre with materials on torture, international events, and human rights, as well as a speakers' bureau. The centre has been represented at conferences in Canada and abroad. In 1993 it honoured 250 invititations to speak at universities and colleges. It also makes public service announcements.

An adult education approach was adopted early on, supported by the Central and Latin American refugees and based on the writings of Paulo Freire. It is complemented by a human rights perspective stemming from the original sponsorship by Amnesty International. The latter perspective has been expanded through ongoing debates, led in part by a member of the board who is a human rights educator (CCVT, Newsletter #7, 1993, p. 17). All these activities contribute to empowering participants and staff.

The CCVT's consultation activities have led to institutional advocacy initiatives. For example, the centre opposed a uniform data collection system on refugees on the grounds that it would be too intrusive and threatening to this population. Also, it has testified at hearings on Canada's new immigration law (Bill C-86) and on the activities of the Refugee Board, and debated the New Immigration and Refugee Board Guidelines on gender persecution (CCVT, Newsletter #8, 1994, pp. 3–4).

INTERNATIONAL ACTIVITIES

The centre's international activities are buttressed by funding from international agencies such as the UN Voluntary Fund for Torture Victims. The CCVT has supported clinics for children traumatized by violence in Central America, as well as the Imbali Rehabilitation Centre in the province of Natal in South Africa. It is currently supporting the Documentation and Rehabilitation Centre for Torture Victims in Ethiopia, the Torture Survivors' Centre in Lithuania, and the Family Counselling Centre in Sri Lanka.

AWARDS

In recognition of its humanitarian and community achievements, the CCVT has received a national award from Health and Welfare Canada and twenty-six volunteers' awards from the Ministry of Citizenship. At the provincial level, the CCVT has received the United Way Award of Honour for outstanding support to the community, as well as the

Norman V. Bowen Humanitarian Award from the Ontario Psychological Foundation. Other awards include those from the Faculty of Medicine at the University of Toronto, Somali Immigrant Aid, and the Somali-Canadian Society of Toronto.

DISCUSSION

The activities of the CCVT reveal the simultaneous development of inner and outer circles of community that actively engage survivor victims in diverse activities. As these circles of involvement multiply, they reach increasingly outward toward the larger society.

CD for survivors of torture takes many forms, from responsive normalization to leadership training in community and organizational skills. One of the key indicators of a newcomer community's integration to the host society is the degree to which it forms linkages with mainstream institutions (Breton, 1991). Personal and institutional networks of solidarity adapted to contemporary urban conditions, once established, come to replace lost traditional networks (Beiser, 1990; Wellman, Carrington, & Hall, 1988).

The notion of empowerment, currently advocated as a central principle of community psychology in personal and collective terms (Rappaport, 1987), has been shown to be associated with community participation (Zimmerman & Rappaport, 1988). Empowerment results in individual and collective health (Wallerstein, 1993). The 'socio-environmental approach' taken by the centre provides conditions where development can occur, through 'a continuum of empowerment strategies' relating to personal empowerment, small-group development, community organization, coalition advocacy, and political action (Perkins, 1993).

The CCVT helps vulnerable populations while addressing collective responsibility. In doing this, it has made a remarkable contribution. 'By recognizing the extent of torture, opposing its practice and offering support for survivors, communities can begin to mitigate its effects and create a more humane world for the next century' (Simalchik, 1993, p. 45). Community education is but one facet of the centre's societal direction, which also includes linking survivors with their ethnic and geographical communities and building advocacy coalitions around immigration, antiracism, and gender issues. This combination of local and international activities, concomitant with the active involvement of the centre's staff and participants in articulating a philosophy that integrates earlier forms of conscientization with the current debates worded in terms of human rights, democracy, and pluralism (Turner, 1993), has contributed to the success of this model.

The CCVT is developing its activities and policies in increments, and in doing so is actively contributing to the formulation of principles to shape our changing civil society (Kumar, 1993). In conclusion, the CCVT is at the vanguard of the encounter between CD, the new social movements (Cohen, 1985; Diani, 1992), and the current debate on civil society.

DIRECTIONS FOR RESEARCH

The separate strategies developed by CCVT should be evaluated. Further inquiry into this multifaceted approach to CD points to several directions: examination in philosophical and action terms of the compatibility of the multiple methods used, in particular of internal and external CD; assessment of the cultural 'fit' of these strategies for the various ethnic and national communities, and assessment of the balance between ethnospecific and gender-specific forms of CD; consideration of linkages between ethnospecific and mainstream community actions; and evaluation of the possibilities and limitations of NGO structures in pursuing these recent developments. A participatory research approach should be taken when such inquiries are conducted.

B. The Entre Nous Femmes Housing Society, Vancouver:
Single Parent Women and Community Economic Development
Leslie Stern, Leslie Kemp, and Michael Clague

WHAT IS ENTRE NOUS FEMMES?

Becoming a single parent changes many women's lives dramatically. We were all perfectly fine until we became single parents. (ENF founding member)

For many women in Canada, becoming a single parent means a drop in income, poor housing, and increased responsibilities. In Vancouver, the Entre Nous Femmes (ENF) Housing Society was established in 1984 to change this situation for its members. ENF (which means 'among us women') is about creating 'space' – safe space where the needs of women as single parents are recognized and validated and from which organizing can take place. In this story of CD, housing was the organizing tool. A group of women shared their personal circumstances and decided to act.

The purpose of ENF is 'to create and manage safe and affordable housing communities which provide a base from which female led single parent families can move forward, through and beyond the stages of poverty.' There are eight ENF housing communities in the Greater Vancouver area, the first completed in 1986 and the eighth in 1993. Each community is named after the mother or grandmother of someone involved with ENF, in acknowledgment of 'the extraordinary lives of ordinary women.'

ENF is more than a housing society. As indicated in its purpose, housing is viewed as integral to the empowerment of single mothers, who are likely to find themselves in poverty: 'Our experience has shown that once basic needs are met, lives stabilize, while work and income opportunities increase.'

Women living in ENF housing have the opportunity to participate in the management and operation of their own housing community, at both the board and management level and as volunteers. Also available to them through the society are employment and skills development opportunities in building maintenance and in landscaping and property development and management.

The ENF Housing Society is managed by a board of directors composed of tenants elected from each housing community and from the community at large. The volunteer efforts of these participants enable ENF to translate its philosophy into action and CD. The commitment to personal empowerment and responsibility is expressed through a nonhierarchical structure that promotes co-operation and innovation. ENF hires a property manager for each community in consultation with a representative of the tenant community. The society's philosophy is evident in its views on tenant participation:

Tenant participation in community management is encouraged, but not mandatory. Single parents are often burdened with multiple responsibilities, and non-resident property managers provide a practical means of support in the daily operation of communities, while still encouraging the ENF philosophy of individual empowerment and responsibility. (*Entre Nous News*, 1993)

Tenant committees may include maintenance, mediation, social activities, gardening, and recycling. The ENF housing communities are located in neighbourhoods ranging from the inner city to middle-class suburban districts. In designing these communities, ENF works to incorporate the realities and experiences of single-parent families. Every development tries to be sensitive to different family lifestyles, particularly as this relates to those who choose to stay at home and raise their children and those who choose to work part or full-time outside the home.

The design criteria for each community include the following:

- safety
- light and livability
- easy maintenance
- ability to monitor children
- accessible common room and play areas

Most buildings are constructed around central courtyards or play areas. A sense of privacy and ownership is maintained within the security of community living. There are also innovations that reflect the needs of parents and small children – for example, child-height view-holes on doors, and dining room floors that are easy to clean.

ENF is a housing society 'plus.' Housing is the core activity; around this are a range of other activities that provide residents with greater control over their lives and new opportunities in work, education, and quality of life.

HOUSING AND SINGLE PARENT WOMEN

In 1991, one out of five families with children in British Columbia was headed by a single parent, and most of these parents were women. In 1985, 50.9 percent of B.C. families that were headed by women lived at or below Statistics Canada's low-income line (Statistics Canada, 1990). The number of women and children living in poverty has continued to increase.

The typical single-parent family consists of a mother with one or two children. In Vancouver few single-parent women, whether employed outside the home or receiving social assistance, have been able to obtain housing at less than 30 percent of their total income, which is the Canadian standard measure for housing affordability. When the cost of child care is considered, it becomes plain that it has been almost impossible for most mothers to manage financially.

The only affordable options have been government-supported housing (which involves waiting up to five years), moving in with friends or family, or putting up with unsuitable living conditions. Young single moms with infants typically end up in drafty, damp basement apartments. For the most part, society has viewed housing as an investment and treated it as a commodity to be governed by the law of supply and demand. This reflects a patriarchal system of interests. Though women generally view housing as the centre of life, few earn enough to afford the housing they require without assistance from a mate or the government.

Throughout the 1970s and 1980s in Canada, women of all backgrounds and from all economic levels were likely to enter poverty as a result of divorce or other failed relationships. These women faced increased financial and emotional responsibility, yet their wages and life circumstances were governed by cultural assumptions from the 1950s, when men were seen as the primary providers and most 'women's work' went unacknowledged and unpaid or underpaid. Though half of female single parents were poor, few people recognized the extent of the 'feminization of poverty.' By custom, single mothers were viewed as deserving their lot: they had somehow broken the boundaries of society's norms.

Faced with these realities, a small group of women in Vancouver wanted to develop a supportive, interactive housing community that responded to the social and economic realities of single parenthood.

THE PERSONAL IS POLITICAL

Becoming a single parent changes one's life drastically in ways one might never expect. There is never enough time, never enough money, nor ever enough hands to meet the emotional and physical needs of one's children and the various demands of society. (ENF member)

At the beginning of the 1980s, the Vancouver YWCA was sponsoring support groups for single mothers. These groups provided an opportunity for mothers to meet while their children were looked after by others. They provided a respite from the rest of the world and a relatively safe place for a 'single mom' to be. Some of the women began to talk about breaking down the stereotypes projected by the dominant culture. The research the women did found that single parents come from all backgrounds: 24 percent had never been married, 10 percent were widowed, and the rest were either divorced or separated. However they became single parents, most women seemed to need from six months to two years to recover from the emotional impact of what they and their children were experiencing. Their experiences were rarely recognized or validated.

The YWCA support group decided to put what they were learning into action. They used the 1982 provincial election to focus on two issues: income and housing. This was a valuable education in the political process. The following summer, some members were invited to plan the next annual YWCA Single Mothers' Symposium. A workshop called 'Uniting for Change' was held that focused on political strategies and working with the media.

Out of these initiatives the Single Mothers' Action Committee was formed. It researched and investigated four issues: income, child care, housing, and women and the law. The group decided to concentrate its efforts on housing, which had been an issue for every member. They realized that until one's home is safe and secure, one cannot deal effectively with anything else.

The group believed that given the resources and the opportunity, single mothers could develop housing that truly met their needs. The vision here was of an interactive community based on women's values and the establishing of a firm base from which single mothers could move forward.

The first step was for women to stop acting like victims and begin to believe that things could be made better through mutual effort and self-determination. The next was to create an organizational structure and a workable strategy. The personal would be transformed into the political through an action agenda for women's housing.

THE CREATION OF ENF

They were always pushing the edges ... they were relentless. What I remember most is 'tenacity,' which you have to have. (Former Inner City Housing staff member)

ENF, an offspring of the Single Mothers' Action Committee, undertook something that had never before been done in Vancouver – the planning, development, and management of affordable housing for single mothers, *by* single mothers. They had no previous experience in housing development. They had to overcome scepticism, disinterest, and rejection. They had to remain firm in their own conviction that they could do it. They succeeded by building on their own life and work experience.

ENF was born of necessity and idealism. Members asked themselves: 'How can we meet women's housing needs?' The key factors were affordability and safety. But there was also a desire to generate a community of interest, a supportive environment, and increased opportunities for paid employment. Especially important was the desire to carry into the housing community the philosophy of mutual support and consensus decision-making that had proved so valuable in the support group and the action committee.

The vision was to build and manage safe and affordable housing for female-led families. At the same time the group wanted to create an environment of opportunity and empowerment. It would be a healthy community composed of a cross-section of family types and lifestyles. The goal was that 60 to 70 percent of the households would be led by single parents, with a few of these headed by men. This was where the need was greatest and where the options were most limited. The remaining units would house two-parent families, seniors, and some singles.

At the time ENF was organizing, the Canada Mortgage and Housing Corporation (CMHC) was the primary instrument of support for subsidized, affordable housing in Canada. Once it had CMHC approval, ENF would have funds to develop its project, a guaranteed mortgage, and ongoing operating subsidies.

An organization that was to provide significant assistance throughout ENF's efforts to develop housing was the Inner City Housing Society. Inner City was an established resource group that helped develop nonprofit and co-operative housing. With ENF, it was breaking new ground. Inner City agreed to split its fee income with ENF, if the latter was successful in obtaining a project development grant. This meant that ENF would have the resources to participate directly in the development work. It could use its one-third of the fee to hire an ENF member to do the tenant development and management planning that Inner City would normally do.

TWO POSSIBLE TYPES OF DEVELOPMENT

There are three types of publicly supported, affordable housing in Vancouver:

- Government financed and managed (though little has been built of this housing type since the 1970s).
- Co-operatively owned and managed by the residents.
- Owned and managed by occupants (renters) of a nonprofit housing society.

ENF chose the nonprofit option. The members reasoned that most single parents were already overworked and needed choices about their degree of participation in the management of their housing. The co-operative model was inviting, yet demanding of time. The nonprofit model was seen as more flexible – as allowing for participation but not demanding it. Also, the nonprofit society might be able to lend extra support and encouragement to the families it housed.

Another feature in favour of the nonprofit model was the opportunities it might offer for paid work for women. The group knew that a single mom's fight for self-esteem is never-ending. To the rest of the world, she has 'blown' her relationship. It's a no-win situation: If she works full-time, she's ignoring her children. If she stays home with her children, she's lazy and a drain on the system. Part-time work is ideal, but usually a financial disaster. A rental building had the potential to create real jobs close to home; at the same time, it would provide service rather than load on another set of demands.

ALMA BLACKWELL: THE FIRST ENF HOUSING COMMUNITY

These women were not afraid of not knowing. The group didn't have a chance to sit back and examine itself ... The goal was housing, and each time a door opened we walked through it. (ENF member)

CMHC did provide the development funds to ENF. However, when ENF and Inner City submitted the final development plan, the project was turned down. It seemed that CMHC had changed the emphasis of its housing policy to take less account of social values and more account of cost efficiency. However, the ENF members persisted. They met with the regional manager for CMHC in British Columbia and presented their case. They gained the support of the local Member of Parliament, who was a woman and a former community organizer. Letters backing their campaign came from prominent community organizations, including the YWCA and the United Way. The ENF case was raised in the House of Commons. A consistent argument was presented:

social values had to be supported in CMHC programs, and housing for single parents was of utmost priority.

ENF's strategy was to take action on several fronts at the same time. These fronts included pressuring politicians and bureaucrats in Ottawa, the federal capital; lobbying housing officials in Vancouver intensely; gaining public support from key organizations; and using the media. The strategy worked. ENF also got CMHC to approve the payment of child care costs from the capital fund so that women could be free to work on the project while their children were being looked after. The Alma Blackwell Housing Community became ENF's first nonprofit, affordable housing community. It was named after a grandmother of one of the founders, who herself had been a single parent.

CMHC required that 25 percent of the units be subsidized at below market rents. However, knowing what they did about the need for affordable housing, ENF's members were determined to subsidize at least 50 percent of the units. In order to spread the subsidy further, ENF asked that families pay 30 percent of their monthly income on rent rather than the minimum 25 percent allowed within the CMHC operating agreement. ENF also developed an informal policy that at least half of the subsidized units were to be occupied by parents employed outside the home; the other half might depend on government for income assistance. The goal was to encourage self-determination and self-sufficiency whenever possible. The success of this approach became evident two years after the project opened, when it was found that more than half of the families originally dependent on government income assistance had become self-supporting.

Designing a housing community for young single-parent families was a special challenge, given the very tight budget. The design for Alma Blackwell encourages a unique identity for each household in the community, while at the same time fostering interaction and communication among residents. Each unit has a separate and distinctive entrance from the courtyard. One courtyard features play equipment for young children; the other is flanked by a bike shelter and a grassy field. Both laundry rooms look onto the play areas, as do most kitchen windows. There are also offices for community members and for the ENF Society. The common room is meant to be a community living room. Bright and roomy, it is used for meetings, parties, workshops, and craft fairs. Its use is managed by the residents.

ENF wanted to ensure that residents could participate in the management of the society (and in forming the policies governing Alma

Blackwell) if they wished. The residents of Alma Blackwell were asked to elect a representative to the board of ENF. In this, according to a former Inner City Housing staff member, they 'were way ahead of their time in terms of the management of a nonprofit board.'

The Alma Blackwell Housing Community was completed in 1986. It was an intense and demanding experience: one of endless meetings and a constant search for consensus. Members steadfastly refused to give up on the vision of housing for single-parent families, despite the external obstacles. 'It definitely said that you can change the system,' said one of the original ENF tenant board members. 'It gave me a lot of hope and knowledge about what you have to do and about the awful lot of work involved.'

TEN YEARS LATER: ENF TODAY

Seven more such communities have since been developed, which demonstrates a remarkable integration of learning, empowerment, and social action. ENF has become a dynamic example of the ability of single mothers to meet their own needs, given the opportunity and the access to resources. Over the years the group has pushed the accepted definitions of housing development and management to embrace a broader perspective, one that includes community and personal development. There have been tensions between the ideal and the possible, between the desire to continue to develop new communities and the need to strengthen what already exists. There has also been steady debate about how to promote continued growth without sacrificing ongoing maintenance, and about how to balance the perspectives of tenants, staff, and board. While funding is available for property management, there is little available for internal community or board development.

ENF is still engaged in a process of refining, re-evaluating, and reforming its methods. It is looking at the roles and responsibilities of the various members of the ENF community, with the focus on tenant participation, decision making, and the transmission of values. This process was initiated at the group's most recent annual retreat and is 'very much in progress,' according to the society's current president. She describes the process as difficult in terms of the amount of time and energy it takes and the different levels of commitment of the various participants. This is what makes the outcome difficult to predict. However, this type of process is an integral part of what CD is about – action, and then reflection leading to further action.

TENANT PARTICIPATION

Tenant participation has always been a key aspect of ENF's role in CD. Residents have been encouraged to take responsibility for day-to-day decisions by working closely with the property managers and establishing their own internal structures. In addition, residents are invited to sit on tenant selection and staff hiring committees. The society endeavours to include residents' perspectives in its decision-making process by welcoming tenant input and including a representative from each building on its board of directors.

The society also fosters CD by encouraging communication among the tenants through its newsletter and by providing offices and meeting spaces. Tenant initiatives in areas such as child care, food co-ops, and recreational and educational programs are encouraged. In addition, ENF has offered several job-training programs in building maintenance, property management, and office administration. This has helped residents develop skills in new areas; for some, it has provided a stepping-stone to paid employment.

Prospective tenants were included as part of the design and management process during the development of ENF's first project, the Alma Blackwell Housing Community. Tenants also helped develop later projects by providing design and organizational ideas. In doing so they looked beyond their own interests in order to envision future communities. Initially, the society nurtured and developed the communities. Now each community has strength of its own and nurtures the society by providing fresh perspectives and new sources of leadership for the group as a whole.

A key issue was this: 'How much say and control can and should tenants have in their own communities over selection of new tenants?' (*Entre Nous News*, November 1993). It was suggested that 'this is often a balancing act between the financial stability of the community, moral and ethical issues, government requirements, the existing society policies such as the internal move policy, and the desired demographics and character of the community.' ENF held a workshop around this issue, to which all residents and members of the society were invited.

Other questions posed to members of the society and the residents of its eight communities asked:

What is the difference between property management and CD? Can/should ENF do both? What does community mean to you? What works about the community you are in? What do you think is the most important to change and why? What contribution could you make toward that change? What holds you back? What would CD in your community look like? How could this be funded? (*Entre Nous News*, November 1993)

All of these questions illustrate a desire to reach beyond the accepted functions of housing development and management to a broader role for the society in CD.

CONNECTING TO THE BROADER COMMUNITY

In addition to the links it has fostered within its own communities, ENF has established networks with the broader community. This has been facilitated through membership and participation in organizations such as the B.C. Women's Housing Coalition, the National Action Committee on the Status of Women, the Cooperative Housing Federation of B.C., the Canadian Housing and Renewal Association, the B.C. Working Group on Community Economic Development, and the B.C. Non-Profit Housing Association. In addition, ENF residents have established strong links with day care centres, schools, community centres, and groups and businesses within their local communities.

WHAT HAS BEEN ACHIEVED: A RETROSPECTIVE

ENF's main intention was to build and manage safe and affordable housing for female-led families while promoting a vibrant mixed community with a variety of lifestyle alternatives. By and large, ENF has achieved this goal. A demographic profile of its tenants shows that in May 1993, of 326 adult tenants, 159 were single parents (156 of them female), 69 were couples, and 19 were seniors. Also, 7 tenants had disabilities, and 39 spoke languages other than English.

Another of ENF's intentions was to achieve a balance between tenants who required government income assistance and those who were employed either full or part time. ENF reasoned that single parents need to be able to choose between caring for their children full time (thus requiring income assistance) and accepting paid employment and putting their children into day care programs. The May 1993 profile showed a rough balance between those who derived their income from employment and those depending on government assistance. Of 264 residents, 85 were employed by the private sector; 16 were employed with public sector agencies; 17 were students; 17 were retired; and roughly half (129) received income assistance from government.

If ENF did nothing else but construct and manage housing, it would have achieved its goal. It has provided 256 units of housing for people with low incomes, many of them women with children. However, ENF has achieved much more than this:

- It has provided opportunities for women in areas such as employment and skill development, and given them the freedom to go back to school or to take time to regain physical or emotional health.
- It has reduced tenants' worries about lack of income security, and lessened their fears of being evicted because of inability to pay or other problems.
- It has provided a safe place to raise children.
- It has removed the social stigma of being a single parent.
- It has provided women with choices and self-esteem.
- It has created eight distinct communities.
- It has provided a model of organizing for other women.
- It has enlarged the boundaries and the social perceptions of women's abilities to meet concrete goals.

Women emphasized the importance of stable, safe, and affordable housing for their own and their family's health and well-being:

I can hardly begin to express how valuable it is to me to have comfortable, stable, convenient and affordable housing for my family. 'Home' is the foundation that we build our lives upon; the base starting point from which we venture out into the world to make social contacts, to achieve employment goals, work on educational aspirations, etc. The feeling of dignity and self-respect that comes along with having a good home environment to take pride in, is crucial to mental health, the ability to conquer challenges, and to feel like a valued and valuable contributing member of society. Unfortunately, what ought to be a right seems like a rare privilege, considering the scarcity of good family accommodation, especially for low-income earners, and the length of the waiting lists. (Quoted in Geary, 1992, p. 88)

This sentiment was expressed over and over again in interviews conducted to document the history of ENF.

In the 1990s the Conservative federal government stepped back from its role in providing affordable housing. The programs through which ENF developed its eight communities, are no longer available for new projects. At the same time the provincial government is redefining its role in relation to affordable housing. While single parents are now widely recognized as a 'high need' category, little is being done in the way of policies and programs to address those needs. While Vancouver grows at an accelerated pace, the supply of low-cost housing dwindles. Women must continue to make their voices heard and to fight for social equity, or they will be overlooked by the forces behind mainstream global economics.

ENF is continuing its process of renewal. The board, staff, and tenants are willing to participate in a process of carrying forward the society's organizational culture and assessing the values and practices that have shaped and defined ENF. The future will reveal the outcomes of this process.

What is certain, is that ENF is a group of women actively working to improve the lives of women. They have found their voice as women in the housing sector and they are using this voice in effective ways to create change. It is a voice that creates excitement and enthusiasm, it 'hooks' people because the energy behind the voice is so encompassing, and it provides a vision and model for other women to reach out and find encouragement from. The story of ENF serves as an example and inspiration, not only to Canadian women and men, but also to people from other countries, who, like us are struggling to create safe, secure, affordable and accessible housing which reflects and responds to the needs of its users. (Geary, 1992, p. 95)

ENF AND COMMUNITY DEVELOPMENT

ENF is a story of self-reliance and self-empowerment. No outside individuals or agencies initiated this organization and its work, though a number turned out to be key sources of support. The women of ENF were their own CD workers. The motivation, the conviction, and the vision were theirs. They applied their skills and abilities to this complex undertaking. Some of the members brought previous work and educational experiences to the task; all, regardless of education or training, became self-directed learners. Conflicts and issues of power were dealt with strategically. Road blocks were regarded as setbacks and not as defeats. The inertia of the bureaucracy required them to identify key points for intervention and advocacy instead of simply meeting the housing 'system,' with all its rules and regulations, head on.

ENF has enlarged the boundaries for what women are able to achieve in creating safe, affordable, and appropriate housing. It has done so by successfully communicating its values within its own community and in the community at large. It has acted from a belief in self-determination. It has struggled self-critically to balance the creation of change with the limits of what is possible. To sustain its ideals, ENF has had to avoid becoming a building development 'institution' itself. These are the characteristics of ENF's experience that may be of relevance to groups involved in CD. ENF is an example of effective social change for the advancement and well-being of women who were marginalized – led by the women themselves.

ENF AND COMMUNITY ECONOMIC DEVELOPMENT:
CONTRIBUTION TO THEORY

It is often the unaddressed needs in women's lives that serve as a catalyst for them to play an active role in CED. A 1993 study focusing on women and CED (Alderson et al., 1993) found that women often organize themselves to meet a range of needs such as affordable housing, child care, transportation, and wholesome food, and to create a supportive environment for those women who are new to Canada or facing isolated circumstances. In the case of ENF, single-parent women chose housing from among a range of important issues, in the belief that providing housing would address a number of other needs for single mothers (e.g., affordable shelter, stability, and an opportunity to address employment and educational opportunities).

CED activity is also seen as a means of gaining control over local resources, and as an opportunity to build permanent institutions (MacLeod, 1984; Swack & Mason, 1987; Alderson et al., 1993; Shragge, 1993). In the case of ENF, women started with their own experience and needs as single mothers. The motivating factor was to help women in similar circumstances gain control over community resources through the building of permanent structures within the community that were relevant to their particular needs.

Women describe their vision for CED as holistic. To them, the goal is to integrate, with social, economic, cultural, and ecological objectives; this is often referred to as the 'multiple bottom-line' (Alderson et al., 1993). ENF had an explicit multiple bottom-line in its approach to organizing. The goal of affordable housing was meshed with training women as housing developers and property managers, with providing quality child care and child-friendly homes, with providing opportunities for women to re-enter paid employment or education, and with providing ethnically and culturally rich communities.

Self-reliance is another explicit goal of CED (Wismer and Pell, 1984; B.C. Working Group on CED, 1992; Alderson et al., 1993). The B.C. Working Group on CED (1992) indicates that 'CED contributes to self-reliance by encouraging the acquisition of relevant skills and the development of supportive structures and institutions.' Further, 'CED builds on local strengths, creativity, and resources, and actively seeks to decrease dependency on, and vulnerability to, economic interests outside the community and region.' Through their involvement in ENF, women had opportunities to develop and build on their skills as organizers, housing developers, and property managers; this fostered self-reliance and increased their independence. However, women were not seen as powerless or unskilled at the outset; women's own experience, commitment, and enthusiasm were seen as strengths when it came to beginning CD activity.

The Women and CED study reinforces the importance of women as a resource for CED activity:

Women themselves are the most important resource for women's CED! We have learned that the unique set of skills and experiences women bring to CED work make us experts in our own communities. Women approach CED with determination and commitment that comes from a deep concern for themselves and for the future of their own communities. Women are often good problem-solvers who can figure out how to get something done with limited resources and when there is no one else around who is willing to take up the challenge. (Alderson et al., 1993, p. 34)

C. Kindling Community Capacity: Onward Willow
Ray Peters and Gary Cameron

A GOVERNMENT PROJECT INITIATIVE: 'BETTER BEGINNINGS, BETTER FUTURES'

The Better Beginnings, Better Futures Project (BBBF) is a community-based, government-initiated prevention project that has three major goals: to prevent serious social, emotional, behavioural, physical, and cognitive problems in young children; to promote the social, emotional, behavioural, physical, and cognitive development of these children; and to enhance the abilities of families living in socio-economically disadvantaged communities to provide for their children. The case of 'Onward Willow' that follows this introduction illustrates a CD approach to achieving these goals.

The project is funded by three Ontario provincial ministries (Community and Social Services, Health, and Education) and by the federal Department of Indian and Northern Affairs and the Secretary of State. Better Beginnings is the first long-term project of its kind in Canada. It grew out of a number of primary-prevention initiatives that had been introduced by Ontario's Ministry of Community and Social Services (ComSoc) since the late 1970s.

The focus is on children up to the age of eight living in eleven socio-economically disadvantaged communities and neighbourhoods in Ontario. These communities are being funded for four years to provide services tailored to local circumstances. The progress of the children, their families, and their neighbourhoods will be followed until the children reach their mid-twenties.

The BBBF project is composed of the following: community research sites, consisting of project co-ordinators, project staff, parents, community residents, service providers, and educators, established under local sponsorship in twelve Ontario communities; a government committee, consisting of representatives from the co-funding ministries and departments; and a research co-ordination unit, consisting of a core team of academic researchers and locally hired site researchers in each of the twelve communities.

Community Research Sites
The major responsibilities of the twelve BBBF project communities are to develop and implement high-quality prevention and promotion programs for young children and their families. These programs are to be characterized by meaningful, significant involvement of community residents in all aspects of program development and implementation, and by integration of new services for children and families with the existing ones.

Of the twelve participating communities, eight have developed prenatal/preschool models for children from birth to age four – these are the 'younger cohort communities' – and three have developed a preschool/primary school prevention model for children between the ages of four and eight – these are the 'older cohort communities.'

Government Committee
This committee consists of approximately fifteen representatives from the co-funding/cost-sharing partners of the BBBF Project. The purpose of the committee is to support and oversee the BBBF on behalf of the

funding ministries and departments, the twelve research communities, and the research co-ordination unit. The committee representatives also report the research findings back to senior management in government.

Research Co-ordination Unit
This unit, the RCU, does what its name says – it co-ordinates research across the selected research sites. It consists of a core research team and research director, site research teams, central support staff, and advisers. It is incumbent upon the unit to address three general questions:

- Is the BBBF model effective?
- What structures and processes are associated with project results?
- Is the BBBF model affordable?

In developing the research plans, the RCU established a process of broad consultation. In each BBBF community, the RCU site researchers and site liaisons consulted with neighbourhood residents, service agency personnel, educators, and project staff members. These discussions often took place in meetings of local research committees that were established to facilitate community-level review and feedback concerning the RCU's research plans and reports.

In addition to these community consultations, the government committee systematically reviews all research plans. Finally, a BBBF ethics review committee at Queen's University, consisting of several university researchers and community representatives, ensures that all research procedures meet ethical standards. There has been little documentation of the structure, processes, activities, and organization of those programs which are associated with positive outcomes for children. In the BBBF project, by contrast, investigating project development and program implementation at the local project level is an important research objective.

CASE STUDY
ONWARD WILLOW, GUELPH
Jassy Narayan and Jim Vanderwoerd

HISTORY

In the darkness of a winter afternoon in January 1990, excited conversation filled the air as more and more people crowded into the church's basement meeting room. They were coming from schools and mental health clinics, from child welfare agencies and health centres, from day care centres and preschools, from government offices, and from the university. Some greeted old friends and colleagues, while others saw new faces; all had taken time from their usual work to gather to hear about a project named 'Better Beginnings, Better Futures.'

What was all the excitement about? Why did staff representing such a wide range of social, educational, and health services all come together? The news of BBBF was refreshing to many communities that had long been accustomed to hearing only bad news. Many had long felt frustrated from working in a system that divided peoples' lives into neat categories, and that arranged and organized services in a rigid, complex system. Here was a project that offered the possibility of something new, something innovative – something that might in some small way hold the key to more effective helping.

Thus was born in the small Ontario city of Guelph the Onward Willow BBBF project. Many of the people who came to that first meeting continued to come, and a committed and enthusiastic steering committee was formed to develop and submit a proposal for funding. The mood was optimistic. While the work was hard and the challenges were great, the potential rewards were significant: ensuring the best for children, transforming a neighbourhood, and creating a partnership between parents and professionals.

The members of the steering committee worked on their proposal, spending long hours collecting information, brainstorming, debating ideas, and deciding on the best way to satisfy the requirements of the government sponsors. Despite their excitement, their energy, and their commitment to the ideas of community involvement and neighbourhood empowerment, something was missing. No neighbourhood residents were involved, and with the deadline for submitting the proposal only ten weeks away, there was a feeling that without active community participation, the proposal would not receive funding.

Guelph was one of a handful of communities across the province that had been approved for a $5,000 grant to develop a final proposal. The group decided to take a risk: instead of hiring a professional to help write their proposal, they used the money to hire a CD worker whose primary task was to engage residents in the process. The person they hired shared many of the experiences of the people in the neighbourhood: she had lived in public housing; she was a sole-support mother; and she had experienced first-hand what it was like to receive some of the same services now represented on the steering group.

Within a month she had organized two neighbourhood meetings and invited the participation of about a dozen community residents. They were unfamiliar with the language of community organizing, committees, steering groups, chairpersons, quorums, agendas, funding proposals, and government ministries. What could they possibly offer to the steering group?

The CD worker brought them together every week and invited them to talk about their lives and their communities, about their children and their neighbours. They shared their experiences as new parents raising young children, and then were asked what would have been helpful. Their ideas were incorporated into a draft proposal that was sent back to them for their comments. After some tentative beginnings, they soon were eagerly going through it section by section, adding ideas, taking out obscure words, and making it clearer. The neighbourhood organized a petition in the community in support of the proposal, and hundreds of signatures were gathered. Many other agencies were contacted, and their letters of support were attached. Finally, the package was ready. With only hours to spare, a member of the steering group drove to Toronto, the province's capital, to personally deliver the proposal. The waiting now began.

After more than six months and several delays, the announcement finally came that the Guelph community had been chosen to participate in the BBBF project. Onward Willow received high marks for its proposal, particularly for the way in which community residents had participated. The $5,000 gamble had paid off. The steering group and the community now faced the challenge of doing what their proposal said they would do.

The steering group was disbanded, and in its place a board was established to run the project. The board was made up of neighbourhood residents and representatives from various social, educational, and health services in the city. Hiring staff was one of the board's first tasks, but at the same time the members also began to think about how to implement the programs that they had dreamed about in the proposal. The critical first step in this process was to clarify exactly what they were trying to accomplish, and for whom. The government's expectations were clear enough: the project was to demonstrate and document prevention programs for young children in one of two age groups – from birth to age four and from four to eight – and to foster the active involvement and participation of community members.

While the Onward Willow project had been designated as a 'birth to age four' project, many community members had children older than four. A central challenge facing the new board, therefore, was to develop programs that met the government's criteria but at the same time fulfilled the needs and expectations of community members. The solution arrived at by the board was to broaden the project's original goals (outlined in the introduction to this case study) to accommodate a more inclusive CD approach. These broader goals will be discussed in the following section.

TURNING THE PLAN INTO ACTION:
THE DEVELOPMENT OF THE PROGRAM MODEL

The task of turning the proposed plans into concrete programs dovetailed with the hiring of the project co-ordinator. Before assuming the position and in the first few weeks after being hired, she spent many hours meeting and talking to community members and staff to establish trust, and also to undertake a preliminary assessment. She observed that community members were showing renewed pride in their neighbourhood, which before the funding was received had had a generally negative image in the city of Guelph. Furthermore, there was a sense of accomplishment in having one community member hired for the project. The expectation was that other community members would follow.

At the same time, the process was not without conflicts. A rivalry began to develop between those community members who were considered to be part of the in-group (involved from the start) and others (late joiners) who were viewed or who viewed themselves as outsiders.

The relationship between the community members and the service providers had its difficulties. The community members indicated their discomfort with the impersonal attitude and formal language of the professionals. Many of the service providers referred to community members as 'clients' or 'targets' rather than as 'partners.' The project board, with its formal operations, was seen as a forum for service providers. Board meetings were compared to a dinner party at which community members were to be on their 'company behaviour.' In contrast, neighbourhood group meetings were like having dinner at home; at times they were disruptive and noisy, but everyone had a say and felt an equal part of the gathering.

Exploratory meetings with service providers revealed different levels of concern and commitment. Some had been involved in BBBF-related activities from the beginning, while others joined later. Quite a few were aware of the issues of conflict between community members and staff and were sensitive to the fact that community members often disliked or even feared agencies. Generally, their level of discomfort in working face to face with community members was as high as that of community members toward them. On the basis of these observations and personal contacts, the project co-ordinator was able to analyse the situation and resolve the issues.

Moving the project from ideas to implementation required an approach that combined task goals (what to do) with process goals (how to do it). Process goals focused on qualities that would enhance relationships: empathy, respect, genuineness, and concreteness. Empathy is the ability to understand, appreciate, and accept the other person's feelings in a way that highlights interdependence. Respect emphasizes the worth of the individual. Genuineness is the ability to reflect openly about one's thoughts and feelings toward others. Concreteness is the ability to be specific, clear, and direct in sharing facts and feelings.

The model of CD for this project was developed over eighteen months. The outcome was a document for the government funders known as 'Schedule A' – a term rarely used by project participants. Instead, various metaphors were used to help people understand the primary importance of the particular CD approach taken: 'It is like a patchwork quilt, or a vision, or a pie, or a meadow, or a map.' All the activities to meet the objectives were organized and categorized into three program parts. Each program part had a particular focus: the child, the family, or the community. Each part was staffed by a team consisting of a supervisor and a lay person from the neighbourhood, who was selected for particular qualities and attitudes. The supervisor had to have formal training in the relevant area of expertise (e.g., community nursing, child care, family support, CD).

Since the model developed in this project is a partnership model, the struggle over language and meaning has been ongoing, with staff playing a translating and mediating role. The program model means many things to many people. To the funding ministries, it is Schedule A. To service providers, it is 'integrated program components.' To community members, it is something very personal – food, relief from child care responsibilities, a bus ticket or taxi fare, talking to other mums on a particular day, being asked an opinion, or participating in decision making. Neighbourhood staff see the model as 'imposed order' but feel obligated to focus on the particular component they are working in.

Team supervisors view the model through their respective areas of responsibility, but they also see the interrelatedness of concepts and process. They are called upon to translate and interpret information and processes for community members, service providers, and the community at large. For the supervisors and the co-ordinator, there are multiple levels of accountability, which operate simultaneously: accountability to the community members, to the service providers, to the board, to the other staff, and, in the case of the project co-ordinator, to the government-appointed site supervisor and the researchers. To work at these various levels requires flexibility, confidence, competence, and personal contact with community members.

The process of developing the program model was guided by four theories that had evolved from practice in similar projects pioneered over many years in children's and mental health centres in this region of Ontario. These theories relate to CD, adult education, social support, and social competence.

Community development is perceived as the process by which community members create an organizational structure for collective action with respect to decision making and leadership training. The structure facilitates needs identification and the development of the resources to change a stressful environment. The CD process develops a sense of preparedness in the community and promotes community cohesion. It establishes associational space and identifies guides and natural leaders.

Adult education is defined as the process by which adults continue to learn. Adults have cumulative knowledge that integrates life experiences with new knowledge. Their knowledge and experience are a resource to the community. Adults are able to learn and teach at the same time through a peer education process. Because adult education does not depend on formal learning or school learning only, community members with low literacy are included and valued. Reciprocity is a key factor.

Social support is viewed as an effective buffer against acute stress and distress. A person who feels supported copes better and is also more likely to seek and accept help when in need. Social supports relate to a range of concrete and psychological factors, including food, child care relief, transportation, friendship, and opportunities to participate in the community. Reciprocity and mutuality are key ingredients of social support. Social support is seen from an ecological perspective – that is, everyone needs it to survive and thrive.

Social competence is a process by which individuals gain more control over their lives. They develop the ability to express their feelings, and they become more sensitive to others. They develop problem-solving skills and learn to find alternative solutions. They gain a greater understanding of systems and of how to negotiate for their family and community needs. Social competence is the process through which adults learn to reframe things, try out new ideas, take risks, and speak as individuals.

These theories were turned into practice, as could be observed in the everyday activities of the project. For example, at a meeting to plan an activity, CD practice established a partnership in which community members, staff, and service providers worked together. It established structures and leadership roles and ensured that the content of the meeting would fit with the overall goals and objectives of the project. Through adult education, leadership roles were learned. The study materials were adapted to various levels of literacy. Social support was provided by peers and staff; often this involved arranging child care, providing rides to meetings, and similar. Social competence focused on concerns of inclusivity, sensitivity, and feelings, and on ways of communicating.

PRACTICE ISSUES

Assumptions and Principles
Underlying the project is a vision of strength, health, and mutuality. These are not merely guidelines but the foundations of the project; as such, they must be translated and transformed into observable behaviour. For example, if parents and community members cannot be present at planning and evaluation meetings, those meetings are postponed. It is assumed that community members must speak for the community. Some of the key assumptions and principles include these:

- Communities have the capacity, strength, wisdom, and insight to nurture and support families.
- Communities have an abundance of natural leaders and guides who know what is best for the neighbourhood.
- Contrary to being apathetic, communities always have their own interests at heart.
- Communities have the ability and capacity to work in partnership with the formal helping system to nurture and sustain families.

- The informal and formal helping systems work from different feeling states, have different languages, and are guided by different maps.
- The community plays a mediating role between families and the formal helping system.
- Families must be connected with and supported by formal and informal community settings if their various needs are to be met.
- Interventions to promote healthy child and family development should build on and strengthen existing community resources and supports.
- Families and service providers must work in a partnership based on information sharing, trust, and mutual respect in the community empowerment process.

Leadership Style
Because the leadership style is collaborative rather than expert-driven, alliances are possible with all the primary stakeholders – community members, service providers, staff, and funders. A collaborative style is inclusive and participatory, and thus maximizes the opportunities for everyone to contribute.

There are many parts to the leadership role – co-ordinator, facilitator, educator, enabler, resource developer, organizer, follower, partner, broker, negotiator, and advocator. The leadership role changes according to context, and a clear distinction is made between having expertise and being an expert. 'Expertise' suggests a blend of experience and knowledge, while being an 'expert' suggests an attitude of being right or having the right answer.

Collaborative, participatory leadership requires a different use of language and a reframing of words, perspectives, and information. It is based on the assumption that everyone has a unique perspective, that solutions evolve out of dialogue, and that decisions are made through consensus. Thus, collaborative leaders ask for help, are guided by others, listen to feedback, check out feelings as well as information, and generously share credit. This style of leadership allows for a blending of task and process so that *how* something is done is as important as *what* is being done.

Teamwork
In the BBBF project the words 'team' and 'teamwork' play a central role. Partnership among community members, service providers, and

staff had been set out as one of the funding criteria – it was not negotiable. Teamwork is seen as involving relationship building, a spirit of co-operation, a context for learning new roles and responsibilities, and a combining of expertise, experiences, community wisdom, skills, and knowledge. The primary focus of teamwork is the *work* of the organization rather than the play or leisure activities. Teamwork also provides a context for mediating conflict and balancing power.

Committees of the board are assigned as teams to specific areas of responsibility – finance, programs, research, and leadership – and are accountable to the board. In a broader sense, *team* implies belonging, inclusivity, involvement, and leadership as well as hours and hours of hard work and, for some, stress and burnout. *Teamwork* fosters an attitude of partnership, whereby each member is important and makes a unique contribution. At the personal level, a climate of affirmation and acceptance has been created; this meets individual needs of safety, affection, belonging, and reciprocity. At the task level, attention is paid to clarifying the parameters for decision making, naming the task, making a plan, assigning roles, and monitoring outcomes.

Power and Conflict
As can be expected in a project this diverse and complex, with multiple relationships and roles, power and conflict issues are ongoing. BBBF encourages participants to view conflict as a normal part of organizational life and as an opportunity to negotiate for change.

In practice, an innovative model for mediating conflict has evolved that is based on an image of overlapping circles, as opposed to the traditional triangle representing the roles of victim, persecutor, and rescuer. The circles suggest fluidity, inclusivity, and dynamic interaction. A problem-solving approach is used in mediating conflict, with the expectation that if there is agreement on the global principles of CD, there will be some agreement on solutions. The approach combines task with process skills, and the personal safety of each person involved is considered as important as the outcome.

The guidelines for mediating conflict are based on these assumptions:

- Conflict is normal.
- Conflict is to be expected.
- Conflict can be mediated and can have positive outcomes.
- A partial solution is better than no solution.
- There is always more time.

IMPACT OF THE PROJECT ON THE NEIGHBOURHOOD

BBBF is intended as a longitudinal research demonstration project in which the long-term well-being of children is enhanced through partnership between communities, service providers, and government. However, those residents in the neighbourhood who have been actively involved in the project have already benefited in a number of ways.

Many neighbourhood participants have experienced some level of positive change or growth as a result of their participation. This growth or change has been in two main areas: individual growth and development, and improvement in relations with those around them, including family and friends. Some residents say that they have learned new skills and acquired new knowledge, while others say they have gained from the experience of being listened to and respected.

People are actually listening to my opinion [says one resident]. They want my opinion. Before it was 'Who cares?' but they actually come up to me and ask for my opinion and that really gives me self-esteem.

One of the most powerful changes has been that some residents have noticed an increase in their own satisfaction with their lives and with themselves:

I probably feel better about myself in the last year than I've ever felt about myself, ever, and that's because of the project.

I am really ... I am satisfied. I can honestly say that I am satisfied and I like what I do. And I haven't been for a long time.

It has built my self-esteem.

Definitely it has built my self-esteem and my self-confidence back up again.

[My] self-confidence has increased quite a bit ... I've increased my self-confidence, I can work with other people and even try to present a speech and I've never done that in my life, so ... it's given me some backbone.

In addition to individual growth, many also have sensed an improvement in their personal relationships with family, friends, and others. Some feel that they have learned new ways of appreciating and accepting people different from themselves:

I've learned so much about issues that I didn't think applied to me. So I think it makes me an overall better whole person. Learning about racial issues, native issues, and being involved with native communities – I think it just makes me a better person.

[The project] gives me a better outlook day to day on different people around me.

Others feel that their involvement has improved their parenting and their relationships with their children and others:

It's changed me, it's made me a better parent, made me a better friend.

I found out that I have more friends now that I can go to if I have a real emergency – I can give someone a call.

Changed me? Well, I guess because of the way it changed the kids. They were just crazy, wild tantrums, screaming, they were out of control and then coming here and meeting more and more, and being with other kids they have calmed down a lot and there isn't the screaming that used to happen ... I'm a lot calmer.

Some participants have also found that their involvement in the project has given them new insights and knowledge into social patterns that affect their own relationships. For example, issues around gender equality and poverty have given some participants new perspectives from which to view their own situations. Some have made changes in their lives on this basis.

Another significant result is that this district, which had a reputation for crime, poverty, and vandalism, has come to be viewed more positively by outsiders. The name Onward Willow is now respected within many organizations and businesses in the city. Indeed, many project participants have reported that using the name Onward Willow has resulted in increased co-operation when it comes to dealing with various organizations and agencies. One resident said:

I find it is easier to call [an agency] if you have a problem, and they'll listen. Before it would take six months to get them to respond basically to you. But I found that agencies are more willing to be involved, more willing to come out and try and help out with stuff than they were before.

The project has operated for nearly four years, and in this short time significant changes have occurred in the community, in the city of

Guelph, and in the lives of many participants, both inside and outside the neighbourhood. Although the impact of the project on the lives of young children is not yet known, it is clear that CD and the partnership approach has already paid rich dividends for the community and its residents.

D. The Quebec Experience

CD ISSUES AND TRENDS
André Jacob

Quebec is the heartland for Canada's French-speaking people. To understand how and why CD there went through a historical process different from that of the rest of Canada, one must bear in mind that 6 million Quebecers (a large majority) are Francophones.

First of all, it is important to note that from 1935 to 1959 (with a one-term interruption), Quebec was governed by Maurice Duplessis, a right-wing conservative. His gov-ernment was characterized by a high level of corruption, a strong belief in free enterprise, a heavy reliance on foreign investment to develop natural resources, centralized social and political control, and a narrow relationship with the Roman Catholic Church.[1]

After Duplessis's death in 1959, a new government was elected with a completely new perspective. The ensuing rapid change meant a new opportunity for CD. Two ambitious programs of regional development emerged under the responsibility of the state. One was carried out in the eastern part of the province, in a poor region where most workers were fishermen, lumberjacks, miners, and farmers. This project aimed at involving people in a vast integrated program of development. The second program was initiated in the Saguenay region of northern Quebec, another depressed area of farmers, miners, and lumberjacks (though there were also some big industries, such as an aluminum smelter). This program's purpose was to promote adult education. These two

---

1 At the time, the vast majority of Quebecers belonged to the Roman Catholic Church, which was markedly conservative in Quebec. A significant number of priests, brothers, and sisters had escaped from France after the French Revolution. Most were considered loyalists and favourable to the old regime. To them, Quebec was a paradise where they enjoyed favours from the British Crown – including the right to develop their Church – in exchange for helping to control the population.

programs did much to determine the future direction of CD in Quebec, and served as models for further restructuring by the state, especially in the areas of education, cultural affairs, and health and social services.

The focus for development shifted to *participation*. This was at the inspiration of a French priest, sociologist, and philosopher, Father Lebret, who proposed 'human development' and 'human capitalism' as alternatives to socialism. CD in Quebec followed this course for at least a decade. However, in spite of widespread consultation on the 'process' and 'content' of development, the plans for change that were developed were limited and disappointing. The process was managed largely by bureaucrats; the people did not feel they really participated in decision making. When the government decided to close down a hundred villages, the people reacted strongly. In response, the government discontinued the consultation process.

This experience and others showed that programs of development managed by the state are usually based on strategies of integration, as opposed to real participation, even when the latter is a declared principle. Many different approaches have been tried since then to influence government, including political pressure, popular education, participation by bureaucrats, and social animation.

SOCIAL ANIMATION

During the same period in Montreal, the largest city in the province, a new approach emerged called '*social animation*' that was based on two North American styles of community organizing: the confrontational model of Saul Alinsky (1946), and the more consensual model of Murray Ross (1967). These two authors became more widely known in Quebec a few years later, as a result of a book published in 1969 by a French sociologist, Jean-François Medard.

The new movement of social animation was taken up in 1966 by a young social worker named Michel Blondin. The guiding principles were very simple: to start from a very concrete and specific issue, such as promoting a park; and to mobilize people to participate in a process that involved advocacy and the application of pressure to promote the project. Blondin published widely on his experiences (1966a, 1966b, 1967a, 1967b, 1967c), and the movement gained considerable momentum, spreading into many districts of Montreal and into other cities in Quebec. However, people quickly became aware of the limitations of social animation as they met with resistance at city halls and other institutions. This radicalized many in the movement, who turned to political action for solutions. A new municipal movement was formed in 1970 called FRAP (Front for Political Action), which eventually transformed itself into a municipal political party that espoused a strategy of participation. FRAP was the governing party in Montreal from 1986 until the fall of 1994. An almost identical process occurred in Quebec City.

In the meantime, the consensual approach had been subjected to strong criticism from radical sectors inspired by Marxist positions. They were active in the 1970s and at the beginning of the 1980s, led by progressive leaders in trade unions, co-operatives, peace movements, womens' organizations, and immigrant workers' associations. A French sociologist, Alain Touraine, exercised significant influence on the progressive militant movement with his writings on the theory of social action (1985).

'Conscientization' and 'liberation theology,' two innovative intellectual movements of the 1960s and 1970s that originated in the work of Brazilian popular educator Paulo Freire and Peruvian liberationist theologian Gustavo Gutierrez respectively, exercise considerable influence in community work within certain sectors of Quebec society even today. This is especially true for practice with the elderly, with the unemployed, with those on welfare, and with residents of social housing. As adapted to Quebec society, which like Latin American societies is still deeply influenced by Roman Catholicism, their contribution is very significant in terms of literacy, advocacy, popular education, and social and political action. Many organizations and coalitions have adopted such approaches to mobilize people and train popular leaders.

As for the government, it has been introducing significant reforms in social and health services and in education since the beginning of the 1970s, following principles and structures under which participation is controlled by the state and imposed on all institutions. A recent reform undertaken in those services retained this perspective.

Thus, participation is clearly delimited and controlled by the state, which apparently sees the mass of people generally as incapable of participating effectively in the design of organizations and the formulation of policies. In other words, the process remains reserved for the élite. In such circumstances, efforts at popular empowerment can hardly be considered a radical departure from the official process of participation. Apart from the structures of participation, there are public-sector community organizations, such as the CLSC (Local Centres of Community Services), that are active in developing local services and doing some advocacy work (Hurtubise, 1991a).

In conclusion, there are many frames of reference for the analysis of CD. In Quebec the models of Touraine (1985) and Rothman (1970) have been used the most. However, recent writings on the subject provide a different interpretation of that specific page of history. It would be very difficult, however, to cover in this brief overview the vast panorama of community organization and development without omitting other important developments. Only some hints to understanding that evolution have been presented here.

CASE STUDY
CONSCIENTIZATION AS A SPECIFIC FORM OF COMMUNITY PRACTICE AND TRAINING IN QUEBEC
Gérald Doré

'Organisation communautaire' (community organization) is the term most commonly used in French-speaking Quebec to refer to community development. The case discussed next focuses on 'conscientization' as a practice experience within a specific community organization model. The social and theoretical context of community organization in Quebec will be examined first. This will be followed by a discussion of conscientization and of the circumstances in which it came to influence community organization in Quebec. The author describes the collaboration between, on the one side, community organizers opting for the cause expressed by the idea of conscientization, and on the other, professionals deeply rooted in established practices with welfare recipients. In Quebec this partnership has come to be thought of as the 'founding experience' of conscientization, the utilization of which has contributed to existing theory and methods of community organization. The final section identifies current issues faced by proponents of conscientization after sixteen years of its practice in Quebec.

SOCIAL AND THEORETICAL CONTEXT

The government of Quebec passed a law in 1971 pertaining to the public social services that established local community service centres and set the stage for the institutionalizing of community organization. As part of collective bargaining involving unionized health and social service workers, the term 'community organization' was officially designated an organizational function, and 'community organizer' a professional title. In the 158 local centres in Quebec in 1994, no less than 340 of the approximately 2,000 staff had a function defined explicitly in terms of community organization. In the private nonprofit sector, at least an equal number of people practice community organization under a wide variety of job designations, ranging from 'intervenant communautaire' (community intervention agent) to 'permanent' (staff member) and 'personne-resource' (resource person) (Doré, 1992, p. 144; Doré & Larose, 1979, p. 70–1).

Community organization began to be seen as a specialized field of practice in the early 1960s. This came about through a gradual differentiation between direct forms of practice with communities experiencing social problems, and the more indirect practices of social planning and the administration of voluntary sector agencies. Before this time community organization had mainly been a synonym for resource and organizational development (Doré, 1992, p. 133–4). Later, during the social animation period, a new practice identity began to emerge that was based on the principle of social participation and collective action with the goal of achieving social rather than personal change.

Community organization, as a practice separate from social planning and administration, evolved into a diverse field of practice in which various models or strategies of intervention were represented (Doré, 1985, pp. 215–16):

- The *integration model*, which is oriented toward the community's integration and promotes a kind of social participation that is compatible with the existing power structure in the community.
- The *pressure model*, which is oriented toward developing effective bargaining power among marginalized people in the community (whether majorities or minorities), using mass mobilization to make explicit the conflicts of interest that have to be solved at the local level.
- The *self-management model*, which is oriented toward the promotion and development of community ventures that are owned and controlled by the people who work in them, or who consume their goods or services.
- The *politicization models*, which are aimed at linking local community action (either of a pressure or self-management nature) to change in society's power structure.

Conscientization belongs to this last family of models.

CONSCIENTIZATION FROM BRAZIL TO QUEBEC

The term conscientization was coined in the early 1960s by a team of professors at the Higher Institute for Brazilian Studies (INODEP, 1971, p. 20) to describe a new way of viewing and approaching the marginal people of society and the oppressed. The word was later translated into many languages, including French and English. Paulo Freire, one of the institute's members, was at the time leading his famous literacy campaign in northeastern Brazil. He adopted the term to express the kind of successful educational strategy he was pursuing with illiterate peasants and agricultural labourers. The strategy involved learning with the words most significant to one's own social reality; learning to read not only the words but also the social reality to which the words refer (learning to analyse one's own reality); and learning to write not only the words but the reality to which the words refer (learning to act upon one's own reality).

One could say that conscientization first entered French-speaking Quebec in the suitcases of missionaries and international co-operants returning from Latin America. Later, Latin Americans arriving in Quebec as refugees or immigrants contributed further to the advancement of the practice. As Freire's books (1970, 1971, 1978) were translated into French, conscientization quickly became an integral part of the theory of community organization.

In 1974, on the initiative of a group of professors, including myself, community organizers in search of a professional and ideological identity started to meet occasionally at the School of Social Work at Laval University in Quebec City. In 1976, ROCQ (Reconstitution of Quebec's Community Organizers) was founded. In 1977 our group adopted a manifesto which stated that its strategy of politicization consisted of 'the creation of pressure groups and co-operatives that could serve (among other things) as opportunities for members of the working class to "conscientize" themselves to their own class interests and consider autonomous political action.' At that time, the dogmatic and sectarian vanguardism of the Marxist-Leninists had a very strong presence in Quebec. Our group decided to focus instead on the 'literacy-conscientization' of Paulo Freire, because we considered it something concrete and within our reach as community workers to when it came to addressing the immediate problems experienced by the working class (ROCQ, 1977, art. 98 and 99).

THE FOUNDING EXPERIENCE: WHEN CAUSE MEETS GRASS ROOTS

Freire's experience was a source of inspiration to us. At first, though, we did not see how we could put it into practice in our own social context. The answer came from grass roots practice. In the course of a research study undertaken to examine social struggles and their relationship to social policy issues (including social welfare issues), a member of ROCQ met with women belonging to a neighbourhood welfare-rights organization in Montreal. These women, who were in their forties, had left their kitchens and developed, through skills training and by reflecting on their own living conditions, a critical consciousness – a capacity to take charge of their organization and to see their specific struggle as part of the whole struggle of the working class.

The central figure of this experience was a freelance community organizer, Gisèle Ampleman, who had once worked in institutional social services. Since 1972 she had been involved in neighbourhood welfare-rights organizations – a practice enriched by her personal commitment and by her immersion in the popular culture. Recognizing the advantage of an alliance between ROCQ and her grass roots organization, Ampleman agreed to write about the pedagogical tools she had developed. Her strategies were now accessible to other groups, militants, and organizers.

The politicization process experienced by these women could not be taught in the form of lectures; this would have been inconsistent with the practice under observation, as well as contradictory to Freire's pedagogical assumption that content must be accompanied by process. Instead, the collaboration between ROCQ and the neighbourhood organization took the form of a task group that was commissioned to plan a training session for professional community organizers. The task group was composed of three members from ROCQ and four from the neighbourhood organization (two community organizers and two women who were welfare recipients). The presence of these local women contributed significantly to the development of both the content and the process of the task, in accordance with the principle of the educator being educated (Freire, 1970, p. 67).

The training session was conceived as an application of the pedagogical strategies developed in the neighbourhood organization in the previous six years. A full account of this first session of 'sensitization to conscientization' has been published (Doré, 1983); so has a detailed description of its more recent state of development (Barnabé & Brosseau,

1994). The following section highlights some of the theoretical and methodological elements that have emerged from the training session, and describes the ways in which the approach has influenced community organizers who have chosen conscientization as a reference model for their practice.

ON THEORY AND METHODOLOGY

The definition of conscientization that has emerged from its practice in Quebec is the following: a process of cross-cultural and mutual learning between people who are immersed in oppression, and who are struggling from the inner or outer circle for liberation from oppression and are aiming for changes in the power structure of the whole of society (Ampleman, Doré, Gaudreau, Larose, Leboeuf, & Ventelou, 1983, p. 291).

'The freedom to be an educator educated by the same persons one intends to educate' is a premise of this process. In day-to-day practice, as well as in intense training under the supervision of oppressed people – who are themselves involved in their own liberation – this cannot be taken for granted. One has to overcome the sense of cultural superiority that has been internalized through the process of academic socialization. Such attitudes and behaviour cannot be quelled through cognitive discussion alone. The process requires a willingness to become involved in concrete changes and to enter into dialogue with those who are oppressed.

Conscientization requires a recognition of the structural contradictions that one bears, whether as a result of social class, gender, ethnic group, age, sexual orientation, health, marital status, religion, or any other identity parameter in which oppression can grow. This is a prerequisite for the creation of an open and nonpaternalistic alliance between oppressed people and community organizers.

Conscientization implies a commitment of self in identifying one's own path into consciousness-raising. A fairly precise typology has been developed, based on the work of Freire (1971, pp. 109–10; 1974, pp. 157–58) and Humbert (1976, pp. 128–37), that includes attitudes, explanations, actions, and visions of society corresponding to levels of consciousness-raising. In addition, some transitional steps have been formulated between these levels for use by community organizers and the people with whom they work (Collectif québécois de conscientisation – CQC, 1990).

Awareness of the other's culture is also a key. Culture is here defined according to Freire, as 'a set of answers developed by a particular human group to respond to the challenges posed by its environment' (Humbert, 1987a, pp. 288–9). One cannot assume that just because community organizers and the people they work with are part of the same society, they share the same cultural profile. More often than not, there is in fact a wide cultural chasm that needs to be bridged. A commitment to listening and an ongoing struggle against prejudice are essential to becoming culturally aware.

Paying attention to cultures also means paying attention to the ways that people socialize; these form an integral part of the process of community organization. Groups must work hard to build a pattern of social relations that will make newcomers feel at ease without undermining the sense of belonging of the long-standing members. When a group succeeds in this, the long-timers function as educators while remaining open to being educated by the unique situations of the newcomers. Socialization also means paying attention to rituals of welcoming and greeting newcomers, to symbols of belonging, and to ways of celebrating, as well as assuming appropriate attitudes for dealing with personal problems and interpersonal conflicts.

In brief, socialization should lead to a feeling of togetherness. The stresses that result from trying to change society should not adversely affect life. The new type of society we are struggling for can at least partly be put into practice in the here and now in our relations with others. Warm-hearted relations should be considered essential to the formation of political solidarity.

According to conscientization, to benefit from to the unpredictability of personal and collective emotions in group life, one must pay attention to methodological details. Time taken for planning, social analysis, and the learning of specific intervention skills is well spent. Conscientization does not require collective improvisation. A carefully worked out planning process may involve more time than spontaneous action by the community organizer alone, but in the long term it produces a level of collective autonomy and solidarity not otherwise attainable.

During the planning process, the mobilization target and the requirements for participation must be clearly defined for each activity. Conscientization requires sensitivity to differences in levels of consciousness and abilities. A certain amount of training may be necessary before one becomes eligible for a specific function. For example, if a newcomer feels uncomfortable with his or her social status or is not prepared to be identified with the group by the outer circle, it will not be wise to enrol that person in a protest rally.

The key pedagogical tool of conscientization is what Freire calls 'codification.' 'The coding of an existential situation is the representation of that situation showing some of its constituent elements in interaction. Decoding is the critical analysis of the coded situation' (Freire, 1970, p. 96). The codifications developed by Freire take the form of a sketch, a photograph, a drama, or a brief written statement presenting a problem of life experience (Freire, 1970, pp. 106, 111, 114–15).

In Quebec, community organizers in practice with welfare rights organizations introduced their own approach to codification, which might be called 'blank space codification' or 'ongoing codification.' At the beginning of the group discussion, the codification contains only a few entries, these corresponding to significant life dimensions of the situation under discussion. After discussion, the blanks are filled by key words reflecting the experience of the participants. Consciousness is raised by comparing and linking these elements of experience. This practice of codification is best illustrated in the training session 'Being on Welfare,' recorded by Ampleman (1983) and Ampleman and Desgagnes (1994), which is now widely used in various fields of practice.

The goal of codification is to integrate technical with political aspects of learning. The same idea applies to collective evaluation, which is an ongoing process aimed at consciousness-raising. During the process of conscientization, people learn by visualizing the contradictions in which they live, by acting on them according to their level of consciousness, and by reflecting on the outcomes of their actions. These are only a few of the theoretical and methodological principles that have emerged with the development of conscientization in Quebec.

BUILDING A NETWORK

The training session described above propelled ROCQ toward a practice congruent with its theoretical orientation. Since 1978, sessions have been made available regularly to the members as well as to outsiders who have developed an interest in conscientization. In 1979, Ampleman, who had launched the founding experience, went to France for a one-month training session at INODEP (Ecumenical Institute for the Development of Peoples), of which Freire had been the first president. This visit led to a collaborative relationship between ROCQ and INODEP, primarily under the direction of Colette Humbert. In the first half of the 1980s, Humbert came to Quebec on numerous occasions to give advanced training sessions on conscientization. This contributed significantly to the development of the theory of conscientization in Quebec.

In 1983, ROCQ changed its name to correspond to the model of practice that gave it its identity. It became the CQC (the Quebec Collective of Conscientization). Over the years, CQC has offered a wide variety of training sessions designed to meet the changing needs of community organizers. Both the sensitization sessions and the advanced sessions on conscientization have been maintained and are still in demand.

ROCQ-CQC now has a membership of approximately one hundred, in which most regions of Quebec are represented. Since 1978, more than four hundred persons, including both community organizers and grass roots participants, have been trained in conscientization by the ROCQ-CQC. Also, individual members of ROCQ-CQC have trained many people in the public and voluntary sectors and in university programs. Clearly, Conscientization has had a significant presence in community organization practice in Quebec since the late 1970s. It is not a majority trend, however, and like the communities with which it stands, it must cope with the challenges of marginalization.

PRESENT ISSUES

Since early 1980, Quebec, like many other societies, has experienced major changes, and these have had an impact on how conscientization and other practices of community organization are carried out (Girardi, 1984; Piotte, 1990). For instance, community organizing in the public and voluntary sectors has come to be linked once again with social planning practice and administration. This is most obvious in the practice of the local community service centres, among others (Doré, 1992). As a result, some authors are revisiting the three conceptual models of community organization formulated by Rothman (1970). These authors consider 'social planning' to be functioning at the same conceptual level as 'locality development,' stressing community capacity building as the principal goal of action, and 'social action' as placing emphasis on achieving a fairer distribution in the power of decision-making structures (Doucet & Favreau, 1991). From the perspective of the four models articulated by Doré (1985), it is the 'integration model' that has gained in popularity since the mid-1980s. In 1988, 24.6 percent of community organizers in the public sector defined themselves primarily in relation to 'concertation du milieu' or neighbourhood partnerships (Hurtubise, Beauchamp, Favreau, & Fournier, 1989, p. 83). Ten years earlier, in answer to a comparable question, the proportion was 3.2 percent (Doré, 1985, p. 223; Doré & Larose, 1979, p. 92).

The theoretical discourse that has been built to legitimize this new course of events has tended to discount the role of conscientization (Alary, 1988, pp. 78–9; Hurtubise, 1991b, pp. 151–9; Vaillancourt, 1993, pp. 5–6). As a result, conscientization has decreased in popularity in the field of public-sector social services. In 1988, 14.5 percent of the community organizers in the public sector identified conscientization as the ideological trend influencing them most (Hurtubise et al., 1989, p. 83). Ten years earlier, the proportion was 19.4 percent (Doré & Larose, 1979, p. 92). No recent data is available for the voluntary sector, but a significant *increase* in popularity rather than a decrease might be expected, when one considers that 90 percent of the present members of the CQC come from this sector. It is also encouraging to note that in the last ten years, conscientization has played a central role in many different fields of practice: women (Barnabé, 1985, 1987; Leboeuf, 1991; Gaudreau, 1994a), literacy (Comeau, 1987; Saint-Cyr, 1994), politics (Doré & Gaudreau, 1987; Gaudreau, 1994b), health (Ampleman, 1987; Duhaime, 1987), public housing (Lacroix, 1987), mental health (Arsenault, 1991), immigrants and refugees (Oxhorn, 1993), and First Nations (Belleau, 1994).

It is likely, therefore, that conscientization will survive the neoconservatism of the 1990s, as it survived the Marxism-Leninism of the late 1970s and early 1980s. Such optimism is based on the fact that conscientization does not depend on intellectual fashion or on the irrational forces of historical change. Instead, it is nurtured by ethical commitment and by community action that is based on the dialectical analysis of existing social conditions.

3. SUPPORTIVE INSTITUTIONS IN CANADA
Nathan Gilbert

The relative deterioration in economic and social conditions in Canada in recent years, and government efforts to reduce social program expenditures, have together fuelled the development of organizations committed to the promotion and practice of CD. Whether they are involved in intervention, or advocacy, or the provision of services, these organizations require research and information services to be more effective.

Areas of special attention must include health, unemployment, and child poverty.

In Canada, solutions must be found to unemployment and poverty. In the formal sector, fewer new jobs are being created that pay a family wage. After a recession that saw hundreds of companies 'downsize' or go bankrupt in the general trend toward de-industrialization, Canada has entered a period of jobless recovery. This guarantees that unemployment will stay at high levels.

Two Canadian parliamentary reports in 1991 underlined the relationship between childhood poverty and certain significant social problems. It is now widely accepted that adults who were born into poverty are more likely to be unhealthy, unemployed, and badly fed, housed, and educated. In 1991, one Canadian child in five was living in poverty. While 60 percent of the children in single-parent families were living in poverty, 54 percent of poor children lived in two-parent families. Standardized child poverty rates were at least twice as high in Canada during the mid-1980s as they were in the Netherlands, France, Sweden, and Germany. The child poverty rate in Great Britain was slightly lower than in Canada, while the American rate was double that of Canada.

While the health of Canadians is among the best in the world, it has reached a plateau. Health expenditures, which account for slightly more than one-third of all provincial government spending, can no longer be sustained at current levels; as a result, spending may have to be restricted in those other areas that contribute most to good health.

It is now generally acknowledged that healthy communities can evolve only if all the social determinants of health are recognized and addressed. In this regard, programs that benefit the community as a whole rather than specific groups, and that address such issues as adequate income, employment, and early childhood experience, are needed.

THE NONGOVERNMENT FUNDING SECTOR

In Canada, different government agencies provide selective support for CD work; otherwise, CD is financed by nongovernment sources, including foundations, corporate and individual donors, and volunteers. In 1990, 850 foundations were active in Canada; some of these specifically supported CD types of activities, but most did not. These foundations had combined assets of over $3.2 billion and disbursed 32,718 grants totalling $304 million, of which an estimated 1 percent went to CD projects.

Health and social services receive the largest share of foundation grants (24%), followed by education, (17%, mostly to private schools and universities) and religion (14%). Support to the international sector has recently doubled from 1 to 2 percent. Funding for CD would be subsumed under any of these major sectors.

In 1991, Canadian corporations, which reported $31 billion in profits, channelled $406 million in donations to the following sectors: education (26.9%), social services (20.2%), health (19.5% to hospitals and health/disease campaigns), and arts and culture (13.4%).

In 1991, 30 percent of Canadian tax filers claimed charitable donations totalling $3.1 billion. Individual donations, combined with volunteering, provide a major source of support, which includes support for CD. A study undertaken for the Secretary of State in 1989 estimated the value of volunteer work contributed in 1986/7 to be $13.2 billion in 1990 dollars – equivalent to 6 percent of all full-time jobs in the Canadian labour force. In 1990, 43 percent of all Canadians claimed that they did volunteer work for a charitable or community organization.

SELECTED ILLUSTRATIONS OF SUPPORTIVE INSTITUTIONS

In every province in Canada there are institutions, charities, and NGOs that are committed to mutual support and co-operative action, inspired by a vision of justice and a critique of the structures that contribute to injustice, poverty, and ecological degradation. These groups directly engage in and support research and practice of a socially transformative nature. They seek to engage the broader NGO, private, and public sectors in the discourse of social change; they also bring their own experience to the field to influence social theory and practice. The following are only a few examples:

Inter-Pares ('Among Equals').   A Canadian NGO, founded in 1975, that focuses on social and economic issues in Canada and in the Third World. It links social action and CD at home with social change abroad. Rather than implementing its own program, it builds relationships and supports community-based self-help programs. It applies the principles of participation, sustainability, leadership by women, and respect for cultural values. It believes that for international assistance to be effective, it must help people do what they are already trying to do with their own means. Effective assistance recognizes and nurtures the qualities of people and their communities and supports their strength and vision.

Better Beginnings, Better Futures Project (BBBF).   Funded by three Ontario ministries and two federal departments, this is the first long-term project of its kind in Canada. The focus is on children up to the age of eight living in eleven socio-economically disadvantaged communities or neighbourhoods in Ontario. Onward Willow, one of the practice cases in this part, was drawn from BBBF.

Calmeadow.   Established in 1983, this nonprofit charitable organization is dedicated to serving the credit needs of low-income, self-employed people in Canada and has working relationships with groups in Africa, Asia, and Latin America. Calmeadow provides low-income people with access to modest amounts of credit so that they can sustain or start small businesses. Calmeadow lends small amounts of money, ranging from as little as $100 up to $5,000, at market rates using a peer-lending model fashioned by Dr Muhammad Yunnus of the Grameen Bank in Bangladesh. Instead of providing traditional forms of collateral, borrowers form 'loan circles' in which each member vouches for the others' commitment to repay. By applying this method of cross-guarantees and mutual support, Calmeadow has achieved an overall payback rate of 98 percent. Borrowers do not need assets, a credit history, or a long-range business plan.

In Canada, Calmeadow has created new community-based lending models. Loan funds have been created in Nova Scotia (Partnership Assistance for Rural Development), in Vancouver (Peer Assisted Lending), in Toronto (MetroFund), and in sixteen native communities across Canada (First Peoples' Fund). The goal is to make the loan funds and programs as self-sufficient as possible. In 1993, Calmeadow received donations and loan-guarantee support from twenty-seven foundations, twenty-eight corporations, the Canadian International Development Agency, and five financial institutions and other organizations, as well as from churches and unions and over 700 individuals.

The Ontario Prevention Clearinghouse (OPC).   Established in 1985, this organization helps empower groups and communities so that they can work toward achieving their own social, emotional, physical, and environmental health and well-being. The OPC is a nonprofit charitable organization that receives most of its funding from Ontario government departments. It was designed to be an easily accessible resource for consultation and information on disease prevention and health promotion. It also facilitates networking, project development, project support, information exchange, and professional development activities.

Healthy Cities/Healthy Communities. This is part of a worldwide movement promoted by the World Health Organization. Two provinces, Quebec and British Columbia, developed Healthy Communities programs; Ontario then followed suit by funding a three-year project. The Ontario Healthy Communities Network was initiated by municipal governments and by a diverse group of people that included urban planners, public health officials, environmentalists, social development advocates, health centre staff, physicians, and landscape architects. The primary goals of this project are to build up community capacity and to make it easier for communities to share their experiences.

Centre for International Statistics. This uniquely organized research facility serves a highly specialized clientele in the fields of community services and social development. Established in 1991 with the assistance of the Laidlaw Foundation, the centre collects, analyses, and disseminates Canadian and international data pertaining to the economic and social welfare of families and children. Its mandate is to provide statistical research services to community organizations, among others. The centre maintains or has direct access to a collection of more than 25 national and international databases, which are regularly updated and expanded. As a research division of the Canadian Council on Social Development (CCSD), the centre supports the mission of developing and promoting progressive social policies.

4. EDUCATION AND TRAINING
Ken Banks and Helen Ball

INTRODUCTION

Canada has a chequered history in CD, largely as a result of its demographic composition; there are massive areas of sparse population as well as much more densely populated urban centres. The country's geographic, cultural, and economic diversity makes centralized approaches unrealistic. In Canada, as in other countries where rural and urban conditions vary greatly, CD must involve responding to a wide range of conditions.

Currently, Canada is also caught up in the trend toward globalization and under pressure to reduce the role of the state in the economy and in people's welfare. Consequently, community planners are looking for innovative ways for local communities to assume greater responsibility for their needs and institutions. To this end, academic and professional disciplines are taking an increased interest in the education and training of CD workers.

Academic interventions are often theory-driven and can be out of touch with demands from the grass roots for education and training that reflects local concerns. In Canada, many activists want community workers to be trained in mobilizing people for engaging in mutual aid and social action, and in implementing co-operative forms of community economic development (CED). Unions and co-operatives are leading the way by educating their own people in these areas (Fairbairn, Bold, Hammond, Ketilson, & Ish, 1991). In a different vein, economic development interests in business and industry have been pressuring governments to provide certificate to university level training for a profit-centred form of CD. Involved in this are agri-business and business improvement associations (BIAs) across Canada.

Clearly, the skills needed for grass roots process-oriented CD (which aims at mutual aid or social action) are different from those needed for sustainable development programs and for the packaged programs of the BIAs and agriculture groups.

CONTEXT

Within official agencies and universities in Western countries, throughout the development decades, CD has been the focus of massive international activity. Much of this activity has been modelled on the idea of 'rural extension work' that was developed during the early part of this century at American and Canadian universities. This model has its roots in the nineteenth century, when itinerant scholars, as an extension service of universities, would travel to rural communities to speak with farmers about their experiences and to discuss the latest farming technologies. Agricultural societies, for their part, provided educational forums that brought rural communities together. These activities evolved in time into CD programs that involved organizing, educating, and training rural populations in need. In Canada these programs are still sponsored by the Ministry of Agriculture.

CD was seen by successive administrations in the United States as a tool to fight Communism and promote American interests in the Third World. Thus, development-oriented faculties were often encouraged to work in primarily rural countries in order to 'raise the welfare of the common people without imperilling the dignity and the liberty of the individual' (Ruopp, 1953, p. viii). For almost forty years, the Canadian

International Development Agency (CIDA) has also funded university and private agency work 'overseas' (Bean, 1991). The emphasis has been principally on 'development as increase' – in resources, human capacity, and productivity levels.

In contrast, the urban CD that was practised in Canada and the United States during the 1960s and 1970s was more often than not closely linked to the pursuit of a more equitable reallocation of resources and power; this necessarily involved activist approaches in harness with community groups. In the current context of the changing relationship between the state and civil society, and of recent budget cuts in statutory services, the option of 'development as increase' is being actively rethought. More and more attention is being given to the reconfiguration of existing services through self-help and mutual aid. In Canada, in terms of staff training, the organizational skills that workers need in order to support these self-help and mutual aid efforts are often provided under the rubric of CD.

METHODS AND TECHNIQUES

CD and CED amount to a distinct set of strategies for addressing community issues, shared needs, and interests. These strategies include a range of techniques aimed at involving local interest groups in the process of cultural and community change. The methods of process-oriented CD tend to emphasize knowledge of group processes, social learning, social mobilization, and formal and informal organizations, as well as strategies for planned change at the grass roots of society. These strategies have gained popularity among a surprisingly wide range of academic disciplines, community organizations, and even co-operative business groups.

At the same time, business interests call for a type of training that prepares local people to conduct economic development programs. Such programs are less likely to be process-driven, relying instead on more didactic training formulas. The image of local consultation is attractive to those business groups and government agencies who want to invite the participation of local people without necessarily sharing ownership of the design process. Here, implementers are trained in the particular skills required to reproduce a prefabricated program.

Labour unions offer mostly process-oriented CD education for their own staff who work in Canadian communities or overseas. Organizations involved in the women's movement educate women to work co-operatively and collectively in centres and shelters for abused women across the country. Organizations for mental health and for people who are developmentally challenged give community education courses to their own people to work both as staff and as volunteers (Lord, 1987).

Many of these organizations or community groups hesitate to turn to universities for professional training in CD practice because of their concern that such educational institutions would appropriate their gains in local power and dominate the process. However, the lines of division between these methods of education and training may not be drawn simply between the university and the community. Rather, it is the *approach* to learning that makes the exigent difference in how CD will be practised. Experience and formal knowledge are two different approaches to learning, and they can conflict. People who have worked through a process that has raised their level of critical awareness can see this difference; those who simply implement programs are less likely to have the insight to discern the broader implications of their work.

WHAT WE FOUND: CENTRES OF TRAINING

Education in CD seems very alive in undergraduate and graduate programs of social work. We found that no less than nine of twenty-two faculties and departments of social work were involved in preparing students for this form of practice. We also found a vibrant interest in CD and CED training in aboriginal studies in at least three centres. Overall, CD techniques are being taught across Canada at centres for rural studies, urban and community studies, and recreation and adult education.

Among the schools and faculties of social work, Wilfrid Laurier University and Carleton University (Ontario), and the University of Regina (Saskatchewan), conduct courses that aim at having students develop a critical perspective on CD. The native studies programs offer training in doing business in aboriginal languages and understanding the white culture. They also offer educational courses on natural healing and aboriginal traditions that will enhance self-understanding and mutual aid. In addition, there is a women's studies program at the University of British Columbia that offers courses in conscientization that are quite innovative in fostering mutual aid.

Many programs focus on facilitating social change in areas of society that they define as unique to their specific discipline. For instance, the University of Calgary has a Centre for Liveable Communities. Mount

Allison University in New Brunswick has a Rural and Small Town Research and Studies program that is linked with the Department of Geography and focuses on CD. Those faculties of social work that offer courses in CD at the graduate level attempt to balance theory and field practice in institutional (urban) and rural settings.

The University of Quebec at Hull has completed an extensive study in support of community development corporations (CDCs) and community economic development corporations (CEDCs) (Favreau & Ninacs, 1993). Funded by the National Welfare Grants Directorate, this study addressed the dualism of the job market in Quebec that resulted from the loss of traditional employment in the face of global economic restructuring. The findings are of particular interest as they relate to CD training. It was found that contrary to what many community activists believe, community projects often flounder when local leaders have not received training in CD. The study strongly recommends that universities play a more extensive role in CED training 'by including CED courses within existing curricula and by setting up specific undergraduate and graduate CED programs' (Favreau & Ninacs, 1993, p. 7).

Again we see the apparent dichotomy between educators who promote institution-based formal training, and supporters of grass roots based experiential learning. While educational institutions tend to train for specialized expertise, grass roots organizations encourage social learning and the building of solidarity among fellow learners.

The educational program at the Faculty of Social Work at Wilfrid Laurier provides an interesting example of graduate-level studies in CD. This two-year Masters-level program was introduced in 1975 as an integral part of the graduate social work curriculum. It focuses on education and training for CD roles in a range of social services, such as health, child and family welfare, and housing. The original goal was to train graduates to engage in a form of planned change that would organize marginalized populations into community groups and enable (or empower) them to participate in those planning processes that affect their daily lives. Thus, CD courses and supervised field practica focused on building co-operative groups and community, fostering citizen and consumer participation, developing local institutions and leadership, and mobilizing essential resources. More recently, an effort has been made to establish appropriate linkages between planning efforts and broader social movements within Canada and across national and cultural boundaries through the training of workers to intervene in a manner that is critically reflective.

RURAL–URBAN DICHOTOMY

The logistics of Canada's massive geography have historically led to a split between the rural regions, which depend on agricultural and resource development, and the urban clusters along the southern border with the United States. Even so, there has emerged over time a fair degree of overlap in urban and rural practice, education, training, and research pertaining to community. The duality in earlier approaches was apparent in the focus of educational centres. Those in urban settings gave priority in their community practice training to citizen participation and local involvement in community and institutional development. Rural and agricultural colleges, on the other hand, stressed initiatives in functional literacy among the rural population.

While there is a strong trend toward the use of grass roots CD methods and techniques across the country, there is an absence of communication between and among those disciplines that are using and/or teaching conscientization techniques.

CONCLUSION

Our study suggests that in Canadian CD, there is a profound respect for diversity. As we approach the twenty-first century, powerful international stakeholders have become fascinated with the mass media. Their fascination has included a preoccupation with the global standardization of relations. CD has the potential to counterbalance the negative effects of unitary-mass society because it appreciates the uniqueness and peculiarity of the means that people find to solve their own problems. If we want people to be responsible for their own lives, we must prepare them to celebrate uniqueness and support collective action.

It is our concern that the globalization will neutralize people's strengths. The challenge that faces us will be to counterbalance the negative effects of the technologies of a mass society. The continued focus on development that advances the values of collaboration and communication, and that recognizes the importance of human diversity, will be critical in this process.

This review of issues related to education and training in Canada suggests the need for a more balanced approach to learning – one that combines the critical perspective and specialized expertise that formal university education and training can bring to CD, with the experiential learning arrived at through a cumulative process of practical experience at the grass roots level.

5. RESEARCH
Ken Banks

Research methods that are compatible with CD in Canada are often, like practice methods, divided into two fundamentally different approaches. In this section I will identify these approaches as 'applied,' an approach that tests promising interventions, and 'engaged,' an approach that describes and develops relationships. Applied research provides the information institutions need to serve their clients and is regarded as an essential activity in social planning (Cameron, 1992). This approach is well established in the field and has a history within university faculties and social service agencies. It is usually associated with methods based in scientific paradigm – quantitative measurement and analysis, experimental designs, surveys of community needs, and so on. The other approach, engaged research (Banks & Mangan, 1993), begins with a more open agenda and is usually less directly connected to existing social agencies. Using methods drawn from ethnography, interpretive social science, and action research, engaged approaches start from the perspective of persons in need and attempt to facilitate their knowledge-based action. Engaged forms of research have received increased recognition in grass roots CD in recent years (Banks & Mangan, 1995).

The differences in the two approaches are grounded in the relationship between the researched and the researcher, and are also affected by the sponsors of the study. This section briefly describes the two approaches, offers current Canadian examples of each, and gives an in-depth description and analysis of an engaged approach that I will suggest overcomes the fundamental problems and traditional contradictions of doing research on CD processes.

The term *applied research* is often used as part of research done in concert with CD programs. To quote Hedrick, Bickamn, & Rog, 'the applied researcher often receives research questions from a client (sponsor) ... The client is often in control, ... through a contractual relationship' (1993, p. 6). Drawing on theoretical work in sociology, psychology, geography, and other disciplines, applied CD research attempts to analyse relevant data with the goal of developing an analysis and an action plan for the sponsoring agency. Unlike engaged research, it emphasizes the defining of objectives and the measuring of outcomes, and is conducted by highly trained personnel.

Engaged research supports the efforts of local people, who conduct much of the project. In this approach one establishes a process of participatory dialogue that attempts to produce 'close' descriptions of the problems of everyday community life (see Smith, 1974) . The dialogue is between the researched and the researcher(s). Banks and Mangan point out that such dialogue seeks to narrow the distance between common sense and scientific discipline, but not out of a naïve belief that some form of inoffensive compromise can be attained (1994). Engaged research has a distinct action orientation, in both its research methods and its goals for CD.

ILLUSTRATIONS OF RESEARCH APPLICATIONS

Canadian researchers have recently taken major steps in the field of child welfare by using applied research methods to construct self-help programs in high-risk neighbourhoods. At the same time, feminist and native practitioners are employing engaged research in gender and culture/race specific contexts.

The Women's Research Centre at the University of British Colombia conducted an action research project for isolated and otherwise vulnerable women in learning to build friendship ties (Lovell, 1991). In a more economic mode, the native studies program at Trent University (Ontario) encourages graduate students to focus their research on processes of CED that use qualitative approaches. Service-oriented social movements also find that these approaches suit their needs. The Centre for Research and Education in Human Services (Lord, 1987) conducts engaged research that involves people who are developmentally challenged, their families and friends, and the professionals who provide services to them. This research attempts to accurately report what members of this community perceive as appropriate action for their problems.

The environmental studies program at the University of Waterloo (Ontario) conducts applied research in Indonesia that has an ancillary CD component. The team members observe and record the process of professional CD/education that is designed to help local people adapt to new economic conditions. These conditions reflect the impact on the economy and local culture of a government-sponsored, windmill-driven engineering installation near the village that provides electricity to agribusiness in the area. CD work in the local village seeks to ameliorate the effects of newly introduced wage labour. Applied social research is best suited to the task of measuring the effectiveness of these programs.

The Centre for Social Welfare Studies at Wilfrid Laurier University and the School of Social Work at the University of Manitoba have separately conducted extensive applied-research projects. They take different approaches, but both focus on social support for families and have as a goal finding methods to moderate multigenerational trends. They both apply social engineering approaches that involve participation in self-help initiatives by families in high-risk neighbourhoods.

The methodology of both these projects draws on basic research designs: testing models that take the form of progressive programs that incrementally develop increased autonomy through development strategies. Creative ideas culled from earlier studies of families in high-risk communities are in this way brought to the field of family support.

The sponsors – the Canadian government and a large private foundation – offered a range of guidelines, which the government followed as a means to focus the study. However, much of the design work was left to the research team, which decided to establish a series of family-support initiatives that removed stress from individuals in the community. Primarily, they established mutual-aid groups among parents from a designated neighbourhood who were likely to be abusive toward their children. They used lay staff, introduced multiple-support services, increased the availability of professional and paraprofessional services, and developed groups of peers. All of these approaches were drawn from existing research findings. They then introduced a series of independent variables and measured the results. For instance, they encouraged the formation of 'created relationships' through mutual-aid groups for families with weak social networks. This was much faster and more efficient than 'embedded' relationships, which evolve without social worker support. They found that social supports leading to social integration and mutual support for families can relieve stress in a variety of ways. However, agencies must maintain an investment in ongoing supports for the groups (Cameron, Hayward, & Mamatis, 1992, p. 28).

THE COMPANY OF NEIGHBOURS RESEARCH PROJECT:
AN ILLUSTRATION OF ENGAGED RESEARCH

The Company of Neighbours, an exploratory/descriptive/action research project in suburban Ontario, is led by Ken Banks (the author of this section) and Marshall Mangan. The project asks this general question: 'How do families engage in formal and informal helping relations?' In the exploratory stage, the research team sought to identify the helping relations in local peoples' personal networks. In the second phase, a CD process was engaged. Local people were recruited and trained to conduct interviews; the interviewees were then given the opportunity to reflect on the meaning that the research team attributed to the interview data. This reflection was built into this phase to ensure that the researchers accurately interpreted the interview data. In the third phase, on the basis of 'themes' that emerged from the data, a process of social change was facilitated, grounded in the agenda for community action that came out of this ethnographic research process.

Where possible, the research team combined the approaches of CD with the methods of ethnography. First, a community influence survey was conducted using open-ended interviews with people in the community who had been previously identified as most likely to have a direct interest in the field of study. These 'key informants' included local professionals and business people, who helped identify issues, and people who would have strong networks and would likely be interested in acting as research assistants.

Initially, five local people agreed to be trained as research assistants, and a training group was formed to learn basic interviewing skills. This group also helped to construct the interview question script and to code and interpret the data. A 'reflective group' was then formed from among the interviewers and interviewees. The group has met to discuss community issues identified in the data, such as the need for a community newsletter, which they could operate at very low cost. Contact was made with the local high school, where one of the teachers showed interest in establishing a dialogue between the young and the older people in the community. A 'history group' was assembled when we found that there was a strong sense of historical community in our research site. The history group assembled memorabilia and took pictures and stories to schools and a local nursing home. They also held open-house gatherings at our site office, during which they tried to attract newcomers to the town and show them the potential for rekindling a strong sense of community through participation. The power of community narrative is evident here. The high school teacher and a member of the history group discovered a mutual love for music that eventually resulted in the newsletter being used to advertise music and family sports nights at a local park. A further development occurred when a member of the reflective group heard some of the students say that they would like a place to gather and listen to their music and read poetry. This older citizen encouraged the young people to draw up a proposal for using the gymnasium at his church, as he sat on the church board and would speak on their behalf.

The identification of needs, and the interpretation and analysis of these articulations of needs, all happened in the local community. The action that emanated from the research process engaged the experience and knowledge of diverse local participants.

A CRITICAL COMMENT ON APPLIED RESEARCH

Applied research has traditionally been situated within a positivist paradigm of social inquiry (see Winter, 1987; Lather, 1991). Even the less traditional and more innovative approaches to research on CD practice have inherent difficulties for the researcher and practitioner. I would argue that the objective stance required of positivist researchers estranges them from the subjectivity of the everyday lives of the community being studied. While objectivity has its place in community work – for instance, in negotiating or mediating crisis situations – a preoccupation with applying this approach to all practices has nullified opportunities for understanding, reporting, and interpreting the perspective of those being studied. Recent postmodern critiques (Winter, 1987; Lather, 1991) of traditional applied approaches have provided a way to understand why positivist research designs have led to a form of self-defeating epistemological loop. In CD, lasting success is predicated on the involvement and empowerment of the local community. However, in applied research, local involvement is subservient to external expert leadership. The possibilities of achieving involvement and empowerment are limited in the extreme by the external authority assumed by researchers using the objectivist approach (Lather, 1991). In contrast, engaged research raises the consciousness of the life conditions in the subject community, so that a praxis of local experience and knowledge becomes the platform that informs their social action.

CONCLUSION

The applied research paradigm described above amply served the cause of CD in terms of the resource and program developments pursued by social agencies during the heyday of the welfare state. The funding for these agencies is being withdrawn in the present era of fiscal restraint; as a result, the possibilities for this form of research and action have been reduced. At the same time, challenges to positivist approaches to social and community research are being mounted on both ethical and epistemological grounds. The 'engaged research' approach offers an alternative. An ethnographic strategy in CD requires a bridging of community experience and 'action research' knowledge and techniques. Instead of data being removed from the community to be processed and analysed by experts, the community maintains ownership of the data and turns them into relevant actions. The trust necessary to do CD is also required in ethnography. With this approach the agenda for social change is drawn up by community members in a way that constantly reaches out to gather and interpret community opinion.

I feel that having action researchers enter into partnership with the community, as was done in the case illustration above, is even more consistent with the facilitating tradition of CD than the action research cycle espoused by Carr and Kemmis (1986). While their ethnographic research design facilitates close description and reflective analysis, it also maintains the role of the researcher as 'expert,' thereby creating social distance between the researcher and researched and making it less likely that the community will collaborate fully.

The two major approaches to research in CD discussed above have specific applications. Applied research is necessary when measurement and evaluation must be attempted. Engaged research is necessary when the quality of processes and relationships needs to be described. We suggest that this community work modified approach to ethnography provides a vehicle for reporting local perceptions of need as well as the meanings, and themes for action, that local people take from their environment.

6. THEORY
Harvey Stalwick

PRACTICE CONTEXT FOR GENERATIVE THEORY

The chicken-and-egg dilemma of theory and practice is hindered by the boundaries of Western positivism. We need to be alert to pretentious, theory-driven attempts to codify facts, rigidly control knowledge development, and use supposedly value-neutral discourse to predict how our world ought to unfold. Even a sideways glance at practice reveals that this approach doesn't work. CD is a delightfully misshapen square peg in the neat round hole of positivism and other variations of scientism.

Our best hope for finding useful theory for emancipatory action must involve a process of inquiry that is open, interpretive, value-anchored, and co-operative.

How do we detect differences among CD theories and shake ourselves loose from those which are shallow or a hindrance? What can make possible social change that is both real and long-term, cultural encounters that alter for all time one's view of the world's peoples, and a realization of lasting human relationships? I like the way that this six-country study is organized to emphasize case studies, since this approach places practice front and centre. This provides an opportunity for us to learn from others' trials and errors and to reflect on the value of existing CD theories.

CASE STUDIES

The four Canadian case studies covered the following:

- Refugee survivors of torture creating a self-help, nonmedical model of integrated community services (Canadian Centre for Victims of Torture, Toronto).
- Women in poverty taking hold of an economic development strategy featuring safe, affordable housing as a community-creating base (Entre Nous Femmes Housing Society, Vancouver).
- Children and families overcoming 'high risk' labels and tendencies toward social breakdown through a prevention-driven neighbourhood development program (Better Beginnings, Better Futures Program, Guelph, Ontario).
- Community organizers creating a network for self-teaching of critical awareness as a form of resistance (Community Organizing and Conscientization, Quebec).

Combined, these case studies highlight numerous CD issues, including these: the two-sided problem of experts representing a community and the 'disabling' effect of professionalization; the struggle of NGOs and their constituencies to stop being marginalized in society; the downside of diverse funding and double goal-setting (i.e., one goal for the funder, and one for the CD process); the need for the educators to be educated by immersion in popular culture; the need to find a language of inclusion to offset the jargon of bureaucrats and professionals; and the tendency of government and research funders to assume the mantle of standard-setting positivist rigour and then distance themselves from grass roots development.

Instead of falling into the positivist tendency to dwell on a list of issues, we might be better off considering what these case studies can contribute to theories of hope.

What lights up the world and makes it bearable is the feeling which we usually have of our links with it – and more particularly of what joins us to other people. (Halladay, 1992, p. 3)

For an idea to change the world, it must first of all change the life of the person bearing it. It must be transformed into an example. (Camus, 1966, p. 37)

WHAT JOINS US TO OTHER PEOPLE: CIRCLES OF SOLIDARITY

The heart of CD – possibly too often overlooked as trite – is the co-operative maxim: 'Together we stand, divided we fall.' The authors of the case study on the Canadian Centre for Victims of Torture (CCVT) remind us that the aim of persecution is to break down the community first, then personalities. The challenge for CD practice is to build up what the CCVT calls circles of solidarity. That organization does this in a number of ways: by providing convivial meeting places, by developing committed long-term relationships in a befriending program, by respecting the rich diversity of cultural backgrounds, and by maintaining a referral network to provide professional help. For this type of CD initiative, and for other co-operative models for transforming society, the theoretical directive seems simple: Be Human First. Humanity is what joins us to other people.

The people quoted in the case study on Entre Nous Femmes give concrete expression to the same rule of conduct as was stated above. They suggest to us some basic requirements for a practice that leads to co-operative, community-based alternatives to development. For instance:

They have found their voice ... It is a voice that creates excitement and enthusiasm, it 'hooks' people.

You can change the system – it gave me a lot of hope and knowledge about what you have to do.

The group didn't have a chance to sit back and examine itself ... The goal was housing, and each time a door opened we walked through it.

Though their circumstances differ remarkably, the women in the ENF housing project have similar needs to the people in the CCVT project: they, too, yearn for connectedness with a co-operative community, for a regained sense of self, and for convivial places for themselves and their children.

However, the case studies do not make sufficiently clear what values are necessary to support this yearned for connectedness. Some inspiration for this task may be found in North American native peoples' long experience in CD (or more accurately, community survival). The prayer '... and all my relations' is an expression of community. It comes from a theology of nature seeking life and becoming complete. One metaphor for this is the medicine wheel, which is laden with cultural values and is used in a process that enhances cyclical awareness and promotes creative education. Compare this with the values and the notion of education introduced by the Brazilian social reformer Paulo Freire. As explained by Cajete:

Freire's central message about education is that one can only learn to the extent that one can establish a participatory relationship with a natural, cultural, and historical reality in which one lives. This is not the same as the Western-schooled authoritarian style of problem solving, where experts observe a situation from the outside and at a distance, then develop a solution or dictate an action or policy ... Freire's thesis is that the critical consciousness of the cultural and historical roots of a People – as expressed and understood from the perspective of the people themselves – is the foundation of their cultural emancipation. (Cajete, 1994, pp. 215–16)

CHANGE THE LIFE OF THE PERSON: CULTURAL ENCOUNTER

Respectful culture-specific CD practice, featuring ways to learn from and be aligned with people in the midst of ethnic struggles, is central to any consideration of theories of hope (Howse & Stalwick, 1990). A practice that respects cultures seeks positive alternatives to cultural clashes; these alternatives may in turn guide the co-existence of majority and minority community members. 'Cultural encounter' is understood to mean a living interaction with others that becomes a decisive event in the process of changing one's outlook. It can happen that there is no escape from this change, which becomes decisive in one's practice (Bugge, 1994).

The CCVT case study illustrates this in some depth. First, the composition of the CCVT's board changed over time; in the beginning most members were white professionals; its membership now includes people from most of the countries served by the centre. Then, more significantly, the organization matched volunteers with survivors through its befriending program. This seems to have had remarkable results, as previously stated in this case study:

To the befriender, the program opens up new horizons, a rich opportunity to learn about the cultures and experiences of the survivors. In the process, new friendships are established. Also, the program encourages people to reflect on the values of democracy and cultural diversity, and promotes social justice. Collectively, the befriending program directs the community to respond appropriately to the plight of survivors of torture, and fosters movements that challenge inequalities while reinforcing the concept of human rights.

These words speak eloquently of the benefits of a respectful, culture-specific form of CD practice that is steeped in the history of the co-operative movement's social transformational experience. Any failure to embrace such an approach should be regarded as scandalous. One word long associated with the Canadian government's policy in regard to native peoples is assimilation. This notion of progress and civilization, which is intertwined with the North American dream of the melting-pot, is flawed in a major way: it denies an opportunity for people to be enriched by learning about another culture (Sioui, 1992, p. 106). Learning, as a living interaction, should be a two-way street. Providing and celebrating opportunities for cultural encounter can become a hinge for the development of theories of hope in CD practice.

TRANSFORMED INTO EXAMPLE: LEARNING ACTION

Telling stories about CD practice – thought and action – pushes beyond the boundaries of Western positivism. Narrative can be the postmodern key that opens up an interpretive, value-anchored process for understanding change. A meaningful example of this is found in the Chicano metaphor of *resolana*, a Spanish word that refers in this context to the south side of a building or plaza where, in the warmth of the sunlight, men, women, and children reflect on their experiences. Atencio describes the metaphor as representing a pathway to open knowledge featuring

a creative process of building knowledge. It does not build scientific knowledge that leads to technology; rather it creates practical knowledge applicable in social action. Its ultimate role in society is to help humans make decisions ... Initially we began to rename our own world, starting with Resolana itself as a way to build knowledge from our experience. (Atencio, 1988, p. 3)

The case study 'Conscientization as a Specific Form of Community Practice and Training in Quebec' addresses many of the same critical issues and illustrates how practitioners and educators need to provide a place and space for discourse. The theoretical direction for this case study was guided by Paulo Freire's critical awareness methodology, which can be summarized in the terms 'conscientization' and 'codification' (Freire, 1973, pp. vii–xiii, 41–6; Taylor, 1993, pp. 52–72). As described above in the Chicano experience of storytelling, discourse is central. In Quebec the reflected experience of women living on welfare became the narrative and resource base for the educators of community organizers. Such a learning action model has much to offer the field of CD.

In the case study 'Kindling Community Capacity,' the empowering influences in people's lives are revealed in the reported narratives:

I've learned so much about issues that I didn't think applied to me ... Learning about racial issues, native issues, and being involved with native communities. I think it just makes me a better person.

I probably feel better about myself in the last year than I've ever felt about myself, ever, and that's because of the project.

One resident commented on a shift in community attitudes:

I find it is easier to call [an agency] if you have a problem, and they'll listen. Before it would take six months to get them to respond basically to you.

The challenge for CD practitioners is not only to endorse the centrality of narrative discourse but also to advocate for the legitimizing of the knowledge gained from it. In Canada during 1993–4, the Royal Society of Canada and the University of British Columbia Institute of Health

Promotion Research were involved in efforts to determine criteria for participatory action research projects so that mainstream funders would become more sympathetic to this alternative way of producing knowledge.

RESISTANCE AS ASSOCIATIVE ACTIVITY

Even the oxen under the weight of the yoke complain. And the birds in their cage lament ...

Resolve to serve no more, and you are at once freed. I do not ask that you place your hands upon the tyrant to topple him over, but simply that you support him no longer; then you will behold him, like a great Colossus whose pedestal has been pulled away, fall of his own weight and break into pieces. (de la Boetie, 1975, pp. 52–3; original 1553)

While the heart of CD may be described as 'together we stand' to stand only is insufficient. Forward movement, as a process of associative activity that is driven by the values of co-operative development, is needed and becomes the genius of CD (Craig, 1993, p. 127). 'Associative activity' here is understood as people voluntarily coming together to act on the basis of a shared understanding of needs. However, to enter the next century with this quality of genius intact, some rethinking may be necessary to establish a helpful theory of hope.

The four case studies selected for the Canadian contribution to this comparative study represent only a few definitions of community. Case studies from other countries will suggest still more definitions. Each country must, however, look within its own borders and ask, 'Who is missing?' To assume a unity of understanding as to what it means to stand together and act together is folly; it is certainly out of step with the invitation of postmodernism to rethink our accustomed ways (Miami Theory Collective, 1991, pp. ix–xxvi).

The cutting edge of future CD may be sharpened through resistance-forming associative activities by people who are now undervalued and marginalized in society. An open process of seeking out differences and dissent among those who reject the status quo can only encourage participation in a strengthened democratic society. Ideally, the same open process should seek out and involve those who are now in a position to control knowledge and power; thus, a third way of analysis and change may be realized. To fail in this attempt at full participation in civic leadership stifles hope and contributes to apathy and a form of voluntary servitude.

Practices and theories are needed that challenge individualistic conceptions of society and promote an associative or fellowship process with a personality of its own (Heiman, 1977, pp. 5–9; Boldt & Long, 1984, 1992). Within this context, a deeper meaning of empowerment may be realized – one that rises above the all-too-common technical use of the term and expands the notion of co-operative associative activity as a form of resistance. Empowerment involves speaking of 'we' in the way intended by the composers of the Civil Rights rallying song, 'We Shall Overcome.' Perhaps, if we accept that meaning, our practice will more clearly point out a destination that offers increased hope to all involved. Why settle for less?

While in the day time birds always look as if they are flying about aimlessly, in the evening they always seem to find a destination again. They fly towards something. (Camus, 1966, p. 49)

Contributors

Mulegeta Abai
Executive director, former volunteer co-ordinator, Canadian Centre for Victims of Torture, Toronto.

Helen Ball
Doctoral candidate, Faculty of Social Work, Wilfrid Laurier University, Waterloo, Ontario.

Ken Banks
Principal investigator, Company of Neighbours research project, Cambridge, Ontario; part-time professor, School of Social Work, Ryerson Polytechnic University; and former assistant professor, Wilfrid Laurier University, Faculty of Social Work.

Gary Cameron
Director, Centre for Social Welfare Studies, Wilfrid Laurier University; and associate professor, Faculty of Social Work, Wilfrid Laurier University, Waterloo, Ontario.

Adrienne Chambon
Associate professor, Faculty of Social Work, University of Toronto; and Coordinator for Social Work of the university's multi-disciplinary program in Ethnic and Pluralism Studies.

Michael Clague
Past president of the Canadian Council on Social Development; former executive director, Social Planning and Research Council of British Columbia; and currently a consultant in social policy and community development.

Gerald Doré
Professor, École de Service Social, Université Laval, Quebec City; and member of the Quebec Collective of Conscientization.

Nathan Gilbert
Executive director, Laidlaw Foundation, Toronto; former executive director of the Ontario Municipal Social Services Association; and active member on the board of several community organizations and national networks.

Leslie Kemp
Senior program associate, Social Planning and Research Council of British Columbia.

Jassy Narayan
Community worker and program director, Onward Willow Neighbourhood Project of Better Beginnings, Better Futures, Guelph, Ontario.

Ray Peters
Research director, Better Beginnings, Better Futures Projects, Ontario; and professor of psychology, Queen's University.

Joan Simalchik
Former executive director, Canadian Centre for Victims of Torture, Toronto; and currently pursuing doctoral studies in human rights and collective memories at the Ontario Institute for Studies in Education, University of Toronto.

Leslie Stern
Founder and former board director, Entre Nous Femmes Housing Society, Vancouver.

Jim Vanderwoerd
Site researcher, Onward Willow Neighbourhood Project of Better Beginnings, Better Futures, Guelph, Ontario.

Co-ordinators

Harvey Stalwick
Joint co-ordinator, Canada country study. Founder and professor (until 1995), Faculty of Social Work, University of Regina. Currently director of the

Department of Social Work and Sociology, Concordia College, Minnesota. Received his doctorate from the London School of Economics in 1969. He is known for his progressive contributions to community-based social work education, for promoting self-governance in native people's education, for the leadership he has provided to the Community Folk School Movement in Saskatchewan, and for his active involvement in a Canadian and American network of participatory researchers.

André Jacob

Joint co-ordinator, Canada country study. Professor and former director, School of Social Work, Université du Québec à Montreal, where he obtained his doctorate in political science in 1982. Received also a doctorate in sociology from the Sorbonne, Paris, in 1990. He has been publicly acclaimed for promoting human rights and social justice for ethnocultural minorities in the province of Quebec and across Canada, and has been active throughout his professional career in community work and international co-operation, especially with Chile and Tunisia.

References

Abai, G. (1992, May). The therapeutic role of volunteer befrienders. *CCVT Newsletter* (earlier version presented at the 1991 International Conference of Centres, Institutions and Individuals Concerned with the Care for Victims of Organized Violence: Health, Political Repression, and Human Rights. Santiago, Chile).

Alary, J. (ed.). (1988). *Solidarités: Pratiques de recherche-action et de prise en charge par le milieu*. Montreal: Boréal.

– (ed.). (1990). *Community care and participatory research*. Montreal. Nu-Age Editions.

Alderson, L., et al. (1993). *Counting ourselves in: A women's community economic development handbook*. Vancouver: WomenFutures Community Economic Development Society.

Alinsky, Saul D. (1946). *Reveille for radicals*. Chicago: University of Chicago Press.

Allodi, F. (1991, April). Torture victims and service evaluation. Paper delivered at a seminar of the CCVT.

Allodi, F., & Cogwill, G. (1982). Ethical and psychiatric aspects of torture: A Canadian study. *Canadian Journal of Psychiatry*, 27 (March): 98–102.

Amnesty International (1994). *Annual Report*. New York: Amnesty International Publications.

Ampleman, G. (1983). Le bien-être social: pas un choix, mais un droit. Session de formation sur la loi d'aide sociale. In Ampleman et al., *Pratiques de conscientisation*. Montreal: Nouvelle Optique. 41–75.

– (1987). La formation des intervenants en santé communautaire en milieux populaires. In Ampleman et al., *Pratiques de conscientisation 2*. Quebec: Collectif québécois d'édition populaire. 179–213. (318 rue Bagot, Quebec City, PQ, Canada, G1K 1W1)

Ampleman, G., & Desgagnes, J.Y. (1994). *Insécurité maximum garantie. Session de formation sur la loi de la sécurité du revenu*. Quebec: Collectif québécois d'édition populaire.

Ampleman, G., Doré, G., Gaudreau, L., Larose, C., Leboeuf, L., & Ventelou, D. (1983). *Pratiques de conscientisation. Expériences d'éducation populaire au Québec*. Montreal: Nouvelle Optique. (Free translation of the definition, p. 291, by Gérald Doré.)

Ampleman, G., et al. (1987). *Pratiques de conscientisation 2. Logement, alphabétisation, aide sociale, féminisme, syndicalisme, santé publique*. Quebec: Collectif québécois d'édition populaire.

Arsenault, R. (1991). Conscientisation et santé mentale: Une pratique en région. *Service Social*, 40(3): 53–67.

Atencio, Tomas. (1988). *La Resolana: A Chicano pathway to knowledge*. Ernesto Galaraza Commemorative Lecture, Sanford Center for Chicano Research.

Banks, C.K., & Mangan, J.M. (1993, June). Inquiry, education and action: Implications for engaged social research. Paper presented at the Annual Meeting of the Canadian Sociology and Anthropology Association, Ottawa, Ontario.

– (1995). Researching social networks in action. *Journal of Sociology and Social Welfare*, 22(3): 69–87.

Barnabe, J. R.♀.S.E. du nord: Une pratique de conscientisation avec des femmes de classe populaire. *Service Social*, 34(2–3): 249–68.

– (1987). Féminisme et conscientisation. L'expérience d'un groupe de femmes de classe populaire. In Ampleman et al., *Pratiques de conscientisation*. Montreal: Nouvelle Optique. pp. 79–107.

Barnabe, J., & Brosseau, F. (1994). *Sensibilisation à la conscientisation. Session d'accueil au Collectif québécois de conscientisation*. Quebec: Collectif québécois d'édition populaire.

B.C. Working Group on Community Economic Development. (1993). *Report of the provincial consultation and follow-up meeting on community economic development*. Vancouver.

Bean, W. (1991). *Planning adult education programs: A brief manual*. Antigonish, NS: Coady International Institute.

Beiser, M. (1990). Mental health of refugees in resettlement countries. In
  W. Holtzman & T.H. Borman (eds.), *Mental health of immigrants and refugees*.
  Austin, TX: Hogg Foundation for Mental Health, University of Texas.
Belleau, M. (1994). *Jeunes et autochtones. Les défis de l'oppression dans une forma-
  tion à l'intervention*. Quebec: Collectif québécois d'édition populaire.
Better Beginnings, Better Futures. (1991). *Description and lessons learned: 1993
  progress report*. Toronto: Queen's Printer for Ontario.
Blakeney, J., da Costa, G., & Dirie, F.J. (1991). Mutual support model: The basic
  premises. Unpublished manuscript. Toronto: CCVT.
Blondin, M. (1966a). L'animation sociale en milieu urbain: Une solution.
  Recherches sociographiques, 1(3): 283–304.
– (1966b). La formation en service social. *Bulletin de la Corporation des
  travailleurs sociaux professionnels de la province de Québec*, 15 (décembre
  1965–janvier 1966): 7–8.
– (1967a). Notes sur l'animation sociale en milieu urbain. *Les cahiers de
  l'I.C.E.A. (Institut canadien d'éducation des adultes.)*. Numéro spécial sur
  l'animation, 4–5: 51–71.
– (1967b). Quels changements apporte l'animation sociale? *Les cahiers de
  l'I.C.E.A. (Institut canadien d'éducation des adultes)*, 4–5: 165–7.
– (1967c). Vie urbaine et animation sociale. In M.A. Lessar, & J.P. Montminy
  (eds.), *L'urbanisation de la société canadienne-français*. Quebec: Presses de
  l'Université Laval. 111–19.
Boldt, Menno, & Long, J. Anthony. (1992). Tribal philosophies and the Canadian Charter of Rights and Freedoms. *Ethnic and Racial Studies*, 7(4): 478–93.
  (Included in an extensive collection, David R. Miller et al., *The first ones:
  Readings in Indian/native studies*, Piapot Reserve #75: Saskatchewan Indian
  Federated College Press.)
Breton, R. (1991). *The governance of ethnic communities: Political structures and
  processes in Canada*. New York: Greenwood Press.
Bugge, K.E. (1994). The school for life. The basic ideas of Grundtvig's educa-
  tional thinking. In A. M. Allchin et al. (eds.), *Heritage and prophesy, Grundtvig
  and the English-speaking world*. Norwich, Norfolk: The Canterbury Press.
  271–81.
Cajete, Gregory (1994). *Look to the mountain: An ecology of indigenous education*.
  Durango, CO: Kivaki Press.
Calmeadow. (1993). *Annual Report*. Toronto.
Cameron, G., Hayward, K., & Mamatis, D. (1992). *Mutual aid and child
  welfare: The parent mutual aid organization in child welfare demonstration
  project*. Waterloo, ON: Wilfrid Laurier University, Centre for Social Welfare
  Studies.

Campfens, H. (1987, April). *Nurturing community: The individual and community in development practice*. Keynote Address at the Community Development Conference, Social Planning Council, Edmonton, Alberta.

– (1990). The role and future of non-governmental organizations (NGOs) in settlement and integration. In S.A. Yelaja (ed.), *Proceedings of the Settlement and Integration of New Immigrants to Canada Conference*. Waterloo, ON: Wilfrid Laurier University, Faculty of Social Work and Centre for Social Welfare Studies. 147–73.

Camus, Albert (1966). *Carnets, 1942–1951*. London: Hamish Hamilton.

Canada. Immigration and Refugee Board. (1989–94). *News Releases*. Ottawa: Immigration and Refugee Board.

Canadian Centre for Philanthropy. (1993). *Charity facts: 1993–information on giving, volunteering and the charitable sector in Canada*. Toronto.

Canadian Centre for Victims of Torture Newsletters. #6 (May 1992); #7 (April 1993); # 8 (January 1994). Toronto: CCVT.

Canadian Centre for Victims of Torture. (1993). *Volunteers guide*. Prepared by M.G. Abai. Toronto: CCVT.

Canadian Directory to Foundations (1993). *Demographic overview of foundations in Canada, tenth edition*. Toronto: Canadian Centre for Philanthropy.

Canadian Task Force on Mental Health Issues Affecting Immigrants and Refugees. (1988). *After the door has been opened: Mental health issues affecting immigrants and refugees: report*. Ottawa: Multiculturalism and Citizenship.

Carr, W., & Kemmis, S. (1986). *Becoming critical: Education, knowledge and action research*. Philadelphia: Falmer.

(CCSD) Centre for International Statistics on Economic & Social Welfare. (1993). *Countdown 93: Campaign 2000 child poverty indicator report*. Ottawa: Canadian Council on Social Development.

Chambon, A. (1989). Refugee families' experiences: Three family themes – family disruption, violent trauma, and acculturation. *Journal of Strategic and Systemic Therapies*, 8(1): 3–13.

Child Poverty Action Group. (1993). *Campaign 2000: Child poverty in Canada*. Toronto.

Cohen, J.L. (1985). Strategy or identity: New theoretical paradigms and contemporary social movements. *Social Research*, 52(4): 663–716.

Collectif québécois de conscientisation (CQC) (1990). *Grille Niveaux de conscience*.

Comeau, Y. (1987). Une entrée dans un réseau de solidarité. L'alphabétisation-conscientisation. In Ampleman et al., *Pratiques de conscientisation*. Montreal: Nouvelle Optique. 43–77.

Craig, J. (1993). *The nature of co-operation*. Montreal: Black Rose Books.

de la Boetie, Etienne. (1975). *The politics of obedience: The discourse of voluntary servitude.* Montreal: Black Rose Books. (Original 1553)

Diani, M. (1992). The concept of social movement. *The Sociological Review,* 1.

Doré, G. (1983). Des militants et militantes petits-bourgeois à l'école populaire. Les sessions de «sensibilisation à la conscientisation» du ROCQ. In Ampleman et al., *Pratiques de conscientisation 2.* Montreal: Nouvelle Optique. pp. 101–29.

– (1985). L'organisation communautaire: Définition et paradigme. *Service Social,* 34 (2–3): 210–30.

– (1992). L'organisation communautaire et les mutations dans les services sociaux au Québec, 1961–1991. *Service Social,* 41(2): 131–62.

Doré, G., & Gaudreau, L. (1987). Parlons politique! Une enquête conscientisante avec des militants et militantes de classe populaire. In Ampleman et al., *Pratiques de conscientisation 2, Québec: Collectif québécois d'édition poulaire.* Montreal: Nouvelle Optique. 247–81.

Doré, G., & Larose, C. (1979). L'organisation communautaire: Pratique salariée d'animation des collectivités au Québec. *Service Social,* 28(2–3): 69–96.

Doucet, L., & Favreau, L. (1991). Mise en perspective autour de trois «modèles». In L. Doucet and L. Favreau (eds.), *Théorie et pratiques en organisation communautaire.* Sillery: Presses de l'Université du Québec. 5–31.

Duhaime, R. (1987). Le projet O.L.O. et la conscientisation. Une expérience terrain en périnatalité en milieu populaire. In Ampleman et al., *Pratiques de conscientisation 2, Québec: Collectif québécois d'édition populaire,* 215–45.

Entre Nous News. (1993, May and November). Vancouver: Entre Nous Femmes Housing Society.

Fairbairn, B., Bold, J., Fulton, M., Hammond Ketilson, L. & Ish, D. (1991). *Co-operatives and community development.* Saskatoon, SK: Houghton Boston Printers.

Favreau, L., & Ninacs, W. (1993). *Community economic development in Québec: From social experimentation to the first signs of an economy based on solidarity.* Executive Summary of a research project funded by the National Welfare Grants Program, University of Québec at Hull.

Freire, P. (1970). *Pedagogy of the oppressed.* New York: The Seabury Press.

– (1971). *L'éducation: pratique de la liberté.* Paris: Cerf.

– (1973). *Education for critical consciousness.* New York: Continuum.

– (1974). *Pédagogie des opprimés.* Paris: Maspéro.

– (1978). *Lettres à la Guinée-Bissau sur l'alphabétisation.* Paris: Maspéro.

– (1980). Entretien avec Paulo Freire, 19 juin 1978, Genève. Propos recueillis par Yvon Minvielle, *Pourquoi?* 151: 50–7.

Gaudreau, L. (1994a). *Violence en héritage? Une session sur la violence conjugale au carrefour du féminisme, de la conscientisation et de la pastorale.* Quebec: Collectif québécois d'édition populaire.

- (1994b). *Parlons politique! Session de formation sur le passage à la politique partisane.* Quebec: Collectif québécois d'édition populaire.

Geary, V. (1992). *Choices and challenges: Uniting for change. A history of Entre Nous Femmes Housing Society.* Vancouver: Entre Nous Femmes.

Girardi, G. (1984). La crisi del '68. In L. Berzano et al., *Uomini di frontiera.* Torino: Cooperativa di cultura Lorenzo Milani. 833–57.

- (1994). *La militance et ses défis aujourd'hui.* (Available from Collectif québécois d'édition populaire.)

Halladay, Allan. (1992). An apologetics of hope for social work and social policy: An invitation to dialogue. Unpublished manuscript, University of Queensland, Brisbane, Australia, Department of Social Work and Social Policy. 1–8.

Hedrick, T., Bickamn, L., & Rog, D. (1993). *Applied research design.* London: Sage Publications.

Heiman, George. (1977). *Otto Gierke, associations and law: The classical and early Christian stages.* Toronto: University of Toronto Press.

Hossie, Linda. (1991, September 10). Hiding our eyes from horrible truths. *The Globe and Mail,* Toronto. A1.

Howse, Y., & Stalwick, H. (1990). Social work and the First Nation movement: Our children, our culture. In Brian Wharf (ed.), *Social work and social change in Canada.* Toronto: McClelland & Stewart. 79–113.

Humbert, C. (1976). *Conscientisation: expériences, positions dialectiques et perspectives.* Paris: L'Harmattan.

- (1984). Évaluation par rapport à la conscientisation. In A. Morin (ed.), *L'écriture collective. Un modèle de recherche-action.* Chicoutimi, PQ: Gaëtan Morin. 423–5.

- (1985). Éducation populaire et politique: l'urgence d'un renouvellement des modèles traditionnels de la gauche. *Service Social,* 34(2–3): 308–27.

- (1987a). La pensée et le cheminement de Paulo Freire. In Ampleman et al., *Pratiques de conscientisation 2, Québec: Collectif québécois d'édition populaire,* 283–309. (Translation of definition, 288–9, by Gérald Doré.)

- (1987b). L'enquête conscientisante. In J.-P. Deslauriers (ed.), *Les méthodes de la recherche qualitative.* Sillery: Presses de l'Université du Québec. 91–105.

Humbert, C., & Merlo, J. (1980). Éducation populaire et pédagogie militante. *Revue internationale d'action communautaire,* 3(43): 17–23.

Hurtubise, Y. (1991a). L'organisation communautaire en CLSC (Centre local de services communautaires). In L. Doucet & L. Favreau (eds.), *Théorie et pratiques en organisation communautaire.* Québec: Presses de l'Université du Québec.

– (1991b). L'action conscientisante. In L. Doucet & L. Favreau (eds.), *Théorie et pratiques en organisation communautaire.* Sillery: Presses de l'Université du Québec. 147–59.

Hurtubise, Y., Beauchamp, G., Favreau, L., & Fournier, D. (1989). *Pratiques d'organisation et de travail communautaires en CLSC.* Montreal: Regroupement québécois des intervenants et intervenantes en action communautaire en CLSC (RQIIAC).

Illich, I. (1977). Disabling professions. In I. Illich et al., *Disabling professions.* Boston: Marion Boyars. 11–39.

INODEP (1971). *Conscientisation. Recherche de Paulo Freire.* Paris: Institut oecuménique pour le développement des peuples.

Inter-Pares Annual Report (1993). *Creating change: The option of hope.* Ottawa.

Jacob, A. (1985). Des enjeux pour l'action militante des années 80. *Service social,* 34(2–3): 353–68.

Kumar, K. (1993). Civil society: An inquiry into the usefulness of a historical term. *BJS,* 44(3): 375–95.

Kurtz, L.F., & Chambon, A. (1987). A comparison of self-help groups for mental health. *Health and Social Work,* 12(4): 275–84.

Lacroix, J. (1987). Conscientiser par le placotage dans le cadre d'une expérience avec un comité H.L.M.. In Ampleman et al., *Pratiques de conscientisation 2, Québec: Collectif québécois d'édition populaire,* pp. 13–42.

Lather, P. (1991). Research as praxis. *Harvard Educational Review,* 56: 257–75.

Lamoureux, H., Mayer, R., & Panet-Raymond, J. (1984). *L'intervention communautaire.* Montreal: Éditions Saint-Martin.

Leboeuf, L. (1991). Les femmes et la pauvreté. *Service Social,* 40(3): 24–41.

Lord, J. (1987). The voice of the people. *Canadian Journal of Community Mental Health,* 10(1).

Lovell, M. (1991). *The friendship group: Learning the skills to create social support. Report of the Social Support Training Project.* Vancouver: University of British Columbia, School of Social Work.

MacLeod, G. (1984). Community control. In Dorsey and Ticoll (eds.), *The Nuts and bolts of Community Economic Development.* Edmonton: Edmonton Social Planning Council.

Marr, W.L. (1992). Post-war Canadian immigration patterns. In S. Globerman (ed.), *The immigration dilemma.* Vancouver: Fraser Institute. 17–41.

McKnight, J. (1977). Professionalized service and disabling help. In I. Illich et al., *Disabling professions.* Boston: Marion Boyars. 69–91.

Médard, Jean-François. (1969). *Communauté locale et organisation communautaire aux États-Unis*. Paris: Armand Colin.

Miami Theory Collective. (eds.). (1991). *Community at loose ends*. Minneapolis: University of Minnesota Press.

Miller, J.G. (1994). Cultural diversity in the morality of caring: Individually oriented versus duty-based interpersonal moral codes. *Cross-Cultural Research*, 28(1): 3–39.

Mollica, R.F. (1988). The trauma story: The psychiatric care of refugee survivors of violence and torture. In F.M. Ochberg (ed.), *Post-traumatic therapy and victims of violence*. New York: Brunner-Mazel. 295–314.

Oxhorn, M.R. (1993). Popular education in Montreal: Organizing Hispanic refugee and immigrant women. *Intervention*, 96 (October): 19–25.

Perkins, F. (1993, October). *Social interventions: The socio-environmental approach*. Paper presented at the Physicians for Human Rights, International Rehabilitation Council for Torture Victims, Survivors International of Northern California and Centre for Victims of Torture.

Peters, Dr Ray DeV., & Russell, Dr Carol Crill. (1994). *Better Beginnings, Better Futures Project: Model, program & research overview*. Toronto: Queen's Printer for Ontario.

Piotte, J.-M. (1987). *La communauté perdue. Petite histoire des militantismes*. Montreal: VLB.

– (1990). *Sens et politique. Pour en finir avec les grands désarrois*. Montreal: VLB.

Premier's Council on Health, Well-Being and Social Justice. (1991). *Nurturing health: An understanding of what makes people healthy*. Ontario.

Rappaport, J. (1987). Terms of empowerment/exemplars of prevention: Toward a theory for community psychology. *American Journal of Community Psychology*, 15(2): 121–48.

ROCQ (1977). *Manifeste*. Quebec: Regroupement des organisateurs communautaires du Québec. (Quotations translated by Gérald Doré.)

Ross, M.G. (1967). *Community organization: Theory, principles and practice*. New York: Harper & Row.

Rothman, J. (1970). Three models of community organization practice. In F.M. Cox, J.L. Erlich, J. Rothman, & E. Tropman (eds.), *Strategies of Community Organization*. Itasca, IL: F.E. Peacock.

– (1979). Macro social work in a tightening economy. *Social Work*, 24(4): 274–81.

Ruopp, P. (ed.). (1953). *Approaches to community development: A symposium introductory to problems and methods of village welfare in underdeveloped areas*. The Hague, Netherlands: W. Van Hoeve.

Saint-Cyr, F. (1994). *Alphabétisation-conscientisation dans un Nicaragua en transition.* (Available from Collectif québécois d'édition populaire.)

Shragge, E. (1993). The politics of community economic development. In Eric Shragge (ed.), *Community economic development: In search of empowerment.* Montreal: Black Rose Books.

Simalchik, J. (1990, November). *A community response to global repression: The Canadian centre for victims of torture.* Paper presented at the Conference of the Association for Moral Education, Notre Dame.

– (1991). *The role of public education in the development and delivery of the services of the Canadian Centre for Victims of Torture.* Paper presented at the Third International Conference: Health, Political Repression and Human Rights, Santiago, Chile.

– (1993). Torture victims are part of the refugee picture. *Compass,* 11(4) (September/October): 45.

Smith, Dorothy. (1974). The social construction of documentary reality. *Sociological Inquiry,* 44.

Sioui, Georges E. (1992). *For an Amerindian autohistory: An essay on the foundations of a social ethic.* Montreal and Kingston: McGill-Queen's University Press.

Statistics Canada (1990). *Women in Canada.* Ottawa: Statistics Canada.

Stein, B.N. (1986). The experience of being a refugee: Insights from research. In C.L. Williams & J. Westermeyer (eds.), *Refugee mental health in resettlement countries.* Washington, DC: Hemisphere. 5–23.

Swack, M., and Mason, D. (1987). Community economic development as a strategy for social intervention. In Edward Bennett (ed.), *Social intervention: Theory and practice.* New York: Edwin Mellen Press. 327–8.

Taylor, Paul V. (1993). *The texts of Paulo Freire.* Buckingham: Open University Press.

Touraine, Alain. (1985). An introduction to the study of social movements. *Social Research,* 52(4): 749–87.

– (1991). *Critique de la post-modernité.* Paris: Fayard.

Triandis, H.C. (1993). Collectivism and individualism as cultural syndromes. *Cross-Cultural Research,* 27(3–4): 155–80.

Tsuzki, Kei. (1994). Calmeadow: Giving credit where credit is due. *Perception* (publication of the Canadian Council on Social Development), 17(4).

Turner, B.S. (1993). Outline of a theory of human rights. *Sociology,* 27(3): 489–512.

Vaillancourt, Y. (1993). Trois thèses concernant le renouvellement des pratiques sociales dans le secteur public. *Nouvelles pratiques sociales,* 6(1): 1–14.

Wallerstein, N. (1993). Empowerment and health: The theory and practice of community change. *Community Development Journal*, 28(3): 218–27.

Wellman, B., Carrington, P.J., & Hall, A. (1988). Networks as personal communities. In B. Wellman & S.D. Berkowitz (eds.), *Social structures: A network approach*. Cambridge/New York: Cambridge University Press. 130–84.

Winter, R. (1987). *Action research and the nature of social inquiry: Professional innovation and educational work*. Brookfield: Avebury.

Wismer, S., & Pell, D. (1984). Community self-reliance in the age of 6 and 5. In Dorsey and Ticoll (eds.), *The nuts and bolts of community economic development*. Edmonton: Edmonton Social Planning Council.

Wolfensberger, W. (1972). *The principle of normalization in human services*. Downsview, ON: National Institute of Mental Retardation.

Zimmerman, M.A., & Rappaport, J. (1988). Citizen participation, perceived control, and psychological empowerment. *American Journal of Community Psychology*, 16(5): 725–50.

Zolberg, A. (1989). The next waves: Migration theory for a changing world. *International Migration Review*, 23 (Fall): 403–30.

Part IV

The Netherlands

Co-ordinated by CEES DE WIT

The Netherlands

1. INTRODUCTION
Fred Stafleu

The Netherlands is a small, densely populated, highly developed country situated on the North Sea at the estuaries of three major European rivers – the Rhine, the Maas, and the Scheldt. Many Dutch people earn their living in shipping, tourism, and commerce, and in the transportation of goods to countries inland.

The country covers 41,500 square kilometres and has over 15 million inhabitants, for a density of 412 people per square kilometre. The labour force consists of about 6 million people, 67 percent of whom work in the services sector, 28 percent in industry, and 5 percent in agriculture and fishing. Population pressures in the Netherlands make planning of urban and rural areas a matter of special urgency.

The Netherlands is a constitutional monarchy with a parliamentary system of government in a federated state of twelve provinces. A large part of policy is made and executed by municipalities.

Characteristic of Dutch society is what the Dutch themselves call 'compartmentalization' (a vertical differentiation of society), by which is meant the co-existence in political, cultural, and social life of organizations with similar or identical objectives but different religious and ideological bases. This phenomenon can be found in almost all sectors, including broadcasting, the press, education, political parties, trade unions, hospitals, and sports and social clubs. This compartmentalized social structure started to disintegrate in the 1960s; the process accelerated during the 1970s and continues up to this day. Nevertheless, some structures have remained stable, especially among the new minorities from former colonies and among the immigrants from the Mediterranean areas, who aspire for the continuation of their compartmentalized programs and services, which are subsidized by the state. This has presented particular challenges when it comes to integrating these groups, of whom there are sizeable numbers in the large cities, with the mainstream to form a multicultural society.

The year 1973 was critical in the development of the postwar Dutch economy. The first oil crisis, which struck that year, had been preceded by a long period of economic expansion during which the average annual growth of GNP was between 6 and 7 percent, and the average annual unemployment rate was only 2 percent. After 1973 economic growth slowed down, as it did in most industrialized countries. Industry, which had accounted for a large number of jobs before 1973, became less labour intensive, and the number of jobs declined rapidly. At the same time, the labour force was growing at a much faster rate than in most other countries. One reason is that more and more women were seeking paid employment. Unemployment rose from 3 percent in 1973 to 17 percent in 1983. Fortunately, from 1983 onwards there was a new period of expansion, and unemployment gradually decreased. However, the recession that began in the early 1990s, which is expected to be long-lasting, has increased the unemployment rate dramatically again, as well as claims for social security benefits.

This economic stagnation (in a European and international context), combined with the expansion of the social security sector, has led to growing doubts that the Dutch welfare state can be sustained. Further, people seem to be less and less willing to accept the concept of mutual solidarity that is the underlying principle of the welfare state. Before the current recession, most people believed that low-income groups should receive broad social and economic support, paid for by more affluent groups. The instruments to achieve this end were a fair tax system and an impressive bundle of social security legislation that included safety nets for the most disadvantaged. The assumption that the state had an active, far-reaching role was universal.

The welfare state reached its zenith at the end of the 1960s; by then it was providing complete care of people from the cradle to the grave. It was believed that structural poverty no longer existed, thanks to the fact that full employment was a reality.

In such a climate, central and local government felt responsible for introducing and paying for a wide range of social programs, most of them undertaken by voluntary organizations and agencies. These included

CD projects in both rural and urban areas. There were programs that focused on, for example, educational backwardness, neighbourhood development (particularly in urban renewal areas), and the beneficiaries of social assistance. Some programs worked better than others.

The economic recession that followed the 1973 oil crisis made people reconsider the socio-economic structure of society. In the wake of the cultural revolution of the 'activist sixties,' awareness of self and individualism were on the increase, the process of secularization accelerated, and traditional frameworks were abandoned. Community building and mutual solidarity were no longer basic assumptions.

The deep recession put pressure on the government and the political parties to review the concept of the welfare state. Doubts increased about the state's ability to finance all the demands placed on it. State expenditures (the collective sector) reached an unacceptable level – over 60 percent of GNP, a figure that included the extremely high bill for social security.

Since then a number of fundamental socio-political changes have taken place (or at least been aimed at), such as these:

- A gradual decrease in government expenditures.
- Transfer of central state power to provincial and local authorities.
- The take-over of government tasks by independent institutions and by the market sector ('less state, more market').
- Drastic cuts in state subsidies for nonprofit organizations in the medical, social, educational, and cultural sectors.
- Pressure on wages, primarily in the collective sector.
- A stronger check on the volume of social security benefits (for the unemployed, the disabled, and others) and on social assistance (for the poor).

The last item in particular – social assistance – is associated with the welfare state. Along with the economic necessity of reducing social benefits, it must be emphasized that those who were working increasingly began to rebel against the personal burden they had to carry for the benefit of their nonworking neighbours. They considered the extent of abuse and fraud taking place as unacceptable. Workers looked at the 'gap' between their gross salary and their net income and felt that the high social premiums were a waste of money. The low-income workers of the past had succeeded in increasing their income levels, thanks to better education and training and to the fact that more spouses (i.e., women) were employed. Thus, while the lower working classes moved upwards on the social ladder, they were leaving nonworkers behind. This explains why the welfare state is at risk of losing its political support from a sizeable sector of the population.

For CD, mutual solidarity is a basic principle that translates into activities that seek collective action to resolve common social problems at the community level. In the early 1990s a new government policy called 'Social Renewal' provided a new context and support for CD activities. In combination with another policy, 'Administrative Renewal,' Social Renewal programs encouraged citizens and groups to participate in joint actions as a means to improve their living conditions. In a great number of urban districts, particularly those in decline, local groups have set up a variety of small-scale projects related to such problems as unemployment, pollution, crime, vandalism, and multicultural relations. In many of these programs, community workers play an essential part.

This country study will provide an overview of the present state of CD in the Netherlands. It will then discuss a number of specific cases representative of current practice. The cases relating to environmental protection, the integration of the elderly, and the reduction of poverty address policy issues in which CD is often strongly involved. Discussions of the organization of CD, and of training, research, and theory, will round off this study.

2. THE ROOTS OF CD WORK IN THE NETHERLANDS
Cees de Wit

EARLY HISTORY

CD work in the Netherlands has deep roots. We know that in Leiden, a small university town, predecessors of today's CD workers were active as early as the seventeenth century. It was their task to ensure the smooth functioning of everyday life in their neighbourhood. They generally mediated between individuals and the social structures, which produced problems that even then were not easily resolved. The clergy were engaged in this kind of mediation in the areas of religion and work. Apart from this, the so-called neighbourhood lords had to guard and if need be arrange the orderly course of practical matters of daily life, such as (social) security. They also settled arguments, arranged funerals, guaranteed free passage, organized festivities, and cleared dung and dirt. The neighbourhood lord was selected by the neighbourhood's residents. He had to have an air of authority and preferably be self-supporting. He had to have helpers or be rather muscular himself, since he sometimes had to get involved in turbulent arguments and settle them 'as a lord should' or arrange a reconciliation by 'eye contact and shaking hands.' This on penalty of providing a barrel of beer or a ham for the neighbourhood festivities.

The neighbourhood lords disappeared for many reasons, including the expansion of the duties of the local town councils and the rise of police forces, insurance businesses, and sanitation departments. Still, in the course of history this characteristic CD worker continues to surface in other forms. Sometimes the community involved isn't local (i.e., of shared interests), but a community of a different kind, and the CD worker appears as a 'categorical worker.' For instance, during the first industrial revolution, which arrived late in the Netherlands (i.e., at the turn of the last century), he was most often a union foreman. In the next period, community work was joined by a new development in the civic sector – the rise of housing corporations. 'People's education' became the focus of intervention up to the Second World War. This education took place in public housing estates, following the example of Ebenezer Howard's Garden City Movement, and in 'people's houses,' which were semipublic schools for adults. Rural CD took place through provincial organizations (Broekman, 1987, pp. 38, 43).

AFTER THE SECOND WORLD WAR

During the postwar reconstruction of the Netherlands, industrialization reappeared at the same time as a wave of modernization. The impact of these large-scale developments on local communities, professional roles, patterns of education, household situations, and traditional opinions was significant. Also, areas for living, working, and recreation began to spread geographically. Furthermore, the housing shortage caused by the war led to a system of distribution that disrupted kinship networks as it spread out across the urbanized regions. In this context, Dutch CD work in the period 1945–60 detached itself from social work focusing on case work. The task of CD was to help reconstruct the Netherlands and 'steer the influence of industrialization and modernization in the right direction.' It was feared that industrial growth and urbanization would create an anonymous society, and lead to moral decay and a growing class of antisocial elements. It was thought that these threats might be averted if social education was reinforced, and social planning was democratized, through grass roots work in the community and through improvements in social services. The ancient, rural pattern of social relations served as a model for the stimulation of mutual and harmonious relations. Also, a distinction was made between the functional and categorical dimensions of the 'new' profession (Boer, 1968, pp. 155–94; Tienen & Zwanikken, 1972; Besteman, 1974).

As noted in the introduction, the compartmentalized Dutch welfare state played an important part in these developments. It provided the subsidies for appointing CD workers and establishing compartmentalized local socio-cultural facilities such as community centres. These were co-ordinated at the national level by representative consultant bodies, which were also financially supported by the state. In those days important organizational supports to CD work were the clubhouses and community houses. Community organization and cultural work linked up with the existing networks and activities of villagers and neighbourhood residents, with recreational and educational activities being developed on the basis of the neighbourhood's own culture and needs.

Traditionally, recreation and education oriented CD work started from the community centre and the networks it identified or created. But in practice it went beyond these activities, discovering and exploring the internal resources of a network or group that might serve as a basis for developing effective organizations and strategies, which were essential if innovative improvements were to be achieved. Since citizen participation in institutional decision-making was largely lacking during this period, local groups had to develop special strategies for finding the required external resources to undertake projects that would improve living and employment conditions.

URBAN RENEWAL IN THE 1970S AND 1980S

In the 1970s and 1980s a large-scale urban renewal program was introduced to deal with deteriorating city neighbourhoods. Neighbourhood organizations, supported by CD work, played an important part in this, and CD work acquired a steady base (Haberer, 1978). From the perspective of emancipation, countless neighbourhood organizations were developed based on residents' own abilities and supported by young architects and CD workers. These were organizations of and for residents, and project related, functioning often as important partners in the process of neighbourhood reconstruction and renovation. They had their own offices, provided by the town council, and a budget for activities such as training, excursions, and the development of alternative plans. They usually published a district newspaper and had voting power (sometimes a decisive vote) in the renewal projects. In this reconstruction process, residents and CD workers paid special attention to improving their social position as residents vis-à-vis the construction industry, which often tended to act with impunity, being driven by profits. Not surprisingly, linking the physical reconstruction to the process and activities of CD was controversial (Kleijn, 1978). While the vanguard of the neighbourhood organizations achieved some spectacular results, the reconstruction process often moved too fast for most residents to keep up, despite planning, phasing, and 'contract management' (Kleijn, 1985).

INTERMEZZO

CD work managed the urban renewal situation from an 'us/them' perspective. Although there were various competing rival agents, the municipal councils assumed the 'demon' role as local representatives of the state. The main CD approaches were to start a fight with a visible opponent to seek co-operation with the council. 'Us' were the residents of the threatened neighbourhood and their helpers, and 'them' was the council, with its good friends from the building industry. CD's role here was to serve as both social inventor and campaigner, and as network developer, organization builder, and broker for the residents in their dealings with the various council departments and others.

The situation has since become much more complex. 'Us' is no longer the (former) working-class residents of Dutch heritage. 'Them' is no longer the council, with its power to distribute subsidies from the state and the construction industry. Resident's organizations are now created by various ethnic and socio-cultural groups who have lost their community, and by those countless other people who are excluded economically, socially, and politically. What is being aspired to is what Jane Jacobs describes as 'integrated diversity' (in Angotti, 1993, p. 203).

The entire ideological, political, and administrative situation has become rather complex. For some years the welfare state has been attempting to fill the ideological hole that was created when knowledge, power, and income were redistributed. But with the end of the traditionally narrow concept of labour, the disintegration of compartmentalization, the end of the 'big ideas' of the world ideologies, and the accompanying rise in the ideology of cutbacks, the state's role as moralist, or normative agent, seems to be over. The national government is stepping back and splitting off in two directions. It supports the centralization of states in the form of the European Community; yet, local authorities are now assuming the principal responsibility for welfare and welfare-political conditions (albeit with fewer funds at their disposal).

In other words, society no longer provides clear guidelines in terms of what is expected of CD, except that it should provide something new, with the people themselves restoring the solidarity that binds people. This presents a special challenge for CD work, as neighbourhoods are no longer socio-culturally homogeneous, but have become extremely heterogeneous. And the people on whom CD work is focusing – that is, the excluded – are growing in numbers, becoming active only when they perceive their involvement as potentially leading to concrete benefits. For these people, 'diversity without integration' means that they have become alienated not only from labour, but also from each other and from themselves. They step back, ritualize, calculate, or defraud, and start their own little subsocieties with their own subcultures (Engbersen, 1994). Only for the notoriously criminal elements is there social interest, or rather fear, to such an extent that the state is prepared to engage in social experiments. Under these conditions we find police officers at the neighbourhood level assuming social work roles in addition to their law enforcement duties. It is still unclear where the social and/or government support for more constructive, innovative movements will come from. In short, this is a difficult period for CD workers, as they realize that more than ever they will have to prove their worth. There is an increasing demand for their services, but the sources of subsidy are drying up.

THE NECESSITY FOR SOCIAL RENEWAL: EARLY 1990S

Many of the problems noted above, which are the result of a radical transformation in the economic and social structure, will be tolerated by people as long as they happen in somebody else's back yard. Further, in the past, spatial proximity was important for the development of social relations, and territorially oriented CD work was able to respond in kind. But this spatial relations thesis has become much more complex. To many people, living conditions in the neighbourhood are no longer a factor promoting social participation. They work elsewhere and the pressure at work is often so high that at home they want to be left alone. For social, recreational, and care issues they do not need either their neighbourhood or their relatives. Instead, they rely more on their networks, or functional communities. In these 'communities of social practice' (Heraud, in Plant, 1974, p. 38) only fragments of the individual's identity manifest themselves. These networks in turn have their own sectoral, interest-promoting organizations. The result is a social structure whose solidarity is fragmented (Vilrokx, in Coenen & Leisink, 1993, p. 211).

At the same time, there are countless people who do not have and never will have paid work. They live in the lowest-rent areas and stay at home for fear of losing their benefits, since the income from any work they find would be deducted from their benefits. Thus, they are not rewarded for showing initiative. In these areas people develop their own coping strategies, sometimes aided by CD work. They may and often do undertake socially useful work, on a voluntary basis, taking on projects that rank high as social but not economic priorities. While the economic sector understands the significance of social order and stability, it has not reached the point where it will economically reward tasks that promote them.

Policies and strategies were urgently needed to prevent the growth of an underclass and the social and economic exclusion of a significant sector of the population. This challenge was taken up at the end of the 1980s by the movement for social and administrative renewal, initiated first in Rotterdam, which has the world's largest harbour and a high concentration of unemployed people.

Business was booming in the city as a result of its harbour activities, and some of the profits were redirected to reward social innovations that would cut across sectoral lines and provide a basis for new policy development. The small projects planned and implemented by people in various districts and neighbourhoods demonstrated that co-operation was possible not only among neighbours but also among government agencies. Encouraged by the success of these initiatives in Rotterdam, the national government decided to follow suit and introduce a social and administrative renewal program for the whole country, focusing on three main areas:

- Employment, income, and education.
- The quality of the physical environment for everyday living.
- Innovations in the social and cultural fields.

Municipal authorities were expected to implement this program at the local level. The purpose was to seek integrated initiatives that would involve a pooling of financial and other resources of different city departments and organizations. This would counteract the compartmentalized bureaucracy and fragmented organizational structure that then existed.

Because of their proven ability to innovate, and to activate and work with both the community and the system, CD workers were approached to lend their support in carrying out this program (Leur, 1991, pp. 35–9). Persuading them was not an easy task, however. The attempts to do so raised questions about the foundations and renewal of the profession that we will return to in the last section 'Theoretical Developments.'

SOCIAL MANAGEMENT OF DISTRICTS: THE MID-1990S

An emerging issue of great importance is the social management of districts (Hooijdonk & Raspe, 1993). 'Neighbourhood maintenance,' understood as housing estate management or urban management, often has to deal with many different phenomena, and relates to the earlier role of the seventeenth-century neighbourhood lord as landlord. The quality of the physical environment and especially the quality of life are important points of interest here that touch both managers and residents, and involve CD work. Neighbourhood management is not easy, because residents cannot play government, nor do they have the financial means to assume full responsibility for the self-management of the neighbourhood. The CD worker differs in turn from the seventeenth-century neighbourhood lord in that he or she must direct matters as little as possible. It is essential, therefore, to consider carefully what can and cannot be associated with CD.

Neighbourhood management in general includes the decisions and activities of proprietors and users of a certain area aimed at counteracting what is undesirable and promoting developments that maintain and improve the quality of the environment and living conditions. There are four aspects to this:

- Physical-technical management (building, street, and greenery improvement, and maintenance and sanitation).
- Spatial-functional management (what, where, and why).
- Financial management (estimates, budgets, expenditures, adjustments, and monitoring of costs).
- Social management (quality of life, co-management, and partial self-management by residents).

Social management concerns those decisions and activities that are important to the socio-cultural and socio-economic functioning of a neighbourhood. It involves relations between residents, the managers of buildings, the living environment, and neighbourhood facilities. It aims at co-operation in reducing and overcoming social problems linked to unemployment, the aging of the population, the arrival and settlement of immigrants, and the rise in crime, vandalism, and pollution (Os & Haeften, 1988). CD's role in this compares to the functions performed during the period of urban renewal. However, the challenges are different. As a *campaigner* and *network developer*, the CD worker now has to activate more diverse groups in pursuit of a common goal. As a *broker* and *organizer* he or she needs to draw individuals whose ties are less obvious (though they are in similar positions) into groups or organizations, thereby creating more fruitful relations between them and other relevant agents.

CONCLUSION

CD workers in the Netherlands are aware of their own professional responsibilities and are concerned with quality performance and educational upgrading. Evidence of this can be found in the development of a professional profile (Attema, 1991), the publication of several books, the creation of a special chair for the scientific study of CD work at the Department of Philosophy at Erasmus University in Rotterdam, and the setting up of a national register of senior CD workers who are qualified professionals and serve as consultants to younger colleagues.

We perceive the following as the main themes of Dutch CD work:

- *Territorial* work, which is concerned with the quality of life of neighbourhoods. This may include many functional aspects that attempt to counter the loss of social identity and cohesion, neglect, nuisance, and insecurity.
- *Categorical* work with the elderly, women, immigrants or minorities, young people, and the handicapped, leading toward emancipation and increased independence.
- *Functional* work, which involves working toward the development of relevant policy frameworks and programs related to housing, health, education, unemployment, social security, and poverty alleviation, with a special concern for the economically and socially excluded. In this task the CD worker functions principally at the interface between the system and the community.

The three cases selected from the current practice of CD in the Netherlands provide examples of each.

3. PRACTICE

A. CD Work and Physical Environment Protection (PEP)
Eric Canjels with Cees de Wit

INTRODUCTION

Former urban renewal areas and areas where the cost of living is lowest house a mixture of people from different income groups and from very different backgrounds. Quite often the question arises: How can the quality of life be maintained in such a neighbourhood in terms of adequate social involvement on the part of citizens, a well-functioning public order, the absence of pollution and neglect, and a considerable degree of tolerance? Sometimes this is possible. When it is not, inhabitants find themselves in an unenviable position, characterized by social isolation, intolerance, crime, environmental decay, and helplessness in the matter of acting on these problems. The CD worker, who is expected to contribute to the development of social relations in such neighbourhoods, encounters vague feelings of dissatisfaction and an absence of expressed demand for his or her services from the people themselves.

Much is involved in promoting solidarity and in helping form links. First of all, the CD worker must get a clear picture of what issues are at stake and what individuals, groups, and institutions are affected. Usually the worker will encounter mutual prejudices that must be dealt with before anything else can be tackled. Furthermore, he or she must offer a perspective on possible improvements that is clear in content, modest in vision, and manageable. The perspective should not only activate people but also provide a picture of how joint action will redefine people's positions and result in a permanently improved situation (i.e., for the marginalized). It is also essential, if CD work is to be socially recognized and supported, that the worker set high personal standards as a professional and have the proper qualifications. To help turn general feelings of dissatisfaction into constructive, innovative action, the CD worker must take a thoroughly professional approach. He or she must avoid taking undue risks, acting as caretaker, playing the 'working class hero,' and making negative remarks.

In choosing a concrete focus for action, neighbourhood projects are the obvious choice. There may be a request from the residents or agencies to deal with some issue, and there are usually plenty of social and policy questions that call for exploration and experimentation at the local level. In addition, from the point of view of public administration, the neighbourhood is the smallest feasible territorial unit in which policy measures can be integrated.

PHYSICAL ENVIRONMENT PROTECTION (PEP): EXPERIMENTAL CD WORK

An example of a theme that sufficiently appeals to most residents and fits into the policy vision of agencies and organizations is the protection of the physical environment. We will expand on this theme and take a closer look at the Netherlands Project for Experimental CD Work concerning the Physical Environment Protection (PEP) project in six urban areas.[1]

On one level, CD environmental work can be viewed as the promotion of district interests vis-à-vis the environment. But it is also a way to realize the environmental goals of others, such as the municipal council or the housing corporation, in co-operation with the inhabitants. The 'district interest model' is most in keeping with regular CD work. Here, the environment is first of all a point of departure for district improvements, to be termed 'social management.' This may involve improving local living conditions, activating inhabitants on environmental issues, focusing on environmental tasks in work or education projects, and persuading authorities and others with environment-based arguments to do more than just their 'environment' job. Practice has shown that with this strategy, much can be achieved in a neighbourhood.

1 This project is being executed by a project team consisting of the CD workers of six districts. These districts or neighbourhoods are demonstration sites for residents' participation concerning the physical environment. The community workers involved are Johan Bodd (Arnhem), Gerard van Jaarsveld (Breda), Joop Hofman (Deventer), Ans Knook (Roermond), Jaap Noordman (Oldenzaal), and Hugo van der Steenhoven (till 1 April 1994, then town councillor) and Geertje Raadsveld (from 1 May 1994) (both from Utrecht). The rest of the team is composed of Freerk Veldkamp (project leader for the National Centre for Community Development Work/National Consultants Group PEP Community Development Work, LCO/LAMIGO), Henni Bunnik (project leader for the Foundation Physical Environment Education, SME), and Gretha van der West (project co-ordinator, LCO/LAMIGO). We thank them for the information they have provided and for the discussions this article is based on.

SOME EXAMPLES

In the small neighbourhood of DeThij, in a former textile town in the eastern part of the Netherlands, residents' organizations aided by a CD worker have activated the neighbourhood to achieve environmentally friendlier management of their surroundings, starting with the self-management of public greenery. Greenery management is small-scale, operating in some ten areas the size of a square or part of a street. More or less spontaneous initiatives in self-management – such as taking care of a neglected bit of greenery in one's immediate proximity – are publicly noted and held up as examples. An inventory based on areas has been made of residents' wishes and willingness to take care of the greenery themselves. For the town of Oldenzaal this willingness is a point of departure to negotiate agreements with the town council on matters of self-management. The council makes sure that dominant groups listen to others and do not monopolize the discussions. For specific locations, agreements between the council and the residents' organization on overdue maintenance, on facilities and help for residents, and on ecologically correct handling are laid down in a contract. Similar collaboration with the housing association is achieved on the second action point, which relates to housing and living conditions.

Another middle-sized town, Arnhem, in the district of Klarendal, has had many years of experience with district management and environmental initiatives. Each district has a 'platform' on which residents and council representatives serve. This platform draws up an annual district plan with all kinds of measures for improving the quality of life. The council has followed suit by organizing management on a district basis. Each district has its own budget, with which smaller projects can be financed. The environmental initiatives in Klarendal came about because one resident insisted on an environmental approach to a renewal project. This initiative inspired other residents and the CD worker. It resulted in many more projects, such as greenery management, environmental education in schools, and campaigns against advertising flyers. For some years now, environmental measures have been included in the district plan. Some examples:

- An annual budget of Dfl 1,000 has been reserved for the stimulation program 'Greenery and Tree Adoption.'
- Safe pedestrian and cyclist routes to the shopping centre have been laid out.

- District managers and neighbourhood caretakers have been issued with bicycles to do their rounds (i.e., so they don't use cars).
- The district management platform publishes a booklet on environmentally friendly jobs around the house.

The interesting aspect of this case is that district needs and council policy are linked through a municipal district co-ordinator, who consults with residents and the CD worker on what the council should do to achieve its own environmental targets and how to involve the district population.

In Deventer, a town on the river IJssel, a district environment company named Cambio Company is being created in the neighbourhoods of Driebergen and Red Village. Here the living environment is managed by the residents themselves, in consultation with the town council, in a businesslike and environmentally friendly manner. This includes the maintenance of public greenery and the collection of waste (vegetable waste for compost, glass for recycling, etc.). New forms of environment-friendly employment are also being developed, such as a repair workshop and shops for second-hand goods and clothes. Through Cambio Company, environmental targets are being set and employment and education are being provided for a number of residents. It is expected that when formerly unemployed residents are seen to be active in the neighbourhood, others will make an effort to contribute to an active, cleaner neighbourhood. A number of qualified people manage Cambio. The CD worker does not assist on the commercial side of the enterprise but gives advice on education, organization, and strategy – specifically, on objectives and tasks, required skills, and resources available from sponsoring authorities (e.g., subsidies, empty buildings, social benefit funding) and from the Chamber of Commerce and companies in the neighbourhood. This is valuable advice, since plans only begin operation after lengthy negotiations between the residents' organizations and the town council on the tasks and financing of Cambio. Part of the plan includes training social benefits recipients (job poolers) for employment in the company.

In the cities of Utrecht, Breda, and Roermond there have also been attempts to promote better conditions in the living environment through citizen participation. Yet there are differences as to local approach and effect.

In Utrecht, in the neighbourhood of Vogelenwijk/Tuinwijk, the objective is to reduce the nuisance level of motorized traffic. People are aiming to stop through-traffic, put up more bicycle sheds, turn some streets and squares into pedestrian zones, and build better parking facilities and a district environment centre for information and initiatives. In the district of De Heuvel in Breda, the focus is on district environment care, which includes greenery management and the collecting and separating of waste. These are carried out as joint ventures between residents and town council. In the Planetenbuurt in Roermond, we find a mixture of CD-type activity and citizen participation in social planning. Despite social changes, this approach suits the predominantly law-abiding nature of the people in that part of the country. An 'eco-team' has been started for people to learn how to save water and energy, limit the use of cars, purchase less polluting products, and so on. To this end, courses are being held, and companies are being approached to produce and sell goods in an environmentally friendly manner.

OBJECTIVES AND CENTRAL CONCEPTS

In all of the above cases, the same objectives are being pursued: a better environment, an improved social situation, and permanence. From a CD point of view the three guiding principles are quality of life, participation, and permanence.

'Quality of life' is an abstract concept that is difficult for public administrators to grasp. However, for the CD worker, it is a helpful conceptual tool by means of which the many complaints about general decay, environmental neglect, poverty, insecurity, and crime can be focused and turned into positive actions that will also serve to reduce feelings of social insecurity. A neighbourhood's quality of life can be said to have returned when spatial, social and economic circumstances are such that people no longer feel threatened. Simply by being involved with one another through participatory action, they will feel more at peace. For CD work, it is a sensitizing concept that becomes a concrete reality on the job; it allows unbearable situations to be reversed through small, perspective-rich, context-driven projects with readily visible outcomes.

'Participation' is another vague, sensitizing concept, and one that is open to several interpretations. Participation is considered to be a prerequisite for a functioning democratic society (Hendriks, 1978, p. 47). Its basic presuppositon, which is common to all major ideologies, is that citizens should be socially active one way or another.

'Permanence,' another sensitizing concept, refers to taking care of social and material environments, which cannot be replaced except at high cost. Whether these costs are material or immaterial, or both, does not need to be discussed here. All three concepts, which are central to all community work (though being discussed here in relation to environmental protection), play an important part in shaping permanent living conditions and social patterns.

We will now discuss the objectives mentioned above in terms of CD work. Environmental objectives are often important, too, but they are not the touchstone for CD projects. The questions are these: How do environmental objectives become operationalized? And how can CD objectives be integrated with environmental ones?

Starting from the perspective of the environment:

- As a precondition for ensuring a safe and permanent material environment, the use of herbicides to tend flower-beds will no longer be allowed.
- Fewer cars means less carbon dioxide emissions, more space available for children to play, and an increased opportunity for social encounters.
- A sound ecology and a sound quality of life often go hand in hand.
- The introduction of waste collection by the community provides an opportunity to reduce street litter.
- Environment-friendly employment and education contributes in a modest but conspicuous way to reductions in unemployment, boredom, and vandalism.
- The area's residents (i.e., though participatory action) and the town's council and other institutions (who can provide funds and partnership) are valuable resources to be mobilized.

The important issue here is not to what extent the environment will benefit from these things, but rather how much the neighbourhood as a community will gain from them.

CD is primarily concerned with promoting quality of life, participation, and social permanence. In this process the CD worker is the expert in the field of participation. This expertise is used to achieve behavioural changes that result in a higher quality of life and environmental friendliness. The notion that participation is an effective way to bring about these things is based on several principles, which will be listed here:

- The CD worker seeks to link his or her interventions to citizen initiatives. This improves both the quality and the effectiveness of the environmental measures taken, and the participants' willingness to co-operate in achieving quality of life and permanence.
- When citizens participate in preparing plans or projects, decisions become more effective, since their experience and expertise is being used.
- A participative approach, if it is taken in a professional way and linked to needs, offers people a chance to take concrete actions. Experience has shown that such an approach is more effective than moralizing and making public appeals.
- In shaping opinion, using existing (or newly formed) social networks gets better results than resorting to mass communication. Also, new networks that are created in this process can have significance for other fields besides.
- When citizens and officials participate together, environmental targets can be linked to other issues in the district. The same goes for self-management projects.
- Participation increases the support base for project measures, as people will co-operate in a more intensive and permanent way.

ROLE, POSITION, AND METHODS OF CD WORK

How do these insights affect the role, position, and methods of CD work? In Table 4.1 we have listed some points, most of which speak for themselves.

However, we want to draw particular attention to the question of whether environmental objectives should be included in CD's normal practice or considered a new specialization. From a community interest point of view, the former seems an obvious tack. When the environment is the principal target, then the latter might seem preferable. But this reasoning is not sufficiently convincing, because in creating a basis for environmental action it is crucial to know the community, which might prefer a CD worker who already works there. On the other hand, the integration of environment-focused targets with CD work requires special knowledge, which not every CD worker will have. This might be a reason either to invest in knowledge about environmental policy to ensure strategically correct advice, or to find a community worker who knows how to appraise policy frameworks.

TABLE 4.1
Environmental Objectives and CD Practice

Aspect	Environmental goals set by the authorities	Environmental interest from community perspective
Strategy of change	Marketing information	Empowerment, CD
Mandate	Municipal council	Residents
Definition of environment	National plan for environmental targets	Local plans for safe, well-maintained environments
Function of CD worker	Environment targeted	Community targeted
Role of CD worker	Broker, campaigner, networking	Social innovator, campaigner, organizer, resource person
Methodology	Training for behavioural change	Promoting community interests
Goal determination	Top-down	Bottom-up
Goal formulation	Environment as goal	Environmental actions as instrumental
Criteria for success	Long-term benefits to environment	Quality of life and participation
Funding interests	Policy-driven program implementation	Community-driven program implementation
Solutions	Seeking behavioural change	Improved services through participation
Residents' representative committee	Awareness of environmental issues as priority	Focus on representing community interests

In relation to methods, we would like to touch on a few aspects of the PEP-oriented CD approach. Environmental issues are often described abstractly, in the sense that the community is being subjected to a possible threat in the distant future. To operate successfully, the CD worker must take a concrete approach that is coupled with a clear view of his or her own contribution to a permanent solution. Gaining insight into the residents' subjective perceptions on environmental issues is essential in this.

In recruitment and training, we deal mainly with new staff and with residents who are already active in other fields and may require reorientation. A subject that is unfamiliar to the current staff, and that holds limited interest for them (since they are occupied with other matters), can easily evoke misunderstanding, suspicion, and a sense of being misjudged.

When taking up the town council's agenda on the environment, the CD worker usually assumes the role of 'relations broker' to the residents. However, when supporting residents' interests, he or she serves as co-inventor, network developer, or organization builder. In activating other agents than residents' groups, the community worker will be actively involved in campaigning. Far-reaching forms of participation, such as self-management by means of employment projects and community management companies, not only require a well-devised company plan and a solid organization but also a system of mutual rights and responsibilities.

A major shortcoming of many forms of environmental work is that they stress individual behavioural change without ascertaining whether such change is realistic. For example, more is achieved by improving public transport than by pleading with people to leave their cars at home. Besides physical and organizational changes, social and cultural changes are needed if quality of life and living conditions are to be improved in any permanent way. To this end, the public profile of environmental issues can be raised by linking environmental concerns to other themes and projects, such as the quality of buildings.

CONCLUSIONS

- Environmental issues can become an important and integral part of experimental projects, even if they are not the *main* concern. As we have said, they can serve as preconditions, or as an additional objective, or they can be a source of inspiration or a means for mobilization.
- Focusing on environmental issues leads to a different image of an ideal community, both in the physical sense and when working with residents and agencies.
- To be effective, environmental projects should be linked to the community's interests regarding quality of life, partnership, and participation; also, their objectives should be formulated in a community environmental plan.
- Anticipation that action on the environment will address other relevant policy concerns will encourage communities to get involved

in environmental issues. But it is important to be clear on the residents' own position in this, as well as on the position of the CD worker. For local and national authorities, the emphasis will be on seeking community participation in forming environmental policies, and on promoting the citizenry's own responsibility for environmental protection. In contrast, for CD environmental participation is of less importance as an instrument for concrete, clearly defined behavioural change.

- The emphasis in CD is on new as well as familiar methods. The trend is toward taking more initiative and working innovatively, with the goal of forming partnerships with external sources instead of working (in the narrower sense) in an interest-defensive way.

B. The Flesseman Project: Neighbourhood Services for the Elderly in Amsterdam
Liesbeth Klein-Beernink

INTRODUCTION

Since the Second World War there has been a tradition in the Netherlands of moving elderly people into senior citizens' homes on the outskirts of major cities. People who had spent their entire lives in the older part of the inner city had no alternative but to leave their natural environment. This not only caused an unnatural break at the end of life, but also created an unbalanced and incomplete society, for when a considerable part of an entire generation is removed, the young grow up without any knowledge of and respect for the elderly. The following case study explains how the local people of Amsterdam's inner city, supported by professional workers, succeeded in changing the plans of the local and national authorities.

The authorities had planned a subway with a highway on top for the Amsterdam district called the Nieuwmarkt. This would have split in half a lively community of families who had lived in this quarter for several generations. The authorities also contemplated the demolition of many older, low-rent houses in the area – houses that had been vacated during the Second World War by their Jewish owners. The residents of the Nieuwmarkt decided to organize, feeling strongly that cities belong as much to ordinary people as to those who seek profits from urban renewal and development. They acted at the right time, and succeeded in their joint efforts. The philosophy of the action group was this: 'We want a town with neighbourhoods where living, playing and working, learning and shopping can be done nearby for the young and the old together.'

The Nieuwmarkt is a very lively community that has learned how action should be undertaken – what it can do by itself, and what it needs professionals for. With the intention of providing better care for the elderly, the neighbourhood council created the Flesseman Foundation, named after a company that owned a huge building in the centre of the community. That building became the focal point of resistance against the planned crosstown expressway. Demolishing the building would create sufficient space to construct the motorway, so the neighbourhood council decided to develop an alternative plan for the structure that included an old people's home and social housing for young families. As presented to the city, the plan became a rallying point for the community: 'Either an expressway, or keeping families together.' The community both lost and won. While the residents did not succeed in stopping the subway, they were able to halt the construction of the expressway and get approval for social housing and an old people's home in the Flesseman building. Even after the subway was built in 1988 and some buildings were demolished, the street plan of the neighbourhood remained the same. Today, this inner-city quarter is a dynamic centre with a mixture of social housing, shops, schools, offices, playgrounds, and an old people's home.

In describing the Flesseman Project, we will focus on the elderly. Once the neighbourhood council received permission to create an old people's home, it revised its original plan, wanting to be innovative and creative. Not only did the council want residential care, it also wanted the elderly to be able to stay in their own homes if they so desired, even if this involved some dependence on external help.

We will now turn to the Flesseman Project. We will begin by providing some background information about the elderly in the Netherlands, and follow this with a discussion of the changes in elder care since 1988. We will then describe some specific components of the project, and finish with a brief evaluation of the project and its significance for general policy on the elderly.

THE ELDERLY POPULATION IN THE NETHERLANDS AND THEIR CARE

The elderly (over 65 years of age) make up 13.9 percent of the total population of Amsterdam (720,000) but only 7 percent of the population of Amsterdam's Inner City, of which the Flesseman neighbourhood

TABLE 4.2
Use of Health Care Resources by the Elderly in the Netherlands

Type of care	Cost in billion of guilders	Use of health care resources (as % of total budget) by people over 65
Extramural care		
• Home help	1.8	45
• District nursing	1.0	70
• General practitioners	2.0	75
• Others	3.8	25
Intramural care		
• Old people's homes	4.8	99
• Nursing homes	4.2	94
• Hospitals and specialists	16.1	45
• Mental health care	4.0	10
• Medication and adaptations	4.7	40
• Prevention	3.2	45

Source: Ministry of Welfare, Health and Culture (1990) FOZ: The Hague

forms part. Table 4.2 provides some data on costs to the state for extra-mural and intramural care, both overall and for the elderly. As these figures suggest, structural changes in the Dutch economy and changing views on the welfare state in recent times are having a severe impact on the housing, finances, and care of the elderly, who have been as badly hit as other vulnerable sectors of the population, if not more badly hit. Thus, a fundamental rethinking of policy regarding the elderly is needed.

CHANGES IN PERSPECTIVES ON THE NEIGHBOURHOOD AND CARE FOR THE ELDERLY

Looking back at the recent history of the Flesseman Project, five changes in approaches to elder care can be identified; each one significantly influenced the next. Each has also contributed to the discussion of care for the elderly at a national policy level.

The first change in thinking began with the aforementioned slogan ('We want a town ...'), which was painted on the wall of the Flesseman building by the action group. This philosophy of neighbourhood life opposed the settlement planning policy of the local and national authorities. This policy, introduced in the 1960s, involved building new towns on the 'polders' (lands reclaimed from the sea) that would draw people from the older cities. This plan involved separating the functions of living, working, and recreation. Also, hospitals, nursing homes, and homes for the elderly were to be moved to the outskirts of cities. The Nieuwmarkt neighbourhood action against the official plan started in 1972 and resulted in the official recognition of the quarter's residential functions in 1974. It had turned official thinking away from *reconstruction* and toward *rehabilitation*.

The second change in perspective was in the health care field. The objective of the national policy on health care in the 1970s was to strengthen extramural care (i.e., home care), on the assumption that this would reduce the need for intramural (i.e., insitutional) care. However, it did not have the anticipated effect. Contrary to official expectations, intramural organizations began to grow, because those involved in extramural care selected people for referral to intramural care facilities; in the process the two groups reinforced each other's interests.

The residents' council of the Nieuwmarkt decided to change this pattern and proposed to use part of the intramural budget for providing care outside the planned old people's home – quite an innovative idea at the time. The proposal preceded the change in national care policy on *substitution* introduced in 1983, which involved the shifting of budgets from one government department to another with the intention of stimulating alternative solutions to the more expensive system of intramural care. Government officials were looking for ways to bring about a shift in care giving, from a reliance on highly professionalized forms of care to less professional and cheaper forms. During this same period, the national government decided to decentralize budgets and the responsibility for spending in several areas to local authorities. In theory, the new substitution policy and the move toward decentralization should have created opportunities for experimentation at the local level and led to new forms of care. In actual practice, care providers still retained control over how care was to be defined.

The third change was in the traditional structure and financing of care for the elderly in the Nieuwmarkt neighbourhood. Again, the council anticipated changes that were made later in national policy, aimed at stimulating new forms of care for the elderly in their own homes and based on a closed budget system. The neighbourhood council proposed to create fifty-two places in the planned old people's home in the Flesseman building, instead of the allotted seventy-two, with the extra funds to be spent on neighbourhood facilities for the elderly. The government agreed with the *exchange money concept* in principle in December 1983, and so informed the Amsterdam authorities in August 1984. Ministerial permission to go ahead with the plan was granted later that year.

The fourth change in perspective involved a shift in emphasis from care toward *preventive action*. When the money was being transferred from intramural to extramural care, the neighbourhood council intervened by preventing it from going to established extramural organizations, insisting that it be spent as the council thought best. The council's decision was to support preventive facilities and activities. A professional project leader was appointed to co-operate closely with the neighbourhood on a plan that would allow the elderly to stay in their own homes in the community. This decision also anticipated another change in national policy that would provide flexible/varied care based on the unique situation of each older person.

The fifth and most recent change, in 1989, involved the purchaser of service, the provider, and the elderly as user. The neighbourhood felt that it wasn't enough to merely develop more facilities without looking also at the issue of quality of service. This required strengthening the process of *decision making by the elderly* in three areas: finding out which form of care and which facilities were best suited to the unique situation of each individual user; arriving at the right solution; and finally, allowing the elderly person as user to do a quality check on the service provided. To this end, the neighbourhood introduced senior citizens' consultants who would assist the elderly in decision making. The ultimate objective was to strengthen the ability of elderly people to exercise control over their lives by giving them a decisive voice in matters of care. Providers would have to give up their decision-making power and heed the decisions of the elderly. The outcome of such a change in the relationship between provider and user would permit the elderly person to maintain independence and live in the surroundings of his or her own choosing.

With the introduction of senior citizens' consultants, the Nieuwmarkt once more anticipated the future. It had been common practice to have case managers functioning alongside the care providers. Now, in the Flesseman Project, the consultants operate independently. They do not mediate between client and provider; rather, they work strictly for the elderly to match up requirements with options. Existing care organizations may possibly be providers, but if the care and facilities they provide are not to the client's liking, the consultants will have to look for other options. We need to emphasize again that the consultants are not linked in any way to the providers other than by the client's consent.

This shift to a market orientation also requires a different policy from the purchasers (i.e., the local health care and housing authorities). The news from Amsterdam is that the local authorities and health insurance companies decided to adopt (in April 1994) the full range of principles guiding the working method of consultants, described above, for the handicapped and the elderly all across the city.

THE PROJECT

The first change described above resulted in the Nieuwmarkt in a totally new concept in living and housing: the integration of social housing, community living for the elderly, and an old people's home in one complex.

Neighbourhood Foundation

To conduct this conversion, the neighbourhood council created the Flesseman Neighbourhood Foundation and appointed members to the board. This foundation functioned as a legal entity vis-à-vis the authorities, and had the power to make contracts – something that a local neighbourhood council without legal status cannot do. The foundation was thus able to take on one professional worker for the neighbourhood, paid for by the housing association. It was his task to supervise the whole process, and to participate on behalf of the neighbourhood in all important decisions relating to the construction phase. As supervised by the neighbourhood foundation, his functions were to make sure that the neighbourhood's philosophy was upheld, and to prepare regular reports on activities to the neighbourhood council.

The reconstruction of the Nieuwmarkt area began in 1986 and ended in 1989. The old people's home was opened at the end of 1988. A project leader was appointed at the start of the reconstruction phase to devise projects financed by the 'exchange money' that the foundation received from the city (Dfl 500,000 annually). Her task as community worker was to develop ideas on preventive facilities for the elderly in collaboration with the neighbourhood. Having been active as a social worker in the area, she was well acquainted with the people and organizations, and had their trust. An office was made available to her by the foundation and the neighbourhood council. Being on the payroll of the Neighbourhood Foundation made her independent of such care organizations as home care, social work, and district nursing. All of these organizations made claims on the exchange money, arguing that they had been active in the area for a long time and therefore were in the best position to spend the money well. The neighbourhood council decided otherwise.

With the exchange money, many projects were started, such as the following:

- A handyman from the neighbourhood was employed to make adaptations and repairs in the homes of elderly people.
- Day activities were organized for isolated and handicapped elderly people.
- A local transportation system was established for the elderly.
- Personal alarm systems were installed, and a security project was begun.
- The elderly were informed about the proper use of medication.
- A newsletter was launched to inform local people about Flesseman projects.

Centre for the Aged
Services for elderly people living independently in the neighbourhood improved significantly with the opening of the Flesseman Centre for the Aged. Besides accommodating and providing care for fifty-two people, the centre provides facilities for elderly people living in their own homes in the neighbourhood. They can make use of the following:

- Dinner served every evening at the centre, or delivered to their homes.
- Respite care for those recovering from hospital treatment.
- A sheltered garden.
- Assistance with bath facilities, when needed.
- A hairdresser.
- Recreational activities.
- A spare bedroom in the centre for visiting relatives and friends.

The centre is open twenty-four hours a day, seven days a week, and thereby provides a sense of security. When it opened in 1988, a separate foundation was created called the Flesseman Foundation Centre for the Aged. This centre has its own sources of income and budget, in conformity with the laws relating to old people's homes. The residents themselves must pay for their housing and care, unless their income is insufficient. In such cases, social benefits will pay for residential care.

Consultants for the Elderly

A third foundation, created in 1989, is the Flesseman Foundation of Senior Citizens' Consultants. This is also an independent body, with its own board and budget. It is funded by the exchange experiment, among other sources. The director of the neighbourhood foundation also serves as the director of the consultants' foundation, principally because of the lack of funds to support two directors. Nevertheless, the consultants remain independent and will, if necessary, criticize any actions taken by the Neighbourhood Foundation just as they would other organizations.

The consultants' main objective is to ensure that the elderly receive proper advice that is independent from the advice given by care givers or providers. Consultants contact senior citizens by visiting everyone over 80. For all other persons over 55, their office is open from Monday to Friday during regular daytime hours.

The consultants main tasks are these:

• To address all kinds of age-related questions.
• To advise the elderly on how to stay independent.
• To assess the need for care.
• To provide advice on budgeting.
• To make preventive house calls.

The working principle is that as people get older, their problems may increase while their ability to solve them decreases. If consultants can intervene while the problems faced are still within the ability of the elderly person to solve, then the moment of deciding to move into residential care may be postponed.

The following are the priorities of the consultants:

• Helping the elderly stay independent.
• Providing outreach (40 percent of those assessed who were not currently receiving help were found to be in need).
• Providing services based on demand rather than supply.
• Supporting consumers.
• Providing information on social and commercial service systems.
• Searching for creative ways to maintain independent living.
• Following up on advice.

EVALUATION

The Plan

The board of the neighbourhood council decided to undertake a form of evaluation that would serve as an instrument for policy develop-ment. It was felt from the start that the exchange experiment could only be considered a success if the elderly felt that they were better off and able to manage their own affairs. The evaluation was assigned to a nonprofit market research agency (Jong, 1992). The question for the evaluation was phrased as follows: 'Does the "exchange" experiment in the Nieuwmarkt help elderly people to maintain their independence for longer periods of time and to their satisfaction, than would have been possible without the facilities and service offered?'

Specifically, the evaluation set out the following objectives:

- It was to provide information on whether the increased provision of assistance to the elderly in their homes helped them to stay indepen-dent as long as possible.
- It was to be useful as a policy instrument for the board of the Neighbourhood Foundation, by providing the kind of information that would enable the board to modify projects developed during the experiment.

Other functions of the evaluation included these:

- To make findings accessible to anyone who wished to learn about the results.
- To serve as a means of studying and following through on the aims of the experiment.
- To facilitate critical reflections on the experiment.
- To develop a management and marketing information system to acquire ongoing information about the project.

The Results

The evaluation produced its first and very important results in the early stage of research in 1987. It found that too many elderly people in the neighbourhood still had insufficient knowledge about the possibilities of assistance, and about other available facilities. This finding led to the creation of the senior citizen's consultants' service, described earlier.

The overall evaluation results presented in 1992 found that 98 per-cent of the elderly in contact with a consultant were very enthusiastic.

They expressed confidence that they were able to get all the help they needed (with the assistance of a consultant), and that the quality of their life had improved. A number of elderly people changed their mind about wanting to move into residential care, while many others postponed intramural living. Some care providers used the information received from the consultants to improve their service.

The general evaluation of the Flesseman projects was quite positive. These positive results led the local authorities to request that the neighbourhood foundation continue its innovative activities in the field of care for the elderly. In 1993, Flesseman was chosen, as one of the more innovative projects for the elderly in the Netherlands, to take part in an international network of the European Union.

CONCLUSIONS

We will conclude this case description and analysis with some observations on certain factors that may have contributed to the project's success and innovative character.

- *Scale.* The area is not too large (16,800 inhabitants); this facilitates residents' identification with the neighbourhood.
- *Commitment.* A strong commitment to the community on the part of the elderly was demonstrated in the organization of a neighbourhood council. Members of the foundation's board were appointed by the council.
- *Change in policy.* The neighbourhood council took advantage of every opportunity offered during a time when fundamental changes were taking place in government policy.
- *Budget.* The budget for the projects was generated by the neighbourhood itself, which chose to have twenty places designated for the old people's home exchanged for money. That money was used to finance all kinds of projects during the eight-year experiment. Although the amount is fixed, the city council decides annually which areas and projects it will be spent on.
- *Long-term experiment.* The experiment extended over a period of eight years. To obtain optimum benefits, it is important to have many years available to experiment.
- *Research/evaluation.* Market research was considered a more useful type of research for making adjustments in the experiment than the traditional after-the-fact form of evaluation.

• *Professionals*. The professionals involved in the Flesseman Project were flexible and innovative, and this contributed to the improvements in the quality of care provided and in the satisfaction felt by the elderly.

Finally, the Flesseman case demonstrates an interesting process of CD. Although the focus is on the elderly, in fact, the entire Nieuwmarkt neighbourhood has been and continues to be involved. The role of the neighbourhood council as a community organizing agency has been crucial. Its objectives are definitely not restricted to keeping the elderly in their familiar surroundings: it also works vigorously to protect the original dynamic character of the neighbourhood, and to maintain positive relations between diverse groups of citizens.

C. Project European Community (EC) Anti-poverty Action Program: An Integrative Approach
Carel Tenhaeff

INTRODUCTION

The third European program to combat poverty, or Poverty 3, was implemented from 1990 to 1994. Its purpose was to advance the social and economic integration of excluded persons and groups. This experimental program consisted of 42 projects: 14 'innovative initiatives' and 28 'model actions.' The innovative initiatives were aimed at specific target groups; the model actions were to develop an integrated approach to the problems of the disadvantaged in specific geographic areas. The Netherlands had one project of each type. This case concerns the Dutch model action project, which was carried out in three towns – Den Helder, Eindhoven, and Hengelo – and co-ordinated by the Netherlands Institute of Care and Welfare (NIZW), a national NGO.

Three basic principles were central to the Poverty 3 Program: participation, partnership, and multidimensionality (Abou Sada, 1991). Multidimensionality was the most important of the three. Problems relating to poverty and social exclusion are not one-dimensional but consist of a tangle of smaller problems relating to income, housing, knowledge, work, welfare, health, and environment. Therefore, it is essential to use an approach that dispenses with ritual boundaries between sectors (compartmentalization) and between ordinary citizens and professional workers (bureaucratization).

Furthermore, problems created by poverty manifest themselves on different levels: the micro level of the individual problem itself, the meso level of the disadvantaged areas, and the macro level of social and economic discrepancies. Consequently, an approach needed to be developed that would co-ordinate activities at the community practice level as well as policies at the local, regional, national, and (where necessary) international levels.

This means that besides horizontally co-ordinated activities among the underprivileged on the practice level, vertically co-ordinated poverty-related policies also were to be implemented. Generally speaking, CD is concerned with the establishment of horizontal links. The establishment of vertical links is the responsibility of decision-makers, who may be advised by those involved in CD.

Multi-dimensionality, as the central idea of the Poverty 3 Program, was implemented on the basis of two other concepts: participation and partnership. *Participation* means that the least privileged are not merely passive beneficiaries of the program, but should also take an active part in the selection, supervision, and implementation of the program's activities. In this regard, the aim of Poverty 3 was to create new relationships between users and services in which self-organizations were seen as indispensable partners. *Partnership* means seeking new forms of co-operation in order to arrive at a truly integrated approach to solving poverty-related problems. Partners are those who make visible and significant investments in the program. Partnerships between the social sector and the private sector and, as already mentioned, between professional and self-organizations, are thus regarded as truly innovative forms of co-operation.

This section presents a general picture of the new, co-operative networks that were developed in three quite different project areas. First, the problem is described: How can there be poverty in the Netherlands? How does it occur in the project areas? And how do we want to tackle it? Next, most of the activities developed by the project are summarized and grouped together to show how they were – or became – interrelated.

The project resulted in what seem now like widely varying developments in the three project areas, even though the basic principles, general analysis, and overall goals were shared by the program as a whole. This diversity is evident in both the horizontal and the vertical links that were established. To some extent, this has to do with differences in the professional backgrounds of the workers who were involved in establishing horizontal links at the community level. In the Netherlands, CD has become a separate profession. In this project, however, other professionals performed CD functions as well – social welfare workers, health education workers, and field researchers.

THE PROBLEM: SOCIAL AND ECONOMIC EXCLUSION

How can there be social and economic exclusion in a rich and seemingly well-organized country such as the Netherlands? Modern poverty is defined as the lack of any prospects as a result of low income and social isolation. The new poor are, therefore, a vague and broad target group, and one that cuts through the usual classifications for deprived groups. Social exclusion also includes a failure to use the facilities available. Criticism of the system of facilities is justified here, as it reaches our target group insufficiently. In the project areas of the program, this modern poverty is observed as follows:

Social Exclusion in Nieuw Den Helder
Nieuw Den Helder, built after the Second World War, is divided into two districts, which in turn are subdivided into fourteen neighbourhoods. The problems were concentrated in a cluster of nine neighbourhoods, with a total population of 10,463. Officially, at least 10 percent of the residents were living on social benefits.

The problems were caused mainly by an undiversified economy and by geographical isolation on the country's northern periphery. The sea has always been the main source of income for Den Helder. Even today, the Dutch navy and fishing together account for two-thirds of the labour market there. The husbands of many married women (the 'blue widows') are, therefore, away from home for long periods of time, which explains the high divorce rate. There is no growth in this part of the . labour market, because of Den Helder's peripheral location.

The fact of a lopsided and stagnating labour market has specific negative consequences. Among men, unemployment is slightly lower than the national average; among women it is higher. Among young people, unemployment is very common, and this mainly affects women as well. Because of the absence of industries, only a small number of 'guest' or migrant workers have settled here. There are, however, relatively large groups of refugees, and immigrants from the former colonies – a result of the Dutch government's policy of spreading these groups out when they arrive in the Netherlands. For some of these groups, there is virtually no place in the local labour system. These excluded people tend to be concentrated in the Nieuw Den Helder district, where rents are low. Many of them had debts, and there was a lot of vandalism, addiction, and petty crime.

Social Exclusion in the Kruidenbuurt in Eindhoven
The Kruidenbuurt is one of the neighbourhoods of Eindhoven where problems related to social exclusion were concentrated. The population of 3,699 is spread over 895 households. It was not known exactly how many households were living on a minimum income. We did, however, know that about 25 per cent of the people able to work were registered as unemployed, and that about 35 percent were registered as disabled. In both groups, the majority had great problems surviving. This was also true for one-quarter of the elderly, especially for the single elderly living on an old age pension only. The number of people over 65 was 387 (10.5%).

The Kruidenbuurt is an old neighbourhood with few newly built houses, little room for children to play, and no industry. The houses are mainly cheap, rental accommodation, and this has led to a rather lopsided population. In addition, there is a lot of neglect of privately owned houses because the owners or renters can't afford to maintain them. Demolition of houses was becoming an issue. All of these conditions bred pollution of the living environment, petty vandalism, addiction, and prostitution. These visible symptoms of poverty were – and still are – concentrated in a number of problem streets. There was also growing tension between certain groups of the population: not only between the more and the less deprived, but also between people of Dutch origin and those belonging to ethnic minorities.

There was a sharp increase in the percentage of long-term unemployed people. There were three specific problem groups: older production workers from industries in and around Eindhoven who had been made redundant; unemployed young people who had never finished their schooling; and single-parent families. A large percentage of the first two groups in particular – which were directly interconnected – could no longer be reached. This was clear from the project on employment mediation for unemployed people, which had been running here prior to Poverty 3. About 17 percent of the unemployed could not be reached at all, and for about 30 percent, mediation seemed impossible. This was mainly a result of physical and mental problems, relationship problems or addiction to alcohol, drugs, or gambling. These problems were particularly serious among the ethnic groups.

Social Exclusion in Hengelo

The municipality of Hengelo had, at the outset of the project, a population of 76,187. The number of households living on a minimum income was 7,576 (25.6%), involving 14,644 people (19.2%). This was a consequence of the high rate of unemployment in the Twente region, the old industrial region where Hengelo is located. Hengelo's policy toward people living on a minimum income had up till then been part of a general urban policy, which it wanted to implement in certain concentrated neighbourhoods in the town. Unemployment had increased from approximately 1,500 people in 1978 to approximately 4,000 by 1988. More than half the unemployed were long-term unemployed. These people were suffering from apathy and had stopped applying for jobs altogether. The number of people receiving disability or widow's benefits was 3,688; an estimated 80 percent of them lived on a minimum income. The number of households of elderly people living on a minimum income was 3,798 – 50 percent of the total number of such households.

The rise in unemployment was largely a result of the dominant role played by the region's metal and textile industries, in which many cuts and changes had taken place. Specific groups of unemployed to whom we paid particular attention were women living on welfare (805), 80 percent of whom were single mothers, and foreign nationalities (70% Turkish), 85 percent of whom were unemployed.

Almost one-quarter of all unemployed people had completed their secondary education or higher. This highlighted that local educators were failing to gear courses toward the regional labour market. Clearly, unemployment affected the whole population.

The rise in living costs during the preceding years was another contributing factor to poverty. Housing had become too expensive for most people to pay for without hardship; people were now having to pay user fees for health care, and so on. Almost half of the people living on a minimum income had debts that could be claimed immediately. Furthermore, many people, especially the more poorly educated, were quite unfamiliar with the services and benefits available to them; as a result, about 10 percent had to live on less than a minimum income.

THE PLAN: STRATEGIES FOR THE DEVELOPMENT OF COHESION

The project plan (1989) specified how the model action plan would merge various aspects of exclusion into a strategic plan, as follows:

Integrative Approach

What is important is an integrative approach that addresses several aspects of the situation at hand. Living on or under the poverty line has, after all, different causes and different consequences. The plan primarily addressed the following aspects of poverty: unemployment, housing and environment, health, knowledge, and social isolation.

Unemployment affects people who either have been excluded from the formal labour market or have never actually participated in it. A person who lacks (paid) work finds closed many doors to social advantages and services. *Bad housing* and *a bad environment* are characterized by low-rent and often dilapidated accommodation. Draughty and noisy houses have negative effects on health. This may lead to absenteeism from school or work, and to chronic illness. In areas where this is a particular problem, the living environment often shows signs of neglect and is unhealthy and unsafe. *Ill health* is related to bad housing and habits, and to more limited care facilities and greater reticence to use them (Withagen & Jonkers-Kuiper, 1993). *Social isolation* is the product of limited financial means and a lack of prospects. Together, these give rise to nonparticipation in social life and lack of concern on the part of the individual for his or her health. Lack of *knowledge* – that is of training, education, and information – is relevant to all aspects mentioned above (World Development Report, 1993, pp. 14, 37–51). In fact, the aspects mentioned are *all* interconnected and were, therefore, integrated into the project plan.

Two Interrelated Areas for Improvement

The plan tries to bring about improvements in two broad areas:

- *Improving participation*, which involves mobilizing, motivating, and organizing target groups and improving their opportunities for problem-solving.
- *Improving conditions*, which involves creating better chances and opportunities through measures such as improving co-operation between organizations and institutions and, where necessary, modifying policies.

Improving participation is essential, because if social participation were to dwindle away, somewhere along the line we would no longer have a society. However, attempts to activate the most deprived groups have no realistic chance to succeed if we do not at the same time improve social conditions. Improving participation means breaking through a fixation on the negative values mentioned earlier (Brugman, 1994). The participation process must aim at concrete and realistic objectives that are determined partly by the target group itself and toward which professional organizations can gear their practical policies. Otherwise, participation will only lead to greater cynicism.

Participation and Individual Self-determination

Re-establishing social participation – that is, activating and mobilizing people as well as enabling them to take responsibility (once again) for their own lives – was a primary objective. This involved creating conditions wherein the process of activation and enablement could be developed and implemented, as well as increasing people's support by setting up projects and activities that directly involved them.

Co-operation between Professional Organizations

Years of experience in tackling this problem have shown that different organizations and institutions often seek solutions to related problems in a fragmented and independent way. One innovation of the project plan related to changing compartmentalized working methods to form co-operative ventures between the relevant organizations and agencies. These co-operative ventures had to be functional with respect to the concrete objectives that issued from the participation process. In particular, forms of co-operation had to be devised that could bridge the gap between different social practices and policy areas.

Detecting Structural Problem Areas

The plan was set up in such a way that we could systematically detect structural obstacles that needed to be tackled on a policy level. Our activities were directed at the following:

- A variety of 'classic' target groups: the long-term unemployed, the 'disabled from work,' single parents, schoolchildren, immigrants, addicts, tenants, and low-income senior citizens.
- Various 'classic' sectors, as mentioned earlier: housing, environment, work, training and information, and health and welfare.
- Three 'classic' levels of action: the level of individual assistance and care, the level of community organization, and the level of municipal or regional policies.

Central to our work was the development of cohesion between all these activities. The following paragraphs present three pictures of what this cohesion looks like after three-and-a-half years of development work. Within each of the selected areas, most project activities have been clustered around a focal point. These focal points, which differ for each project area, may be considered the 'anchors' of the project:

- The District Centre and Infoshop in Nieuw Den Helder.
- The Neighbourhood Development Plan and the Infoshop in Eindhoven.
- The role of a 'catalyst' in relation to low-income groups in Hengelo.

These anchors are described below for each project area. The activities discussed serve to illustrate how cohesion had been developed as of January 1994, when the project still had half a year to go.

NIEUW DEN HELDER: DISTRICT CENTRE AND INFORMATION SHOP
AS ANCHORS

History
In the Nieuw Den Helder neighbourhood we have, mostly in collaboration with local residents' groups, organized various activities to get in touch with deprived persons and groups. Through these activities, people meet each other (with or without specific tasks) or are brought in touch with organizations that could be helpful to them.

Generally, in view of the importance of building groups and networks, special attention was given to the socio-cultural dimension. For instance, management training was provided for volunteers, a Health Market was organized by our working group on health and was visited by approximately 200 residents, and a neighbourhood committee was mobilized. With two existing self-organizations, Striving for a Better Life (SNBL) and the Living Environment Group, we have co-operated actively. SNBL consists of three groups from different neighbourhoods. In collaboration with our project, SNBL has run a number of activities, including a supervisory residents project, a sewing course with Caribbean women, a painting group, a video team, and an open-space planning project.

District Centre
Groups and networks that have developed in this manner must be given the opportunity to develop further into a team that can continue to influence services and other organizations in the area. Mainly for this

reason, we have worked hard to establish a district centre, where a number of project-based activities are being offered or developed. The centre is based on the co-operation between a variety of service providers (both public and private) and self-organizations. The building granted for this purpose was in very bad shape. The necessary repair work was carried out mainly by long-term unemployed youths, as a step toward permanent work, and was made possible by grants from the local authorities and from a private-sector housing association. The centre was officially opened on 15 May 1993 and offers a variety of possibilities:

- Services by three 'district masters' of the housing association and by the 'quarter warden' appointed by the local authorities.
- Comprehensive services from the Information Shop, which is staffed by volunteers and a multidisciplinary team of professional workers.
- A meeting place where residents' groups can plan and implement activities.
- Play-o-thèque Nieuw Den Helder.

The groups and services concerned were mostly leading separate lives in the area. Before being accepted as partners by the district centre, they had to show willingness to co-operate with others – professionals and self-organizations alike.

Information Shop
The Information Shop is a working group of volunteers and professional workers who are carrying out a number of activities. Regular consulting hours are kept by the job mediation agency Work-Again, by the regional agency for educational support, by social counsellors, and by the regional agency for social counselling. The volunteers take care of the reception desk five days a week. They may be asked to provide information on health, consumer affairs, and social rights. Their function of referring clients to appropriate services is equally important.

Participation Platform
To secure the decisive support of local residents for the centre's plans and activities, a 'participation platform' was introduced on which every self-organization in the area, small or large, could have one representative. It should develop into a multicultural council for the centre.

For the centre to thrive, socio-cultural activities must be organized in and around it. One way of doing this is through the partnerships that have been developed with socio-cultural agencies, such as the regional training centre for women. Another way is to open a neighbourhood restaurant, to be staffed by some of the many long-term unemployed women in the area. This plan has not yet been realized.

Improvement of Individual Situations through Intermediaries
The neighbourhood centre and Infoshop are intended as intermediaries – that is, as places where direct links can be established between the social system and excluded residents so that made-to-measure support can be provided for solving problems. This approach requires first, that the real needs and problems of people be known, and second, that professionals and volunteers *recognize* those real needs and problems, so that appropriate plans of action can be worked out.

For us, the concept of a made-to-measure approach refers not only to demand-oriented methods of working with *individual* clients, but also to demand-oriented methods of working with *groups* (through courses and management training) and with *categories* of citizens (through the centre, the Information Shop, and public meetings). In this respect, influencing the policies of existing services and institutions to change their working methods has been a core aspect of our work. Clearly, this involves equipping not only *citizens* (for instance, through management training courses for volunteers), but also *professionals*.

These matters, though small-scale, are important. For instance, addiction to drugs is a serious problem, not only because of the negative health effects but also because it is an escape mechanism that blocks progress in various ways. For this reason, our working group on health devised a training course for professional workers who are confronted with chronic drug abuse. This training has helped them find ways to reduce social isolation. This small-scale example is provided to show that developing a made-to-measure approach is not only an *ideological* concept, to be operationalized through different forms of empowerment, but also a *methodological* concept that has practical consequences for how services are delivered, organized, and co-ordinated.

From the methodological perspective, the integrative approach that we are developing is a *cross-sectoral* one that results in *made-to-measure* responses. Links have been established between various sectors (work, training and education, health and well-being, housing, environment). The many *volunteers* have a general information and counselling function for people with problems in various spheres of life. A made-to-measure approach is realized through this 'one desk' system, whereby volunteers refer visitors to the right professionals as and when necessary.

How to Continue

The results of the project are being 'transferred' in four basic ways: by handing over project-based activities; by passing on methodological know-how; by continuing to participate in European social programs; and by influencing policies. Several 'loose' activities of our project served as an example for others – for example, the course for single parents and the management training courses. The evaluations of these activities have led to follow-up activities by regular services, or to policy proposals (e.g., on social renewal, professionalization of volunteers, and integrated district development).

Partnership is an essential condition for initiating and (if necessary) co-ordinating change. We have developed this partnership by setting up a working group. The members of this group are the agency for job mediation Work Again, the regional health service, and the working group on housing. The latter is based on a partnership between local authorities, the housing association, and residents' committees.

These groups are well equipped to continue working with the results of the model action. At a local conference held in June 1994, decisions were made on the basis of an evaluation in which the experiences of the model action were transformed into 'lessons' for the future. The main issues were district development, planning on the basis of participation, and cross-sectoral action.

EINDHOVEN/KRUIDENBUURT: NEIGHBOURHOOD DEVELOPMENT PLAN AND INFORMATION SHOP

History: Housing Committee and Infoshop

At the start of Poverty 3, there was in Kruidenbuurt a housing committee consisting of five persons. Though a partner in urban development policy, this group had limited support. That was why we enabled the committee to conduct a survey among the local residents, in which 295 of the 1,199 households were interviewed. This not only gave us an exact picture of the residents' situation, needs, and grievances but also resulted in fifty people offering their services as volunteers.

Subsequently, we set up a partnership with the committee, establishing an Information Shop to be used as a base for the following activities:

- Supplying 'low threshold' information on a daily basis.
- Incorporating the housing committee.
- Initiating new working groups.
- Organizing a job pool in the neighbourhood.
- Establishing a form of self-management by groups.
- Consulting with four other neighbourhoods in the municipal planning framework of integrated neighbourhood management.

Since 1991, various organizations have been providing counselling sessions at the Infoshop: the housing committee, the local police, the environmental inspectorate, the legal aid centre, and an advocacy group for elderly people. The two largest housing associations for the area provide information during the period in which applications for individual rent subsidies must be filled in by low-income tenants.

Area Analysis and Neighbourhood Development Plan
In January 1993 the Infoshop was running so well that we had to look for bigger offices. Also, the housing committee was receiving widespread support and various other self-organizations were working very hard.

Around that time, we completed an analysis of the area's problems. The analysis shows which groups are to be regarded as the most excluded, and how integrated neighbourhood development may increase their participation and lead to their being accepted as partners. In our opinion, acceptance of the most excluded groups as partners in development is the crucial test.

This analysis evolved into a neighbourhood development plan, which was accepted by the management committee of the Foundation Neighbourhood Management Kruidenbuurt (SBK) in May 1993. The plan indicates which problems must be solved at short notice and which in due course.

Foundation Neighbourhood Management and Neighbourhood Platform
The SBK was founded in October 1992. At the same time it assumed a key role as the neighbourhood's voice and became responsible for managing the Infoshop. In that role, it takes on those issues which are not being dealt with by a local working group or action group. It also organizes meetings of the Neighbourhood Platform, and works with the platform.

The municipality of Eindhoven allocated to the SBK a budget of some 45,000 ecus in 1992, and 65,000 ecus in 1993. This money is meant for neighbourhood management. The Neighbourhood Platform decides how to spend this money. The platform started in December 1991, at the initiative of the residents' committee. Its purpose was to assemble all local groups of active citizens with the goal of influencing the policies of housing associations, local authorities, and private services in a co-ordinated manner. After several meetings, it was decided to found SBK.

The platform consists of 25 to 40 participants. Participating groups are the local housing committee, six groups working to improve specific blocks or squares in the area, a working group for senior citizens, two parents' committees (primary schools), and professional organizations including the Deacony of Stratum, the local primary schools, Welfare Work for Senior Citizens, the district centre, and the local foundation for CD work. Any participant can place items on the agenda. Besides 'opinion setting,' important goals are to exchange information and to learn to look 'across boundaries.'

Implementing the Neighbourhood Development Plan
Many different projects have been implemented by these groups as part of the neighbourhood development plan. About half of these activities are concerned with the physical planning and control of the housing and living environment, but children are also very important to these groups. We list the projects in which children play a central role:

• The Working Group Lavendelplein Playground.
• Children's pocket money fund.
• Holiday work for children.
• The Playground Foundation 'Kindervreugde.'

Other projects, in the field of housing and environment, are these:

• Tackling the back alleys.
• The Working Group Living Environment.
• The Edelweiss Straat/Floralaan Neighbourhood Association.

Two other activities involving children are carried out in the district centre: cooking lessons and 'Snotver3.' The cooking lessons project, which is carried out in co-operation with the Eindhoven Healthy City program, is a course for children, young people, and adults from low-income groups that concentrates on 'eating well at low cost.' Snotver3 is a children's theatre group supervised by a professional in the neighbourhood centre.

Economic Integration

Contributing to the fight against unemployment was a crucial test for the project: we wanted to prove that we could play a crucial role in this particular field. Our research in 1991–2 showed that most of the area's unemployed had been unemployed for more than one year and were surviving on one allowance only. Also, 75 percent no longer expected any improvement. In addition to these people, there were those disabled from work (400) and women re-entering the labour market (150). Thus, of the total working population, 38 percent could not find work or had great difficulty keeping it.

In tackling this problem, we sought co-operation with the social service and regional labour offices for a pilot project, 'Mediation for Work at the Neighbourhood Level.' We formed a 'supply network' in which a number of professionals and volunteers helped between ten and fifty people find paid work (depending on demand). On top of this, we conducted an elaborate labour-market survey in the Stratum district. In this, we were casting our net wide, because economic development at the neighbourhood level had virtually no scope. The survey was conducted beginning in May 1993, with two tasks:

- To map unemployment in the area ('who,' residence, age, employment record, duration of unemployment, etc.).
- To find existing or soon-to-exist vacancies. We were surprised to find several hundred of these – none were known, or had been made known, to the employment office.

The job mediation team, its directors, and the economic affairs counsellor have all agreed to continue to work on the basis of the survey results. The team checks vacancies, assesses the educational requirements, and then posts them through the Infoshop.

HENGELO: INSTITUTIONALIZING A CATALYST FOR SOCIAL AND ECONOMIC ACTIVITIES BY LOW-INCOME GROUPS

Overall picture

Ultimately, the cohesion of all activities of the project lay in the way we sought to achieve change. To this end, we institutionalized the role of catalyst, which led to a great number of activities, most of them in the form of interventions aimed at specific actors and specific results. Many activities followed three steps:

- Recognition of problems and potentialities of the socially excluded.
- Mobilization of target groups and public and private organizations.
- Activation of existing structures to discover and expand the opportunities for new coalitions.

This role of catalyst was our anchor for consolidating and transferring certain results of the model action. Hengelo needs a small, rather independent group of change agents, a group that works across levels and sectors in developing activities, discovering problems and potentialities, building new coalitions, and influencing policies with links to neighbourhoods but also to the regional level. This approach is required in Hengelo because of the way in which social exclusion manifests itself there: it is concentrated less in neighbourhoods, as in Den Helder and Eindhoven, and is more dispersed over the population in general.

Local Situation

In our work we had the advantage of a direct link with the local council and the local authorities. On the one hand, this created a certain freedom to act; on the other, however, this highlighted resistance to change – some actors and organizations were very good at protecting their own vested interests. Actually, quite often they had to be. Prior to Poverty 3 there had been severe cutbacks in socio-cultural work, and now, suddenly, a new actor was appearing on the socio-cultural scene.

Generally, we found that non-administrative staff endorse the importance of developing new ways to tackle exclusion, but that their managers often simply do not have the means to provide for that development. It is the duty of politicians to find a solution for this problem. In this context, we have put a number of issues on the agenda, in two ways: by showing results (i.e., that a different approach is better); and by showing prospects (i.e., that there are many more potential resources). These results and prospects can be found in four areas:

- Networks that operate flexibly.
- Effective methods for demand-oriented work.
- Capacities of self-organizations.
- Opportunities for the media and research institutes.

Networks around Social Integration

The links between social and economic integration play a central role. However, we observe that often in neighbourhood networks the emphasis is more on social integration, in the sense of creating a social fabric in the neighbourhood. To hold out the prospect of economic integration, we needed an additional urban/regional network in which different actors function. In 1990–1, two complementary networks were set up in Sterrenbuurt, a low-income neighbourhood. The first, Agencies Around the Table, is a multidisciplinary platform, made up of experts working in Sterrenbuurt and neighbourhood representatives. The objective of this group is to exchange plans, ideas, methods, and other information that is relevant to an integrated approach to problems. This was necessary because of fragmentation, overlap, and mutual prejudices.

The second, the Self-management Network, developed into the Star Gazers, a residents' association, which has already introduced several plans. As was always intended, these two networks are self-supporting, and have been since 1991. We did, however, continue to have close links with them to deal with problems or opportunities at the urban level.

The agencies around the table together carried out a health inquiry in the neighbourhood to gain insight into possible points of action. It appeared that in particular, children and young people were not being reached sufficiently. We concluded that social exclusion should be given a higher place on the health care agenda and that extra efforts should be made to improve co-operation with target groups. Building on the Self-management Network, we brought together actors at the municipal level to discuss affordable housing. Housing costs had risen enormously between 1989 and 1993, and we wanted to investigate how people with serious problems making ends meet could be helped to find affordable accommodation. The actors in this were a steering committee on policy for minimum-income people, the Department for Urban Development, housing corporations, and a tenants' association, Housing Consumers. Also, we helped to improve the Town Workshop. This was one of our first activities, started in September 1991. Run by a supervisor, two paid staff (formerly unemployed), and two volunteers, it was intended as a place where people living on a minimum income could have things repaired or buy low-price goods.

Networks around Economic Integration
Three urban networks focusing on jobs were established:

The *Employers' Network* was a plan, proposed by employers, to reserve one hundred vacancies for long-term unemployed people from ethnic minorities. Provided they completed the necessary training, these people would be guaranteed steady jobs. This proposal was announced at a conference, Involvement in the Local Community as a Company Strategy, prepared by a working group in 1992 in which various large companies took part. It took a lot of time and effort to end resistance to this job plan, which was able to start only in 1993. From then on, we focused on other social responsibilities for employers. For this purpose, the working group set up a foundation called Work Givers.

The *Jobs Network* focused on setting up a centre for 'made-to-measure' employment mediation similar to the Nieuw Den Helder plan. To introduce these methods in Hengelo, we set up a working group consisting of the Regional Employment Agency, the Regional College for Secondary Vocational Education, and the social services. Various experiments with the method have been conducted, but the plan to found an agency for this purpose has not yet materialized.

The *Women's Network* relies on contacts with other European projects, the most important of which is New Opportunities for Women (NOW). This network focuses mainly on work in the care sector, where the little that is being done is carried out by informal caregivers at great cost, because of a lack of paid care staff. This network offers opportunities for paid work for single parents, provided training and child facilities are made available (which also generates employment for them).

STRENGTHENING THE CAPACITIES OF SELF-ORGANIZATIONS

In addition, activities were set up to reach socially isolated people in co-operation with key figures from self-organizations. Our tasks included analysing specific causes, bringing together the various actors, developing ideas, and promoting involvement. Our key function was training and preparing volunteers. Two examples of activities will be illustrated here.

First, the Information Project for People from Ethnic Minorities, which focused on educational opportunities, was carried out in Sterrenbuurt, Eindhoven. It concluded with a forum discussion in October 1992. The project was continued and expanded by the regional educational agency, by self-organizations, and by Echo, a local information centre. For this purpose, a permanent working group was set up that is fully controlled by self-organizations. A second activity in Sterrenbuurt was the formation of a group of disabled people. This resulted in a research project, Self-investigation into the Situation and Prospects of the Disabled from

Work. The investigation is being conducted by the disabled people them-selves through participatory research; as such, it is an important part of the empowerment process.

CONCLUSION

We have been trying to develop forms of *participatory planning*. This concept does not appear in the terminology of Poverty 3 (as described in the introduction), but outside Europe, it is at the centre of literature about integrated development programs to fight poverty. Since the 1970s, practically all poverty programs have included provisions to involve the underprivileged themselves, through community participation in the planning, execution, and maintenance phases (Wit, 1992, pp. 57–75). This means creating forms of development planning that set out not from a given solution, but from a given problem. The problem of poverty cannot be solved by social planning alone; solutions must be sought, at least partly at the community level (Korten, 1984a, pp. 176–88; Shubert, 1986, pp. 207–36).

Participatory planning means more than the decentralization of poli-cies: it also involves a redistribution of power between politicians and government bodies on the one hand, and target groups and NGOs on the other (Valk & Wekwete, 1990, pp. 3–12). When this does not hap-pen, community participation is restricted to the implementation of policies whose purposes are to legitimize solutions that have been de-vised by others, and to increase the "clout" of government (Paul, 1987; Marsden & Oakley, 1991, pp. 315–28).

The participatory approach to fighting poverty and exclusion was expounded in the Third World much earlier and much more thoroughly than in the West. This had to do with resistance, at first to colonialism, and later to the Westernized, urbanized, local élite. From the very out-set, one of the goals of this resistance was to further the self-reliance of disadvantaged groups through community organization (Valk & Wekwete, 1990). In Europe, this approach only became topical in the 1980s as the result of a far more abstract discussion, namely, whether the existence of the 'new poverty' could be put down to the gap be-tween the system on the one hand and the real-life world on the other; or between politics, which is oriented toward economic matters, and citizens, who are oriented toward spontaneous matters (Lange, 1992). This entirely different discussion led, however, to the same outcome, namely, a plea for participatory planning whereby a central role would be given to networks of professional and nonprofessional mediators, or intermediaries, between the system and the real-life world (Korten, 1984b, pp. 299–309; Yeung & McGee, 1986).

The Project EC Anti-Poverty Action Program attempted to give tangible form to these mediatory networks. The project was not implemented on the basis of a blueprint, but rather on the basis of a global strategic plan that accounted for both *product* and *process*. In other words, it offered room to experiment, to make mistakes but also to react to unexpected opportunities quickly, and to adjust course on the basis of self-evaluation.

One important thing that the three projects had in common was this: CD work was restricted neither to the work of one profession (CD workers), nor to the boundaries of specific neighbourhoods or districts. The variety in professional backgrounds of the workers involved explains why the results of the three projects look quite different.

4. INSTITUTIONS SUPPORTING CD
Wil van de Leur

In the past a broad range of NGOs were responsible, on a national level, for the support of CD work in the Netherlands. This reflected the various religious and political denominations of Dutch society. They all belonged to one or both of the national umbrella organizations – the National Council on Social Welfare and/or the Council for Cultural Work.

In the 1980s the character of national supporting institutions changed dramatically. As a result of the devolution of responsibility for many tasks and budgets of the Ministry of Social Welfare to local and regional authorities, the number and size of the national supportive institutions has decreased. Furthermore, the policy of the 'retreating government' led to severe cuts. Efficiency measures led to the dissolution of some of the above-mentioned institutions, to the regrouping and merging of others, and to the creation of new ones.

Most notable was the discontinuation of the National Council on Social Welfare, which for many decades had been the active representative of the private social welfare institutions in the Netherlands and also in the field of CD. Of equal importance was the creation, by government decree, of the National Institute of Care and Welfare (NIZW). In this institute many functions relating to the maintenance and development of professional services, which had previously been under the jurisdiction of many smaller institutions, have been merged. The NIZW is divided into sections for young people, the handicapped, and shelter and local social services. It also maintains a Centre for Professional and Vocational Training Affairs and a Documentation and Information Centre. The section for shelter and local social services section is especially important with regard to CD work.

In the early 1990s, national organizations devoted to community work, under threat of dissolution by government decree, were saved by parliamentary intervention. As a result of this intervention the National Centre for Community Work (LCO) was created, which specialized in two things: disseminating knowledge about local practices and experiences; and seeking innovative approaches to community problems and challenges through several networks of local CD projects. For example, there are networks consisting of local groups and organizations of people with disabilities, co-operating in eleven regional platforms. These regional platforms work together in a national network called LSV/WAO. Another national network consists of organizations from a number of deteriorating urban areas. The recent merger of the two national institutes for social scientific research has resulted in the Verwey Jonker Institute, which combines two areas of research expertise: social work and social care, and CD.

The above description is not intended to provide a complete picture of the range of supporting institutions in the Netherlands. Rather, it reflects the efforts of the Ministries of Health, Welfare, and Sports to provide incentives to national consumer organizations in the fields of health and welfare. In this context, mention must also be made of the ongoing experiment with the National Centre of Social Policy, which aims to create a national platform on issues of marginalization and to provide intersectoral answers to questions of social policy.

The central government's retreat from the field of CD, combined with decentralization, has led to supportive tasks being concentrated in regional institutions. Each of the twelve provincial governments makes its own policy. Although there are many differences, these policies have generally led to the formation of large and highly professional organizations. In general terms, these regional institutions cover social work and social care, as well as CD and socio-cultural work. They emphasize consultation and quality improvement issues.

Another effect of the government's retreat in this field is that professionals in social work and community work are striving to install professors at various universities, using funds from industry, churches, and local authorities. In this, the goal is to increase scientific attention to and support for their work.

It is important to state here that, given the complex nature of Dutch institutions, many undertakings in the broad field of CD can be found in other governmental and nongovernmental structures and institutions. For example, the Ministry of Justice runs extensive programs with regard to crime prevention and social self-reliance. Similarly, the recently installed Foundation Society and Police runs a program that focuses on the improvement of social self-reliance. A policy introduced in the early 1990s called Social Renewal aims at stimulating institutions and non-profit organizations and bureaux to engage in forms of networking. The primary objectives in this are to get a 'bigger bang' from the considerable public money that is being spent to alleviate the hardships caused by unemployment and to reduce the overlap of services and benefits.

5. EDUCATION AND TRAINING
Jos Cornelissen

INTRODUCTION

In the Netherlands, education aimed specifically at CD takes place within Higher Professional Education (Vocational Education 18+), in particular advanced social work education. Higher Professional Education is a typical Dutch form of education, aimed at training people for professional practice.

Since 1991 these educational systems have converged under the term 'social and cultural development' (SCD). This is a broad-range, generic program in which students choose one of four fields: social development, basic education, arts, or culture and recreation. A core principle of SCD is that students are taught to initiate learning and development processes that enable people to model and shape their cultural and social situations independently. In the social development stream, students are mainly taught how to initiate and support people's activities to improve their living, housing, and working conditions by promoting their own interests through grass roots organization.

The education for SCD normally takes four years, with an additional two years for students who are specializing in social development. The first year of the four-year program is a generic year. The program includes one year of work placement, during which the student is provided with personal supervision. The program has a full-time and a part-time version. Part-time students work a minimum of twenty hours each week in an education-related job.

Higher professional education in the Netherlands is of equal value to a university education, although it is different. Graduates are eligible to continue on to doctoral studies. Everyone who shows interest and can meet the requirements is admitted to the program. Selection takes place mainly during the first year. At present there are twenty colleges offering SCD studies to approximately 1,400 students, one-third of whom are engaged in social development studies. In 1992, about 85 percent of the graduates were employed in a related field within one year. Since the early 1990s, the number of students has increased somewhat, after a drastic decrease in the mid-1980s. This increase is the result not of greater social demand, but rather of a shift in the social climate stimulated by, among other things, the national policy of 'social renewal.'

Each of the twenty colleges has one or more teachers with specific expertise in CD work. About 150 teachers are involved in SCD education.

ADVANCED TRAINING

Post-graduate courses are offered in – among other subfields – employment, intercultural work, information technology, and social renewal. Support organizations to CD also provide several courses aimed at professional practice.

A number of professions are represented in the field of CD – for example, sociologists, policy scientists, lawyers, employment mediators, health information officials, housing experts, and environment experts. In general, those workers who have a different educational background, and who then take additional training in CD, possess more narrowly specialized and concrete knowledge of the field; while the workers with specific training for CD acquire process abilities and knowledge.

PROGRAMS

The education system for CD in the Netherlands focuses on two areas: providing support to people's initiatives; and social modelling. The first area presupposes abilities in the field of social-organizational service, strategic consultancy, and educational activities. The second, which focuses on initiatives to counteract poor environmental conditions and is becoming more and more important, emphasizes abilities in the field of project development, project management, and research.

CD graduates are engaged in the execution of CD activities at the professional level, and in the improvement of methods.

PRACTICE METHODS

Graduates must demonstrate aptitude in these areas: methods of activation, problem solving, competence improvement, and policy influencing. In addition, they must be able to analyse a situation with regard to the relevant issues, to develop an appropriate action plan, and to facilitate and supervise group processes. It is important that the professionals be very flexible. Increasingly, project-oriented community action is being deployed, and this requires flexibility with respect to target groups and methods. In more complex situations, an integrated 'territorial' or 'route' approach may be called for. In such cases the CD worker is called upon to function as an intermediary between several agents.

QUALITY CHECK

In principle, the schools are autonomous in modelling their education. There are no guidelines from the government or from a national co-ordinating institution. The schools do arrive at agreements between themselves through a national consulting body that has a separate association for social development. A national organization, the Accreditation Body for Care and Welfare, was created in the early 1990s in which all relevant partners (field practice departments, employers, employees, institutions for the improvement of work methods, and representatives of professional education) attempt to come to terms with one another. Also, professionals in the field of community work have developed 'profiles,' which schools are encouraged to use when they are setting their requirements for graduation.

In the collective labour agreements, employers stipulate the qualifications that employees must have. Usually, every school has practice field committees, in which representatives from the practice field in that region comment on relevant aspects of the study program and the organization.

Most schools participate in an annual national poll of graduates, one year after graduation. The participants are questioned about their employment situation and the utility of their education for professional practice.

Every six years an external 'visitation' takes place, in which a committee, composed mainly of experts from the field, judges all educational versions of one discipline. SCD's turn was in 1994; the committee will present its findings in a public report. On the basis of repeatedly negative reports, the minister can decide to withhold from a certain school its subsidies.

Also, an increasing number of 'consumer guides' are appearing in which the various schools are classified according to various criteria based on, among other things, these visitation reports. Most colleges of higher education try to achieve some degree of international rapport by joining and participating in the International Association of Schools of Social Work (IASSW), and/or by taking part in an international network of similar schools. There are no international networks aimed exclusively at CD; instead, the networks are more general, aimed at social work, social pedagogics, or social development.

6. CD AND RESEARCH
Koos Vos

The relationship between CD and research has three levels. First, the CD worker uses research as a tool of the profession. Second, research helps to improve methods of CD practice. Third, studies have examined general practices of social development, of which CD forms a part. We will present some examples of each level.

RESEARCH AS A TOOL OF CD WORK

In a recent handbook on CD work, Broekman (1991) describes five types of research that CD workers can use on the job: the making of a 'social chart,' policy analysis, polls, community self-survey, and action research.

Which of these (or other) techniques is chosen depends on what the CD worker hopes to achieve. The main point of research in a CD process is to gather and analyse information that suggests what action to take. Also, research findings may help to influence decision makers. In addition to this, Broekman mentions two secondary effects of research in the CD process: mobilization and activation. Broekman's discussion of the five techniques is such that a professional can make a well-reasoned choice for any situation at hand. He discusses factors such as the objective, mode of operation, means (time, money, people), and expected results.

For example, a social chart will indicate the quality of life in a certain area by providing data on history, demographics, income and employment, environment, housing, social relations, organizations, and public administration. Workers create a chart at the outset of a project, making use of existing data sources as well as their own observations and discussions with participants; this process enables CD workers to become acquainted with the views of both professionals and citizens, and to find out what the 'pressure points' are in the quality of life of a certain area. Pressure points are clues to improvement activities.

Broekman describes policy analysis, polls, and community self-surveys in a similar way. However, for the purposes of this discussion, we will focus only on a form of future-oriented or action research called the 'LENS method' (Attema, 1991). A social chart, in actual practice, provides a static picture of the situation; the 'LENS method' takes a dynamic approach to quality of life. It describes not only the views of all the people involved in an area, but also the possibilities of change and improvement. The central concept is no longer the 'quality' of life but rather its 'viability.' This is a much more fluid concept. Villages or districts are viable when they are able to improve their quality of life, either on their own or with the aid of external resources (Attema, 1991). The LENS method includes several forms of future-oriented research: the future workshop, the Delphi method, and scenario building.

RESEARCH AND THE IMPROVEMENT OF WORK METHODS

Research can also be used to improve or renew professional action. We will give three examples (Lieshout, 1992).

The first focuses on the CD worker's mode of operation, or role, as researched by Broekman (1988). He defined 'role' as a professional's ability and inclination to act in a goal-oriented and situation-determined way in CD processes, guided by ideas on effectiveness and surrounded by expectations in regard to his or her own effectiveness. He constructed seven roles, which cover the full range of practice in CD processes: mobilizer, oracle, catalyst, course determinant developer, mediator, advocate, and activist. In choosing among these roles, he argued, practitioners must weigh theoretical presuppositions as to what is practical in a certain situation (or 'impact model') – that is, as to which role is likely to be more effective in a certain situation, given the underlying factors.

The results of Broekman's research (1988) showed that Dutch community workers in the second half of the 1980s were engaged primarily in educational, organization-building activities. Advocacy and activism were rare. His research also identified methodological gaps: the notion of the relationship between the initiative group and supporters appeared to be weak, while distinctions between the initiative group, the target group, and the beneficiary group appeared to be completely lacking in the CD workers' awareness.

The second example of research on work method improvements relates to the search, started in the 1980s, for an integrated approach to work with the elderly (Pacilly, 1988). The search for such a model was guided by a commitment to the emancipation and participation of the elderly, and by the notion that the elderly are to be treated as 'users of service' and not merely as 'recipients of care.' To this end, experimental research was carried out in several service locations. This work, together with input from outside experts, resulted in the development of a perspective on the social position of the elderly; this perspective in turn provided the basis for integrated elderly work. Integrated elderly work was defined as 'a strategy of change which starts from problems pointed out by the elderly; problems which make it difficult for them to grow old successfully' (Pacilly, 1988, p. 112). These general suggestions of the elderly were the starting point; the abilities and resources of the elderly and their network were incorporated into a solution. This strategy sought also to improve the functioning of service organizations and the cohesion between private enterprise and public administration. Furthermore, attention was paid to the way in which participation of the elderly could be stimulated. For this purpose, platforms were created for the elderly. The experimental mode of operation showed that the work of the authorities, service providers, and professionals in the field of care for the elderly was adequate only when it was based on the needs and interests that were expressed by the elderly themselves (Pacilly, 1991).

The third example concerns the application of a self-survey method developed by the Verwey Jonker Institute (Foolen, 1993) for an antipoverty study. The program planners, in searching for a model for integrated action at the local level, outlined three points of departure for action: the multidimensionality of poverty; a partnership between the public and the private sector; and the participation of the poor themselves in policy design and program execution. The survey method that was developed helped local teams reflect on daily practice before, during, and after the action. In turn, the project researcher gathered, analysed, and compared the material that was produced by self-survey in the different locations and presented his conclusions to the National Institute for Care and Welfare (NIZW), which had the task of constructing the model of integrated work. A similar method was used in the development of an approach to improve the accessibility to general provisions for elderly immigrants.

RESEARCH INTO CD WORK AND SOCIAL DEVELOPMENT

Research into CD Work

Kramer, back in 1970, noted that CD work in the Netherlands was too narrowly focused on population groups, and that it ignored the important work to be done on citizen participation. This narrow focus, he argued, was primarily due to the unique political and social situation in the Netherlands at the time – the country was dominated by an élite faction that was organized on an ideological basis. Peper (1972) held government responsible for not being clear as to what forms of participation it wished to promote; and criticized institutions supporting CD for serving essentially as a buffer between the political system and the population in such a way that political democracy was not being promoted. Vos (1985) observed that CD workers at the end of the 1960s and the beginning of the 1970s were guided principally by the ideology of nondirectionality (i.e., a concern for 'process'). It was not until the prevailing system of political and social élites (the system of 'compartmentalization') began to disintegrate that action groups from the population appeared on the political stage, joined by CD workers. The same observation was made by researchers evaluating rural projects involving CD work (Elsch & Raspe, 1976; Vos & Brink, 1983).

At the beginning of the 1980s, NIMO (currently part of the Verwey Jonker Institute) started the 'trend investigations' into CD, relying on polls. These studies focused on CD workers and institutions supporting CD work, on the fields in which CD workers initiated projects, on the groups they worked with, and on similar issues. The results of the tenth trend investigation were presented in 1994 (Hooijdonk & Raspe, 1993). The authors found that there were some 303 institutions supporting CD work – twenty less than during the 1980s. The number of CD workers (predominantly male) remained relatively stable at about 1,000 (equivalent to 700 full-time). Most had received a technical or vocational education. In terms of content, district-linked work had increased significantly, especially in urban areas, and housing and related issues were still the main focus of interest. Furthermore, priorities had shifted from urban renewal to issues of governance and participation.

Also in the 1980s, CD work began to receive considerable attention from science, as evidenced by the creation of special university chairs for CD and by the number of doctoral dissertations that had CD themes.

Veen (1982), for instance, compared four activation approaches in CD and socio-cultural education work: animation, social action (Alinsky style), the radical approach of the left, and locality development. Schuyt's study (1985) connected local welfare policies to the role of CD work. Broekman (1987) published his organizational analysis of the first institution for CD work in the Netherlands, Community Development Foundation Drenthe. He showed how the socially innovative approach of this institution could still serve as an example to contemporary CD workers. Finally, Dijkstra (1989) examined the effects of CD work on the local level. His conclusions, not flattering to CD work, were that the non-active part of the population did not appear to get served.

Research into Social Development
Beck (1974), whose concern was with local democracy, reported on neighbourhood actions in rural areas of the Netherlands. The antithesis 'populations authorities' was central in this analysis. Subsequent studies by the Department of Studies in Social Development at the University of Amsterdam focused on the concept of 'promotion of interests by self-organization,' in which the concept of 'strategy' was an important analytical instrument. Professional CD work was mentioned in this line of studies, but only as one among several actors. The same was true for a later study by this department, which focused on 'conflicts between interests in a working class area.' Specifically, this study considered the impact of a proposal by the Amsterdam City Council to build an opera house in that area. In their research, Beck and Blom (1980) attempted to develop a model for analysing local actions that would do justice to the dynamic nature of social reality. For instance, they asked what impact the strategies pursued by the various actors had on the decision making about this issue. This study also showed clearly the evolution in how the 'authorities' were perceived. Analytical studies were still quite simplistic at the beginning of the 1980s; even so, they had become sophisticated enough to begin to identify the presence of various factions within 'the authorities,' each having its own strategy and networks.

During the urban renewal period of the 1970s, the government commissioned special research to locate pressure points in the practice of urban renewal. The study of various residential areas resulted in the design of a theory on the CD process. De Kleijn (1978, 1985) chose *emancipation* as the key normative concept for his theories. A CD process is an emancipation process, he stated, in which inhabitants and users of underprivileged districts and neighbourhoods join forces in an organization in order to get a better grip on their common housing and living conditions. Armed with this perspective, De Kleijn developed a model of elements that impede or promote a CD process. This model became a source of inspiration for the new movement of 'building for the neighbourhood,' and for professional CD work, which has incorporated de Kleijn's model into its own body of knowledge.

Thus, research and theory development during this period provided cause for optimism. Neighbourhoods could be mobilized, and it seemed possible to construct a common front. However, a later study by Beck and Blom (1980) showed that the district or the neighbourhood were becoming 'fictions' in the sense of becoming increasingly diverse and heterogeneous, with various groups often at war with one another.

Several research studies in the later 1980s began to document the growing fragmentation in social relations and the search for new action orientations. With the aid of Gidden's conceptual framework, Wit (1987) studied the reorientation processes in a district that had lost not only its steel factories but also two big churches. Loo, Loozen, and Oosterman (1988) took Elias and Bourdieu for their guides in outlining how a working-class neighbourhood developed, through urban renewal, into a neighbourhood with different but coexisting lifestyles.

Anderiesen and Reijndorp, in their study on social segmentation in urban districts (1989, 1990), were also guided by Bourdieu. They showed how lifestyles of groups of people in districts can be interpreted as variations in economic, social, and cultural capital, and how these variations create very separate worlds in the same neighbourhood.

In the second half of the 1980s, studies on poverty began to appear. These were precipitated by a major economic crisis that the country suffered at the beginning of the decade, which resulted in a considerable loss of employment. Although the economy rebounded in the second half of the decade, and new employment was created, more and more people were experiencing long-term unemployment and being forced to live on a minimum income for long periods of time. Studies by Engbersen (1987), Kroft et al. (1989), and Engbersen (1990) provide a clear insight into the life of these unemployed and point also to the diversity of this group. The six types of long-term unemployed identified were the conformists, the ritualists, the retreatists, the active, the calculating, and the autonomous. They were distinguished from one another in terms of their endorsement of employment objectives, search behaviour (formal and informal), and use of opportunities offered by the social security system.

Some recent research has begun to focus on the implementation processes of the Social Renewal program, which looks beyond urban and
economic renewal toward the social participation of (especially) the
'excluded' citizens. Social Renewal is a process that will allow social
relations – the social connective tissue of local society – to flourish
again. How does this process develop? Fortuin (1991, 1992, 1994) followed this process closely in three Rotterdam areas. He was mainly
interested in reconstructing the meaning of social renewal for the civil
servants, policy-makers, and policy consumers involved. He found that
the issues that arose in the three areas of the city differed considerably;
these might include (among others) provisions for and by women, district management, and the reintegration of the long-term unemployed.
In spite of these variations, some common priorities emerged, with participation being the most important. In Fortuin's words, 'Involving inhabitants in policy programs puts the pressure on the logic of a policy'
(1994, p. 74).

Research into CD shows an increasing interest in gaining an insight
into the living environment of citizens and into public administration,
specifically in urban areas. This interest is not limited to researchers,
but can also be found among administrators.

7. THEORETICAL DEVELOPMENTS IN COMMUNITY WORK IN THE NETHERLANDS
Cees de Wit and Peter van Lieshout

THEORY IN CONTEXT

The Netherlands has an extensive and diverse system of care and welfare provisions. The various contributions to this Dutch study show
that CD work holds a special position in this. In this section we will
sketch an outline of the theoretical tradition relevant to CD, focusing on
the political context and on scientific developments. Let's begin by stat-
ing that although the Netherlands indeed has a highly developed welfare state, there is no advanced up-to-date theory on the welfare state.
Earlier attempts in the 1960s and 1970s (Thoenes, 1962; Heek, 1973)
built on the work of Beveridge (1942), Carr (1951), Myrdal (1958), and
Bruce (1961). Apparently, to many scientists the Dutch welfare state
was so self-evident that theorizing on it wasn't much of a challenge. It
wasn't until things went very wrong that scientists began to reflect on
their relation to reality (Ortega y Gasset, 1975). Apparently, Dutch theo-

reticians had felt that more was wrong with the divided understanding of knowledge of the social domain than with the social practice of the welfare state. This changed under the Thatcher regime in the United Kingdom, and later when the Lubbers government came to power in our country.

Theory on social phenomena first of all functions as an instrument in the discovery and acceptance of what is hidden. In the second place, social theory functions as an advocate for those new practices by which questions in the economic and social fields can be solved. Now that the welfare state in the Netherlands, as in many other Western countries, is more and more the subject of discussion, interest in theory development on social and socio-economic policy is increasing. One of the first points to be made is that hardly any research has been done on the social necessity and the social effects of the social security system in the Netherlands. And this when the system, in terms of money, bears extremely heavily on the national product.

If theoreticians have shown little interest in the social security system as the important spine of the welfare state, this does not apply to a number of care and welfare provisions that are characteristic of the Dutch welfare state. We should make reference here to a relevant publication that distinguishes, for important comparative reasons, between three types of welfare state: the liberal (Canada, the United States, and Australia); the corporatist (Germany, France, Italy, and Austria); and the social democratic (the Netherlands, Sweden, Norway, and Denmark, with the United Kingdom a mixture of liberal and social democratic) (Andersen, 1990). Theoreticians focusing on care and welfare provisions were interested first in the humanizing and pacifying of modernization, and second in the emancipation of marginalized individuals and underprivileged groups.

In view of certain tendencies such as secularization, individualization, and fragmentation, the profession of social work wanted to better understand its helping function. In this context, intensive efforts have been made to achieve a better theoretical articulation of social work's functioning. The most interesting theoretical initiative in this domain, however, related to higher education. This discipline wanted first of all to provide a theoretical reflection on help in general. In an international perspective, it was a unique attempt to create a new form of social pedagogy that was relevant to the rapidly changing times. In the mid-1970s, independent departments appeared at various Dutch universities in the new social science of 'andragology' or 'agology' which focused on the promotion of personal, social, and cultural welfare. They did not last long, as they were the first to fall victim to the budget cuts at the beginning of the 1980s. This was not just related to the fact that social workers and welfare work were falling out of favour with policy makers (Achterhuis, 1980). It was also related to the fact that the new branch of study did not succeed in formulating a clear research program. The basic idea – that there ought to be one general theory on human action – never got beyond abstract, hollow phrases. In addition to this, social workers in the field of care and welfare often felt criticized rather than supported by the 'higher education theoreticians.' Thus, the specialty went down for want of legitimacy. It was a pre-theory 'on' social work, rather than 'for' social work, despite all notions of action orientation (Gastelaars, 1990, pp. 346–67).

In this respect it is relevant to note that the Netherlands makes a relatively strong distinction between institutions for higher professional training, and universities. Institutions for higher professional training only provide education and do minimal research, whereas universities link research and education. It matters greatly to the chances of development for any specialty whether it is counted as belonging to the professional institutions or to the universities. Many types of social work have ended up in the field of higher professional education. Thus, case work and CD work are not being taught at the university level, and have not been the subject of research or thorough reflection. This means that there have been no centres of knowledge for these important parts of the social sector until recently. In the past few years, however, the authorities have tried to introduce forms of research in schools for higher professional education. At the instigation of professionals in the field, initiatives from the voluntary sector have led to the establishment of chairs at universities to achieve theory development.

PRACTICE/THEORY INTERACTION

Until recently, the actual development of knowledge took place outside the educational systems, within institutions that, besides engaging in actual service and social work, did knowledge building 'on the side.' This was a fruitful interaction between practice and theory; this approach is characteristic of the Dutch situation even today.

For instance, Hendriks, a frequent visitor to and speaker at foreign conferences, and a productive writer, was director general of the Ministry of Culture, Recreation, and Social Work and in that position commissioned extensive theory development research; the goal in this was to promote an intellectual, reflection-oriented attitude among the staff of his department. He was particularly keen on improving the profession of CD. His point of departure was what today would be termed participatory social planning. Broekman and Canjels (1989, pp. 55–81), in writing about Hendriks, summed up his image of society as 'large groups with unsolved social psychological problems, pollution of the environment, persistent poverty, an inequality of income, bureaucracy and technocracy resulting in alienation.' Key notions were participation, decentralization, and the development of one's abilities. His intervention repertoire had three important elements: social research, social planning, and CD work as found also in North America.

FROM COMMUNITY ORGANIZATION TO SELF-ORGANIZATION

Tienen and Zwanikken (1972) during the 70s paid attention to modernization issues such as technological development and urbanization, trying to understand them and how the problems inherent in them might be corrected through community organization. They looked upon society mainly as a cultural phenomenon in transition, and discussed whether it was possible to control change within it. In their opinion, CD workers were not suited to do more than bring about a few minor corrections. They argued that CD workers should assist in the realization of what is generally felt to be important – that is, the designing and constructing of one's own society.

Besteman (1974), who also saw modernization as the central idea of people's transformation, focused on structural rather than cultural forces. He felt that problems could best be solved by working as much as possible according to method and project. He favoured an action system, consisting of residents (staff), field experts, and CD workers, in which 'the population' participated as much as possible. Self-activation was not emphasized. His line of approach was to contribute to the emancipation of the underprivileged, and of people at risk such as those becoming unemployed. By linking problems to achievable goals, a 'problem project method' with alternative solutions could be created. The CD worker would take a directive role that emphasized effectiveness of action in relation to goal achievement.

Kleijn (1978), with others, was against this approach, feeling instead that if CD workers were going to take seriously the residents of labour districts, they must disassociate themselves from abstractions such as 'the population.' He focused on the neighbourhood organization as the means to bring about emancipation. Urban renewal was a useful direct cause, in his opinion. Without access to facilities to serve as a base of power, a neighbourhood organization could not contribute to the improvement of the residents' position or, for that matter, to their personal development. He advocated an explicit approach to democratization and emancipatory conditions that referred to both material and social improvements. He saw the CD worker's mode of operation as position-linked and, in principle, 'bottom-up' instead of 'top-down' oriented. In order to achieve a power base of any kind, the internal organization had to be in order, there had to be sufficient support from the community, and there had to be sufficient knowledge of the circumstances among those providing support. Only then could a strategy against the opposition be useful.

He distinguished four modalities to this effect: control of the opposition, negotiations on points of difference, joint responsibility, and a neighbourhood organization that could make plans and direct their execution. In his conclusions he made no attempt to assess the extent of the model's universal applicability, but he recognized that CD work is full of dilemmas that have to be handled through a situation-linked approach. Emancipation, in his opinion, was not a job for outsiders, and not even for CD workers. Rather, it was something that people themselves must do. In this he linked up with the critical thinking of the Frankfurters, who saw alienation as arising in large part from modernization. Kleijn (1985), who developed his theory from an emancipatory perspective, also identified conditions that made the CD process more likely to succeed, and factors that functioned as obstacles.

ACTIVATION VIA DIALOGUE

Two more developments must be mentioned. The first of these is 'liberation theology,' which guided the actions of radical priests and vicar–labourers. This approach, however, had no significant theoretical follow-through in CD work. Second, we must point out the ecclesiastical 'social activation' work, and more specifically the dissertation by Baart (1986) that focused on the question of how church members could be activated. Baart advocated that believers should not be persuaded or manipulated into community work, but rather should be activated through dialogue based on stories. Dialogue to him is more than conversation – it is a way of understanding one's own actions and taking a critical personal position instead of focusing on organizational modelling. Starting from the idea of being situated in a communicative and social sense, he characterizes dialogue as a symmetrical interpretative relationship from which activation work can be created.

All of the above describes developments in theory up to the mid-1980s. The movement has been away from project-bound theories and toward more emancipation-oriented theories within the tradition of practice/theory interaction.

NEW CHAIRS

The welfare state in its general development has moved toward what Beck (1992) describes as a society at risk, in which people in a disadvantaged position are sentenced to social exclusion by socio-economic developments, or isolate themselves from a world they no longer feel is theirs. This phenomenon has arisen so quickly that 'social activation' and 'solidarity work' have been placed on the agenda of many institutions and local authorities.

Thus, at the end of the 1980s and the beginning of the 1990s, the search for new theoretical insights into CD as well as social work was once more receiving a great deal of attention. This search took place first in the voluntary sector and in professional circles; soon after, there were developments at the university level – specifically, several chairs were created. Those relevant to CD include a special chair at Erasmus University in Rotterdam for the study of the scientific basis of CD work, and a chair at the Catholic Theological University of Utrecht focusing on the discipline of CD and activation work as it relates to church and society. Also, there was an initiative at the University of Utrecht that led to the establishment of a new interdisciplinary group within the social sciences; this group is attempting to integrate action with the development of framework theory involving psychology, anthropology, sociology, and social philosophy. Also at the university level and at research institutes, there have been recent initiatives to reassess the welfare state; and to examine new forms of citizenship, work, social security, and care; and to advance the theory and practice of spiritual work and of social work in general.

In connection to the above developments, questions have arisen whether lines of convergence can be found in recent thinking linking the social to the economic; and in the philosophical debate between those espousing individualism, enlightened communalism, and republican thought on 'the good life.' If such convergence is found, what implications will this have for theory development in the interventive professions? Here we end our summary of current theory development in the context of the Netherlands, and take a broader perspective.

DUTCH DEVELOPMENTS IN A NORTHWESTERN EUROPEAN PERSPECTIVE

German, British, and French theoreticians have been a source of inspiration to many generations of Dutch students. It must be noted here that a single, coherent theoretical vision does not exist in these regions. American mainstream functionalism and the thoroughness of the Frankfurter School both influenced Dutch theory development in the early 1970s. Ten years later, French theoreticians like Foucault, Castells, and Donzelot were major sources of inspiration. Another ten years later, 'grand' deterministic theories lost popularity, and interest shifted toward theories on human resources and the hermeneutic and dynamic approach to social phenomena.

It is often said that nothing is as practical to social work as a good theory. Such a statement does not just express the need for a somewhat objective appraisal of action; this appraisal must also be correct, or adequate to reality. Since a detailed survey of every theoretical development of interest to CD work would be impossible, we have decided to focus on the work of the German philosopher and social theoretician Jürgen Habermas; the British psychologist and sociologist Anthony Giddens; and the French sociologist Pierre Bourdieu.

Recent developments in social theory in northwestern Europe are a synthesis in the sense that on the one hand they are linked to hermeneutic, interactive/communicative, action-oriented schools of thought; while on the other hand they are linked to framework/theoretical ones. They aim at some sort of connection between a communicative (sense-oriented) and a strategic (goal-oriented) rationality. In this context the new social sciences are not so much 'value-oriented' (normative or value committed) as 'value inclusive.'

COMMUNICATIVE ACTION: FRAMEWORK AND LIVING ENVIRONMENT

Habermas (1981, 1985) is of interest to CD work, because he does not just describe the crises of modernization and reproduction, but also provides a way out of the fundamental dilemma of social theory, which is the relationship between normative and cognitive aspects of the acquisition of knowledge. He shows the link between communicative action and rationality, and argumentation. The fundamental question of how social order can be achieved can be answered by referring to the definitions of social reality that are created communicatively in daily contacts (Kunneman, 1985). Habermas's analysis of communicative action is not limited to the level of action theory. He is aware that action theoreticians have a preference for original stories, life histories, unstructured interviews, and participant observation as instruments for discovering meanings; and that in following this course they develop an empirically based theory that is not just being forced upon a situation, but *rises from it* according to strict protocols for the acquisition of knowledge and the 'life world.' These action-oriented approaches overlook, according to Habermas, the problems of material reproduction of societies. They overlook factors that, in a manner of speaking, influence their action. He takes a 'framework theory' approach. By analysing the symbolic reproduction of society's action theoretically, and by describing the material reproduction in 'framework theory' concepts, Habermas is able to show the costs that accompany the process of modernization in Western societies.

'Social evolution' is analysed by Habermas as the interlocking of two rationality processes. On the one hand there is rationalization of the life world, which liberates communicative action from the coercion of tradition. On the other hand there is an increase in efficiency based on the level of material reproduction. The process of rationalization of the life world holds primacy, as it provides the social basis for the economy and the state as subsystems. The life world, Habermas points out, is polarized between the private and public environment, with communication and argumentation on the one hand, and on the other hand the economy and state frameworks, which are moved by strategic goal-oriented action and dominated by money and power. The toll prosperity pays in Western and other societies is the colonization and penetration of the life world; the economy and the state encroach upon it with money and power. This, without recognizing that the issues present here can in the long run be solved only by communicative action and mutual agreement, through argumentation rather than through strategic action. CD workers who help people oppose these forces must consider that there are at least three levels functioning simultaneously in social action: those of culture, society, and the individual. In the process whereby the life world is rationalized, Habermas considers 'loss of meaning' an important point of interest on the level of culture and for the disturbances it produces in cultural reproduction. 'Loss of meaning' translates into 'problems of legitimacy' at the societal level and into an 'orientation and education crisis' at the individual level. Here the 'rationality of knowledge' is the proper standard of judgment.

When there is a question of disturbances of social integration, the insecurity of collective identity becomes an important point of interest. In the context of social integration, the central issue on the level of society is 'anomy,' or pluriformity of standards. At the individual level, issues of 'alienation' are at work. Here, the standard according to Habermas is that of solidarity of those affected.

In the case of disturbances in socialization, the point of concern at the cultural level is the breakdown of traditions. At the level of society these disturbances produce problems of motivation. And on the personal level they are defined in terms of 'psychic pathologies.' The standard of judgment here is the accountability of the agents involved.

DUALITY AND STRUCTURING

The Englishman Anthony Giddens (1984, 1990, 1991) is also important to CD, particularly in times of fundamental social change, as he has introduced new concepts to the rather static and deterministic relationship between culture and structure. Like Habermas, he has tried to achieve a synthesis between the familiar action theory approaches on the one hand, and the framework theory on the other hand.

He also focuses on communication, which he defines as 'the exchange of meanings in interaction.' In this regard, he sees people as having three options: acceptance, amendment, or reinterpretation of the meaning of interaction. Meanings in exchange relations, according to Giddens, are linked to power and to sanctions that are structurally embedded in dominance and legitimacy. He calls particular attention to three modalities that are important to CD work: first, the role of 'symbols' as schematic meanings; second, 'facilities;' and third, 'standards.' These have not always been handled with success by CD workers, because they allow dominant agents to impose their images and symbols, or because claims being made on facilities or resources are not being honoured, or because they naïvely focus on standards. Thus, the limits of interaction and structuring are also the limits of CD work.

Another interesting point made by Giddens that is of relevance to CD relates to three types of consciousness influencing social action. We will look first at the three types of consciousness. These are 'reasoned action,' based on discursive rational consciousness; 'practical action,' based on practical consciousness; and 'routine action,' which is habit-determined, affecting most daily activities. Practical action, he argues, can be changed by changing the knowledge base that links discursive and practical consciousness. However, this is not true of unconscious action, which is directed essentially by motives derived from a moral conscience that may minimize concern about right action to bring about change. In this context, routinized action lies between practical and unconscious action, in that people frequently follow familiar modes of behaviour because of the sense of security it gives them. This concept of consciousness is important to CD work, since it helps workers respond appropriately to those feelings of insecurity which often produce either violent or apathetic reactions.

Much of development work unfolds within a spatial setting like a development area, a disadvantaged district, or a transition zone. The positions of the people within the setting are often interpreted in terms of space. We have illustrated this in the examples taken from the field of practice. Where social positions and relations are expressed in terms of space, and where people with different characteristics live next to one another experiencing either comfort or nuisance, one has to deal with the spatial characteristic of the profession.

The spatial concepts Giddens uses are 'locales' and 'regions.' These he links to 'sequences of action within time.' He rejects the notion of 'place,' since he finds it too specific and too much linked to types of activities and levels of scale. He also rejects 'space,' considering it too broad a term. He favours a historically determined multilevel 'locality' in which the combination of the various encounters ('regionalization') can be or have been put into effect. He points out that in most locales, the borders that separate the various regions are often determined by overlapping symbolic and physical markings.

These two spatial notions he links to four concepts of time in order to avoid the misleading 'snapshot science' (as he terms it) of society. A good understanding of these four concepts of time is important for successful CD work, since residents often operate in a very different space of time than do municipal authorities or institutions, for instance. Giddens's four concepts of time are as follows:

- Duration of 'interactions' in a stream of immediate experiences that have a beginning and end, that are immediately observable, and that are usually of a short duration.

- Duration of 'overlapping human lifespan,' such as stages in the life cycle and generations that involve distant notions of time, reciprocity, and structuring.
- Duration of 'institutions,' which have more or less ready-made patterns of action and long duration, and involve structured frameworks.
- Duration of an 'episode' placed in historical context involving certain circumstances or crises.

The structuring of social relations, extended in space and time, takes place, according to Giddens, through the duality of social structures. He describes this duality in *The Constitution of Society* (1984) as both medium and outcome of behaviour it organizes. In other words, the behaviour of people is determined by social structures; at the same time, their actions determine those social structures through the use of symbols, facilities (or lack of them), and standards.

DYNAMICS OF CAPITAL AND CONTEXTS

Now briefly about Bourdieu (1977a, 1977b, 1984) and his meaning for CD work. He focused on the functioning of symbolic power and its demythologization. For him it is important that people be their own true spokesmen about their social reality, instead of being spoken to. People need to develop the art of defending themselves against the words that legitimize power, especially the language of modern science and business. This is to argue not for an antiscientific position, but for creating the conditions for a new scientific and political mentality that has a liberating effect and that itself has been liberated from censure.

Bourdieu, however, is not just interesting to CD because he lashes out at the manipulation of the political economy by leaders governing on the basis of socio-economic science. He also has carefully developed a conceptual framework that enables us to describe social dynamics in the most fundamental empirical way, in which we first seek information about the meaning of social reality and the experience of people at the community level as expressed by them, understand it, and then look for new theoretical insights that can be useful for developing effective action.

His central notion, 'symbolic power,' refers to the value that clings to words. That symbolic power is linked to persons in a certain position within a certain context or 'field,' and with certain 'habits' of functioning. By 'field' Bourdieu means 'world' – a relatively autonomous social universe with an irreducible logic, for example, the 'welfare sector' or 'artistic circles.' A field is a network of 'objective' relations between 'objectively' defined positions that exercise coercion on the agents that hold these positions. The agents are bound to the game that is played on a field by 'evidence of complicity.' The struggle is about the division of specific power (or the specific capital), and therefore also about the preservation or change of the structure and the definition of who can or cannot join the game. 'Field,' to Bourdieu, means the external and compulsive structure of relations between positions.

'Habit' concerns the internally 'embodied' dispositions that lead individuals to observe reality situations in a programmed fashion and take practical action. In other words, habit concerns the internalization of a field. In order to play the game in a certain field, one has to possess, according to Bourdieu, a 'practical sense' of habit. This stands midway between the conscious and the unconscious, and is a kind of practical feeling for the game to make certain social and cultural investments (more or less unconsciously) that are linked to interpretation and power. Bourdieu sees these investments as contributions to previously accumulated efforts through which one can appropriate social energy.

Thus he creates a relationship with both the concept of labour and the concept of capital. In addition to economic capital, he distinguishes social capital and cultural capital. 'Social capital' is defined by him in terms of social connections such as kinship, friends, acquaintances, and similar. In order to maintain these connections and make them work – that is, in order to profit by them – one has to invest in them. This involves making an effort. For instance, in relation to networks it involves focusing on their reproduction, recognizing them for their functions and exclusive activities, and confirming one's gratitude for their contributions. At the personal level it has to do with exchange, defending weaker members, and developing reputation, spokesmanship, and representation.

Cultural capital is characterized by the appropriation of knowledge, preferences of taste, and standards of civilization by an individual, in the course of time and in the spirit of a willingness to sacrifice. The accumulation of cultural capital takes a great deal of time and cannot take place by mandate or be delegated. Cultural capital manifests itself first of all in an *embodied* state through 'cultivation.' Incorporated, it becomes a physical quality of the individual, a 'habit'; or a 'having' that has changed into a 'being.' This form of personal capital, unlike money or proof of ownership, cannot be easily transferred as a gift, inheritance, purchase, or exchange. Contrast this with cultural capital in its *objectified* state; this kind is about cultural goods such as paintings, books, instruments, and machinery, which of course *can* be transferred. Then there is a third form of cultural capital, which is *institutionalized* and relates to the guaranteed presence of cultural capital such as a school diploma.

Finally there is *symbolic* capital, which can be capital of any kind insofar as it is represented by an object of knowledge. In Bourdieu's view, social, cultural, and symbolic capital can in certain circumstances be converted into economic capital and symbolic power, with which the 'game' can be played in one or several fields.

This completes our discussion of the major sources of inspiration from northwestern Europe in the search for relevant theoretical foundations for CD work in the Netherlands.

EPILOGUE

Important new micro and macro insights can be gained from the above review of major European theoreticians that can serve as starting points for professional practice. They can be summarized as follows:

1 Members of a society or parts thereof benefit from becoming actively involved in the development of a democratic society.
2 CD workers are advised to start their interventions by reflecting on the meaning of the 'life world,' and the 'interaction' and the 'habits' of the people they work with, and to help transform the outcome of this process into socially relevant options that will reverse social and economic exclusion and promote participation.
3 The exploration and discovery of relevant framework, structural, and field characteristics is essential. This process must be seen as being linked to the positions people are in.
4 Taking into account points 1, 2, and 3, professional intervention ought to manage concretely the structuring of social relations and the dynamics of different forms of capital as conceptualized by Giddens.
5 This involves paying attention to the identification of sources and facilities internal to groups or networks of people. These are essential for participation.
6 This also involves the need to continuously explore and identify similar sources and facilities, present in other agents, that make

possible productive strategic co-operation aimed at resolving problems and fostering a participatory, democratic mode of social development.

7 Furthermore, carrying out the educational, organizing, and strategic tasks requires a 'practical sense of habit' – that is, an internalized disposition to observe, assess, and act.

8 Finally, the implementation of these tasks is an uninterrupted cyclical process involving a cognitive, and concrete (i.e., material), appraisal of the following:

- The structure in the narratives and stories told by the people themselves.
- The relevance of theoretical concepts, problem formulations, and analyses (in a way that is devoid of professional self-interest).
- The possible alternatives.
- The appropriateness of one's own 'sense of habit,' 'field,' and rules of play in furthering the position and participation of the people one works for and with.

8. CONCLUSION
Cees de Wit

THE DUTCH SITUATION

The various contributions of CD work in the Netherlands can be described in terms of periods of turbulence, permanence, and stagnation. The 1960s and 1970s were turbulent insofar as the development of the welfare state was concerned. Yet there was also permanence, because of the efforts of CD workers to promote the social and economic participation of the least privileged. In recent decades, patterns of solidarity have been changing; moreover, budget cuts and changing circumstances have created some stagnation in the profession regarding its position on citizen and client orientation and participation.

In this country study on CD, we traced its practice from its beginnings to the present. We also looked at organizational and intellectual developments in the context of a highly developed welfare state and growing individualism.

Today, social work and CD are *in*, and social welfare and the centrality of the state are *out*. In this changed environment, professionals have been searching for new identities on the margins of society, supported by responsible politicians when recognize the importance of their work, particularly in this period of transition.

In previous decades the lack of professionalization in the field of CD strengthened the workers' ideological orientation. More recently, ideologization has been replaced by a debate on professional identity in terms of qualifications, recognition, and 'certification' by society. The debate on CD has also been picked up by the stakeholders themselves. The social sciences, in response to these turbulent times, aim to influence the debate on how society should be restructured and organized.

Contributors

Eric Canjels
Project evaluator, LAMIGO (national demonstration project on environmental protection and community development work; and associate of LCO (Netherlands Centre for Community Organizations).

Jos Cornelissen
Director, School of Social Work, Eindhoven; member of the National Council of Higher Professional Education; and former executive board member of the International Association of Schools of Social Work.

Liesbeth Klein-Beernink
Project manager, the Flesseman Project in Amsterdam.

Wil van de Leur
Managing director, LCO (Netherlands Centre for Community Organizations), and secretary general of SBO (Dutch Association of Community Workers).

Peter van Lieshout
Professor, Faculty of Social Sciences at Utrecht University; and managing director, NIZW (Netherlands Institute for Care and Welfare, Utrecht).

Fred Stafleu
Social economist and former secretary, National Council on Social Welfare; and currently with the Gradus Hendriks Foundation, the Hague.

Carel Tenhaeff
Development sociologist; Dutch project manager of the Third European Anti-Poverty Program; and associate of NIZW.

Koos Vos
Research director, Verwey Jonker Institute for Research on Society Issues, Utrecht.

Co-ordinator

Cees de Wit

Honorary professor holding the special Dr. Gradus Hendriks Chair of Community Organization and Community Development, Erasmus University, Faculty of Philosophy, 1989–95; formerly a senior research fellow and associate professor of urban studies at Utrecht University, following doctoral studies in urban sociology and architecture; known for his community work in urban renewal and social housing; and currently a consultant on urban development.

References

Abou Sada, G. (1991). *Europe against poverty.* Lille: GEIE Animation & Recherche.

Achterhuis, J. (1980). *De markt van welzijn en geluk.* Baarn: Ambo.

Andersen, E. (1990). *The three worlds of welfare capitalism.* Cambridge: Polity Press.

Anderiesen, G., & Reijndorp, A. (1989). *Gescheiden werelden, sociale segmentering in 19e eeuwse stadswijken.* Universiteit van Amsterdam: Centrum voor Grootstedelijk Onderzoek.

– (1990). *Van volksbuurt tot stadswijk, de vernieuwing van het Oude Westen.* Rotterdam: Projektgroep Het Oude Westen.

Angotti, T. (1993). *Metropolis 2000: Planning poverty and politics.* London: Routledge.

Attema, F. (1991). *De LENS-method, handleiding voor toekomstanalysewerk van wijk en dorp.* Deventer: Weson.

Baart, A.J. (1986). *Verhalen, de dialoog als grondmodel van maatschappelijk activeringswerk.* Hilversum: Gooi & Sticht.

– (1993). *Het arrangement van de tragiek.* Utrecht: Katholieke Theologische Universiteit.

Beck, U. (1992). *Risk society: Towards a new modernity.* London: Sage.

Beck, W. (1974). *Democratie in de wijken, een onderzoek naar buurtacties in Nederland.* Amsterdam: Van Gennep.

Beck, W., & Blom, M. (1980). *Een cultuurpaleis in een arbeiderswijk? analyse van een belangenstrijd.* Deventer: Van Logghum Slaterus.

Besteman, A. (1974). *De probleem-project-methode in het opbouwwerk; denk-leer-en bijscholingsmateriaal.* Drachten: Wonn.

Beveridge, W. (1942). *Social insurance and allied services: A report.* London: HMSO.

Bodd, J., & Canjels, E. (1994). *Milieuactiviteiten in de wijk.* Zwolle/Utrecht: Project Wijken voor het Milieu.

Boer, J. (1968). *Opbouwwerk; verkenningen op het gebied van community organization in nederlandse verhoudingen.* Arnhem: van Logghum Slaterus.

Borren, S., & Taverne, D. de Wit. (1991). *Het milieu meemaken; De bijdrage van
WVC aan milieuparticipatie.* Utrecht: Stichting Milieu Educatie.

Bourdieu, P. (1977a). *Outline of a theory of practice.* Cambridge: Cambridge
University Press.

- (1977b). *Reproduction in education, society and culture.* London: Sage.

- (1984). *Distinction: Social critique of the judgement of taste.* London: Routledge
& Kegan.

- (ed.). (1993). *La misère du monde.* Paris: Seuil.

Broekman, H. (1987). Sociale innovatie in Drenthe, de ontwikkeling van de
Stichting opbouw Drenthe (1924–1972). *Medelingen Opbouwwerk* (July/
August).

- (1988). *De handelwijze van de opbouwwerker, een inzicht in het interven-
tierepertoire anno 1987.* Drachten: WONN.

- (1991). *Opbouwwerk, methoden, technieken en terreinen.* Den Haag: Dr. Gradus
Hendriks Stichting.

- (1994). *Professioneel opbouwwerk.* Den Haag: Dr. Gradus Hendriks Stichting.

Broekman, H., & Canjels, E. (1989). *Dringende vraagstukken voor de jaren 90.*
Drachten: WONN.

Broekman, H., & Vos, K. (1985). *11 jaar probleem-project-methode in het
Opbouwwerk.* Drachten: Wonn.

Bruce, M. (1961). *The coming of the welfare state.* London: Batsford.

Brugman, H., Engbersen, R., & Tenhaeff, C. (1993). *Contact verbroken? Contact
hersteld!* Utrecht: NIZW.

Buisman, R., de Bass, H., & Didde, R. (eds.). (1991). *Op weg naar een schone
bodem; Verleden, heden en toekomst van de bodemsanering.* Utrecht: Stichting
Nederland Gifvrij.

Carr, E.H. (1951). *The new society.* London: Macmillan.

Coenen, H. (1987). *Handelingsonderzoek als exemplarisch leren.* Groningen:
Konstaple.

Coenen, H., & Leisink, P. (eds.). (1993). *Work and citizenship in the new Europe.*
Aldershot: Elgar.

Craib, I. (1992). *Anthony Giddens.* London: Routledge.

Dahrendorf, R. (1988). *The modern social conflict.* London: Weidenfeld and
Nicolson.

Deelstra, T. (1990). *Natuur in Steden; Voorbeelden uit binnen- en buitenland.*
Rijswijk: Ministerie van Landbouw, Natuurbeheer en Visserij.

Dijkstra, J. (1989). *Opbouw in Spoorwijk, een empirisch onderzoek naar de effecten
van opbouwwerk op locaal niveau.* Delft: Eburon.

Elsch, H. van, & Raspe, A. (1976). *Opbouwwerk in stedelijke situaties.* sHertogenbosch: NIMO.

Engbersen, G. (1987). *Een profaan boek in de openbaring.* Utrecht: RUU.

– (1990). *Publieke bijstandsgeheimen, het ontstaan van een onderklasse in Nederland.* Leiden/Antwepen: Stenfert Kroese.

– (1994). Onderklassevorming in Nederland: De oude stadswijk als Commedia dell Arte. *Tijdschrift voor de Sociale Sector.* 8–14.

Engberson, G., & van der Veen, R. (1987). *Moderne armoede, overleven op het sociaal minimun.* Leiden/Antwerpen: Stenfert Kroese.

Foolen, J. (1993). *Armoede 3 op zoek naar export.* Interne publikatie. Utrecht: Verwey Jonker Instituut. (Commissioned by NIZW, in the context of the EC Action Program).

Fortuin, K. (1991). *Berichten uit de samenleving.* Eerste deelrapportage. sHertogenbosch: NIMO.

– (1994). *Berichten uit de samenleving, syntheserapport.* Utrecht: Verwey-Jonker Instituut.

Fortuin, K., & Hovingh, R. (1992). *Berichten uit de sameleving 2.* Tweede deelrapportage. sHertogenbosch: NIMO.

Gastelaars, M. (1990). Een gedesoriënteerde veranderingswetenschap; Over de geschiedenis van de Nederlandse andragologie. *Kennis en Methode,* 1990(4): 346–67.

Giddens, A. (1984). *The constitution of society.* Cambridge: Polity Press.

– (1990). *The consequences of modernity.* Cambridge: Polity Press.

– (1991). *Modernity and self-identity: Self and society in the late modern age.* Cambridge: Polity Press.

Haberer, P., de Kleijn, G., Nicholas, F., & de Wit, C. (1978). *The neighbourhood approach: Improvement in old neighbourhoods by and on behalf of their inhabitants.* The Hague: State Publisher.

Habermas, J. (1981). *Theorie des kommunikativen handelns.* Frankfurt aM: Suhrkamp

– (1985). *Die neue unuebersichtlichkeit.* Frankfurt aM: Suhrkamp.

Have, T.T. van. (1968). *Klein bestek van de agologie.* Groningen: Wolters Noordhof.

– (1973). *Andragologie in blauwdruk.* Groningen: Tjeenk Willnk

Heek, F. van. (1973). *Van hoogkapitalisme naar verzorgingsstaat: Een halve eeuw sociale verandering, 1920–1970.* Meppel: Boom.

Henderson, P. (1982). *Opbouwwerk in de praktijk.* Deventer: van Logghum Slaterus.

Hendriks, Gradus. (1978). *New trends in social welfare policy in the Netherlands.* Rijswijk: Ministry of Cultural Affairs, Recreation, and Social Welfare.

Hes, J., et al. (1991). *Sociale Vernieuwing en Opbouwwerk.* Den Haag: Dr Gradus Hendriks Stichting.

Hooijdonk, G. van, & Raspe, A. (1993). *Concepties van samenlevingsopbouw, trends 93*. Utrecht: Verwey Jonker Instituut.

HRWB. (1989). *Wijken onder druk: Studie naar de leefbaarheid in wijken met sociaal economische achterstanden*. Den Haag: HRWB.

Huiskens, T. (1988). *Kenniet bestaat niet: Campagne tegen het verval van een na-oorlogse woonwijk te Rotterdam*. Rotterdam: Rio.

Jansen, U., Aalders, A., & Swinnen, H. (1994). *Organisaties van bewoners en schoon bouwen en wonen; een praktijkgericht onderzoek*. Utrecht: Verweij Jonker Institute.

Jong, A. de. (1992). *Verwerven, gebruiken en beoordelen van diensten door ouderen*. Amsterdam: Bureau Welzynsmarketing.

Kleijn, G. de. (1978). *Samen staan we sterk*. sGravenhage: Staatsuitgeverij.

– (1985). *De staat van de stadsvernieuwing*. Utrecht: Vakgroep Stadsstudies RUU.

Koenis, S. (1993). *De precaire professionele identiteit van sociaal werkers*. Utrecht: NIZW.

Koning, E., & Tjallingii, S. (1991). *Ecologie van de stad: Een verkenning*. Wageningen: Platform Stadsecologie.

Korten, D.C. (1984a). Rural development programming: The learning process approach. In Korten & Klauss.

– (1984b). *People-centered development: Towards a framework*. In Korten & Klauss.

Korten, D.C., & Klauss, R. (eds.). *People-centered development, contributions toward theory and planning frameworks*. West Hartford, CT: Kumarian Press.

Koster, A., & Claringbould, M. (1991). *Natuurlijker groenbeheer in Nederlandse gemeenten*. Den Haag: Vereniging van Nederlandse Gemeenten.

Kramer, R.M. (1970). *Community development in Israel and the Netherlands*. Berkeley Institute of International Studies, University of California.

Kroft, H., et al. (1989). *Een tijd zonder werk, een onderzoek naar de levenswereld van langdurig werklozen*. Leiden/Antwerpen: Sternfelt Kroese.

Kunneman, H. (1985). *Habermas theorie van het communicatieve handelen: Een samenvatting*. Meppel: Boom.

Laan, G. v.d. (1990). *Legitimatieproblemen van het maatschappelijk werk*. Utrecht: SWP.

Lange, D. (1992). Partizipation und politikverdrossenheit. *In Dokumentation des 3. Partizipations-Seminars im Rahmen von Poverty 3*. Hamburg: EG-Projekt Eimabüttel.

Leur, W. van de. (1991). Sociale Vernieuwing als 'down to earth' – operatie geschetst vanuit het opbouwwerk. In Joyce Hes (ed.), *Sociale vierniewing en opbouwerk*. Den Haag (G.H.S.).

Lieshout, P. van. (1992). Metamethodiek: de methodiek van de methodiekontwikkeling. *Sociale Interventie*, 1(3): 159–66.

Lijphart, A. (1976). *Verzuiling, pacificatie en kentering in de Nederlanse politiek.* Amsterdam: De Bussy.

Loo, H. van der, Loozen, R., & Oosterman, J. (1988). *Buurt in balans: Levensstijlen in nieuw oudwijk.* Utrecht: Jan van Arkel.

Marsden, D., & Oakley, P. (1991). Future issues and perspectives in the evaluation of social development. *Community Development Journal* (26): Evaluation of social development projects.

Ministerie van Landbouw Natuurbeheer en Visserij. (1992). *Natuur en educatie: Een praktijkbeeld.* Den Haag.

Ministry of Housing. (1993). *The best of both worlds: Sustainability and quality lifestyles in the 21st century.* The Hague.

Ministry of Welfare, Health, and Culture. (1990). *FOZ.* The Hague.

Municipality of Amsterdam. (1993). *Ouderen in Amsterdam.* A Report.

Munters, Q., et al. (eds.). (1983). *Een Kennismaking met de structuratietheorie.* Wageningen: Landbouw Universiteit.

Myrdal, G. (1958). *Beyond the welfare state.* London: Duckworth.

Ortega y Gasset (1975). *Zelfinkeer en verbijstering.* Den Haag: Leopold.

Os, P. van, & van Haeften, P. (1988). *Buurtbeheer veertien keer.* Utrecht: Jan v. Arkel.

Pacilly, C. (1988). *Integraal ouderenwerk, meer kansen voor meer mensen om succesvol ouder te worden.* Sittard: Wozon.

– (1991). *Ouderen aan zet, participatie van ouderen in de ontwikkeling van integraal ouderenbeleid.* Sittard: Wozon.

Peper, B. (1972). *Vorming van welzijnsbeleid.* Boom: Meppel.

Paul, S. (1987). *Community participation in development projects: The World Bank experience.* Discussion papers n° 6. Washington: World Bank.

Pels, D. (1989). *Pierre Bourdieu, opstellen over smaak.* Veldbegrip: Habitus en het.

Plant, Raymond. (1974). *Community and ideology: An essay in applied social philosophy.* London: Routledge and Kegan Paul.

Platform voor Duurzame Ontwikkeling. (1993). *Duurzame ontwikkeling op de lokale agenda 21: Ideeën voor gemeentelijk milieu- en ontwikkelingsbeleid.* Utrecht.

Shubert, C. (1986). Providing urban-based services: A comparative analysis. In G.S. Cheema (ed.), *Reaching the urban poor: Project implementation in developing countries.* London: Westview Press.

Schuyt, T. (1985). *Opbouwwerk en lokaal welzijnsbeleid, modellen van lokaal welzijnsbeleid en de rol van het gesubsidieerde opbouwwerk.* sGravenhage/ Utrecht: VUGA/NOW.

Someren, P. van, et al. (1987). *Criminaliteit en gebouwde omgeving.* Den Haag: VROM.

Stuurgroep Experimenten Volkshuisvesting. (1992). *Vier ecologische woningbouwprojecten vergeleken.* Rotterdam.

Thoenes, P. (1962). *De elite en de verzorgingsstaat.* Leiden: Stenfert Kroese.

Tienen, A.J.M. van, & Zwanikken, W.A.C. (1972). *Opbouwwerk als sociaal agogische methode.* Deventer: van Logghum Slaterus.

Valk, P. de, & Wekwete, K.H. (1990). *Decentralizing for participatory planning? Comparing the experiences of Zimbabwe and other Anglophone countries in Eastern and Southern Africa.* Aldershot: Avebury.

Veen, R. van der. (1982). *Aktivering in opbouw- en vormingswerk, een vergelijking van vier benaderingen.* Baarn: Nelissen.

Veldhuizen, H. van. (ed.). (1980). *De buurt blijft.* Leeuwarden: Oude Stadswijken Overleg.

Vereniging Milieu Defensie. (1992). *Actieplan Nederland Duurzaam.* Amsterdam.

Vereniging van Nederlandse Gemeenten. (1991). *Kaderplan van aanpak.* Den Haag.

– (1994). *Van Glasbak tot zonneboiler; de belangrijkste ontwikkelingen binnen het gemeentelijke milieubeleid.* Den Haag.

Vos, J.T.F., & ten Brink, D.T. (1983). *Opbouwwerk in Noord-Nederland op de keper beschouwd.* Drachten: WONN.

Vos, K. (1985). Bladeren in het PPM-dossier. In Broekman (ed.), *PPPM, een lopend dossier,* 11 jaar probleem project methode in het opbouwwerk. Drachten: WONN.

Waals, M. v.d. (1989). *Methodiek, een nieuwe weg.* Deventer: WESON.

– (1990). *De rede van het opbouwwerk.* Utrecht: Jan van Arkel.

Wit, C. de. (1987). *Niet bij staal alleen, over sociaal-culturele en ruimtelijke veranderingen in het dagelijks leven van Uilen, nu een wijk van Utrecht.* Utrecht: Vakgroep Stadsstudies R.U.I.

– (1992). Stedelijk armoedebeleid in India (Urban poverty-related policies in India). *Derde Wereld* (1992): 4.

Withagen, P., & Jonkers-Kuiper, L. (1993). *Achterstandsbeleid van GGD-en,- analyse en aanbevelingen.* Utrecht: NIZW/VDB.

World Development Report. (1993). *Investing in health.* Oxford: Oxford University Press.

Yeung, Y.M., & McGee, T.G. (1986). *Community participation in delivering urban services in Asia.* Ottawa: International Development Research Centre.

Part V

Israel

Co-ordinated by JOSEPH KATAN

Israel

1. INTRODUCTION
Joseph Katan

The State of Israel, established in 1948, is located at the eastern end of the Mediterranean Sea. It is thus bordered on the west by the sea, on the east by the Kingdom of Jordan, on the south by Egypt, and on the north by Syria and Lebanon. Israel is a very small country, with a total territory of only 21,000 square kilometres (which leaves out Judea and Samaria and the Golan Heights, which have only been under Israeli control since 1967).

The country had a population of 5.67 million people in 1994 of whom 82 percent were Jewish and 18 percent were Arab. Most live in cities, the largest of which are Jerusalem (the capital), Tel Aviv (the economic and cultural centre), and Haifa.

The Jewish population of Israel is extremely heterogeneous, as it is composed primarily of immigrants who arrived after 1948 from approximately a hundred countries. Between 1990 and 1994 alone, over half a million immigrants arrived in Israel, most of them from Russia and other countries of the former Soviet Union. The Arab population is predominantly Moslem, with a minority of Christians and Druse.

Israel is a parliamentary democracy. The head of state is a president elected by the Knesset (parliament) but his functions are primarily symbolic. It is the prime minister who carries the political authority, and this position is filled by the person who heads a majority coalition of political parties. Parliamentary elections are held every four years. Israel is a multiparty state; its 120 members of parliament currently represent eleven political parties.

Israel is clearly a welfare state in its social orientation. The government provides, directly or indirectly, a wide variety of social services in the areas of education, health, income maintenance, housing, employment, and personal services. Many of these services (especially in the realms of income maintenance, education, and health) are anchored in law as mandatory services that must be provided to the population. Services are provided not only by the central government, but also by other organizations, such as local authorities and NGOs. The involvement of these organizations in providing various welfare services has increased in the last few years.

Israel has well-developed agricultural and industrial sectors. The country feeds itself. Textiles, food, chemicals, electronics, and computers are the primary industrial products.

Israel has four major problems. *First*, it has serious defence problems stemming from the animosity that has existed between Israel and the Palestinians and some of the Arab states. These problems have diminished only partially during the most recent peace process. *Second*, there are economic problems such as a large trade deficit and unemployment. The causes of these problems include the huge costs of defence and immigrant absorption and the current international economic situation. *Third*, Israel is beset with social tensions, most of which arise from the relations between religious and secular Jews, and between the various ethnic groups that make up Jewish society. Tensions between ethnic groups have been diminishing recently, but between religious and secular Jews they are escalating. *Fourth*, there are substantial social problems arising from the existence of populations in distress. As a welfare state, Israel provides for the basic needs of its population, but this minimal provision leaves a significant number of individuals and families under the poverty line. This group is composed primarily of the elderly, families with many children, and single-parent families.

Because of Israel's defence and economic problems, and because of the difficulty it has absorbing immigrants from different social and cultural backgrounds, various groups in Israeli society hold the conviction that Israel requires a strong and firmly led central government. Thus, the Israeli government and other central state organizations have always performed key functions in planning and directing the economy, in designing social services, and in initiating various economic and social development programs. Israel's small size has further reinforced the state's pivotal role.

Israel also has certain elements that are essential for the development of a civil society, such as a large number of voluntary organizations that play an active role in various fields, and well-established urban and rural communities that maintain strong local traditions. However, the influence of these elements has been constrained by the strong tenden- cies toward centralization described earlier.

In the wake of various global and national developments in recent years, such as disappointment with government accomplishments, in- creased privatization, the strengthening of local municipalities, and the rise of individualism, Israel's central government has lost some of its power, and certain components of civil society have gained strength. Nevertheless, the government still continues to play a dominant social and economic role.

Community social work, which is striving to generate political decen- tralization, to empower individuals and communities, and to reinforce elements of civil society, is thus confronted with an uncomfortable and discouraging environment in Israel. However, breaches in governmen- tal control and increased trends toward decentralization and local power are providing opportunities for community social work to realize some of its objectives. In the section 'Organizational Structure of Community Work' we will describe and analyse community work in Israel, and the circumstances that influence it, in an attempt to show how such work is carried out in Israel's unique socio-political context. However, this study will begin with a description of three cases that are representative of the practice and issues of community work and development in this country.

2. CURRENT PRACTICE
A. Ossim Shalom: A Community Demonstration Project for Peace and Welfare[1]
Yossi Korazim and Naomi Sheffer

INTRODUCTION

This case study describes a pioneering and innovative community-based preventive project designed to mitigate tensions and hostilities between Jews and Arabs in one of Jerusalem's neighbourhoods.

The project was initiated and carried out on a voluntary basis by a group of Jerusalem social workers who had a strong community work

1 This case study is based on a presentation made by Dr Yossi Korazim and Naomi Sheffer, founding members of Ossim Shalom, at the 12th International Symposium of the International Federation of Social Workers, Washington, DC, July 18–22, 1992.

orientation. In 1990 they founded a grass roots organization called Ossim Shalom. In Hebrew this name has a dual meaning: *ossim* is both the acronym of social workers and the plural form of the verb 'to act'; *shalom* means peace; thus, Ossim Shalom denotes both 'social workers make peace' and 'to act for peace.'

Ossim Shalom is now a steadily growing nonprofit and nonpartisan voluntary organization composed of Jewish and Arab Israeli social workers who view the promotion of peace among Jews and Arabs, as well as among Israel and its neighbours, as one of their basic professional commitments. The organization has decided to advance this goal not only because peace is important in itself, but also because it believes that there are direct links between peace and welfare. Since it was founded, the organization has worked in various directions: convening conferences to discuss issues relating to peace and welfare, organizing workshops on conflict resolution attended by Jews and Arabs, and convening open meetings between Jews and Arabs. Most of these activities have been planned and attended by social workers. The case study described in this paper relates to one of the most conspicuous and concrete activities initiated by Ossim Shalom, that extended beyond professional boundaries and tried to transmit the message of peace and welfare to an external audience: residents of distressed neighbourhoods.

These residents are usually followers of right-wing nationalistic parties, and they are therefore very suspicious of organizations advocating peace among Jews and Arabs. By initiating such a community project, Ossim Shalom has taken on a very complex and difficult social and professional task.

This case study, which describes the main accomplishments of this project and its impact on the community, is divided into four parts. The first places the project in perspective by describing the unique historical, social, and political context in which it was conducted. The second presents the project objectives. The third describes the project's main accomplishments in its first year and the reasons it was discontinued. The summary discusses the main implications that can be drawn from this project.

THE HISTORICAL, POLITICAL, AND SOCIAL CONTEXT

To understand the context of the project, one must recognize the historical framework of the Israeli-Arab conflict. This conflict has existed essentially for over a century and focuses on the control over, and rule of, a small territory. The two nationalities involved differ in terms of culture, ethnicity, and religious heritage. In part, these differences have contributed to the growing support for extremism on both sides. Since Israel's independence in 1948, there have been six wars with neighbouring Arab countries, as well as hundreds of acts of hostility and retaliation across and within borders.

The Arab minority in Israel currently consists of approximately 950,000 in the pre–1967 War territory (within the 'Green Line'), and an additional 1.5 million living on the West Bank of the Jordan (which has been under Israeli control since 1967) and on the Gaza Strip (which has been under Palestinian control since 1994). This is a sizeable proportion of the total Israeli population of about 5.4 million.

The geographic situation of Israel also plays a part in the conflict. Greater Israel is quite small; it takes only eight hours to drive from the north end to the south and one-and-a-half hours to drive from the eastern border to the western, including the occupied territories. Within this area, the potential for daily friction between Arabs and Jews is pronounced, especially in mixed cities but also in Jewish areas, where thousands of Arabs work and commute during the day. An example of such a mixed city is Jerusalem. One-quarter of the city's half million people are Arabs, the majority of whom are Muslims. The Arabs live in separate neighbourhoods with distinct cultural, religious, and social characteristics, but many of them work and shop in the closed Jewish neighbourhoods.

As a result of this physical closeness between Jews and Arabs and the daily contacts among them, Jerusalem became a main location for terrorist acts initiated by Arabs against innocent Jews. Generally, these acts have led to aggressive retaliation by Jews against Arabs. This situation creates an insecure climate, stimulates extremism, and intensifies the hostility between Jews and Arabs.

THE PROJECT'S OBJECTIVES

In this climate of deepening hostility and mistrust, Ossim Shalom sought to develop a preventive community-based project that would try to break this negative chain of events and lay the foundation for better relations between Jews and Arabs. The organization did not pretend that it could stop acts of terrorism against Jews. Instead it acted on its strong conviction that for ethical and pragmatic reasons, retaliation by Jews against innocent Arabs had to be prevented, and that preventing these aggressive reactions could constitute a first stage in the creation of improved relations between Jews and Arabs living in closed neighbourhoods.

The event that spurred Ossim Shalom to initiate and implement the project occurred in the summer of 1990, when two Jewish teenagers were killed by Arab terrorists. Their brutal murder prompted a citywide outburst of violence by Jews against innocent Arabs. In the neighbourhood where the murder occurred, hundreds of Jews attacked Arabs returning home after work.

Ossim Shalom activists understood that in order to make their idea a reality, they had to start with a demonstration project that would focus on trying to change citizens' attitudes and behaviour in one of the neighbourhoods in which the violence had occurred. They also realized that in launching such a project, they faced two main challenges: securing the support and assistance of the municipality of Jerusalem; and gaining the trust and co-operation of the neighbourhood's residents. The activities of the project team were designed to deal with these challenges. Their accomplishments will be described in the following section.

THE PROJECT'S ACTIVITIES

Securing the Municipality's Support
Securing the municipality's support for the project was viewed as vital for three main reasons: first, to enter the neighbourhood and implement the project; second, to secure resources for implementing the project; and third, to encourage residents to co-operate with the project.

In order to get the city's support, Ossim Shalom arranged a meeting with the city's director general. At that meeting, the group's representatives presented the project idea and its main objectives, and asked for support. It was clear at that initial meeting that city officials were deeply concerned about the increase in retaliatory attacks against Arabs, and positively disposed to developing preventive programs that would address this issue. Ossim Shalom had made its proposal at an opportune time.

The city's interest was reflected in the agreements reached in that meeting. The city's director, on behalf of the municipality, formally requested Ossim Shalom to develop a professional intervention program aimed at preventing future outbursts of violence against innocent Arabs in Jerusalem neighbourhoods, and appointed a senior official –

the Director of Social and Youth Services – as the city's liaison with Ossim Shalom. Furthermore, Ossim Shalom and the city agreed that if the intervention model was successful, it would be carried out in other high-risk neighbourhoods.

Choosing a Neighbourhood

Following the meeting, Ossim Shalom and the city established a steering committee. The city's representatives on the committee included social workers and community and youth workers from various city departments. The committee's first task was to select a proper setting for the project.

It reviewed and analysed the patterns of violence in Jerusalem and found that certain districts were more likely than others to be the focus of retaliatory attacks. These sites had four general characteristics:

- They were public gathering areas where Jews and Arabs mingled, such as markets and industrial areas.
- The were 'seam' neighbourhoods – that is, on the border between Jewish and Arab areas.
- They were critical junctions and/or main roads running though Jewish neighbourhoods, and were heavily used by Arabs commuting to and from work.
- They were neighbourhoods characterized by low socio-economic levels and several forms of social distress.

The neighbourhood finally selected for the project was chosen according to these four criteria. It is located next to an industrial and commercial area that serves as a trading and working area for many Arabs, and is situated on a critical main road that Arabs use for commuting to and from work. The neighbourhood also has a low socio-economic profile, with many characteristics of social distress, such as high housing density, low incomes, high rates of drug abuse, prostitution (not necessarily by local residents), frequent community and family violence, and high youth and adult unemployment. Also, the neighbourhood had been the site of both terrorist acts and retaliatory attacks.

However, the neighbourhood also had two assets that turned out to be important in planning and implementing the project: an active and recognized local leadership, and a group of municipal social workers who operated in the neighbourhood and knew it very well.

Gaining the Neighbourhood's Trust

Gaining the neighbourhood's trust was perceived by the steering committee as the project's major challenge. Thus, a series of meetings were initiated between the project team and members of three important local committees: the neighbourhood committee, the women's club, and the neighbourhood youth council.

The first meeting was held with the neighbourhood committee. The project team introduced the concept of Ossim Shalom and its emphasis on the links between peace and welfare, and then described the main objectives of the project. The discussion that followed the presentation focused on two main issues: the political identity of Ossim Shalom, and its potential benefits for the neighbourhood. Ossim Shalom's members described their political inclinations (commitment to peace and welfare), but pointed out that their organization was nonpartisan in nature. They also emphasized their sincere desire to help neighbourhood residents improve their quality of life. The neighbourhood committee members, some of them followers of right-wing parties, were at first suspicious of the project's real nature, but were eventually convinced that it might help the neighbourhood.

A contract was finally agreed upon with the neighbourhood committee. It stipulated that the project team would help the neighbourhood get better and more services and resources from the municipality, and that the neighbourhood committee would co-operate with the team in trying to change the reactions and attitudes of residents towards Arabs.

The meeting with the second community group, the women's club, proved to be the most challenging and exciting. After presenting their ideas, the Ossim Shalom members, accompanied by the neighbourhood committee chairman, were aggressively confronted by one of the women, who said, 'I've been listening to you carefully, and I want you to know that I and some of my friends here [she indicated two or three other women] took part in the stoning of Arabs last year. I was sorry then not to have been a man because I could have thrown larger stones. The next time Arabs murder innocent Jews in Jerusalem, I will make sure that the whole neighbourhood will be organized so that no Arabs will reach their homes alive.' After a long silence, the Ossim Shalom members asked the group if that was how they all felt. A somewhat older woman placed herself in direct opposition to the former speaker and expressed her embarrassment and shame for the violent reaction against Arabs. She spoke about the days before the War of Independence in 1948, when Jews and Arabs lived peacefully in the same neighbourhood. She also expressed her concern about the stigma the violence had attached to the neighbourhood, and its possible negative impact on housing prices. Her forthright comments stimulated other women to state their positions instead of sitting in uneasy silence. At the end of the meeting the group agreed to participate in the project.

The meeting with the third community group – the neighbourhood youth council – was also fruitful, and its members agreed to co-operate with the project. Thus, the Ossim Shalom team had succeeded in overcoming local suspicions and reservations and in convincing neighbourhood activists to support the project and to take part in its planning and implementation.

One of the immediate results of the local activists' readiness to participate in the project was the formation of a permanent Ossim Shalom Neighbourhood Steering Committee (NSC) of fourteen members, including seven delegates from the three community groups, four delegates from the municipality's social services department (which included workers involved at the neighbourhood level), and three members of Ossim Shalom.

The NSC, which met on a monthly basis, decided to concentrate on the four main objectives:

- Understanding neighbourhood needs and problems through local participation.
- Building group cohesion and trust among its members.
- Clarifying personal values and attitudes of those involved in the project.
- Serving as the catalyst for the development of similar projects in other city neighbourhoods.

Team members were able to show their commitment to the neighbourhood's well-being at an early stage of the project's development through an unfortunate event. The collapse of half an apartment building had left forty families homeless, and those remaining in the building were terrified for their safety. Ossim Shalom members appeared immediately on the scene and joined the city's emergency task force in offering assistance to the residents. The trust they thereby established with neighbourhood activists and residents enabled the project team to enter the neighbourhood and helped greatly in facilitating the project.

The two main accomplishments of the project will be described in the following section.

THE PROJECT'S MAIN ACCOMPLISHMENTS

The team's plan for the first year included the following activities:

- The organization of an opening event to mark the beginning of the project's activities in the neighbourhood.
- The setting up of a conflict resolution workshop for community leaders and activists.
- The organization of intergroup and intercommunity meetings with leaders and activists from Arab neighbourhoods in and around Jerusalem.
- The documentation of lessons learned from the 1990 outbreak of violence in the neighbourhood against Arabs.
- The development of a plan for preventive community intervention that could be applied to deal with any future outbreaks of violence against Arabs.

As of July 1992 the project had accomplished two of these proposed activities and was continuing to plan the others.

The first major accomplishment was the organization of an open community meeting designed to introduce the project's ideas, objectives, and specific programs to neighbourhood residents, and to get their support. At the meeting the speakers representing the neighbourhood complained about the lack of adequate services in the community. The Ossim Shalom members emphasized the links between peace and welfare and expressed their commitment to the neighbourhood's well-being. The speaker representing Ossim Shalom faced some strong antagonism from several local residents, who did not welcome the involvement of this 'peace-loving' organization in the neighbourhood. The neighbourhood activists who chaired the meeting handled this confrontation respectfully but assertively. One of the strongest and most heartfelt of the speeches supporting co-operation with Ossim Shalom came from an NSC member who had originally opposed the entry into the neighbourhood of an organization with leftist leanings. This support signalled that Ossim Shalom had succeeded in building bridges with community leaders.

The second major accomplishment of the project was the conflict resolution workshop. The participants included not only neighbourhood activists who were members of the NSC, but also other residents. Guided by members of the project team, the workshop met seven times on a weekly basis for a total of twenty hours. The major goal of the work-shop was to prepare the participants for a leadership role in resolving conflicts. The expectation was that the workshop would change the attitudes of these leaders; and equip them with skills that would en-hance their capacity to improve the neighbourhood; and prevent retali-ation against innocent Arabs following acts of terror.

The workshop emphasized five main areas:

- Interpersonal communication.
- Awareness of the meaning and roots of stereotypical attitudes and their societal and behavioural implications.
- Understanding the sources of fear and anxiety about strangers (especially Arabs).
- Practising conflict resolution methods.
- Setting priorities in dealing with social problems and issues.

At first, the workshop organizers were quite concerned about the considerable differences in age among the group's members. However, that heterogeneity turned out to be an asset: the openness and frank-ness among its members helped to create of a sense of familial intimacy, which added to the group's cohesion. At the end of the workshop the participants expressed their readiness and willingness to take part in a joint workshop or meeting with an Arab community group. Thus, the workshop had achieved one of its major objectives: to lay the founda-tion for a different kind of relationship between Jews and Arabs, in which tensions and hostilities could be mitigated.

However, at this stage, project activities stopped, and plans for orga-nizing a joint meeting between the neighbourhood activists and the leaders of an Arab neighbourhood and for utilizing the neighbourhood intervention model developed in other communities did not material-ize. The discontinuation of the project stemmed from three interrelated factors.

First, the national elections at the end of 1992 and the municipal elec-tions in the middle of 1993 had occupied the full attention of the local public as well as of city officials for more than seven months, and this reduced both support and resources for the project.

Second, the victory of Labour (a social democratic party) in the na-tional elections and the removal of the Likud (a right-wing party) from government resulted in political upheaval. Relative to the Likud, Labour favoured a moderate and compromising approach toward the Arabs.

Among peace activists (including Ossim Shalom members) there was a sense that the new government would assume the job of advancing the cause of peace among Jews and Arabs, and that they could shift their activities to other areas.

Third, for more than a year the Ossim Shalom members had been maintaining a very intensive involvement in the neighbourhood. Often they had devoted two, sometimes three, evenings per week to the project, and this on a voluntary basis. That they withdrew from the project was due as much to their own exhaustion as it was to external circumstances (i.e., the elections and their results).

SUMMARY

The way the project ended demonstrates the inherent weaknesses of an undertaking that is complex and demanding and that depends entirely on the motivation, commitment, and concrete involvement of volunteers and on uncertain and changing circumstances.

However, the difficulties that were encountered in continuing the project and achieving its various objectives do not erase the significance of its accomplishments. It had succeeded in gaining legitimacy from a distressed neighbourhood that at first had been lukewarm in its welcome, with some citizens rejecting any intrusion of peace activists calling for improved relationships between Jews and Arabs. Ossim Shalom had also succeeded in convincing the neighbourhood leadership to take part in an effort to change residents' attitudes and behaviour toward Arabs.

Furthermore, while the vicious circle of terrorist attacks and aggressive reactions in Jerusalem did not end when the project was discontinued, incidents of retaliatory attacks against innocent Arabs did stop occurring in that specific neighbourhood.

These achievements can be attributed at least partially to the professional approach adopted by the project initiators. They made a special effort to gain the co-operation of neighbourhood activists and to involve them in project planning and implementation. And by stressing that the project was primarily designed to help the neighbourhood improve its quality of life, they were able to gain the community's trust. They also stressed that continuous attacks against Arabs would be harmful to the neighbourhood, severely damaging its image in the city, depreciating the value of houses, and weakening the municipality's readiness to invest there. Clearly, Ossim Shalom recognized that suggesting the project's main objective was to improve Jewish-Arab relations might jeopardize the project from the beginning. The group adapted its approach accordingly.

There were two main factors had helped the project's team to convince the neighbourhood activists – and through them the other residents – that the project could really be beneficial to them: the backing of the city and its readiness to develop and improve community services; and the active involvement of city workers (including Ossim Shalom members) in the project.

In sum, this project demonstrates that it is possible to link diverse CD objectives: for example, to improve the quality of life in a distressed neighbourhood while creating more peaceful interethnic relations in that same neighbourhood. At the same time, the discontinuation of the project indicates that professional good will, devotion, and skills are not sufficient by themselves to carry out such a complex project. A more solid and stable organizational basis is needed for such an undertaking.

B. Pioneering Community Work in a Jewish Ultra-Orthodox Community in Jerusalem[2]
Debra Shapiro

JERUSALEM – BACKGROUND AND INTRODUCTION

Jerusalem is undoubtedly the most pluralistic city in Israel. It has over half a million people, of whom nearly 30 percent are Arabs and almost 70 percent are Jews. In addition, the Jewish population is highly heterogeneous: about two-thirds are modern secular and Orthodox Jews, and the rest are ultra-Orthodox (UO). These four groups, although they tend to live separately, are close together geographically: the Arabs in East Jerusalem, the large majority of the UO in the northern part of the city, and the remaining groups spread out in the rest of the city. Among the Jewish population, the UO community is the most rapidly expanding one. This is mainly because of the high fertility rate among UO families. In fact, about half the Jewish children in Jerusalem attend a separate system of UO schools.

---

2 This case study was written by Deborah Shapiro, director of the Community and Youth Unit for the Ultra-Orthodox Population, the Community and Youth Division, Municipality of Jerusalem.

As a city composed of a plethora of neighbourhoods, Jerusalem is characterized by a very active and comprehensive community work department. However, until about five years ago community workers were involved only in secular and Orthodox neighbourhoods. The UO neighbourhoods were considered an unknown land and closed territory for professional community work. This situation has changed in recent years. That community workers are now entering UO neighbourhoods reflects a growing predisposition among UO Jews to utilize services provided by the municipality and other outside organizations.

The UO community, which was once relatively self-sufficient in providing basic services for its members, has recently become more consumer oriented and is increasingly turning to the city for community services and development. In turn, the city has shown an increasing interest in meeting the needs of the UO population, in light of the growth within their neighbourhoods.

This case study describes and analyses the involvement and activities of a community worker in one UO neighbourhood, and is divided into three main parts. The first part portrays the unique social and cultural characteristics of the UO community and discusses its reaction to the appearance of professional community workers. The second part describes the main activities of the community worker in the neighbourhood – the challenges she faced and how she coped with them. The third analyses her success in introducing community work interventions into this unique social setting.

THE CHARACTERISTICS OF THE ULTRA-ORTHODOX COMMUNITY

There are several publications that describe and analyse UO Jews and their communities, and identify their characteristics (El-Or, 1994; Friedman, 1988, 1991; Shilhav, 1991a, 1991b). The UO Jews live in separate and distinct neighbourhoods, where they constitute all or a large majority of the residents. All their religious institutions, such as synagogues and schools, are located within these neighbourhoods. In addition, every UO neighbourhood has a specific name and distinct geographical boundaries. There is a strong emphasis on the strict preservation of religious norms, codes, and modes of behaviour within these neighbourhoods; this is reflected in people's dress, the separation between men and women, and total religious observance on Saturdays and holy days. Even nonresidents are required on entering these neighbourhoods to comply with these strict norms. Furthermore, the

UO community is characterized by a broad, independent network of voluntary and philanthropic organizations that substitute, at least in part, for external services.

The unique nature of the UO community is particularly evident in the relationships between men and women. Most UO men pursue religious studies as a full- or part-time occupation as opposed to earning a livelihood. Because of their involvement in religion-based networks that take care of their social needs, they are somewhat detached from the needs of women and children. This has a strong impact on the status of women. Although tradition instructs them to pursue indoor household activities, economic realities have compelled quite a few of them to enter the labour force. Many women are now the chief breadwinners in their families. Also, because the men have devoted themselves to religion, women have formed their own interpersonal networks.

The preservation of religious norms and modes of behaviour is coupled with the rejection of modern and secular values. The UO community refrains as much as possible from developing social, cultural, and economic relationships with outsiders. Past efforts to safeguard the community's unique identity have led to an almost total isolation from the surrounding environment, and to the formation of autonomous and separate social services (especially charity organizations).

In recent years, though, many UO Jews (although by no means all of them) have grown more willing to utilize external services and to develop relationships with the secular environment. The entry of women into the labour force is one manifestation of this, and has greatly influenced the community's course of development. However, this opening up to the secular world is considered acceptable only as long as it serves the UO community's interests and doesn't threaten its erosion. This increased willingness to 'reach out' is also reflected in the community's increasingly active role in the local social and political arena. While the city's mayor and most of the city council are secular or moderately orthodox Jews, representatives of the growing ultra-Orthodox community have gained a strong influence in the council and control important municipal departments.

These political developments, and the more open approach of the UO community, are guided by several motives, one of which is the community's understanding and conviction that relationships with the outside are vital for ensuring the provision of the external resources needed for maintaining the community's religious, educational, and welfare institutions and improving its members' quality of life.

All of the above suggests some of the factors that hinder professional community work in the UO community. For instance, UO communities have steadfastly refused to support professional interventions that originate in the secular environment. Also, the city has been reluctant to invest resources and develop programs in UO neighbourhoods where the main interest of the residents is to exploit the city's services on an instrumental level rather than an organizational one. Furthermore, there are inherent contradictions between the UO culture and values and the professional values that guide the activities of community workers. One such conflict is between those professional values which stress equality, self-determination, and empowerment and those religious norms which emphasize the unique qualities and roles of each gender and demand total obedience to religious authorities.

Despite these limitations and difficulties, professional community work has penetrated UO neighbourhoods. The factors that have contributed to this change, and the involvement of a community worker in one particular neighbourhood, will be described in the following section.

COMMUNITY WORK IN BUCHARIM-BEIT YISRAEL NEIGHBOURHOOD

Bucharim-Beit Yisrael is a relatively small neighbourhood on the southern edge of the city's UO quarter. It has a population of about 1,800 households (10,000 people). The vast majority of residents (around 85%) are UO, and the remainder are Orthodox and traditional-secular.

The 1983 Census reported that the neighbourhood had severe social problems such as housing congestion, low incomes, and poor services. The neighbourhood's low socio-economic status convinced government and city authorities to include it in Project Renewal (PR), which began in the late 1970s.

Community work and development was an integral component of the project's activities in all the neighbourhoods that were included in its framework. Thus, since the project's inception a community worker has been assigned to Bucharim-Beit Yisrael by the city's community work department.

Over the years, the project's managers and the UO community experienced great difficulties in establishing positive relations, and community work did not succeed in changing this situation. Consequently, many of the project's activities in the neighbourhood catered mostly to the needs of the secular and Orthodox residents.

Thus, when a new community worker was assigned to the neighbourhood in 1988, she faced two main challenges: first, building proper relations with the UO community; and second, improving the poor community services provided to the members of this community. The situation was even more difficult because at that time the project was forming plans to withdraw from the neighbourhood.

The main tasks of the community worker were, therefore, to build meaningful links with the UO community, to develop new relations between that community and both the city and the project, to help organize local resident's groups, and to improve the quality of life in the neighbourhood. Three of the many programs in which the community worker was involved are described below.

Establishing a Community Centre
In the early 1980s, when the project in Bucharim-Beit Yisrael was in its first stages, the mayor of Jerusalem suggested establishing a community centre in the neighbourhood. The initiative encountered strong opposition from religious leaders in both the neighbourhood and the city: they feared that such a centre would promote secular values and threaten the UO culture. The city authorities had done little to find out whether the community wanted such a centre, and had not involved community representatives in its planning; as a result, the community opposed the centre, and it wasn't built.

Following her assignment to the neighbourhood, the community worker decided to re-examine the issue of establishing a community centre, but this time with the full participation of local residents and with sensitivity to the community's values and culture. Her first step was to organize a neighbourhood committee of eight women, whose main function was to assess the needs of women and their children. The emphasis on women's and children's social needs stemmed from the unique situation of UO women, as described in the introduction to this case study.

The committee conducted a needs assessment survey that included one hundred families. Most of those surveyed said there was a need for a community centre that would provide a wide range of social and recreational activities for women and children, including physical education, dance classes, a health club, English classes, parent groups, and arts and crafts and religious study classes.

While these findings indicated real community needs and a desire to cope with them, they also exposed the difficulties inherent in any attempt to introduce new concepts into a conservative religious community.

UO culture rejects the pursuit of universal, recreational leisure activities, viewing them as a threat to the community's full compliance with religious standards. For instance, a recent ruling by the Orthodox assembly (the most extreme ruling authority within the UO community) banned dance classes for women because they could lead to immodest and undesirable physical behaviour. Value conflicts also emerged regarding lectures on health issues and the formation of parent groups. While most of the women expressed a willingness to attend such activities, the community worker understood that in order to establish a viable community centre that would meet women's social needs, she would have to mobilize wide support and legitimacy within the community and take into account its views, expectations, restrictions, and sensitivities. In order to achieve this objective, she activated the women's committee, which assumed the responsibility for planning the centre's activities and shaped its organizational structure. The principle that guided the committee and the community worker was that the centre's activities would generally be supervised by UO authorities and that the programs would comply with religious requirements. For instance, the dance classes would be instructed by UO women and include only women.

Thus, the planning of the centre's activities was conducted with full local participation. Furthermore, it was based on a continual process of dialogue within the UO community and between that community and the city and other external organizations. However, while trying to overcome resistance to the centre within the UO community, the community worker faced another difficulty: the city and project officials were reluctant to support the centre. This reluctance had several sources: lack of confidence in the city's ability to serve the specific needs of the UO community; opposition to the idea of allocating resources to a population that had cut itself off geographically, culturally, and socially from the secular world; and an unwillingness to collaborate with a community that wanted to exploit the state and the city.

The community worker dealt with this problem by opening channels of communication between representatives of the community and city officials. The resulting dialogue succeeded in converting mistrust, suspicion, and apprehension into trust, understanding, and mutual acceptance; and has helped both sides develop meaningful relationships and define common goals.

The community worker had succeeded in overcoming the resistance of both the UO community and the municipality, and in building proper relationships between them; as a result, a branch of a nearby community centre was opened in the neighbourhood. This centre now offers a variety of recreational, cultural, and social activities for women and children, including classes, support groups for disadvantaged mothers, enrichment programs for kindergarten children, a study centre for school-children, a games library, and workshops for training men and women for community leadership. In addition, the centre has helped establish a 'House for UO Women,' which provides welfare and social services to local women. This house is managed by the city welfare department.

Publication of a Neighbourhood Paper
During the 1980s, Project Renewal published a bimonthly newspaper in the neighbourhood. Assuming that the newspaper would stop publishing when the project withdrew from the neighbourhood, the community worker initiated the establishment of a new neighbourhood newspaper, to be managed and edited by the residents themselves. The main objectives in this were to improve channels of communication within the community, to enhance residents' participation in local affairs, and to contribute to the growth of an active local leadership composed of women. To this end, in the summer of 1992 the worker organized and held nine weekly workshops, which were attended by a group of local women interested in taking an active part in the new paper. The main objectives of the workshops were to equip the participants with the knowledge and skills necessary for publishing and issuing a local newspaper, to discuss its character and content, and to organize a board that would be responsible for the newspaper's publication. At the end of the workshop series, a board composed of twelve women was established; eleven board members belonged to the UO community, and one was secular.

Publishing a newspaper in a secular community doesn't raise any special internal problems; doing so in a UO context is a very complicated and complex process. The UO community's religious leaders constantly warn of the dangers of secular newspapers, which practise no censorship and therefore publish news about violence, sex, and other matters considered intolerable in UO circles. Thus, different sectors of the UO community publish their own national and local newspapers and forbid their followers to read secular newspapers or to follow the media, including television. Some groups within the UO community discourage their members from listening to the radio.

These sensitivities and difficulties were made obvious in the board's discussions about the objectives of the newspaper and its policies and content. The board's first meeting was devoted to such questions as these: Who would be the publication authority? Would a religious authority have to be consulted on every publication? Would the contents need to be censored? Would the newspaper have a clear religious nature, and if it did, how would it relate to the needs and interests of the neighbourhood's secular minority? Would the newspaper raise issues – such as alienated youth, homelessness, and alcoholism – that are controversial within the UO community?

With regard to these questions, there were strong differences of opinion among the women that stemmed from their different attitudes toward social conduct and modesty, and their different feelings about secularism (El-Or, 1994). A few board members believed that they could not publish a newspaper without the permission of an Orthodox authority. Most members believed that Orthodox leaders need only be consulted on specific issues, and that the nature of the newspaper should absolutely be determined by the board itself.

The board's decision on these issues was a compromise: the newspaper would emphasize its UO character, while maintaining its autonomy. The board's policy included the following components: First, the board as a group would not involve in its decisions a religious authority who would function as a censor, but members could choose to consult with such an authority on material that they personally prepared for the newspaper. Second, since publication of women's names could be regarded as an infringement on modesty according to religious norms, writers would be allowed to submit articles and information to the newspaper under a pen name. Third, each newspaper would be published with this note: 'Edited by UO women.' After these decisions were made, the only secular member of the board resigned, claiming that a newspaper so clearly UO in its outlook would not represent the interests of the community's secular minority.

The board's approach was that the newspaper had to be accepted by the UO authorities, lest it be banned by extreme UO elements, as Project Renewal's newspaper had been in previous years. The community worker supported this approach because she believed that the publication of a newspaper by a local group of active women constituted a vital social change, and that such a change in this unique setting could not be attained without certain accommodations and compromises. As often happened, she had to remember the cultural context of her work.

The newspaper was published every two months and improved communication within the community and between the community and the municipality. It also promoted further awareness of local needs and problems, and showed that an active group of local UO women could plan and implement a community project.

Activating UO Men
In addition to establishing a community centre and publishing a neighbourhood newspaper, local women took part in other community activities. They convinced the municipality to invest more resources in the neighbourhood and to improve services. The municipality has since developed or refurbished neighbourhood parks, and installed street benches. Also, the city's health department has begun planning a 'mother and child centre' in the neighbourhood that will provide medical services to pregnant women, mothers, and young children.

The community worker understood that without men's participation, broad community grass roots activity would not expand and her success with women would be jeopardized. Thus, while she focused on women, she also encouraged men to take part in various community activities. To this end, she tried to get the support of UO city council members to influence local men to be active in the neighbourhood. The politicians told her they had limited capacity to encourage male participation at the expense of religious studies. After a long-planned publicity campaign in the middle of 1992, a group of twelve men agreed to participate in an eighteen-week leadership workshop. After that time they formed a committee that dealt with issues and problems relating to the neighbourhood's physical environment. This represented significant progress in getting UO men to become involved in community activities.

The above review of community work activities in Bucharim-Beit Yisrael indicates that its major contributions to the community were these: it fostered local leadership, especially among women; it actively involved these women in local affairs; it built bridges of understanding and co-operation within the neighbourhood; and it improved local services. All of this was accomplished without jeopardizing the unique cultural and religious characteristics of the community. The factors that may explain this success are discussed in the following section.

FACTORS AFFECTING THE DEVELOPMENT OF COMMUNITY WORK
IN THE NEIGHBOURHOOD

The Community Worker's Religious and Cultural Closeness to the Community

One of the issues that has been studied in recent years is the relation-ship between social workers' religious and cultural values and those of their clients', and how important shared values are in determining the degree of the clients' growth and change (Loewenberg, 1985). This case study sheds additional light on this issue. The community worker held the same religious values as the people of the neighbourhood. Her personal behaviour, including her dress and speech, was similar to that of most of the neighbourhood residents. Furthermore, she often visited residents' homes and was seen daily on the neighbourhood's streets, so her personal lifestyle was well known in the community. Likewise, her commitment to Orthodox religious practices made it esaier for her to establish trustworthy mutual relationships with the community.

Because of these shared values, the worker understood the meaning and significance of the religious norms, codes, and symbols in the community's life and was able to find proper ways to convince local residents that her initiatives would not contravene religious values, but would in fact serve the community's interests if they were channelled with insight and sensitivity. She accepted and respected community values and often acted on them, even when they differed from her own. The community's residents reciprocated by showing their readiness to co-operate with her. It should be mentioned, however, that although strictly Orthodox, the community worker did not identify with any particular Orthodox group. This was to her advantage, since it enabled her to exercise objectivity in dealing and interacting with various UO groups and mediating between them.

Combining Community Work Roles with Religious Dimensions

In all her activities the community worker took into account the reli-gious dimension and its requirements. This meant, among other things, separating activities between the sexes (such as initiating different local committees for men and women); obtaining the confirmation of a recognized local Orthodox leader for every program that might have religious/ethical implications (such as the recreational activities in the community centre); and supporting the religious character of the neighbourhood newspaper. This orientation didn't always coincide with the worker's professional and ideological beliefs, but she decided to allow UO religious and cultural consideration to take precedence, under the assumption that this was a vital prerequisite for penetrating the community and achieving important professional objectives.

The Worker as a Woman

The fact that the worker was a woman also had significant implications. It is doubtful that a male worker would have succeeded in establishing as close a relationship with the local women, because of the religious restrictions on contact between the sexes. In all likelihood, a male community worker who was religious would have had more success in fostering community activity among the male residents.

However, this case indicates that employing a female worker had advantages: she was able to form emotional bonds with the women, reinforce their ability to take on leadership roles, and promote improvements in quality of life. These improvements were possible because the UO women acted as boundary mediators between the secular world and the UO community. They were contacts for the men in their attempts to accommodate and control the impact of secular norms on the UO community.

The Worker's Affiliation with the Municipality

While the worker's orthodox style of life helped her build meaningful links with the UO community, her affiliation as a municipal employee with Project Renewal and her acquaintance with city officials helped her establish contact between the community and these external bodies and to mobilize the resources that were necessary for developing services and programs in the neighbourhood.

The worker was convinced that the neighbourhood had serious problems that required the city's intervention; therefore, she often acted as an advocate, representing the neighbourhood residents vis-à-vis city officials. This approach cost her some support among PR workers, who believed she was identifying too strongly with the community, but she was supported by the municipality's community work department, which viewed her advocacy role as professionally correct. Her success in building bridges between various city departments and the neighbourhood contributed to a significant improvement in the quality of life of its residents.

The success of community work in introducing several meaningful changes into this unique socio-cultural context originated in the worker's good relationship with both the community and the secular world, and in her ability to build relationships between the two without jeopardizing the community's unique characteristics.

SUMMARY

Until recently, UO neighbourhoods were always viewed as closed to the interventions of professional community workers. In fact, for many years community workers didn't enter these unique neighbourhoods.

Thus, this case describes a pioneering and successful attempt by a community worker to change this situation, and to show that community work *can* play an important role in UO neighbourhoods. Despite the value discrepancies between the UO community and the city, the community worker succeeded in adopting a number of roles such as facilitator, mediator, developer, empowerer, planner, organizer, activator, and advocate, while applying the appropriate professional sensitivity and skill. Community work promoted community leadership and service development that was directly relevant to the UO residents.

In recent years, UO politicians have been seeking to reorganize some municipal services to cater to the UO population; meanwhile, professionals are tailoring the lessons learned from the Bucharim-Beit Yisrael model to meet UO community needs all over the city. The authorities must reinforce the achievements of their community workers by including the lessons of Bucharim-Beit Yisrael in training programs for workers.

This case proves that it is possible to overcome multicultural differences, and to harness deeply rooted conflicts to promote positive action. As a result of this success, the community work approach, which puts an emphasis on resident participation, the growth of local leadership, and the planning of programs and services congruent with people's needs, is currently being applied in other UO neighbourhoods in Jerusalem.

C. Training Local Activists[3]
Joseph Katan with Joseph Pardes

INTRODUCTION

Active and meaningful participation of citizens in their communities is considered to be one of the cornerstones of community work in Israel,

3 This case study is based on four main sources: Pardes (1988, 1989, 1993) and York and Havassy (1993). Additional information was provided by Yosef Pardes, previous director of the Service for Community Work in the Ministry of Labour and Social Affairs.

given this country's unique circumstances as a heterogeneous and complex society facing many security, economic, and social challenges. The emphasis on citizen participation is designed to serve several objectives:

- Strengthening citizens' identification with their communities.
- Improving relations between clients and service organizations, thereby bridging possible gaps between them.
- Encouraging citizens to support various programs initiated by central or local organizations, and mobilizing them to take part in their development and implementation.
- Encouraging citizens to participate in improving the quality of life in their communities.

Thus, citizen participation is viewed as a mechanism for promoting active citizenship, social integration, and a better quality of life.

The following case study describes a program to establish local schools throughout the country for training citizens in community work. These schools are for citizens who are already active in their communities, or who have demonstrated the potential and willingness to be active. The program's main purpose is to improve the skills of grass roots activists so as to strengthen their effectiveness in working with representatives of local and national organizations.

This section has four main parts. The first describes the main objectives of the program, the second reviews the major stages of establishing and developing such a program, the third is a brief look at the scope and dimensions of the program as of the end of 1994, and the fourth summarizes a survey that was conducted of the graduates of the program.

OBJECTIVES OF THE TRAINING PROGRAM

The program was initiated by the Ministry of Labour and Social Affairs. The main objectives of the training program coincide with the expectations emphasized by the ministry's Service for Community Work (SCW), and with its image of what functions a community worker should be able to perform. Those functions include:

- Identifying and assessing local needs.
- Co-operating with local authority workers, and with functionaries of other organizations, in the planning, development, and implementation of services suited to the needs of various local populations.

- Interacting with local residents, mobilizing their support and involvement in various community activities.
- Building proper links with external organizations (such as government ministries and national voluntary organizations) and convincing them to invest resources in the community.
- Managing local grass roots organizations such as neighbourhood committees and self-help groups.
- In the matter of specific local needs, increasing the sensitivity and responsiveness of welfare departments, health clinics, and the education ministry, and similar service agencies, both local and national.
- Strengthening the identification of local residents with the community.

These components of the activist's role reflect the principles, perceptions, and objectives of community work emphasized by the SCW: fostering citizen participation, strengthening local identification, and building proper and consensual relationships between citizens and formal service agencies.

The SCW initiated the idea of developing schools for community activists throughout the country, set the main objectives, and urged community work units in local welfare departments in various cities, towns, and regional councils to adopt and implement the idea. The SCW, in conjunction with Project Renewal, also allocated most of the financial resources necessary for establishing these schools. In fact, the program for training local activists became the highest priority on the SCW's agenda during the 1980s.

While the initiative for the program came from the central government, its actual operations are carried out at the local level, by community workers in welfare departments. The process of establishing a school for community activists at the local level is described in the next section.

PLANNING AND IMPLEMENTATION STAGES

Establishing of a local school for training community activists involves four main stages. These stages, and the central role played by the community worker throughout the process, will be described below.

Informing Community Leaders and Obtaining
Their Support for the Program
The first challenge for the community worker, after getting approval from the local welfare department – which is responsible in most locali-

ties for community work activities – is to sell the idea to key people in the community and mobilize their support for it. To this end, the community worker organizes a meeting, to which are invited officials from the local authority and Project Renewal (where applicable), as well as active members of neighbourhood committees, parent councils, community centres, social clubs, local voluntary organizations, and branches of political parties.

This event is also attended by representatives of the SCW and the institute in charge of the training activities. At this meeting the community worker and representatives of the SCW and training institute distribute information on organizational, administrative, and educational issues, including the following:

- The program's objectives, and its advantages for the community.
- The expected involvement of the local authority, and the functions it will assume in implementing the program.
- The role of the SCW.
- A general outline of the training program and its potential to adjust in response to local conditions and needs.

After the program is discussed and any questions are answered, a decision is made whether to launch a training program in the locality. If the decision is yes, the participants select a steering committee to be responsible for running the program. This committee generally consists of the community worker, who represents the local authority; the district supervisor of the SCW; and representatives of the community itself, of Project Renewal, and of the training institute that will be in charge of the educational activities.

Several factors generally help the community worker and the government representatives gain the support of key local people: the government's willingness (and Project Renewal's) to finance the program; and the feeling that the central government is very interested in the program and therefore would not welcome local refusal to adopt it. Also, the local functionaries realize they will be consulted at all stages and that the program will not threaten their turf.

Selection of Candidates
While the selection of candidates is made by a special admission committee, which includes the community worker, the district supervisor of the SCW, and a representative of the educational institute, it is the community worker who actively recruits participants. Based on his or

her activities and acquaintance with the community, that person identifies potential candidates (members of neighbourhood committees, activists in community schools, etc.) and convinces them to apply to the program. In addition, he or she contacts various local organizations (Project Renewal and voluntary organizations) and encourages them to refer potential candidates.

Since the number of candidates is generally larger than the program can absorb, the admission committee must screen the candidates. The screening process includes interviews with candidates or their representatives and reviews of application forms. Each form includes information on the candidate's background and public activities, and on why the candidate wants to attend the school. The selections are then made, based on three main criteria: the candidate's past involvement in public activities; the likelihood that he or she will continue these activities; and the likelihood that he or she will participate regularly in classes.

Shaping the Program Curriculum

The local steering committee is responsible for adjusting the general curriculum to the unique circumstances, needs, and expectations of the community. Generally, every local curriculum consists of a national part that is used throughout the country and makes up about two-thirds of the whole curriculum, and a second part that is geared to the special needs and characteristics of the locality at hand.

The national curriculum was designed by the SCW and discussed and approved by the council for training programs for community leaders. The SCW formed this national council in order to broaden public support for the program and to strengthen its legitimacy.

The council consists of twelve representatives, who come from institutes of higher education, the Ministry of Labour and Social Affairs, and several NGOs operating in the area of CD. The council also includes several local activists. The council was responsible for setting the program's general policy; it also developed and updated the curriculum and the methods of instruction, prepared instructional materials, determined admissions criteria, established conditions for terminating a participant's studies, and chose for each locality the institute that would conduct the training program. The work this council does emphasizes again the key role played by central bodies in guiding and shaping this program.

The local component was designed by the steering committee. A typical curriculum includes the following main topics:

- General background: structure of Israeli society; values and principles of a democratic society; the essences of pluralism; the central government – its structure, authority, and functions; local government's functions and authority; voluntarism and voluntary organizations; communities in Israel.
- The community and its services: the community's structure and composition; the community's main needs and problems; formal and informal systems in the community.
- Community work's main principles and components: citizen participation; relationships between individuals and their environment; identification and assessment of needs; planning, development, and implementation of programs; disseminating information within the community.
- Special social problems and needs: the aged; women's problems; juvenile delinquency; alcoholism; quality of the environment; intergenerational relationships.
- Working within the community: running local committees; activating local residents; fundamentals of teamwork.
- Specific skills: negotiating, decision-making, interpersonal and interorganizational communication; preparing proposals; writing letters; budgeting.

The Program Teaching Technique and Structure of Studies
Although the teaching techniques utilized in the training program vary from one locality to another, all include the following components: lectures, open discussions, simulation exercises, analysis of case studies, films, trips to other communities, and meetings with formal functionaries (mayors, government officials, service directors, professionals, etc.). In addition, the participants are required to plan a project, under supervision. Generally, a program includes two terms of study, with the first term spread over 23 to 27 meetings, and the second term over 12 to 14 meetings. The meetings are generally held once every two weeks.

The second term is designed especially for activists who have completed the first term and received a certificate. The studies in this term are more advanced; the participants are expected to work more independently, and to prepare and carry out projects, either by themselves or under the guidance of the course instructors or local community workers. The studies in this term are organized into modules of 10 to 30 hours; each participant is required to complete at least three modules and 60 hours.

The actual training is carried out by eight training institutes that have amassed considerable experience in community work and adult educa-

tion: three universities, three colleges, a government institute for training workers in welfare services, and a training institute specializing in
community work.

The first school for community activists was founded at the beginning
of 1980 in the small southern town of Kiryat Gat. Twenty-eight participants successfully completed this program. In the entire country, 259
schools had been established as of the end of 1995. By the end of 1994,
about 5,000 local activists had completed the program and received a
diploma.

A typical school generally operates for about six months and ceases
to exist after accomplishing its mission of training a group of local
activists. In certain localities a new school has been opened after an
interval of several years.

At the beginning of 1989, sixteen schools were operating, and about
eighty were in various stages of planning and development. A phenomenon of the 1990s is the establishment of permanent schools for
local activists in the bigger cities, such as Jerusalem and Tel Aviv. These
schools were established at the initiative of the local municipalities'
community work departments.

As previously noted, the SCW wanted to open schools throughout
the country, especially in towns inhabited mostly by new immigrants,
in distressed neighbourhoods of big cities, and in rural areas; indeed,
about half of the schools have been opened in remote areas in the
southern and northern regions of the country. However, only a few
schools have operated in Arab towns and villages, primarily because
professional community work in Arab neighbourhoods is still in an
embryonic stage.

The above review indicates that the program for training local activists has become a central component of community work in Israel. What
has been the impact of this program on its graduates? Did it achieve its
objectives? A partial answer to these questions has been provided by
York and Havassy, whose study will be summarized in the following
section.

Between 1988 and 1990 York and Havassy, aided and backed by a small
steering committee consisting of the director of the SCW and two other

officials from the ministry, conducted a survey of the graduates of the 144 schools that operated between 1980 and 1988.

The purpose of the survey was to obtain data in four main categories:

- Individual socio-economic and demographic data.
- Base data on the program in which they participated (its location and level, the training institute that executed it, etc.).
- The graduates' current involvement in community activities.
- Self-evaluation of relevant knowledge and skills and the extent to which the training program contributed to the graduates' functioning in general, and community activities specifically.

Questionnaires pertaining to these subjects were sent out, through local community workers, to the 1,800 graduates of the training program. About 800 questionnaires were returned by mail, and some 300 additional graduates were interviewed in their homes. Altogether 1,070 questionnaires (about 59%) entered the database.

On top of this, thirty-five community workers were asked to summarize the programs held in their localities during the 1980s, to estimate the number of graduates who were still involved in public activities, to describe the character and frequency of their community involvement, to assess the average level of the graduates' knowledge and skills, and to indicate the extent to which, in their opinion, the material learned in the training program had been applied in the field. The main findings of the survey of graduates are offered below.

Socio-demographic Background

There were more female graduates (54%) than male. Their average age was 42 (the range is from 15 to 80). Most were married (85%) and had an average of three children each. Their average education was 11.3 years. The graduates were engaged in a wide range of occupations: 42 percent were in white-collar occupations such as academic professions, management, and commerce; over 32 percent were blue-collar workers (skilled, semiskilled, or unskilled); 6 percent were unemployed. Fifty-seven percent of the graduates were born outside Israel, but most of them arrived in the country in the early years of the state, probably as children or young adults.

The graduates lived in 73 different communities: 50 percent lived in urban neighbourhoods, 22 percent in small towns, 21 percent in villages, and 7 percent in Arab towns and villages. Thus, a typical graduate was in his or her early forties, married with children, a high-school graduate, employed in an office or as a blue-collar worker, and living in an urban neighbourhood. The typical community activist shown in the findings belonged to the lower middle-class, which constitutes a minority in most of the communities.

Community Activities

About 70 percent of the graduates (724) indicated that they were involved in public activities in their communities, and many of them were involved in several fields. About 35 percent were active in neighbourhood committees, about 20 percent in parent committees in local schools, and about 17 percent in apartment block committees. Others were involved in political parties, community centres and committees, Project Renewal steering committees and subcommittees, workplace committees, and activities with the elderly and new immigrants.

Through their membership on these committees, the graduates had performed a wide variety of tasks: establishing contacts with community residents, planning and organizing activities, recruiting residents for community activities, building bridges to formal organizations, and assessing community needs. The active graduates had devoted on average about four hours per week to community activity. Thus, the survey showed the existence of a large group of local activists characterized by intense and versatile community activity.

The Impact of the Program on the Activists

Since the survey was conducted after the graduates had completed their studies, it is impossible to say whether the range and intensity of their community activity was affected by their participation in the program. However, the survey was able to suggest that it was.

First, the graduates were asked to evaluate their level of *knowledge* in ten areas (including the local system of services, links between organizations, methods of teamwork, the role of community workers and social workers, the structure of the local political system, and methods of publicity) and their level of *ability* in fifteen areas (including identifying needs, problems and resources, planning activities and projects, working in a team, helping, advising, and activating others, expressing themselves orally and in writing, setting priorities, and carrying out activities and projects). These subjects and skills are all taught in the programs.

The findings were that in most of the knowledge subjects and practical skills, the graduates' average level on a scale of 1 to 5 was around 4.

In other words, the graduates evaluated their knowledge in relevant areas and practical skills as good.

Second, the graduates were asked if they felt that they had managed to apply what they had learned in the program to their community activities and to their day-to-day life activities. On a scale of 1 to 6, the average was 4.1 for community activities and 4.3 for day-to-day activities. Thus, most of the graduates felt that the program had equipped them with knowledge and skills that were relevant to their community activities.

Third, the survey's findings showed a consistent positive correlation between the knowledge and skills acquired in the program on the one hand, and the level of community activity on the other. However, the correlation coefficients were generally very moderate.

While these correlations showed positive links between the variables, they didn't indicate any direction of effect. However, other statistical tests (analysis of variance, and regression analysis) indicated that only one variable – the belief among the graduates that they could apply the knowledge and skills learned in the program – had a direct, causal effect on the level of community activity.

These findings indicate that training of community activists can be beneficial if there is a strong emphasis on equipping these local leaders with concrete practical skills that can help them in their daily public activities.

SUMMARY

This case study described a successful program to train local activists in various communities throughout Israel. The program has two major characteristics. First, the central government is heavily involved: the SCW initiated the program, financed it (together with Project Renewal), developed its curriculum, and closely monitors its daily operations. Second, the program has generated a positive local response. Local organizations as well as local activists have shown themselves ready to co-operate with the SCW and to be actively involved in the program. Local community workers serve as liaisons between the national and local bodies. This co-operation has undoubtedly contributed to the spread of the program throughout the country and to the fact that a large number of activists have taken and completed the training.

The main characteristics of the program accurately reflect the nature of Israeli community work and the pivotal role played by the government. However, as this case study very clearly showed, there is a stable core of grass roots activists in many communities. These activists perform a wide range of tasks and contribute to improving the quality of life in their communities. Furthermore, there are some signs that despite the intensive government involvement, the local activists are becoming a significant independent factor in their communities. The survey findings indicate that the training program has been instrumental in this.

Thus, the training of activists can be viewed as an effective mechanism in building local leadership and a meaningful civil society in a country such as Israel, which is characterized by a powerful state with strong centralist tendencies.

3. ORGANIZATIONAL STRUCTURE OF COMMUNITY WORK
Joseph Katan with Yossi Korazim and Aaron York

As indicated earlier, the Israeli socio-political situation is characterized by conflicting trends. On one hand, the central government and national political parties are pushing toward centralized control; on the other, local authorities and organizations, as well as various citizen groups, are promoting and reinforcing decentralization.

Although the central authorities were very powerful during the early years of statehood, since the beginning of the 1970s local leader and organizations have gradually increased their strength. This has brought about a more balanced division of powers between the state and civil organizations, although Israel's special circumstances continue to promote the maintenance of centralized power. All of this has had a strong impact on the structure and methods of community work and the development and character of its support system.

In this section we will describe the main organizations engaged in and supportive of community work practice and development.

ORGANIZATIONS SUPPORTING AND PERFORMING COMMUNITY WORK

Service for Community Work: Ministry of Labour and Social Affairs

The SCW has six principal functions:

• It funds a considerable portion – between 50 and 75 percent – of the local authorities' community work budgets. These funds are earmarked for community workers' salaries and for various community projects. In 1992 the government helped pay the salaries of 170 community workers and 350 neighbourhood workers. The remaining funds were provided by the local authorities themselves.

- It provides professional supervision and consultation to local community workers.
- It assists in setting up schools for training local activists (refer to the practice case included in this country study).
- It encourages local authorities to initiate, plan, develop and implement community projects and services for populations served by the welfare departments (children and youth, new immigrants, the developmentally disabled, etc.).
- It develops projects promoting local economic initiatives in deprived neighbourhoods.
- It organizes training activities for community workers, and fosters a community orientation among social workers operating in local welfare departments.

Local Authorities
While the central government provides funding and direction, the specific and ongoing activities of community work are performed mostly by community work units, which are found in most of the local authorities in Israel. The nature of these activities depends partly on the unique circumstances of each community; that being said, most of the local community workers perform these functions: surveying needs; planning and developing community projects; organizing neighbourhood committees and providing aid for their activities; consulting with workers in various welfare services; improving interagency co-ordination and consultation with workers in various welfare services; and improving interagency co-ordination and consultation with local leaders.

The Association for Development and Planning of Services for the Elderly
This association provides a clear example of planning and developing community services for a specific population under a model with distinct community work features. The association is administered by two bodies: the government, and the Israel-Joint (an organization representing overseas Jewish foundations that support various social projects in Israel). The association does not provide direct services; rather, it acts primarily as a catalyst to establish local organizations, which in turn advance specific services and projects. These organizations, which operate today in most of Israel's towns, are composed of representatives of

various community agencies that provide services to the elderly as well as representatives of the elderly themselves. The organizations assess the needs of the local elderly and plan, develop, and implement services to meet these needs. The central association provides financial support and professional consultation. Thus, its work is based on four principles: decentralization, planning and developing services responsive to local needs, consumer involvement, and co-operation among various community organizations.

Public Housing Companies
During the 1950s and 1960s the government played a central role in building apartments for the hundreds of thousands of new immigrants who arrived in Israel. Most of these apartments were purchased over the years by their residents, but many still belong to public housing corporations that are owned either fully by the government or co-operatively by the government and some of the large municipalities. These corporations also provide apartments to the poor and elderly and to families living in overcrowded conditions. In the past these corporations employed many community workers – in fact, in the early 1960s the largest government housing corporation employed most of the community workers in Israel. The development of community work in these corporations grew out of the awareness that it is not enough to provide housing to people; one must also encourage proper maintenance of residences, promote the quality of life in residential areas, improve local services, and advance social integration.

Since the early 1970s, these corporations have been doing less and less community work. Today only a few community and neighbourhood workers still operate through these corporations. The view held by their directors that neighbourhood community work is the responsibility of local authorities and community centres is one important explanation for this reduction. Another is that by ending their involvement, the corporations freed up money for other things.

Voluntary Organizations
Large voluntary organizations (VOs), especially national ones like the General Federation of Labour (the main trade union in Israel), have always been very active in initiating, developing, and implementing community projects (social clubs, kindergartens for the children of working mothers, etc.). In recent years there has been considerable growth in the number of small, local VOs, which engage in various community

activities such as planning, developing, and delivering services to specific populations (women, poor people, gays, etc.); advocating for minorities and for populations in distress; and working for social justice and equality.

Funding for these organizations comes from various sources: the government, members' dues, lcoal contributions, service charges, and overseas foundations such as the New Israel Fund, which helps VOs that are promoting social equality.

Community Workers Council
The Community Workers' Council serves as the organizational framework for professional community workers in Israel. The council is affiliated with Israel's social workers' union. The council operates on two main levels: organizing professional meetings and conferences for community workers, and lobbying influential politicians and government executives on social policy issues relevant to community work. Also, several years ago the council initiated a successful project designed to encourage consumers of social services to become involved in shaping policies relevant to their needs. The project was supported and funded by the social workers' union.

SPECIAL COMMUNITY PROJECTS

Development of Rural Communities
One of the greatest accomplishments of Israeli society was the founding of approximately 700 rural communities, of which about 250 were *kibbutzim* and roughly 450 were *moshavim*. A *kibbutz* is a socialist collective based on three principles: common ownership of property, collective decision-making, and equality of rewards for all members, regardless of occupation. *Kibbutz* members engage in agriculture, industry, and tourism. Members of *moshavim* also perform agricultural work, but these communities are structured around family farms; however, decisions affecting community aspects of *moshav* life are made by a committee elected by the *moshav*.

These communities have undergone fundamental changes in recent years. The changes in the *kibbutzim* can be linked with the erosion of the collective spirit and the value of equality, and with the weakening of direct democracy. In the *moshavim*, the crisis is evident primarily in the disintegration of community institutions. These changes stem from developments occurring generally in Israel and other Western countries, such as increasing competition and individualism, coupled with a weakening belief in social solidarity.

Project Renewal

Project Renewal was the most substantial CD enterprise undertaken in Israel after the founding of the state. The aim of this project, which was initiated in the late 1970s by the central government and implemented in about ninety localities, was to rehabilitate Israel's distressed neighbourhoods. The project has three central components: the physical and social rehabilitation of neighbourhoods; meaningful participation by neighbourhood residents in shaping and implementing the project's programs; and co-ordination of the functions of the various agencies (government ministries, local authorities, and voluntary organizations) that are taking part in planning and implementing the project.

The project was financed by government ministries (primarily housing, education, and labour and social affairs), and by Jewish communities abroad.

Community Centres

Almost every local authority in Israel has a multipurpose community centre. Each of these centres has a board of directors composed of local residents and representatives of both the local authority and relevant governmental ministries (especially the Ministry of Education).

A government corporation of community centres, whose board of directors is chosen by the Minister of Education, is responsible for appointing the directors of the local centres (an arrangement designed to reduce the directors' dependence on local politicians), for organizing supervision and training activities for workers, and for mediating between the centres and governmental ministries. The corporation also provides part of each centre's budget.

Each centre has a clear and unambiguous community orientation. All offer local residents various services, especially in areas such as sports, culture, and informal education. They also offer necessary services such as welfare assistance. Moreover, since one of the principles of the centres is to encourage the meaningful participation of the local residents in shaping policies and activities, they are a major arena for CD.

Community Schools

The Israeli educational system is heavily centralized. The Ministry of Education directly employs most of the teaching staff and sets the school curriculum. The present trend, however, is toward decentralization, with the local communities having more say in the education of their children.

A community-oriented school is generally characterized by involvement of the parents in the school's life (shaping the curriculum, organizing social activities), use of the school's facilities for community activities, and acceptance of local traditions in the school's educational programs.

Neighbourhood Administrations

Jerusalem was the first municipality in Israel to institute a program of neighbourhood administration. To this end, it divided the city into small districts and established a neighbourhood administration in each. Tel Aviv and several other municipalities later did the same. These administrations have three basic goals, which are congruent with the principles of community work: to bring municipal services closer to the residents, thereby increasing their responsiveness to local needs; to increase residents' involvement in shaping these services' goals, structures, and patterns of activity; and to improve co-ordination of services at the neighbourhood level.

SUMMARY

This review illustrates the pivotal role played by the central government and other national bodies in financing and providing direction for community work in Israel. A clear majority of community workers in Israel are paid directly or indirectly by the government. Also, most community projects and development enterprises are initiated by the government and funded by relevant ministries (labour and social affairs, housing, education, and culture) and/or by other national agencies.

A large number of these initiatives, such as Project Renewal, community schools, neighbourhood administrations, and services for specific groups (such as the eldery and the disabled) are based on principles of community work such as decentralization, client participation, co-ordination between organizations at the community level, delivery of services congruent with population needs, and promotion of local activists' influence. Even so, in most of the projects the central bodies have maintained their dominant authority. However, the last few years have seen a gradual development of grass roots civil organizations that have no connections with the central establishment. These serve as pressure groups as well as self-help groups. At present their influence is limited, but they are gathering strength and beginning to be a serious factor in Israel's socio-political arena. Thus, a better balance between the state and the various independent societal elements can be anticipated in the future.

4. COMMUNITY WORK RESEARCH
Joseph Katan with Yossi Korazim and Aaron York

Over the last forty years, Israeli and foreign researchers – among them sociologists, economists, political scientists, psychologists, and social workers – have studied various issues relevant to community work and development in Israel. These include immigrant absorption, relations between ethnic groups, social and political processes in urban and rural communities, the development of Israel's political system, and relations between formal organizations and their clientele.

In this short review, we will not be able to cover such a wide variety of subjects; therefore, we will concentrate on studies that have dealt specifically with community work topics. Most of these studies were conducted in universities and research institutes and were financed by the government and a number of Israeli and overseas research foundations.

The studies employed a variety of research methods, including surveys and other quantitative analyses, qualitative investigations that focused on specific communities and organizations, and content analysis of documents. Certain studies combined quantitative and qualitative methods. The following is a short review of four subjects that gained much of the attention of researchers.

CHANGES IN THE PURPOSES AND FUNCTIONS OF COMMUNITY WORK
AND INFLUENCING FACTORS

The first studies on community work in Israel were conducted in the 1960s by Ben Lappin (1971) and Ralph Kramer (1971), who examined the influence of Israel's socio-political context on the functions of community workers during the first stages of the development of professional community work in Israel.

Lappin found that community workers had difficulty in building an independent profession; he attributed this to the nature of Israel's socio-political system. Kramer, who interviewed most of the country's community workers, noted the political impotence that characterized most of them. This impotence was expressed in their lack of knowledge of the political realities in the communities where they worked, and in their reluctance to embrace political tactics. He also encountered a lack of awareness of the importance of political behaviour in promoting social change. Kramer attributed all of this at least partly to the fact that the workers belonged to organizations that were connected to the political establishment and maintained by it.

The political involvement of community workers was studied again about ten years later by Chetkow-Yanoov and Katan (1976) and Chetkow-Yanoov and Nadler (1978). They asked fifty local community workers to report on their political orientation and contacts with local politicians. This time around, the local community workers showed a good knowledge of the local political arena marked by intensive, continuous, and positive relationships with local politicians. These relationships were designed to influence the politicians' decisions and activities. The workers understood that developing good links with local politicians is vital to the professional objectives of community work.

Another follow-up study on community work in Israel was conducted by Friedman (1984). Using content analysis of professional reports and publications, he compared the activities of community workers during the 1950s, the 1960s, and the 1970s, and found that during the first period the workers focused on two activities: development of services, and administrative tasks. During the second period, they continued to concentrate on these but added a number of additional duties, such as planning services and working with civil organizations. During the third period, they assumed still more functions but the development of services and fulfilment of different administrative functions still remained central.

Community workers' roles were later studied by Cnaan and Rothman (1986). These researchers examined the extent to which Rothman's three models of community work – social planning, locality development, and social action – applied to the perceptions of a sample of Israeli community workers. Their findings indicated that Rothman's conceptual framework did not have much relevance to these workers' understanding of their functions and activities. Also, that Israeli community workers focused mainly on locality development. Social planning came second, and social action was only a marginal activity.

An additional aspect of community work was examined by York (1988), who investigated the extent to which workers have a directive or nondirective approach to their work.

These studies, which examined the evolution of community workers' objectives, purposes, and functions over a period of forty years, identified signs of both continuity and change. A clear majority of workers work in organizations that are strongly connected to the political establishment, and the content and direction of their work are both strongly influenced by this. However, the workers have gradually and steadily gained greater political sophistication and autonomy, and this has enabled them to play a more significant role in determining the objectives of their work and the techniques to achieve them.

CITIZEN PARTICIPATION

One of the areas that received considerable attention from the researchers related to citizen participation. In studies dealing with this topic, several basic questions were asked, including these: Is it really possible to involve citizens in a meaningful way in social services and projects? Can their participation be increased in a planned and orderly fashion? Do the citizens who are supposed to represent populations actually do so? What are the goals of citizen participation, and how are these goals achieved?

Studies conducted by Liron and Spiro (1988), Churchman (1988), and Azmon (1988) investigated these questions in the framework of Project Renewal, which sought to achieve meaningful citizen participation on the local committees that directed the planning and implementation of projects at the neighbourhood level.

The studies examined the activities of the residents' representatives on some of these committees and reached the following conclusions: Despite various limitations, among them the presence of central and local government representatives, many residents' representatives took an active part in local committees and influenced their work. Moreover, in many neighbourhoods, the involvement of residents in a project led to the emergence of an active and influential local leadership. But it must also be said that despite these positive developments, the involvement of residents had only limited success in countering, the strong influence of municipal and federal authorities.

Other arenas of citizen participation were studied by Yanai (1988) and by Itzhaki and York (1994), who examined the participation of residents in community centres; by Friedman (1984), who studied parent involvement in local schools; by Katan (1992, 1993), who explored residents' participation in old age homes; and by York and Havassy

(1993), who studied neighbourhood residents who were trained in local schools for local activists.

The studies reviewed above identified the difficulties inherent in establishing meaningful citizen participation in Israel's socio-political climate. But they also documented the emergence of citizen's groups that were both able and very willing to take an active part in community life. This development, coupled with greater organizational responsiveness, has led to the emergence of some authentic forms of citizen participation.

CIVIL ORGANIZATIONS

Studies undertaken in the field of civil organizations examined different aspects of the structure and activities of citizen's groups. Some of these groups are specific to a given territory; others are for individuals who share common needs but live in different territories.

Cnaan and Katan (1986) investigated a sampling of neighbourhood committees, which are very common in and around Israel's cities. They found that the socio-economic and demographic composition of these committees does not match the composition of the neighbourhoods where they are sited. This finding arouses considerable doubt about the extent to which these committees really represent local residents. A number of more recent studies have confirmed this finding. Furthermore, the neighbourhood committees focus their efforts primarily on lobbying external authorities (such as governmental and municipal officials) to improve neighbourhood services. They devote little effort to work within the neighbourhood itself, such as organizing self-help activities and increasing residents' identification with the neighbourhood. This pattern of activity stems from the perception by committee activists that improving a neighbourhood's quality of life depends primarily on building links with external authorities and convincing them to provide more resources.

Another focus of study was citizens' protest groups, which represent the interests of distressed populations. The most prominent among these were the Black Panthers movement, which was active during the later part of the 1960s, and the Tents movement, which operated during the late 1980s and early 1990s. The Black Panthers movement, which was studied by Bernstein (1979) and Leman-Wilzig (1992), was organized by a group of teenagers and young adults in one of the distressed neighbourhoods of Jerusalem. Its aim was to utilize conflict tactics (demonstrations, strikes, etc.) to draw public attention to the conditions of poor neighbourhoods. The Black Panthers' activities led the government to increase expenditures on social services, and this improved the situation of the distressed populations. After several years of activity, the organization dissolved. Part of its membership moved on to the mainstream political arena, to work within the framework of the existing political parties.

Deri (1992) investigated the Tents movement, which represented citizens with housing problems, and attributed its eventual decline to the success of government officials in splintering the movement and breaking its members' solidarity by proposing individual solutions for specific families. The movement's goal – to change government housing policies – was not achieved, but its protest activities gained broad media coverage and generated solutions to many families' housing problems. Thus, although the protest organizations did not succeed in introducing basic social reforms, they did contribute to some improvements in the situation of distressed populations.

Self-help groups were studied by Bargal and Gidron (1983). They described and analysed these civil organizations and documented their development and spread in the city of Jerusalem.

EVALUATION OF COMMUNITY PROJECTS

Many community work projects have been undertaken in Israel over the years, but only a few of them have been systematically evaluated. The most prominent of these was Project Renewal.

The researchers who evaluated this project examined a wide variety of issues, including the project's objectives, and whether those objectives were achieved; the influence of local residents on project policies and activities; and the impact of the project on the neighbourhood's quality of life, and on its external image. The studies demonstrated that a considerable number (although not all) of the objectives were achieved, and indicated which factors were influential in determining the degree to which the goals were obtained.

Hasson (1989) conducted an extensive evaluation of neighbourhood administrations in Jerusalem (which were discussed earlier), and found that the city's heterogeneous character and differences between neighbourhoods led to variations in how these administrations functioned. He also noticed disharmony arising from the city's willingness to promote *administrative* decentralization and neighbourhood residents' interest in *political* decentralization. In certain districts, local leaders become powerful enough to influence the administration and to counterbalance the power of officials.

UTILIZATION OF RESEARCH FINDINGS

As indicated above, many of the studies were solicited by the government or by sponsors of community work projects; for example, evaluations of Project Renewal were requested and funded by the executive board of the project. The evaluation of Jerusalem's district administrations was requested and funded by the Israel-Joint.

The findings of these commissioned studies were conveyed to the relevant authorities not only in the form of research reports, but also in face-to-face meetings between researchers and policy-makers at the national and local levels. In addition, many of the studies were used as a basis for articles in professional journals. Despite the dissemination of the studies' findings and recommendations, there is no clear evidence that these recommendations have actually been utilized, although it can be assumed that the exposure of policy-makers to the studies' findings did influence some of their decisions.

SUMMARY

This review of research shows how far community work has come during the last forty years. Israeli community work is strongly linked to central government and related state organizations that play a pivotal role in initiating and funding various CD programs (rehabilitation of distressed neighbourhoods, creation of community centres and community schools, etc.). These central organizations sponsoring community work have incorporated into their programs a number of community work principles, such as administrative decentralization, citizen participation, and local co-ordination. However, they have always maintained ultimate control. There are clear signs, however, that this strong degree of centralization is being weakened by emerging trends. Local leaders have gained some influence on development projects, and citizens' organizations have begun to make their mark on the central government and local authorities. Thus, Israel is undergoing a slow and gradual transition from a state-controlled society to a society where civil organizations fulfil a significant role.

5. EDUCATION AND TRAINING FOR COMMUNITY WORK
Joseph Katan with Yossi Korazim and Aaron York

Community work in Israel is recognized as an integral part of social work. The basic training for social work is provided in the undergraduate programs of schools of social work at five Israeli universities (Hebrew University in Jerusalem, Bar Ilan University, University of Haifa, Tel Aviv University and Ben Gurion University), and the graduates of these programs are formally recognized as social workers and certified to work in the profession. The undergraduate programs consist of three years of courses. During their final two years, student gain experience in practice through supervised field placements in a social service agency.

UNDERGRADUATE PROGRAMS

All the undergraduate programs include courses in community work; three of them offer community work as a specialty. There are two principal components of community work as a specialty: a set of courses in community work, and at least one year of field training in community work.

Included in the course work are the following subjects: the goals of community work, methods of intervention, and skills (techniques of problem-solving; identification and analysis of needs; planning and evaluation of services; organization of populations; working with volunteers, local activists, and self-help groups; co-ordination of services and organizational change).

Field training is usually performed in agencies such as the community work units of local welfare departments, public housing corporations, and community centres. In these settings, students are exposed to the work of community workers and are expected to implement community work activities such as surveying community needs, planning services, creating change within an organization, and establishing and/or providing guidance for citizen's groups. The field-work is supervised by an experienced community worker authorized by the school of social work to supervise students.

GRADUATE PROGRAMS

Each of the schools also has a graduate program that trains social workers who are already in the field to carry out management, supervision, and advanced practice functions in human service organizations. These programs also provide advanced studies in community work, primarily for students who are already practising community work.

Although there are some differences between them, all of the graduate community work programs offer courses in the following subjects: the theoretical basis of community work; research in community work; intervention techniques and skills; planning, implementation, and evaluation of social services; group work (with emphasis on work with community groups); citizen participation; and social policy and administration of welfare services. These studies also include a supervised practice experience in which the student is expected to execute a community work project at the advanced level. In addition, some of the students may write theses on community work subjects. Graduate studies may extend from two years (full-time) to five years (part-time). At one of the schools (the Hebrew University) there is also a special two-year program for training managers and senior staff of community centres. This program strongly emphasizes courses in community work that parallel courses in the graduate program.

CONTINUING EDUCATION

On top of all this, there are other agencies that provide continuing education for practising community workers and for other workers. The most outstanding of these agencies is the Central School for Social Service Workers, run by the Ministry of Labour and Social Affairs. This school provides workshops for community workers at all stages of their careers.

Continuing education programs for community workers are also provided by the schools of social work and by organizations that employ large numbers of social workers, such as the major local authorities. It should be added that community workers who are just entering the field are closely supervised during their first working years by an experienced professional. In recent years the SCW has initiated special courses for social workers operating in local welfare departments, with the intention of enhancing their community orientation and their understanding of the community work approach. This initiative was guided by the assumption that a community orientation can be very useful to workers who do not ordinarily utilize community work techniques.

SPECIAL TRAINING PROGRAMS FOR NONPROFESSIONAL WORKERS
AND ACTIVISTS

Community work in Israel is performed not only by professional workers, but also by activists in civil organizations and by nonprofessional
workers in urban neighbourhoods and rural villages.

In many localities, the SCW has helped to establish special schools
that train local activists, such as members of neighbourhood committees, for leadership roles. These schools were described in an earlier
case study.

Consultation and training services for activists in civil organizations
are also provided by Shatil. This organization, which belongs to the
New Israel Fund, holds one-day and ongoing workshops on such topics
as administering and directing civil organizations; the legal basis for
these organizations; budget planning; procurement of resources; and
lobbying, advocacy, and marketing. Nonprofessional workers are trained
primarily through the close supervision provided by professional community workers.

During the 1960s, Israel became active internationally in training community workers. For example, Kenya's first school for training community workers was established by Israeli personnel. In addition, the Carmel
Centre in Haifa trains workers to perform various community functions
in developing countries in Asia, Africa, and Latin America.

EDUCATIONAL MATERIALS

What is the basis for training community workers in Israel? What educational materials are used?

During the early years, training for community work in Israel was
based primarily on books and articles in professional journals published abroad, especially in the United States and Britain. Some of the
books and articles were even translated into Hebrew. An effort was
made – sometimes successfully, sometimes not – to adjust these materials to the special social and cultural realities of Israel.

In the past two decades more and more work has been published by
Israeli researchers, teachers, and community workers. This work includes theoretical papers, descriptions of community projects, professional
reports describing community interventions, research reports (including
evaluations), and theses prepared by graduate students. Although publications from abroad are still widely used, these Israeli publications form
the main basis of community work education in Israel.

SUMMARY

The above review described the wide scope and content of community work training in Israel, but it also exposed some of its limitations. Although the training is conducted mainly in autonomous universities, it is strongly influenced by the characteristics of Israeli community work as described in previous sections. This influence is reflected, for instance, in the fact that those field-training agencies in which students are placed, such as welfare departments and community centres, emphasize the dimensions of community planning and locality development, and therefore do not expose the students to social action practices. Furthermore, students are not placed in civil organizations that use protest tactics.

Also, it was the government that established and supported the institutes for training local activists; thus, it has a strong influence on their educational activities and curricula. The only NGO that plays any significant role in training is the New Israel Fund.

Clearly, the system for educating and training professional and non-professional community workers and local activists strongly reflects the present characteristics of Israeli community work. It follows that that system does not contribute to the development of a new breed of workers capable of introducing changes into the objectives, structure and patterns of activity of community work in Israel.

6. THEORETICAL PERSPECTIVE ON COMMUNITY WORK
Joseph Katan with Yossi Korazim and Aaron York

HISTORICAL OVERVIEW

Professional community work began in Israel in 1953, five years after Independence, when farming villages (*Moshavim*) for new immigrants were established in different regions of the country.

This rural-based community work was guided by the classical models of CD, which emphasized self-help, social integration, co-operation, institution-building, and adult education (Batten, 1965). With the creation in the mid-1950s of new towns and new neighbourhoods in the older cities, community work became more urban-oriented, adopting concepts typical of urban CD and community organization such as needs identification and assessment, client involvement, intergroup co-ordination, intergroup relations, local development, and citizens' organization.

A new phenomenon appeared on the Israeli socio-political scene in the early 1970s: the emergence of protest movements that resorted to radical tactics to pressure government to change its social policies. Following this development, different concepts, such as conflict strategies and radical social action (Alinsky, 1945), began to find their way into the community work narrative. However, in the field, these concepts were applied in only a very limited way (Jaffe, 1980).

The concept of social planning gained popularity toward the end of the 1970s and began to affect the practices of community workers. This trend was an outgrowth of Project Renewal, through which the government, in partnership with Jewish communities from abroad, set out to renovate distressed neighbourhoods and towns. Community workers who were intensely involved in this project focused mainly on promoting resident participation in local committees, which were to guide the project in each of the neighbourhoods. But they also took part in planning various services and programs.

In recent years, the emphasis in Israel on decentralization, localism, voluntarism, grass roots organizations, and self-help has had an impact on community work. Workers have begun to take on new roles in old as well as new voluntary organizations, including those engaged in improving neighbourhood relations among Jews and Arabs and promoting peace between Israel and its neighbours. In this, they have drawn on conflict mediation and resolution strategies and techniques.

Despite these different emphases and trends, the four main objectives of community work in Israel have barely changed over the last forty years. These purposes arise from the unique characteristics and circumstances of Israel, which is a heterogeneous society composed of many ethnic and religious groups; and from certain values and trends within the social work profession, with which Israeli community work is affiliated.

MAIN PURPOSES OF COMMUNITY WORK

To foster citizen participation is the first of the four main purposes. This is viewed as an end in itself but also as a means for educating people to act as good citizens and for strengthening their social and political rights as members of a democratic society. One of the principal components of citizen participation is client involvement. Israeli community workers have been in the vanguard of those demanding that clients of human service organizations be involved in formulating the policies and implementing the programs that are relevant to their lives.

The fostering of citizen participation is closely related to a second major purpose of community workers – to form and guide local citizens' organizations, especially resident committees in urban neighbourhoods. The main functions of these committees are to represent the interests of the neighbourhood residents vis-à-vis local municipal authorities and the central ministries; and to pressure those external bodies to invest more resources and provide better services in the neighbourhoods being represented.

Since active local leadership is perceived as necessary for strong local organizations, community workers have worked to establish schools for community activists in various cities and regions throughout the country. The main objectives of these schools are to stimulate citizens to participate in their community and to provide the relevant values, knowledge, and skills that will allow them to carry out various public functions. These schools place a special emphasis on the meaning of democracy and its concrete implications. This special initiative was described and analysed in an earlier case study.

Through its active involvement in fostering client participation, developing citizens' organizations, and training local leaders, community work is helping lay the foundation for a civil society in Israel. The fact that community work in Israel is strongly attached to the state may explain the emphasis community workers place on involving clients in existing service agencies, and linking citizens' groups with national and local establishments. At the same time they pay only limited attention to other tasks, such as the initiation of independent self-help organizations, which constitute the backbone of a civil society. Hundreds of self-help independent groups exist in Israel, but community workers have had only limited involvement in their formation and development.

The third purpose of community work in Israel is to promote social integration. This means maintaining proper and consensual relationships among various groups and organizations within communities, and establishing good working relationships between locally based organizations and the municipal and central governments.

Two of the practice cases presented in this country study showed how community workers helped improve communications among different social and ethnic groups. One case described efforts to build bridges between an ultra-Orthodox neighbourhood and its secular environment. Another case described a neighbourhood project designed to reduce tensions between Jews and Arabs.

Community workers in Israel have rarely been involved in promoting radical social action, and rarely resort to conflict strategies; however, they clearly have assumed leadership in fostering a 'civic culture' characterized by co-operation. This has involved searching for a consensus, facilitating communications, and establishing proper relationships among various organizations and groups.

The fourth purpose of community work in Israel is to raise the quality of life of neighbourhood residents by increasing the resources and improving the services provided to them. To this end, community workers not only strive to foster client participation and organize resident committees, but also to identify local needs, assess them, plan programs designed to cope with them, and take part in their implementation. In their social planning function, community workers establish links between various organizations (local and external) and co-ordinate their activities at the local level.

These four purposes are well reflected in community work at the micro, mezo, and macro levels. The large majority of Israeli community workers operate at the micro (i.e, neighbourhood) level, where they are involved in the following functions: guiding nonprofessional workers in organizing residents' committees in apartment blocks; organizing and guiding neighbourhood committees; linking these committees with municipal and governmental authorities; identifying local needs; and developing programs and services.

At the mezo (i.e., city or regional) level, community workers are engaged in identifying the needs of specific population groups such as the elderly, small children, and battered women, and in planning and developing services designed to meet them. In addition, community workers do liaison work with various service agencies, co-ordinating their activities. In recent years special emphasis has been placed at the mezo level on organizing institutes for training local activists (this project was the focus of an earlier case in this country study).

Community work involvement at the macro (i.e., national) level is still rare, even though many social problems and their solutions are national in character. One exceptional case is a program launched in 1990 by the Israeli Association of Social Workers. The association hired an experienced community worker to help local steering committees in distressed neighbourhoods to organize themselves into a national representative committee, which successfully blocked government attempts to reduce the budgets available to these neighbourhoods. In addition, the worker set up a national body of health service consumers that succeeded in introducing certain amendments to the nation's health insurance act.

Another example of involvement at the macro level is the employment of community workers in several nationwide voluntary organizations such as the New Israel Fund, which supports grass roots organizations operating in the fields of human and civil rights. These practices are more the exception than the rule in Israeli community work, but they may signal the beginning of a possible change in course for community work in Israel.

Contributors

Yossi Korazim
Co-ordinator of planning and research in the Department for Children and Youth in the Ministry of Labour and Social Affairs; received his doctoral degree in social work; teaches courses on social welfare policy and community work at the Hebrew University in Jerusalem.

Debra Shapiro
Director, Community and Youth Unit for the Ultra-Orthodox Population of the Municipality of Jerusalem Community and Youth Division; degree in social work; a former municipal community worker, for five years, in ultra-Orthodox neighbourhoods in Jerusalem.

Naomi Sheffer
Director, Women's Bureau, Ministry of Labor and Social Affairs.

Aaron York
Director, School of Social Work, Bar-Ilan University; has worked as a community worker and consultant to local municipalities and voluntary organizations, and has published extensively in this area.

Co-ordinator

Joseph Katan
Associate professor and chair of graduate studies at Tel-Aviv University School of Social Work; has published extensively in the fields of community work and social policy; has served as a consultant to government ministries and local authorities on these subjects; has also taught in South Africa, the United States, and Canada.

References

Alinsky, S.D. (1945). *Reveille for radicals.* Chicago: University of Chicago Press.

Azmon, Y. (1988). Citizen participation in a project renewal neighbourhood in Jerusalem: A genuine opportunity or just an illusion. *Megamot*, 3–4: 363–83 (in Hebrew).

Bargal, D., & Gidron, B. (1983). *Self-help and mutual-aid group in Jerusalem: An exploratory study*. Jerusalem: Hebrew University, Paul Baerwald School of Social Work (in Hebrew).

Batten, T.R. (1965). *Communities and their development*. Oxford: Oxford University Press.

Bernstein, D. (1979). The Black Panthers: Conflict and protests in Israeli society. *Megamot*, 25: 65–80 (in Hebrew).

Chetkow-Yanoov, B., & Katan, J. (1976). Interrelations between community workers and politicians: An Israeli example. *International Review of Community Development*, 35–6: 137–56.

Chetkow-Yanoov, B., & Nadler, S. (1978). Community social workers and political leaders in municipal settings in Israel. *Journal of Social Service Research*, 1(4): 357–72.

– (1987). *Dealing with conflict and extremism*. Jerusalem: Israel Joint Distribution Committee.

Churchman, A. (1988). Resident involvement in project renewal: Goals and achievements. *Megamot*, 3–4: 342–62 (in Hebrew).

Cnaan, R., & Katan, J. (1986). Local neighbourhood committees in Israel. *Journal of Voluntary Action Research*, 15: 33–46.

Cnaan, R., & Rothman, J. (1986). Conceptualizing community intervention: An empirical test of three models of community organization. *Administration in Social Work*, 10(3): 41–51.

Deri, D. (1992). *Protest, politics and policy innovations – The struggle of the housing disadvantaged*. Jerusalem: The Jerusalem Institute for Israeli Studies (in Hebrew).

El-Or, Tamar. (1994). *Educated and ignorant: Ultra-Orthodox Jewish women and their world*. Tel Aviv: Am Oved.

Freedman, I. (1984). *The school, the parent home and the community in Israel*. Jerusalem: The Sald Institute.

Friedman, M. (1988). *The educated ultra-Orthodox women*. Jerusalem: The Jerusalem Institute for Israeli Studies (in Hebrew).

– (1991). *The ultra-Orthodox society – sources, tendencies and processes*. Jerusalem: The Jerusalem Institute for Israeli Studies (in Hebrew). 115–43, 186–91.

Friedman, Z. (1984). *The development of the function of community social workers in Israel in 1953–1979*. Jerusalem: The Service for Community Work, the Ministry of Labour and Social Affairs (in Hebrew).

Hasson, S. (1989). *Neighbourhood administration in Jerusalem*. Jerusalem: The Jerusalem Institute for Israeli Studies (in Hebrew).

Itzhaki, H., & York, A.S. (1994). Different types of client participation and their effects on community social work interventions. *Journal of Social Service Research*, 19(1–2): 85–98.

Jaffe, E.D. (1980). *Pleaders and protesters*. New York: American Jewish Committee.

Katan, J. (1992). Resident participation in six old-age homes in Israel. *Gerontology* (Summer): 26–44 (in Hebrew).

– (1993). Factors affecting resident participation in six old age homes in Israel. *Social Security*, 39: 67–82 (in Hebrew).

Kramer, R. (1971). *Urban community work in Israel*. Jerusalem: The Hebrew University in Jerusalem.

Lappin, B.W. (1971). *Community workers and the social work tradition*. Ramat Gan: Masada Press.

Leman-Wilzig, S. (1992). *Public protest in Israel, 1949–1992*. Ramat Gan: Bar Ilan University (in Hebrew).

Liron, R., & Spiro, S. (1988). Public participation in planning and management: Evaluation criteria and their application in Project Renewal. *Society and Welfare*, 9(1): 17–34 (in Hebrew).

Loewenberg, F. (1985). Values and ideologies in professional practice. In *Religious and social work practice in contemporary American society*. New York: Columbia University Press. 51–78.

Pardes, Y. (1988). *Training programs for local community leaders*. Jerusalem: The Community Work Service, Ministry of Labour and Social Affairs.

– (1989). *School for urban and rural community activists for promoting local leadership in the years 1980–1988, and forecast for the years 1989–1990*. Ministry of Labour and Social Affairs (an internal report in Hebrew).

– (1993). *Training programs for the development of local community leadership*. Jerusalem: Ministry of Labour and Social Affairs.

Shilhav, Y. (1991a). The influence of religion on cultural ground: The ultra-Orthodox Jews in Jerusalem. In *25 years to the unification of the city, chapters in municipal geography of Jerusalem*. The Jerusalem Institute for Israeli Studies. 102–25 (in Hebrew).

– (1991b). The Shabbat circle or Dizengoff circle? – Between ethnical ground and instrumental ground of the ultra-Orthodox commmunity. In *A small town within a modern city: A geography*. Jerusalem: The Jerusalem Institute for Israel Studies. 33–54.

Yanai, U. (1988). Ideology and reality: Representation and participation in local services management. *British Journal of Social Work*, 18: 75–87.

York, A.S. (1988). Directive and nondirective approaches to community social work and their measurement: Preliminary findings. *Society and Welfare*, 9(1): 35–44 (in Hebrew).

York, A.S., & Havassy, H. (1993). Schools for community activists: A report of the first decades experience. *Journal of Community Psychology*, 21: 124–7.

Part VI

Ghana

Co-ordinated by FRED ABLOH and
STEPHEN AMEYAW

Ghana

1. INTRODUCTION
Fred Abloh and Stephen Ameyaw

Ghana is a small (238,540 sq km) anglophone, West African country bordered on the east, west, and north by the francophone countries of Togo, Ivory Coast, and Burkina Faso, respectively. To the south the Atlantic Ocean washes a 550 km coastline. It is a tropical country with a generally low-lying landscape, divided into three main ecological zones: northern savannah, the forest zone in the centre and south, and the coastal savannah belt.

Between 1960 and 1994, Ghana's population increased from 6.5 to 17 million, with an almost equal number of males and females. There are five major ethnic groups: the Akans, Mole-Dagbani, Guans, Ewes, and Ga-Adangbe. The nonblack population (mainly Lebanese and Syrians) accounts for 1 percent of the total (Johnstone, 1993).

Ghana has experienced a rapid turnover of governments since its independence. Kwame Nkrumah and his Convention People's Party took over the reins of power from the British on 6 March 1957, operating a unitary, unicameral, multiparty government based on universal adult suffrage. This changed in 1964 when, in order to facilitate industrialization and carry out its socialist policies, the Nkrumah regime declared Ghana a one-party state. In February 1966, Nkrumah's government was overthrown in a military coup. The country has since been governed by a series of five military and four civilian governments. In January 1993, Lieutenant Jerry Rawlings was elected president of the Fourth Republic, and introduced a new democratic constitution aimed at promoting local governance.

The country operates a primary sector economy based on agriculture, mining, and lumber – a legacy of colonial rule. Agriculture accounts for about 40 percent of the gross domestic product and 70 percent of the country's total export earnings, and employs 60 percent of the labour force. Ghana, like many other Third World countries, is heavily dependent upon a single crop, in this case cocoa. The cocoa sector employs almost 33 percent of the agricultural labour force, and cocoa exports account for about 60 percent of export earnings. The production of export and local crops is carried out entirely by peasants using mainly traditional farming techniques, and by social organizations. Industry accounts for only about 15 to 20 percent of the gross domestic product. This sector, which focuses on import-substitution industries, has not contributed much to the national economy. In fact, most of Ghana's manufactured exports are agriculture-based – for example, cocoa paste, cocoa butter, and wood products. The industrial sector is highly dependent on imports such as oil, machinery, and transportation. In some cases as much as 80 percent of industry's needs must be imported. Consequently, an important constraint on the growth of the industrial sector is the availability of foreign exchange.

In the early 1960s, in an effort to reduce foreign economic dominance, the government launched an energetic but only moderately successful state-centred economic development program (Hansen & Ninsen, 1989). The country reverted back to a capitalist system after Nkrumah was ousted in 1966. On the whole, the contribution of agriculture and forestry to Ghana's GDP has declined since then. Many Ghanaians make their living in the 'informal' sector because of limited opportunities in the formal, wage-based sector of the economy. However, the informal sector as a whole has been undermined by government policies. Inadequate co-ordination, poor quality of extension education, and meagre credit facilities have slowed the pace of production.

Between 1983 and 1987, Ghana experienced a series of crises – a prolonged drought, forest fires, food shortages, diseases, and social and political instability. It was during these years that the Rawlings government implemented its structural adjustment program (SAP). Key reforms included trade liberalization, private access to foreign exchange, relaxation of import controls, and infrastructure rehabilitation. Though some aspects of the adjustment program helped to ease hardships in the country, its impact on the poor was negative. Life expectancy rates dropped, while poverty, hunger, and disease reached their worst levels since the pre-independence era.

In 1991, CD programs received substantial support from the government and donor agencies (as they had in the 1950s) to develop projects aimed at environmental security, social renewal, and income generation. The goal of these projects was to address the poverty, hunger, disease, and apathy that were endemic among the rural and urban poor. Attempts were made to encourage citizens' groups, communities, churches, and NGOs to participate in projects that could best be handled at the grass roots level. Over the past forty years, peasants have responded in large numbers to some successful government-administered CD programs, such as the mass literacy campaign of the 1950s and the health and family-planning campaigns of the 1990s.

The following section examines the historical development of CD in Ghana and describes the various institutional supports and training mechanisms that are aimed at CD-related programs. The two case studies described in the subsequent sections provide examples of CD processes and programs in operation in Ghana. The section on research examines and describes research activities conducted in the area of CD. The final chapter, on theory, identifies recent trends that are relevant to CD and the status of education and training.

2. A HISTORICAL PERSPECTIVE ON COMMUNITY DEVELOPMENT
Fred Abloh and Stephen Ameyaw

EARLY GOVERNMENT PROGRAMS (1948–57)

The history of government involvement in CD in Ghana (formerly called the Gold Coast) dates back to 1948, after the Second World War, when the British colonial regime established the Department of Social Welfare and Community Development (Sautoy, 1960). The growth of CD during the 1950s was one of the most important factors in the social and economic development of the country. These gains did not come easily. In addition to the efforts of innumerable politicians, civil servants, and churches – all struggling to define an effective CD program for the country – traditional local leaders contributed through their often superior knowledge and skills in the area of village development.

When the Convention People's Party won the general election and assumed power in 1952, Kwame Nkrumah became prime minister of the British colony. Nkrumah gave CD (known then as 'mass education') top priority once he came to power, adopting the general guidelines of the universal education program that had been developed by the colonial administration six years before independence. A detailed plan was formulated and tabled in the legislative assembly in 1952 by the Honourable Kojo Botsio, Minister of Education and Social Welfare, and approved unanimously. The plan stressed literacy education and self-help among the population and signalled the government's readiness to collaborate with those who sought to help combat illiteracy in the country (Sautoy, 1960). An experimental mass-education team, based at the School of Social Welfare in Accra, established a curriculum that included group discussion, drama, physical training, first aid, and music.

CD gained considerable impetus for a number of reasons apart from government resolve. The first was related to the success of the farmers' co-operatives that had been established between 1929 and 1931. Most of the cocoa farmers who belonged to co-operatives relied on traditional techniques of self-help and mutual aid (called *naboa* in Ghana), to prepare the cocoa beans for fermentation and drying. Also, basic services and infrastructure facilities in the rural areas (such as clinics, schools, feeder roads, and water) were poor, and this necessitated a CD strategy that relied on indigenous resources. As well, the high levels of disease and illiteracy among women had prompted the creation of a women's home economics program.

To understand the full ramifications of Ghana's experience with CD, one must examine the programs, philosophy, strategies, objectives, and activities emanating from the Department of Social Welfare and CD. Table 6.1 provides an overview of the five major programs initiated by the department between 1951 and 1957. These programs focused on adult literacy, women's home economics, self-help village projects, extension campaigns, and training. (Extension campaigns are CD activities grafted onto programs of other ministries by request.)

Adult Literacy
As shown in Table 6.1, adult literacy was promoted through CD campaigns. As a first step, the program captured the enthusiasm of the 'educated few' in the villages – including teachers, clerks, and storekeepers – and persuaded them to act as volunteer teachers. These volunteers, who were required to be able to read, write, and do simple maths, were then trained by CD department staff using a variety of teaching methods. At the same time, education and learning were promoted through the use of mobile cinema vans. In addition, weekend courses, one-day school sessions, and seminars were designed to equip

the volunteers with the skills they needed for their teaching tasks. Certificates and badges were provided to successful volunteers, who then played an important role in attracting others to the adult education program. This program was one of the most successful CD programs in the world at the time, attracting experts from many countries in Africa and elsewhere.

Women and Home Economics

Another government priority was to develop basic hygiene and skills among adults and young women through the Women's Home Economics Program. To meet this objective, some of the same training techniques as used in the literacy program were applied. Female staff and volunteers were recruited and trained to develop women's groups in the villages and in the rural training centres that had been established in various parts of the country. In addition, yearly in-service training courses were organized for the female staff. These courses included family menu planning, sewing and handicrafts such as garment making and mending, home improvement and healthy family development, the housewife in the kitchen, the healthy village, and child care, which included care of the expectant mother as well as care for infants and toddlers (Sautoy, 1960). To promote skills development among young girls, vocational programs were provided by the training centres. Some of the village halls that had been built with communal efforts were converted to rural day nurseries for mothers so that they could leave their children while they were busy with farming or with their trades. A considerable number of such nurseries are operating now in many rural and urban areas across the country (Boateng, 1986). Self-help and voluntary action were vital to the success of the adult literacy and women's campaigns.

Self-help Village Projects

Another important program that relied on the CD educational process was the self-help village projects initiative, which responded to the people's desire for concrete results in the form of community facilities and services such as schools and clinics. One of the most popular projects was the Henderson Box. This was a tank that stored water that had been directed from a stream through concrete channels into a coarse filtration tank containing sand and stone. Also, it had a platform for women and children to stand on when fetching water. The Henderson tank had two advantages: it helped remove impurities from the water;

TABLE 6.1
Overview of Community Development in Ghana 1951–1957

Programs	Philosophy	Strategy	Objectives	Activities
Adult literacy	Giving sense of progress and enlightenment to the individual	Adult education carried out with the people and by the people	To upgrade knowledge and skills of mature people	Mobile cinema van education One-day school Bookmobiles Library services Weekend seminars Advertisements
Women, home economics	Women's knowledge and skills development and improvement in their lives	Educational awareness training program for mature women Vocational training for girls	To achieve healthy family living To increase women's participation in development To develop women's skills To institute vocational training programs	Craft production Training courses in hygiene Home economics Maternal and child care Nutrition Establishment of training centres Training of day nursery staff
Self-help village projects	Outward expression of desire to improve life	Self-help projects carried out with the people and by the people	To upgrade community infrastructure To develop and promote self-help initiatives	Henderson's Box type watertank Tree planting Construction of kraals Construction of markets Building of schools, latrines, village halls, clinics, and post offices Construction of roads

TABLE 6.1 *continued*
Overview of Community Development in Ghana 1951–1957

Programs	Philosophy	Strategy	Objectives	Activities
Extension campaign	Teaching local communities types of improvements in their ways of living	Extension education and campaign among villagers and farmers Improved techniques and production	To improve social and economic life To increase participation in new and improved techniques To increase the level of literacy	Tax campaign – "pay your rates and develop your community" (1954) Agricampaign – against cocoa pests and disease (1955) Hygiene campaign – against belharzia disease Roof loan/housing campaign (1956) Land resettlement campaign (1957)
Training	Effective selection and training of staff for organization building	Training program for staff, community workers, and target groups Orientation to CD organizational skills	To develop CD leadership capability To develop trainers of trainers To promote effective problem-solving To train multipurpose generalist CD staff and activists	Social studies courses at the University of Ghana Annual staff training conferences Specialized courses for extension workers Diploma courses Establishment of regional training centres In-service training UNESCO fellowship training for Costa Rica, Sweden, Australia, India and other parts of Africa

and it prevented women and children from stepping in the water as they were collecting it. Requests for these water tanks came from many villages, and this prompted the government to work out a partnership arrangement in which the villagers engaged in self-help efforts, and the CD department provided technical assistance for a nominal fee (Sautoy, 1960).

Self-help projects varied by region. For example, in the northern region there was a high demand for deep wells, tree planting, and the construction of markets, schools, and *kraals* (cattle pens). Popular projects in the Ashanti region were town halls, feeder roads, clinics, and schools. According to government statistics, 386 village projects were completed in 1953, 1,499 in 1954, 844 in 1955, 1,016 in 1956, and 1,210 in 1957.

Extension Campaigns
A fourth major program of the CD department involved extension campaigns, which introduced new and improved techniques designed to enable people, by their own efforts, to improve their general standard of living (Sautoy, 1960). CD staff applied their experiences with adult-teaching techniques and the use of visual aids. Regular group discussions were held focusing on cocoa pest and disease control and stressing the value of cocoa to the farmer and to the country in general. CD, through literacy education and adult education, thus became a useful instrument for extension campaigns.

This CD approach was adopted by other government agencies as well. In 1953 the Department of Agriculture asked CD staff for help in disseminating information on rice growing, the use of fertilizer, and the production of manure for mixed farming. In 1954 the Ministry of Local Government contacted CD staff to launch an educational campaign on paying taxes. There were other extension campaigns in which the Department of Community Development was involved, including those for roof loans, land resettlement schemes, and the control of Belharzia, a parasitical disease (Sautoy, 1960).

Training
The fifth program, focusing on training, served to enhance the other four programs. There were two principal kinds of training: the first aimed at the department's own staff, and the second at volunteer leaders. Staff training varied according to the level of entry. An initial screening was performed on the entry-level staff to measure their enthusiasm and their belief in working with and for people at the village level. This training took six to nine months. Diploma courses were designed by the

University of Ghana to provide in-service training for senior staff. Annual staff conferences were designed and hosted by the university for senior staff. In addition to training, these courses and conferences provided an opportunity for the participants to evaluate the work done during the preceding year and to plan for future programs.

One of the main objectives of the training was to produce multipurpose field workers with the wide-ranging knowledge and skills needed to help in village-level work. The multipurpose workers were taught adult education techniques and the principles and practices of CD. For example, they learned agriculture, basic building techniques, and the use of visual aids. However, the multipurpose CD staff were always backed by field specialists at the regional or central offices.

Rural training centres in the country provided refresher courses. For example, at the National School of Social Welfare in Panfokrom, near Accra, courses were conducted on basic building techniques, on how to conduct literacy days, and on public speaking. Training was an ongoing process, and the department provided it through its extension services to a great variety of groups. For example, it served municipal councillors, lorry drivers, road safety workers, and mechanics. Under UNESCO sponsorship, it trained people from as far away as Costa Rica, Sweden, Australia, and India. As a result, many countries in Africa and elsewhere benefited from the accumulated experience and expertise of community developers in Ghana.

CD Departmental Structure
The CD department in Ghana between 1950 and 1957 had a pyramidal structure. At the base of the pyramid were the villages and individuals receiving the department's programs: adult education, women's work and self-help projects. A mass education officer, assisted by senior and assistant officers, was placed in charge of a number of districts within a region and worked with the people in the villages to implement the department's programs. As a general policy, administrative functions were left to the principal CD officers and their assistants in the regional offices. This approach was taken to permit mass education officers to work as much as possible with and for the people at the village level. A female mass education officer in the regional office co-ordinated all the programs related to women's work in the regions. She was assisted by female mass education officers in the districts. Specially trained CD officers included an expert in visual aids, and an engineer who provided technical advice on road and bridge construction using visual aids. The regional office staff were supported by a technical field unit

that provided equipment, cinema vans, and vehicles to various centres in the region. The CD department in the central office in Accra had a national director in charge of all operations in the country, who reported to the principal secretary, who reported to the minister.

CHANGES IN THE POST-INDEPENDENCE PERIOD (1958–80)

After independence, the CD department found itself caught in a political crossfire as governments and ideologies began to change rapidly. As a result, most of the functions and structures of CD have changed dramatically over time, though the approach is still the same. Immediately following independence in 1957, Nkrumah turned the CD operation into an arm of the new Ministry of Labour and Social Welfare, with the goal of establishing co-operatives that would conform to the government's socialist policies. There were several reasons why this change was made. First, CD activities, particularly the self-help village projects, were seen as controlled by local authorities who had supported the opposition party during the three general elections before independence. Second, interdepartmental jealousies had been rising as a result of the growing popularity of the CD programs, which required different departments to work with CD staff on joint projects. Third, there was pressure to expand government departments in order to create employment opportunities for party supporters. Fourth and finally, the village projects were seen as promoting local rather than national government. Despite all this, CD programs such as self-help projects, adult education, women's work, and extension campaigns continued to be promoted, albeit with limited staff and funds.

Another reorganization of CD activities occurred when the Busia government assumed power in the Second Republic in 1968. The Department of Social Welfare and Community Development, the national service corps, the workers' brigade, and rural housing were placed under the umbrella of a new Ministry of Rural Development. A roof loan scheme that the CD department had managed for the Ministry of Housing was incorporated into the new Rural Housing Department. This reorganization was meant to co-ordinate efforts to alleviate poverty, disease, and apathy; and to create employment through integrated rural development schemes. Most CD programs – adult education, extension campaigns, women's work, and so on – continued to be encouraged and promoted.

The National Redemption Council Party (NRC), which ousted Busia's government in 1972, conducted its own reorganization, bringing the

Department of Social Welfare and Community Development again under the mandate of the Ministry of Labour, Social Welfare and Community Development. During the early months of the NRC administration, CD programs became more popular; the regime heavily promoted self-reliance, and established programs such as Operation Feed Your Self and Operation Free the Industries. The Department of Community Development conducted educational and awareness campaigns throughout the country. In the urban areas people began to plant cassava, plantain and vegetables in their backyards, while the rural people increased their food production. However, because of administrative mismanagement, the self-help ideology did not last long. The Third Republic, under President Limann, did not make any major changes affecting the CD Department.

DEVELOPMENTS SINCE 1981

When the Provisional National Defense Council Party (PNDC) under Rawlings came to power in 1981, the CD department was separated from Social Welfare and placed under the Ministry of Local Government. The goal was to bring together departments that promoted local development so that local people could have more input into decision-making and benefit directly. Most of the CD programs described above are still functioning, particularly the women's work program.

The prevailing conditions of poverty, disease, and apathy have led in recent years to the development of associations, groups, and NGOs. Among these are women's' groups, producers' and traders' associations, environmental organizations, and church groups, which aim to empower the poor and develop intermediate organizations.

The CD department has acknowledged the organizational and structural changes in the public and private sectors, and the increasing activity of domestic voluntary organizations and international NGOs in local development projects, and is responding by attempting to set up partnership arrangements. For example, the New York–based World Education Centre is working with CD staff to promote functional adult education geared toward particular groups, such as farmers, drivers, artisans, and labourers. CD staff have also been working with the Ministry of Health to promote family planning programs and to conduct Health Week activities in the country.

Among the domestic NGOs, the Ghana Rural Reconstruction Movement has been promoting adult education and self-help village projects; it also provides extension services to farmers. In various locales, more informal networks are emerging: these include youth groups, community and ethnic associations, women's groups, and organizations that are involved with particular aspects of CD (Hutchful, 1992). The CD department has established eleven women's training institutes across the country in an effort to promote adult education and provide skilled personnel for the various programs and campaigns being conducted.

SUMMARY

The above review shows the important role CD has played in the public life of Ghana since 1948. As noted by Sautoy (1960), especially important in building an effective public administration is the close involvement of the individuals, groups, and communities who are to benefit. In the 1950s the enthusiasm generated by the mass education initiatives of the government was vital to the success of CD. But equally important were the many highly effective self-help and bottom-up initiatives.

The generally acknowledged success of CD in Ghana between 1951 and 1957 was in great part due to the government's willingness to spend money on project and program development. Another factor was the nationalist fervour in the country as it prepared for independence. However, CD activities also faced problems: the staff had difficulty overcoming the general perception that their programs were in competition with those of other government departments, and they often clashed with local development committees over the use of funds and the selection of village projects.

Since independence, CD initiatives have been undermined by political and ideological clashes that have led to departmental reorganizations and sharp reductions in financial, staff, and technical support. However, it appears that CD remains a priority.

3. CURRENT PRACTICE

A. The Integrated Community Centres for Employable Skills: A Rural Shelter Project
Fred Abloh and Stephen Ameyaw

INTRODUCTION

The provision of housing and shelter responds to a basic human need and consumes a substantial portion of human and material resources. In Ghana, even though local people have traditionally relied on low-cost (local) materials, the development of these materials has been largely overlooked by economic planners, who have tended to focus on modern, imported materials such as corrugated iron sheets, cement, and aluminum window frames.

For decades, Ghana has experienced housing problems. Increasing rural poverty and lack of credit facilities have led to the deterioration of an already inadequate infrastructure in the housing sector. Local building code specifications have long been based on regulations established by colonial governments for European-style housing – regulations that require materials and techniques far beyond the resources of most home builders (Stokes, 1981). Standards that reflect age-old local building techniques are more likely to be within the capabilities and resources of the people of the area and will be more suited to the local climate. Local resources and technologies are relatively simple; in this, they stand in sharp contrast to imported techniques, which tend to employ heavy machinery and few people and are controlled by outside capital (Donkor & Lea, 1980).

Major breakthroughs in the political arena are needed to help raise the quality of local building materials and provide the necessary support for the use of these materials. This has begun to happen in Ghana. The following section outlines the historical context for the lack of development of local resources and describes some more recent CD efforts relating to this issue.

THE CONTEXT

In Ghana the processes of colonialism and industrialization have had a dramatic impact on the housing industry, particularly on design and the use of local materials. Traditionally, many Ghanaians lived in traditional compound homes (enclosures) with simple design features that accommodated the extreme hot and cold weather patterns. For instance, many houses did not have windows, though some had small windows in the shape of pigeon-holes. Door openings had no frames and were covered with mats made of raffia palm or tree bark. Walls were constructed with easily available materials such as mud, wattle, daub, and stone. Workmanship was crude, and finishes and aesthetics were not really important. A house was purely a necessity, to be rebuilt as and when necessary.

The British introduced significant changes in housing design, building materials, and construction techniques. These changes began with the arrival of the first missionaries, who built settlements on hilltops such as Akropong and Akwapim. The merchants who followed built castles along the coastal fringes. Both groups introduced technological innovations in home construction with materials such as zinc, lime, cement, coal tar, corrugated iron, and steel (for locks). The apparent convenience of the new methods and materials was observed and adopted by locals, and this resulted in a gradual but significant change in the way Ghanaian homes were constructed.

In the forest zone, roofs had been made from local bamboo, palm branches, and wattle-and-daub; such roofs kept room temperatures cool, but they also leaked and were a fire hazard (Donkor & Lea, 1980). Ghanaians observed the definite advantages of zinc or iron sheets for roofing.

Soon after it was introduced, Portland cement, formed into blocks, became the main material for house walls and foundations in the urban centres. By the 1940s traditional building materials were looked down upon as either outmoded, rural, and backward. House designs were fast becoming apologetic copies of Western designs built primarily with imported materials. People showed off their wealth by building their homes out of imported materials. The massive dwellings of Kwahu Ridge provide good examples of this. Thus, what has emerged in Ghana is a strong preference for imported building materials, and for the prestige that goes with them, and a rejection of local building materials. For the past twenty years, various attempts have been made to reverse this trend and improve local building materials.

INTEGRATED COMMUNITY CENTRES FOR EMPLOYABLE SKILLS

A new project was introduced in the early 1990s as part of Ghana's Program of Action to Mitigate the Social Cost of Adjustment (PAMSCAD), which was aimed at developing and rehabilitating rural housing. The project originated within the continuation schools program, a pilot scheme developed and funded by UNICEF in 1986. Initially, twelve centres were established across the country. These centres, renamed the Integrated Community Centres for Employable Skills (ICCES), eventually expanded and consolidated. By 1994, ICCES had 40 core, 12 associate, and 18 assisted centres.

The primary objective of the ICCES project has been to teach vocational and craft skills to school leavers so as to make them employable. Training focuses on dropouts from all levels of schooling, and on illiterate young people of both sexes.

The youth project teaches home-building skills at craft-training centres. Each centre graduates twenty trainees after a two-year session; this amounts to more than 1,000 graduates per session. The enthusiasm for this kind of training is very strong. Efforts are also being made to encourage the young people to form their own organizations such as builders' co-operatives, carpenters' guilds, masons' unions, and electricians' teams. Several related research projects have tried to discover new ways to use local materials such as stone, wood, clay, and soil. For example, studies have been undertaken that examine the use of stone to build retaining walls for preventing soil erosion, to build better foundations, and to improve drainage patterns.

The goal of the ICCES project is to create a framework for production-oriented action. Toward this end, it supports rural dwellers with start-up capital, practical knowledge, and public education. It also helps them acquire appropriate skills and undertake self-help projects and activities. The ICCES provides facilities, tools, and expertise and trains rural groups in skills that will encourage the use of local materials in production industries, and in the rehabilitation of existing houses and the construction of new ones. Weekend seminars, radio and television discussions, and popular theatre programs have become important educational tools.

PROJECT ORGANIZATION

Individual projects are community based, managed by local ICCES centre managers. Community groups form the bases of local employment and investment opportunities. Individual contributions are treated as shares. Co-operatives and other investment groups are encouraged to own facilities. Quarterly reports and twice-yearly review meetings are arranged at the regional level, as are annual general reviews. The field extension officers of various government departments provide consultancy services. For example, the Town and Country Planning Department, the Ministry of Health, and the Ghana Water and Sewage Corporation are engaged to see the projects through.

The ICCES project has gained much popularity in communities across the nation because of the low cost of homes constructed from local materials. As a result, many chiefs and NGOs have asked for new centres to be opened. In some areas communities have formed their own associations to promote the ICCES program.

The project selection criteria state that projects must have a training component as well as an income-generation focus for the trainees. They must also aim at training, investment, and long-term employment generation for the community or association. NGOs are encouraged to participate and may contribute funds, materials, and other resources. Collaborative efforts within the PAMSCAD framework have led many government departments to pool resources for implementing of the ICCES program. These departments include the Rural Housing and Cottage Industries, Community Development, the Ministry of Local Government, and the National Council of Women and Development. Since the project is community based, ICCES managers work with the district administration. The core centres are controlled by ICCES town and village development committees. At the associated centres, NGOs organize most of the activities while the ICCES provides instruction and equipment. The entire ICCES program is part of the Ministry of Employment and Social Welfare and is headed by a director, who is aided by a consultant.

The ICCES project falls within the parameters of CD and focuses on youth employment, skills training, voluntarism, empowerment, and co-operation. It educates the public on the use of local building materials for housing and drainage works. Intensive research has been done to improve the quality of local building materials. There have been attempts to promote recycled or value-added products, such as wooden shingles made from scrap lumber. Within the ICCES/CD framework, attempts are being made to address other needs, such as for toilet facilities, drainage systems, and road and bridge repair. The success of ICCES demonstrates the enthusiasm and the will of young Ghanaians to gain new skills and employment.

B. Income-generating Projects in Southern Ghana: Women's Perceptions
Victoria Serwah Poku

INTRODUCTION

Ghanaian women contribute in many ways to the development of the nation. Apart from their reproductive role in bearing and caring for children and ensuring the supply of labour through maintenance of the family, women in Ghana are actively involved in production activities in the areas of farming, manufacturing, and commerce.

Development programs have tended to overlook the important role women have played in national development. An attempt to rectify the absence of women in development planning led to a plethora of special projects for women, popularly known as income generating projects (IGPs). The rationale behind the IGPs was based on studies which showed that when women earned more, they typically used the increase to improve the health and welfare of their families. The goal of the case study described here is to provide information on women's perceptions of IGPs and to evaluate these projects on the basis of those perceptions.

STUDY AREAS

The study was carried out in six different IGP communities whose principal economic activities were farming and trading. These local economic activities provided a starting point for the IGPs and will be briefly described below.

Akobima: Palm Oil Processing
Located in the Mfantsiman district of the central region, Akobima is a small rural community of mainly farmers who cultivate palm fruit, plantain, and cocoa. The primary occupation of the women in the community is palm oil processing, which has been organized by the National Council on Women and Development (NCWD).

Asuogya–Nyame Bekyere: Gari Processing
The people of Asuogya in the Ahanta West district of the western region are mostly food crop farmers. Cassava, a tropical plant, is processed by both men and women into a flour called *gari* (used in tapioca). The cassava-grating machine is available to all members of the community. Their only source of water is a river. There is no health post in the area, and the health of the inhabitants is poor. This group has only recently received assistance from PAMSCAD in the form of credit, so the members' benefit cannot yet be assessed.

Afari: Pottery
Afari is a small community in the Atwima district of the Ashanti region, 25 kilometres west of Kumasi on the main Kumasi–Nkawie road. The inhabitants are mostly farmers who grow food crops and cocoa.

The environment is clean, with good drinking water. There are schools up to JSS level, though there is no health facility in the area. Through their IGP group, a day care centre has been built.

There are clay deposits around the area, so pottery has long been the supplementary occupation. The Department of Rural Housing and Cottage Industries has built a kiln for the community, and the 31st December Women's Movement has supplied a banding wheel.

Dabaa: Bead Making

This is a rural community in the Atwima district of the Ashanti region, 25 kilometres west of Kumasi and 5 kilometres from Akropongon on the Kumasi–Sunyani road. It is a small town with a few concrete, multistorey buildings and other buildings plastered with cement and painted. The people are food crop farmers, with cassava being the main crop. The stalk of that plant is used in bead making, which is undertaken by all the inhabitants – men, women and children. They have good drinking water. Funds from the IGP have been used to renovate the houses of group members.

Essam: Palm Oil, Gari Processing, Soap Making

This is a small community in the Birim district of the eastern region. Its inhabitants are mainly farmers who cultivate palm oil and cassava. With help from NCWD, palm oil is processed into soap and cassava into *gari*.

Oshiyie: Fish Smoking

This is a small community in the Ga district of the Greater Accra region. It is predominantly a fishing community, with some vegetable farming. Women are primarily engaged in fish smoking.

FOCUS GROUPS

Between two and four focus group discussions were held in each of these communities. The groups were composed of women between 17 and 85 years of age. In all, 138 women participated in twenty focus group discussions.

Eighty-six women (62.3%) had no formal education; 49 (35.6%) had some primary or middle school education; and 3 (2.1%) had a commercial, secondary, or B level teacher's certificate. About half of the women were not living with their husbands, who were choosing to stay outside the community. A few were divorced, widowed, or separated. Most members had lived in the community since birth.

GENERAL FINDINGS

Because of economic and political pressures, most rural women in Ghana become engaged in income-generating activities. Interestingly, all six projects incorporate employment, health, and educational features. It is the women's need for survival and their desire to provide food, clothing, health, and education for their families that lead them into the employment opportunities provided by IGPs. The question is whether involvement in the IGPs enables the women to meet their needs.

This study found a general dissatisfaction not only with the technical and organizational aspects of the projects, but also with the benefits gained, which were minimal. The women complained that after taking into account the 'in kind' contributions they made to the project (e.g., mutual aid and reciprocal relations), they worked very long hours on often difficult tasks with little in economic terms to show for their efforts. Generally, their dissatisfaction related less to the nature of the work and more to their continuing inability to meet basic family needs and rise above their condition of subsistence.

Insofar as the IGP activities are concerned, they attributed much of their frustration to lack of access to markets to sell their products, poor transportation, lack of credit, taxes, and the absence of an effective system of agricultural and technical inputs that otherwise might have improved their profit levels.

However, while the cash income generated from these IGPs was low, women experienced some material benefits in terms of goods and services. For example, in Akobima, although women had meagre resources, they were able to at least feed themselves and their families. In Afari, women were able to keep their children in school when the teachers knew that the mothers were involved in IGPs and had wares to sell. Additional benefits resulting from IGP activities related to some limited improvements in clothing, food, housing, and hiring of labour for farming, and to being able to contribute toward development projects in the community. The more important benefits were found to be of a personal and social nature; these will be discussed under 'improvements in women's welfare,' following specific findings on the perceived difficulties of IGPs.

PERCEIVED DIFFICULTIES

Although improved technology has increased output considerably and reduced labour input and input costs in some cases, this has not been reflected in purchasing power. Some women noted that, especially in recent times, it had been difficult for them to pay their children's school fees. In Nyame Bekyere, women stated that they have not been able to buy a scarf, let alone half a piece of cloth, for a whole year. In Dabaa, the high cost of chemicals made the craft of bead making virtually unaffordable. The group there stated that their main capital was often used to buy food. They added that in the 1960s and 1970s, when the chemicals were not so expensive, they had been able to make much money out of their project. The women identified several difficulties they had encountered in realizing profits.

Marketing
With improved technology, women were able to produce more, and this created a glut on the market. The women at Nyame Bekyere found that they could produce a lot of *gari* in a short while, with the result that it was sold at a reduced price. Similarly, at Akobima, the women reported that they could process a ton of palm fruit in a day, but when they took the barrels of palm oil to the market, there were few buyers, and those who came dictated the price.

Transportation
The cost of carting raw materials from the hinterlands to production centres and transporting processed goods to marketing centres was high. Since some of the women did not make enough profit from sales because of the low prices, high transport costs were a source of worry. The fish smokers and *gari* processors were affected the most by the lack of adequate transportation.

Credit
In all the projects studied, women expressed the need for credit. They maintained that without it, benefits cannot be fully realized. In fact, the fish smokers – one group who had no trouble marketing their product – wanted to increase production but often could not obtain credit from the fishermen to purchase more fish. Even when credit was given, the fish smokers were forced to sell at a loss when the fishermen demanded immediate payment.

Taxes

Another constraint to the full realization of benefits from IGPs related to the numerous taxes paid by women in market centres. This particularly concerned the *gari* processors of Asuogya–Nyame Bekyere: every time they went to the market they had to pay way-bills, income tax, and levies for wares.

Inputs

Lack of inputs was also a major constraint in some IGPs. The bead makers at Dabaa, for instance, complained of the lack of chemicals and dye for their work. These had once been sold to the IGPs by the NCWD at affordable prices, but now they were forced to buy them from middlemen at exorbitant prices. They made little profit, if any, since the money they received from sales was meagre and they could not buy the chemicals to store in bulk.

Pay-back Period

Women in the pottery and fish-smoking groups were still paying back the loans for the banding wheel, kiln, and wire mesh. Any money from sales was used to pay for these items. Therefore, they do not consider these earnings to be their own.

PERCEIVED IMPROVEMENTS IN WOMEN'S WELFARE

In the study, improvement in welfare was defined to include a reduction in drudgery, increased time for child care and household concerns, and improved health for women and children. The women also recounted ways in which their participation in the IGPs had been empowering.

Reduction in Drudgery

In most of the IGPs studied, the acquisition of better technology brought about a reduction in drudgery and made work less tedious. In Oshiyie, the women recalled that before the IGP was introduced, they were scorched by the heat of the fire as a result of many hours of pulling wire and drying fish; afterwards, they needed to go near the fire only when the fish was smoked. In Afari, the women commented that the binding wheel had freed them from the waist pains that resulted from having to bend or squat for long periods of time. In the cassava and palm oil groups, the graters and presses saved the women much effort and time.

Similarly, the *gari*-processing groups said that if it had not been for the machine, they would have spent much more time grating, which is very tedious.

Time Saving

Except in Dabaa (bead making), the women reported having more time to look after their husbands and children. They were also able to rest more. With the kiln, once the wares were arranged inside, the fire could be set and left. At Akobima, the oil processing group commented that before the IGP, they had had to get up very early in the morning with their children to pound the nuts: 'Now they and their children enjoy a little more sleep and are able to prepare a lot of oil in less time. They can also have time to plait their hair or travel to other places to visit friends and relatives.'

Health

Another very important aspect of women's welfare is health. In most of the IGPs studied, the traditional processing methods resulted in physical pain for the women. In Afari, the chore of bending and squatting to shape the bowls caused many of the women to suffer waist pain. One member reported that with the new machines they did not get sick, were always healthy, and looked 'like city folks.' Another added that they now looked 'good like young women.'

In contrast, at Dabaa, where they did not yet have access to any improved technology but still used a traditional oven to bake the beads, the women commented that the work was extremely tedious and that they experienced waist pain from long hours of standing. One woman said they were exposed to too much heat, which is especially hazardous for pregnant women. They also developed bruises and sometimes serious wounds in the bead-making process. They had requested an improved oven to fire the beads, but this had not yet materialized.

It should be noted here that the women did not raise health issues until prompted to do so by the researcher. There has not been much change in the way the people look after themselves and their children when ill. Many attend the nearest hospital or clinic, while others continue to rely on herbal medicines. Two groups – Essam (soap makers) and Akobima (palm oil) – were able to put up a clinic with the profits generated by their projects. They commented that they worked hard to get the clinic because it was cheaper. If the nurse was unable to treat them, she referred them to the hospital.

At Oshiyie, members had been taught first-aid measures – for example, to treat their children's diarrhoea with oral re-hydrated salt (ORS) or liquid from rice porridge. They had also been provided with information on personal hygiene and family planning. One woman stated that they had been advised that having too many children at short intervals was not good for their health, or for their children's well-being, so they had learned to space their children.

Empowerment Issues
In the IGPs studied, empowerment issues considered by women can be placed in these four categories: education or literacy, knowledge of rights and responsibilities, empowerment through group solidarity, and economic independence and community management.

Education. In two of the projects – Essam and Akobima (soap making and palm oil processing) – women gained knowledge in literacy and bookkeeping, which they used to improve their trading activities and life in general. They stated that as a result of the training workshops organized for them, they had learned to keep track of their expenditures and sales. When the women were given cheques for the bank, they were pleased to be able to read and countersign them. The Essam group had started a literacy program long before the National Functional Literacy Program was established, so many members could read and write in their language.

In Oshiyie as well as in Essam and Akobima, women noted happily that through seminars and public educational programs they had been taught better housekeeping, child care, and family-planning methods. When asked what they wanted from the projects, they said that they wanted 'to become professionals in order to rub shoulders with other professionals.' This would raise their status and give them a sense of belonging. It would also provide increased exposure to outsiders and boost morale. Four out of the six groups mentioned that through constant interaction with outsiders – in exchange programs, seminars, workshops, and participation in fairs like PAFAM (bead makers) and INDUTECH (palm oil processors) – they gained self-confidence. They were able to talk 'boldly' to outsiders and not hide from them, as they had previously done. In fact, they were anticipating appearing on television soon.

Awareness of rights and responsibilities. In two of the six groups interviewed – Oshiyie and Essam – the women had been empowered through increased awareness of their rights and responsibilities, first and foremost as individuals, but also as a group in the community. In Oshiyie, the fishmongers said that when called on to pay monies to a group for reasons they did not understand, they refused. Instead, the leader said they would seek advice from the NCWD. When a chief imposed a fine on them for failing to inform him about some expatriate visitors, they again refused to pay. In Essam, a man believed to be an agent of some organization wanted the group to append their signatures to resolutions he had prepared. The group refused on the basis that they had not been party to the development of the resolutions.

The women also felt they took more responsibility at home. They took the initiative on matters where previously they would have waited for a husband's direction. During meetings they spoke their minds, often disagreeing with leaders, and voted carefully on major decisions.

Group solidarity. Solidarity among group members was considered to be important in all six projects. Through group solidarity and the perception of a common identity, the women were able to solve group problems and settle quarrels and differences quickly. The group also offered a forum for discussing women's problems in an atmosphere of mutual understanding, respect, and trust. They were able to borrow money from their common welfare fund when in need. The women gained a sense of satisfaction in being identified as members of such a group. They considered it something very special when they were invited to church harvests, and often they wore a common cloth to identify themselves at these functions.

The IGP groups provided an opportunity for the women to learn from each other. In Afari and Dabaa (pottery and beads), where the introduction of new designs was a factor in increased productivity, beginners were able to learn from those already working with a new design.

There was a strong commitment to group welfare. In sorrow or joy – bereavement or child-bearing – the whole group contributed with cash donations and food items. The more experienced members counselled groups and individuals on particular problems relating to looking after their homes, caring for their children and husbands, treating minor ailments and injuries, and dealing with marital problems. Several reported that counselling had been instrumental in improving domestic relations with husbands and children.

Community management. The community management role of women was based on the provision of items for collective consumption through collective effort. In some of the project areas this was clearly manifested. In Oshiyie the group planted a number of coconut seedlings to help the tree-growing program, and as an already organized body, they co-operated with the town committee in arranging communal labour. The IGP group in Dabaa joined with town committee members to plant trees for utility poles and contributed half the funds needed for a local water project. The committee was also able to borrow money from the group when needed. In Akobima, clean drinking water, a clinic, a day care centre, a community centre, and a school up to JSS level were all established through the initiatives and contributions of the IGP. Similarly, through the efforts and profits of IGPs in Essam, a school, a clinic, a day care centre, and a community centre were built. Group profits were used to feed the children at the day care centre and to pay the clinic attendant. Other projects initiated were a multistorey building to be used as both a warehouse and a guest house; feeder roads linking two neighbouring villages; and a literacy program.

FACTORS AFFECTING PARTICIPATION

In the study, a participant in group activities was defined as a registered member of an IGP who attended meetings and took an active part in group decision-making. The women discussed both positive and negative factors that affected participation.

Positive Factors

Expected future benefits. Women joined IGPs because they expected future economic gains. They hoped that they would earn enough to purchase personal and household items on 'soft' terms as a group. Members looked forward to profit margins that would enable them to provide food, clothing, school fees, and household utensils for their families, and to pay hospital bills.

Leadership. At Akobima, Oshiyie, and Essam, women attributed their continued membership in IGPs to the good leadership and co-operation they had experienced from project managers. In these communities, good leadership contributed significantly to group cohesion and solidarity. The personal qualities of the leader – patience, tolerance, and openness – were noted as important to the proper functioning of the group, particularly in financial matters.

Negative Factors

In the early stages of the project, not enough time was spent explaining the project's purpose and the expected roles and responsibilities of the women. Several bureaucratic procedures, such as for the disbursement of funds, were not understood; as a result, unavoidable delays were interpreted as a breach of trust, and this undermined members' confidence in the IGP.

A lot of ill-feeling had been generated by what the women perceived as the inconsistent behaviour of donors. For instance, the group at Afari received a kiln and banding wheels from the Department of Cottage Industries and the 31st December Women's Movement, respectively, believing that these were gifts. But shortly afterwards there was a change of policy and they found they had to pay for them.

The members also blamed the project managers for the destruction of their wares during the rains, claiming that the managers had not listened to their 'felt need' that a proper shed should be put up before the kiln was constructed.

In Oshiyie, the women noted that prompt action should follow all promises by donors. They explained that many refused to join the group because all promises by donors were not kept. In this, they cited the example that wire mesh that had been promised in fact never materialized.

In Akobima, the women would have liked donors to arrange for a soap-making factory to buy their palm oil. The communities at Akobima and Essam requested a tractor so that they could cart their fresh palm nuts from the farm to the production centres. In Asuogya–Nyame Bekyere, the group suggested that the Ghana Food Distribution Corporation ought to buy their *gari*.

More generally, IGPs wanted working capital from the government and donors. The study reported a particular case at Dabaa where the women put up a structure for a bead-baking machine promised by the government. However, when the time came for the machine to be delivered, they could not afford to pay the duty.

The initial investment of labour and time – attending preliminary meetings, cleaning project sites, moulding and laying bricks – also discouraged some women from participating. Others were discouraged by their husbands, who argued that bricklaying was not a woman's job. The new roles that women had to take on during the formation of the group often conflicted with traditional ones. Some of the 'deserters' later wanted to join but 'felt guilty' and were not bold enough to come forward once the group was more established.

The use of project equipment by nonmembers also served as a disincentive for participating in the IGPs. It was apparent that there was a lack of understanding between donors and project managers on the one hand, and the beneficiaries on the other. Though nonmembers were usually charged more money than members when they used the equipment, members felt that others did not join because they could already use the machines any time they wanted to. Suspicion about working for the material gain of others was evident in three of the IGPs studied – namely Akobima, Essam, and Oshiyie, where members were emphatic that they would not work for anybody.

All groups expressed the view that if the government or donors want to help them that help must be complete, taking into account all aspects of any economic venture, including finance, marketing, transport, and inputs. Without a more comprehensive approach, women only end up back where they started.

QUALITATIVE PROCESS INDICATORS

The main findings of the study about appropriate indicators to measure the success of a project, as perceived by the women, can be placed in three categories: women's individual improvement, social and economic development, and CD.

Women's Individual Improvement Indicators
Health Indicators. With the establishment of IGPs, improved technologies were introduced, making work less tedious and hazardous. Women experienced less waist and knee pain and had more time to rest than before. The women viewed these benefits as the mark of a successful project.

Self-advancement indicators. One self-advancement indicator mentioned was with respect to appearance. The following comments reflect the status attached to the urban 'image': 'they should put on weight in order to look like city-dwellers,' 'they cannot always be villagers,' 'they should look like the researchers.'

Another self-advancement indicator related to the purchasing power of the women. This related especially to improvements in the creditworthiness of women, their ability to pay fees and bills (for hospital, school, etc.), and their ability to buy new clothes during festivities.

Literacy was mentioned as an indicator only at Essam and Oshiyie. Some of the women commented that what pleased them most was to see people reading. Some also said they could sign their name and promised that they would soon be able to read the Bible and newspapers.

Social and Economic Development Indicators

Empowerment indicators. Empowerment issues considered by women related to what women should be able to do to improve their lives as individuals and as a group. Group solidarity was perceived as important because it helped the less fortunate members in times of need and brought about good relationships. To this end, having an 'association cloth' that distinguished members as an identifiable group was also seen as important. The women indicated that they had become more diplomatic and self-confident when talking to visitors. They also indicated that well-organized meetings should be held more regularly.

Economic indicators. Women specified the following economic indicators of a successful IGP: availability of marketing avenues; regular access to cheap transport; readily available formal credits; prompt payment of credit; and increased job opportunities in the community. Women in Asuogya–Nyame Bekyere said that they would like to have sufficient capital to purchase a vehicle to cart their goods as well as money to tar their roads. At Dabaa, the women indicated that their children should be able to get employment in the community after their schooling, instead of having to travel to the urban area in search of work.

CD Indicators

The consensus among those interviewed was that CD activity should relate in particular to the following: renovation of homes; construction of new buildings; regular affordable transport; empowerment opportunities; availability of good drinking water; and other new development projects. In all communities, women indicated that they would evaluate a successful project using indicators such as the renovating of homes and the constructing of schools, day care centres, clinics, and so on. Those who had mud buildings would be able to plaster them with cement; those who had thatched roofing would have aluminum roofing instead. Water served to visitors would not be muddy, but clear and clean.

SUMMARY

While most of the participants in IGPs felt that they had not profited sufficiently from their involvement to rise above their subsistence level of living, all perceived some benefit in terms of goods and services. It was generally agreed that the introduction of improved technology had reduced drudgery and made work less labour-intensive. Participants felt that their health had improved, as they suffered less from such 'economic' ailments as waist and back pain. Most enjoyed the increased contact with outsiders that resulted from the projects. Their self-confidence had grown, and they were proud of their ability to relate to outsiders.

The participants also noted some of the difficulties they had encountered in the operation of the IGPs. They cited the need for a more holistic package including marketing, transport, credit, and inputs. In particular, the women felt that the repayment period for credit was too short.

For the IGPs to succeed, motivation was vital, and to instil that motivation, leadership was crucial. Good leadership was associated with frequent meetings, accountability with respect to financial matters, and a democratic structure in which members were able to speak freely. Women were more likely to participate if there was clear understanding between themselves and those who implemented the project. Lack of communication created uncertainties about the purpose of the project and the responsibilities of each partner. Also, frequent changes in personnel and bureaucratic delays were found to be confusing.

In the design and implementation stages of a project, the women were often suspicious that they would be working for the material gain of outsiders. Participation was also affected by the amount of investment in time and money that was perceived as necessary in the early stages of the project. Women were less likely to participate if there was no obvious benefit in terms of visible inputs. Participation was negatively affected when the use of the project's facilities was not restricted to registered members.

Where IGPs were successful, women began to think about the lack of health services in their community and attempted to do something about it. All of the participants valued group solidarity, considering this to be the basis for success. Where it did not exist, they perceived the lack of it to be a problem. Some of the women became aware of their rights and responsibilities as a result of the IGP. In all projects, women were

concerned about problems in the community and the need to do something about them. In the successful projects, women had initiated and
contributed financially to CD projects. Where there were complementary projects, the women felt that their own position in the community
had improved.

4. RESEARCH IN COMMUNITY DEVELOPMENT
Stephen Ameyaw

Research activities of interest to the field of CD in Ghana range from
the macro to the meso and the micro levels and address diverse issues.
The macro and meso studies tend to emphasize issues in the area of
economic development, and help to guide the formulation of rural development policies. At the micro level, research studies have examined
ways of ensuring the flow of new, field-tested technical knowledge that
is relevant to rural production and extension education. There have
been several approaches to participative and action research; their general goal is to develop processes and strategies for promoting interaction and understanding between the researcher and the researched in
data collection and analysis. These research approaches will be examined in this chapter in terms of their relevance to CD practice.

SOCIO-ECONOMIC DATA

Research related to CD at the macro level involves the analysis of general conditions within specific regions. The conditions analysed relate
to the environment, the availability and need for resources, and the
socio-economic characteristics of the region's population. Specific examples are studies in such areas as demography, migration, population, stratification, gender, and developmental conditions in Ghana
(Atim, 1986; Bourke, 1986; Hill, 1986). Generally, the studies show that
rural élites play a dominant role in the allocation of resources, thereby
undermining the ability of the poor to 'get their fair share' (Atim, 1986;
Bourke, 1986). The studies also conclude that women, children, and
other disadvantaged groups have not benefited fairly from past development projects (Hay and Stichter, 1984; Ameyaw, 1987; Ewusi, 1987).
Other findings, from population and migration studies, show that there
is a high unemployment rate among those young people who migrate
to the urban areas (Ewusi, 1987).

Some of these findings have been used to reformulate rural development policies – for example, through the 'basic needs' approach – and to create new projects aimed at helping the poor and the disadvantaged groups. Socio-economic research is conducted mainly by universities or research institutes in the country. In some instances this research is a collaborative effort between Ghanaian and foreign institutions conducted by consultants, graduate students, and/or donor agencies.

TECHNOLOGICAL INNOVATIONS

In the search for ways to increase production, particularly by small farmers, there has been considerable research conducted on traditional and more innovative farming practices (Atim, 1986; Ewusi, 1987). It has been suggested that the sowing of low-yield grains, the use of traditional methods of storage, and farmers' dependence on traditional tools – such as the hoe and cutlass (i.e, machete) – have acted together to impede food production in the country. Consequently, researchers have been looking for appropriate technologies that might increase yields for maize, cattle, yams, and vegetables (Atim, 1986; Dadson, 1973).

The problem with this type of scientific research is that it is often theory-driven, and focuses narrowly on 'quick fix' solutions to development without regard for the impact on the daily lives of the rural poor. There are no known comparative studies that measure the impact where such technological developments have been introduced. Furthermore, knowledge gained from past research efforts is rarely incorporated into the design of new projects. A case example that illustrates well the singular preoccupation with technological development involves the programs to improve maize yields that are being carried out in some regions of Ghana. A pilot project and applied research techniques are being used to measure the effectiveness of these projects. Such pilot projects aim to ensure the flow of new, field-tested, technical knowledge that is relevant to rural production.

However, the applied research approach, though important, has a number of drawbacks: It is conducted to support projects already implemented. The research undertaking does not involve the beneficiaries of the project. Recommendations for modifications in the research approach and design are often ignored, as decisions are based on the efficiency and effectiveness of the project. Finally, the researcher or the agency tends to decide what the problems are and how to solve them: they provide the inputs, manage the project, and carry out the evaluation and monitoring functions to make sure that the objectives have been achieved. The weakness of such a top-down approach to research is that it fails to consider whether the project is sustainable. To determine if it is, the community must be involved right from the start of the research effort.

The approaches used by agricultural extension institutes have the potential for addressing some of the problems identified above, in that they seek to co-ordinate the activities of research, education, and the training of small farmers (Dadson, 1973; Ofori, 1973). Their emphasis is on identifying ways to strengthen farming organizations, demonstrate farm management techniques, restructure cropping systems, and promote integrated uses of technology, credit, and marketing systems. Such approaches still involve gathering quantifiable data to test for efficiency and effectiveness, but they also look at the values, motives, and opinions of people to arrive at the best possible ways to promote technical innovation in the rural areas.

ALTERNATIVES TO APPLIED RESEARCH

'Consultative' or 'dialogical' research provides an alternative approach to the more applied research methods. It calls for a more direct interaction with communities in conducting needs assessment studies and evaluating programs and projects (Ameyaw, 1989; Boateng, 1986). It differs also from the traditional social survey research that government ministries (e.g., health, housing, and agriculture) frequently rely on in making decisions about projects. The consultative or dialogical method requires that scientists and project planners meet with small groups of citizens to discuss relevant health, housing, and economic problems. The conversation, which generally lasts several hours, is taped, summarized, and distributed to the larger community through local interpreters. Additional groups come together to discuss the results, and a final report is then published. The approach stresses a flow of information among experts and between citizens and government officials on a face-to-face basis. Individuals are encouraged to think about their problems and to contribute suggestions. Rather than merely producing a set of statistics, this approach gives decision makers a better idea of the likely social consequences of their decisions and the intensity of peoples' feelings about them. The widespread mistrust among the poor toward research experts, planners, and government officials (a result of past failed promises) serves as an obstacle to this consultative approach. This general lack of trust is reinforced when the poor find that even where this research method is applied, officials still control the outcome of the project.

'Participatory action research,' a method currently being applied in Ghana, attempts to address this problem by involving the poor directly in the process, thereby increasing their understanding of the research and its usefulness (Ameyaw, 1987, 1989, 1990b, 1992a; Boateng, 1986). Many NGOs and community associations are using this newer method to get the people of the community actively involved in defining their problems, designing the research, and interpreting the data. In the case of the maize yield project, for example, research teams are now involving representatives from the various sectors of the communities affected by the change. The team may include external researchers with specific skills in data gathering, group process work, or research skills. Each of these researchers may be hired only for the period in which their particular skills are required. However, the research content and direction is controlled *by the people in the community*. (Koenig, 1986; Pettie, 1981). What has emerged from this more participatory form of research is a set of simplified research tools that make it possible for community people to work with researchers to assess, monitor, evaluate, and interpret both quantitative and qualitative data (Franzel & Crawford, 1987; Salmen, 1987).

'APPRECIATIVE INQUIRY': A CASE ILLUSTRATION

'Appreciative inquiry,' an adaptation of the participatory action research approach, is a method that this writer and others have applied in research studies in Botswana, Ghana, and Canada (Ameyaw, 1987, 1989, 1992a; Bushe & Pitman, 1991; Copperrider & Srivasta, 1990). The Techiman market research project in Ghana (1987) outlines the ideas, methods, and tools used in this approach. A central feature of that particular research project was that group discussion was considered an effective method of collecting the optimum amount of information from large numbers of people within a short time span (Ameyaw, 1987, 1990a, 1992a). These group discussions were held in offices, in the marketplace, and in the homes of key traders. Each group comprised an average of twenty traders. Early discussions were held with groups of traders of specific commodities. The final meeting, however, included all types of commodity traders and producers. Apart from being culturally consistent, the early meetings involving different commodity groups were important because traders and producers had a chance to converse with their peers (i.e., with other meat, yam, vegetable, or manufactured goods traders). As traders entered the group discussions, they were encouraged to converse with others in the room. One of the tasks of the research assistants was to help divide the larger group into a number of smaller, more manageable units for discussion; in this, the intent was to create a relaxed, informal environment.

After a brief introduction, the group leader (chosen from among the traders) and research assistant explained to the traders the purpose of the survey. The participants were reminded that the study was not a feasibility study or a study to increase their taxes or provide them with new services. The purpose was to explore ways to create opportunities for their trading activities. Emphasizing this point was considered important, as most rural people have developed a sceptical attitude toward surveys conducted by government officials and researchers, who often use traders for their own ends and fail to live up to their promises or to the traders' expectations.

Each of the participants was asked at the beginning of the group discussion if he or she wanted to express any particular views or concerns. Following this, the leader probed the group with further questions in order to establish the exact nature and state of the issues put forth. The research assistant kept notes of all the deliberations, and often stepped into the debate with open-ended questions that summoned more detailed information on the issues that had particular significance for the traders, their produce, or their social lives. For example, a discussion developed around the issue of food shortages in the market. This raised other concerns about the lack of transportation, poor rainfall, bad roads, higher prices, and the lack of credit and incentives from the government. These thought-provoking discussions served to shed light on the possibilities for amelioration. In these group sessions, each participant was encouraged to reflect on the questions being posed, to provide feedback, and to prepare other questions for submission to the researcher. It was found that many of the participants withdrew their prepared questions during the review session, since they had been answered or were deemed no longer relevant in light of the discussion.

Once the topic had been sufficiently covered, the researcher would invite the group leader to help summarize the discussion notes and identify the issues explored. The group leader would then read the summary to the group, seeking confirmation that the issues had been identified correctly. Participants were informed that some of them would later be chosen at random to complete a questionnaire. By explaining the process and stages in this way, the researchers brought about an amicable working relationship with the traders. A general questionnaire was designed, based on the information and concerns articulated by the traders in these group discussions, and administered randomly to about 200 men and women in the marketplace and at home. Six female traders, known as key leaders, were also interviewed. A case study framework was used to reflect all the details and insights acquired from these six leaders. Together, these techniques generated substantial quantitative and qualitative data.

The findings from this appreciative inquiry provided a foundation from which generalizations concerning the market traders in Techiman could be drawn and from which policies of interest to their trading practices could be formulated. This participatory form of research emphasizes the need for sharing personal experiences, promoting dialogue, asking open-ended questions, and shaping assumptions in collaboration with the participants. The feelings, thoughts, and actions of the traders were as important and as meaningful as our data collection processes, which included visual explanation, storytelling, and group meetings. On one occasion the group leader used a simple broom as a visual tool to illustrate the need for 'collaborative efforts between traders.' The leader pulled one straw from the broom and gave it to one of the participants, asking him to try and break it into pieces, which he did. He then passed the whole broom to the next participant and asked him to break it into pieces, which of course he could not. The unbroken bundle of the broom became an analogy for 'united we stand, divided we fall.' The leader urged traders, producers, women, and men to work together to promote better trading systems.

CD researchers work on the premise that decisions are seldom based on rational facts alone: people react on the basis of their awareness of the situation, their feelings about the project, and whether the proposed action is consistent with their belief systems. The underlying assumption of this type of CD research is that people do not need to be coerced by the leadership if their experience and knowledge are taken into account. The processes of 'appreciative' research create awareness among people of their own resources, as well as how they can mobilize for action. In short, the traders become the key actors in the decision-making process, having a personal investment in and commitment to the proposed changes. In other words, they assume ownership of the project and its recommendations.

CONCLUDING COMMENTS

The appreciative research approach is an attempt to overcome some of the problems that are endemic in the traditional methods of conducting research in Africa. The need to promote joint efforts between traders is as important as the collection of socio-economic data. When harnessed together, these two processes lead to heightened awareness, and to effective participation in research design and evaluation. The appreciative research process also promotes education of community members in self-development and problem solving. Finally, it enpowers rural traders as effective participants in research and data collection.

Research that encourages interaction between policy researchers and rural groups results in more relevant and sustainable development projects. Unfortunately, there are many external and internal constraints to such an approach, including these:

- The attitude of bureaucrats, both civil or military, who undervalue or disregard indigenous knowledge and systems.
- Top-down decision-making processes that rely on knowledge borrowed from the developed countries without regard for its merit or its applicability to Ghana.
- The lack of adequate knowledge about the basic needs of people in their communities.
- The cultural insensitivity of policy planners with respect to the appropriate application of technology.

To improve long-term development, better co-ordination of research is needed, at all levels. Data collection with respect to specific CD-related activities is often inadequate, partly because workers' concern for 'process' takes precedence over the keeping of data needed to carry out useful research. It has also been found that the data-gathering skills of most front-line CD practitioners are limited due to lack of specific training in research. In addition, development projects do not usually provide funding for data collection and retrieval. And, finally, records of past experiences are undervalued with respect to their ability to contribute to the understanding of present problems.

5. THEORETICAL AND POLICY PERSPECTIVE
Stephen Ameyaw

In this final section an attempt will be made to summarize the main themes of Ghana's CD experience and to examine issues related to CD from a theoretical perspective. It will be argued that the issues, particularly those arising from recent social and economic developments, will have major repercussions for the practice of CD in Ghana. The main themes include these:

- The changing role of the state with respect to government CD programs, structural adjustment programs and training institutions.
- The dominant concepts and values of CD in Ghana.
- The emergence and accommodation of intermediate institutions, such as community groups and grass roots–based social action groups.
- Contemporary social and economic realities in Ghana.

Figure 6.1 illustrates the relationship between the central ideas and concepts of CD (represented in the inner circle) and the emerging trends.

THE ROLE OF THE STATE

During the early years of CD in Ghana (1950–7), the country enjoyed a period of relative prosperity. This was largely the result of the booming cocoa industry, which provided employment opportunities for many. During this period, human development in Ghana was viewed primarily within the context of the traditional, communal forms of societal organization. CD attempted to integrate the group or clan based communities into the larger institutional systems of society (i.e., the political, social, and economic structures). A holistic approach was adopted that promoted mass education, self-help, and awareness programs aimed at mobilizing individuals and groups to address their own needs and problems. CD became a participatory process aimed at raising standards of living, attacking illiteracy, and increasing production (Sautoy, 1960). Early CD efforts attempted to engage all segments of the community in collaborative efforts. Local communities were encouraged to identify their own needs and to participate in meeting them. Efforts were made to nurture local leadership and the development of the community's capacity over time (Commins, 1979).

FIGURE 6.1
Systems Model for Community Development (CD) in Ghana

- Geopolitics
- Bureaucratic organizations

Role of the State

- Government CD program
- Structural adjustment programs and policies
- Geo-economics

CD Awareness Education Voluntarism Self-help Mutual Aid

Contemporary Economic and Social Realities

New Concepts & Values

- Aids & drugs epidemic
- Intertribal and chieftancy tensions
- Desertification & land degradation
- Urban focus
- Gender relations
- Community economic development

Mediating Institutions

- NGOS
- Grass roots–based social action groups
- CD organizations
- Training institutions
- Private sector organizations

- Participation
- Self-determination
- Decentralization
- Poverty alleviation
- Sustainability

For many reasons, the state's role in CD has been transformed in Ghana. The growth of government since independence in 1957 – particularly the expansion of the bureaucracy and its increasingly complex methods for allocating resources to groups and individuals – has reduced the state's effectiveness in developing and co-ordinating CD programs that address the needs of the poor (Damida, 1991). More and more, the political, social, and economic structures in Ghana are characterized by unwieldy expansion and complexity. Many people, especially the poor, regard these institutions as remote and impersonal (Hutchful, 1991, 1992). This perception of the government as indifferent and inaccessible has created a crisis in Ghana.

Government CD Programs

At first, government-administered CD programs were directed at the rural population. The approach taken was based on local communities and drew on the strong cultural traditions of self-help and mutual aid. This enhanced long-standing patterns of loyalty and group identification, and reinforced communal institutions. The growth and expansion of the bureaucracy, with its excessive control over information and resources, undermined the development of CD programs and initiatives (Damida, 1991; Hansen & Ninsen, 1989). Instead of reinforcing or integrating clan-based communities as units for implementing CD programs, politicians and bureaucrats, through a series of organizational and ideological changes, have weakened and in some cases eliminated the power base of local leadership (Ameyaw, 1984; Brown, 1986; Aforo, 1987; Sklar & Whitaker, 1990).

The origins of the Department of Community Development can be traced to the appointment of a social development officer in the colonial administration in 1948. Soon after, CD came to be affiliated with the Department of Social Welfare. Over the years, relations between CD and social welfare became strained as a result of numerous administrative changes that were often politically motivated. Since 1980, the two departments have operated independently. But in theoretical as well as practical and educational terms, the objectives of the social welfare worker and the community developer often overlap. Strategies and methods for implementing CD programs – including adult education, village projects, and women's development – may strengthen family ties and improve living conditions, thus preventing villagers from becoming the disadvantaged and distressed clients of the welfare case worker. The community-based rehabilitation program for the disabled – introduced in various rural villages across Ghana by the Department of Social Welfare in 1992, with the assistance of the Norwegian Association of the Disabled – demonstrates the usefulness and compatibility of CD methods and techniques in social welfare programs.

Structural Adjustment Programs and Policies

Structural adjustment programs (SAPs) as a means of economic organization are not a new phenomenon in Ghana. However, the gradual shift from state capitalism to a free market economy is having a dramatic impact on CD practices and priorities (Damida, 1991; Chazan, 1992; Cornia & Helleiner, 1994). In the past, the state was the most active player in articulating the needs of the poor through national and local programs. This meant that village projects, the acquisition of clean water, and road building were integrated into national economic development plans. Under SAP, the state functions as regulator and controller, with a focus on macro-economic reforms such as trade liberalization, improved private access to foreign exchange, relaxation of controls, and infrastructure rehabilitation (Ake, 1990; Sklar & Whitaker, 1990). The market, for its part, co-ordinates all the intermediate production and distribution processes (Cornia & Helleiner, 1994; Lindblom, 1977). Under this system, the multinational corporations and international trade organizations (OPEC, WTO, the European Community, and so on) have come to dictate the geo-economic and geo-political circumstances to which the state must respond in terms of exports and economic diversification.

CONCEPTS AND VALUES

The traditional communal system in Ghana provided extensive cultural experience in the area of self-help and mutual aid activities. Instead of utilizing this experience, however, the government has replaced it with alien forms of education, technology, and community that show questionable results. We argue here for the need to capture the indigenous entrepreneurial skills and the strong cultural traditions of community self-help, mutual aid, and leadership. These can be important tools for the alleviation of poverty.

Programs such as the women's income generation projects (see case study), and those operated by the Ghana Reconstruction Movement and the 31st December Women's Movement (see Figure 6.2), demonstrate the effectiveness of NGOs in working with communities to enhance their entrepreneurial skills for their own development. Church organizations such as the Brong Ahafo Catholic Co-operative Society for Development (BACCSOD) have introduced programs that help maize farmers analyse their production techniques, provide education for prospective members of co-operatives, and extend credit. These efforts all illustrate how the poor can be empowered and how their living conditions can be improved through the provision of loans, technical assistance, business and skills training, funds for affordable housing, and related employment activities. These informal sector initiatives can go a long way if government and financial institutions establish workable credit programs for NGOs and community groups. In short, the private and public sector organizations by working together could produce innovative, co-operative community projects that result in meaningful economic development.

The central issue for CD is not which needs should be addressed, but rather whether CD processes should be managed primarily by government bureaucrats and experts or by the poor and disadvantaged themselves, through effective bottom-up planning – albeit with support and assistance from government and other sources.

MEDIATING ORGANIZATIONS AND INSTITUTIONS

Grass Roots Social Action Groups
A number of community and grass roots social action groups are beginning to appear, and this is providing a different challenge to CD practice. Their emergence is largely the result of a growing collective awareness that a small élite class is unjustly exploiting the general population. This élite dominates the social, economic, and political scene and is perceived as contributing to the growth in mass poverty, unemployment, and inequality (Donkor & Lea, 1986; Aforo, 1987; Ewusi, 1987). Community-based groups, which are found across a wide variety of socio-economic issues and tribal concerns, pursue various strategies to empower themselves, with the goal of changing the country's power dynamics at the grass roots level. In this, they differ from traditional social-action groups, which function along more vertical lines in attempts to influence government policies (e.g., in relation to minority rights, civil rights, children's rights, and child prostitution).

NGOs
International NGOs such as UNICEF and OXFAM have played a major role in bringing the issue of poverty alleviation to the attention of government and donor agencies (Cornia, Jolly, & Stewart, 1987, 1988). This heightened awareness led to the design and approval of the PAMSCAD program. UNICEF also initiated a youth continuation program, which was later incorporated into the ICCES program. The success of such collaborations between international and local NGOs and governments highlights the advantages of linkages and co-operation.

Some NGOs and church groups emphasize the need for personal development, stressing that the first step toward empowerment is made when the competency of individuals as community change agents is emphasized. In this light, a number of training programs in life skills and leadership have been introduced (Ameyaw, 1992a). For example,

FIGURE 6.2
Dimension of 31st December Women's Movement

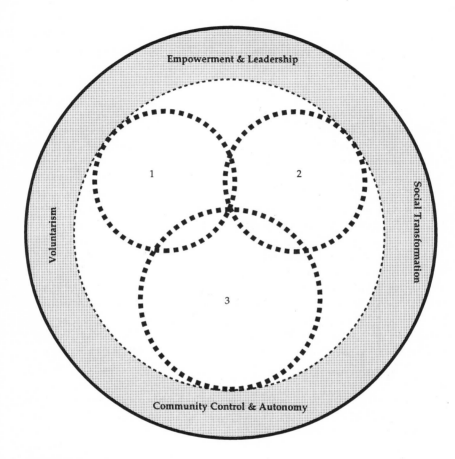

1 Organizational Capacity
- National, district, local leadership & branches
- Workshops, conferences, & seminars
- Villages, towns, & workplaces
- In-service training for staff & volunteers

2 Methodology
- Convention campaigns
- Extension campaigns
- Communication programs
- Participatory democracy

3 Program Content
- Education – research, planning, implementation & evaluation, adult education, conscientization & mobilization, civic rights, equity & justice
- Family planning – child care, nutrition, women's welfare & development
- Economic – income generation projects, cottage industries, co-operatives, credit & productivity programs
- Training – skills development, vocational training

the National Council of Women and the 31st December Women's Movement have designed various programs that enlist CD officers to educate and train women, particularly in the areas of research methods and the planning, implementation, and evaluation of projects. The process, outlined in Figure 6.2, enables participants to become effective problem solvers, leaders, and mobilizers in their communities (Aforo, 1987; Ameyaw, 1987; Hirschmann, 1991).

For example, Ghana's marriage and inheritance laws traditionally favoured men. The women of the 31st December Women's Movement, empowered by their educational programs, campaigned successfully at the national level to have these laws changed.

The case study reported by Serwah Poku demonstrates that women involved in IGPs apply the skills they have acquired in production projects to wider community issues such as health, education, and employment. Informal education in basic legal rights, training in leadership and group dynamics, and heightened awareness (i.e., 'conscientization') regarding issues of equity and justice have all contributed to the growing ability of women not only to change their immediate living conditions, but also to influence government policies.

Training Institutions
The role of the state is changing in Ghana, and at the same time rural and urban population trends are shifting. This means that training practices for CD workers have had to be adjusted. CD leaders, especially those in urban areas, find themselves working increasingly in a pluralistic environment; thus, they now require skills in conflict resolution and mediation based on a broad knowledge of cross-cultural, class, gender, and political issues (Dawson, 1992; Hirschmann, 1991).

With respect to training methods, the linking of research and action is a major positive development. The appreciative inquiry method (see research section), as an example, proved effective in mobilizing market traders to form their own associations. Then, with financial and material support from the Canadian High Commission in Ghana, these traders were successful in building their own day care centre. Thus, research and action were linked. A number of foreign NGOs have directed their many resources toward designing similar programs, with the concomitant goal of helping local NGOs train CD workers. Programs such as these provide valuable learning experiences, and serve as laboratories for training of CD leaders in the field, through action, rather than in the classroom.

Because of the impact of structural adjustment programs (SAPs), CD workers must now acquire greater literacy in basic economics, including knowledge of supply and demand forces, strategies for establishing income-generating and profit-oriented small businesses, and a general understanding of marketing and entrepreneurship. However, budget restraints and the high cost of servicing debt limit the government's capacity to provide the funds and resources that are essential for maintaining and developing training institutions.

CONTEMPORARY ECONOMIC AND SOCIAL REALITIES

Health

Ghana, like most developing countries, must deal with the emergence of two devastating threats: AIDS and drugs. The homeless and poor are especially at risk. If preventive measures are not taken immediately, the country's limited health resources will be quickly depleted. CD can play a central role in preventive education and awareness-raising on both AIDS and drugs.

Intertribal Conflict

Ghana is currently experiencing unprecedented intertribal tensions. In the northern region, tribal conflicts among the Konkombas, Nanumbas, and other groups have led to many deaths. In other regions, rivalries between chiefs are draining the limited financial resources available and undermining local infrastructural development. Such conflicts divert attention from the problems of survival that many people face. CD workers must be trained thoroughly in conflict resolution and mediation techniques if their programs are to address successfully the broader issues of health care, education, and employment.

Desertification and Land Degradation

Given the environmental challenges that confronted Ghana in the 1980s – forest fires, desertification, lack of rainfall, and soil erosion – CD must involve helping the poor manage natural resources more judiciously. Poor cultivation techniques, ignorance, population growth, and the inequitable distribution of resources are major causes of desertification and land degradation in Ghana. Farmers do not have access to the capital required for restoring overused and poorly cultivated land. CD approaches and strategies have played an important role in rehabilitating degraded lands and deserts through awareness and education campaigns which focus on the conservation of resources, the control of marketing, and the economic and legal rights of land users. Other social action groups have been involved with campaigns to preserve the tropical forest. Women's and youth groups are engaged in planting new trees and in educating farmers about the long-term benefits of preserving trees.

Community Economic Development (CED)
In the early years of CD experience, many communities embraced the cocoa industry as a vehicle for social and economic growth. Since then, communities in Ghana have suffered decades of economic decline and change. In the rural areas the pronounced shift away from export crops (i.e., cocoa, coffee, and timber) has posed severe problems. In the urban areas the slow development of technology and the decline in manufacturing are leading to severe unemployment.

The options open to Ghana's government to generate economic development are limited. Current government policies include a myriad of economic and job creation schemes for assisting corporate and individual business development. However, such programs undermine economic initiatives undertaken by the poor, who utilize community-based resources. Yet there are strong arguments for seeking an alternative economic development strategy in the 'informal' sector of the economy. First, in the absence of employment opportunities in the formal sector, the informal sector provides options for income-generating activities for the poor (Serwah Poku's case study illustrates this point). Second, nearly 80 percent of Ghana's people are engaged in some form of informal employment activity, which they have developed largely by mobilizing themselves (Ameyaw, 1987). Third, such projects demonstrate that community groups have 'home grown' entrepreneurial talent and the potential to create their own opportunities. Local groups can be key players in promoting economic development (Ameyaw, 1987).

Local Production
Equally significant in the new reality of Ghana is the need for the government to stop promoting the use of imported products over local ones (Donkor & Lea, 1986). The case study on housing showed how Ghana's dependence on imported building materials discouraged job creation, skills training, and local initiatives.

Rural-Urban Migration

As recently as the late 1950s, individual families and clan-based towns and villages played a vital role in Ghana in the maintenance of personal and community well-being. This is no longer the case in many areas of the country. In 1994 about five million (or one-third) of Ghana's population resided in urban areas, compared to less than a million (or one-sixth) in 1958 (Census Ghana 1960, 1994). Increasingly, the community has become a workplace rather than a place of cultural festivities and family celebrations, mutual aid and self-help. For example, in the traditional, clan-based system of extended families, grandparents played a vital role in child care. NGOs, community groups, and churches are now attempting to relight this tradition and promote interaction among disadvantaged groups through foster grandparent programs, home visits, sport groups, and storytelling.

Migrants and refugees who settle in Ghana's urban centres, such as Accra, Kumasi, and Sekondi/Takoradi, often differ from the main population of those centres in language and lifestyle. This makes it especially difficult for them to find employment and training opportunities. CD programs that focus on skills training, and on group work and community organization, enable such groups to participate more effectively in the decisions that affect their lives. This in turn increases the opportunities for these groups to find work or to engage in income-generating enterprises.

The ICCES youth program and the IGPs for women are two examples of the state's shift toward addressing the needs of urban populations. This shift in emphasis from the rural to the urban setting has resulted in competition between various levels of government, traditional institutions, and community leaders in terms of prioritizing programs and allocating resources for CD.

CONCLUSION

This chapter has examined a number of emerging themes as a basis for building a framework for CD theory and policy in Ghana. A number of theoretical points have been outlined indicating ways in which the institutional systems – economy, education, resources, industry, community groups, and government – are changing and are having a dramatic effect on societal governance. The more holistic approach to human development that CD took in the 1950s was successful because the institutional systems adapted to local cultures and focused on the relatively stable values of mutual aid and self-help in small, clan-based communities. However, after Ghana attained independence, socio-economic and political changes gradually undermined these collective efforts. The rapid turnover of governments, the tension between free market and centralized planning ideologies, and the migration to urban centres all helped to weaken the link between the government and the community as an instrument of social and economic organization.

Increasingly, NGOs are developing various participatory processes that involve the poor in the researching, implementing, and evaluating of projects. These organizations are well placed to take on administrative functions developed from the centre. Perhaps more importantly, however, they provide an intermediary structure for articulating the interests of the poor. While developing new relationships with citizens, institutions, and other government departments, the CD department should also attempt to make its own administrative procedures more participatory, and to promote interdepartmental collaboration.

This discussion has developed several guiding principles that relate to the participation of local groups in planning efforts:

- Sensitivity to others' interests.
- Promotion of joint efforts and collaborative work.
- Provision of freedom, equity, and enhancement of culture.
- Opportunities for building intermediate institutions.
- Effective collaboration with the disadvantaged and the poor to eradicate poverty.
- Creation of opportunities for generating economic activity through the provision of training and technical and financial resources.

Positive forms of participation in CD will address these problems: unemployment; intertribal tensions, manipulations, and co-optations; and environmental threats such as desertification and land degradation. CD in Ghana calls for effective participation by all levels of government, as well as by NGOs, churches, and communities. These must collaborate in planning and implementing programs that will help the poor and the disadvantaged to help themselves as much as possible. The fundamental organizational units for addressing the emerging social and economic issues should be groups made up of representatives from government, NGOs, and the communities involved.

A critical issue for CD practitioners in the twenty-first century will be how to deal effectively with urban and rural groups with different values and world views. The decades ahead will demand a new set of skills for community and social development workers. The involvement of foreign and local NGOs will continue to make a critical difference in addressing the urgent needs of the poor.

Contributors

Fred Abloh
Joint co-ordinator and contributor to the Ghana country study; former professor and Dean of the Faculty of Environmental and Development Studies, and head of the Department of Housing and Planning Research, University of Science and Technology at Kumasi; former community development officer and head of the research unit of the Department of Social Welfare and Community Development; and currently director of the Integrated Community Centres for Employable Skills (ICCES).

Stephen Ameyaw
Joint co-ordinator and contributor to the Ghana country study; currently teaching at the Community Economic Development Centre, Simon Fraser University, and at First Nations institutes in British Columbia; received his doctorate from the University of Waterloo, Ontario, with his thesis focusing on women and development issues in Ghana based on extensive field research.

Victoria Serwah Poku
Senior program officer in charge of the Women in Development component of ICCES; received a degree in social administration from the University of Ghana.

References

Adul, Febiri F. (1994). *Tourism and Ghana development process*. Doctoral dissertation, University of British Columbia, Canada.

Aforo, K. (1987). Grassroots participation in rural project planning and implementation in Ghana. In S.B. Amissah (eds.), *Planning for development in the Third World: Problems and solutions*. Kumasi, Ghana: LARCUST.

Ake, C. (1990). *The long-term perspective study of sub-Saharan Africa: Sustainable development on the indigenous people*. World Bank Background Papers, 3.

Ameyaw, S.K. (1984). *Ideology and culture: The case of Ghana*. Master's thesis, University of Waterloo, Ontario, Canada.

– (1987). *Female entrepreneurship and indigenous food markets in Ghana*. Doctoral dissertation, University of Michigan, Ann Arbor, Michigan.

– (1989). Rural development perspectives: Conducting policy and constraints in practice. In E.A. McDougall (ed.), *Sustainable agriculture in Africa*. Trenton, NJ: Africa World Press Inc. 87–96.

– (1990a). Dynamics of female entrepreneurship. *Women in International Development* (Series No. 205). Lansing, MI: Michigan State University.

– (1990b). Poverty and sustainable development. *Participatory Development Review*, 1(1): 5–6.

– (1992a). Sustainable development and community lessons from Botswana. *The Environmentalist Journal*, 12(4): 267–75.

– (1992b). Alberta as viewed by the Third World. *Proceedings of the Conference of the Arctic Institute of North America*, University of Calgary, Alberta, Canada.

Arko, K. (1994, August). Exploitation of children. *West Africa*, No. 4012, p. 1416.

Atim, B.A. (1986). Low-cost technology and the promotion of rural industrial development. In C.K. Brown (ed.), *Rural development in Ghana*. Accra: Ghana University Press.

Beckman, B. (1991). Empowerment or repression? The World Bank and the politics of African adjustment. *Africa and Development*, 6(1).

Boateng, I.K. (1986). *Planning for development in the Third World: Problems and solutions*. Kumasi, Ghana: LARCUST.

Bourke, B.E. (1986). Rural employment and labour productivity in Ghana. In C.K. Brown (Ed.), *Rural development in Ghana*. Accra: Ghana University Press.

Brown, C.K. (1986). Governmental and voluntary participation in Ghana's rural development programmes. In C.K. Brown (ed.), *Rural development in Ghana*. Accra: Ghana University Press.

Bushe, G., & Pitman, T. (eds.). (1991). Appreciative process: A method for transformational change. In G. Bushe and T. Pitman (eds.), *Organizational Practitioner*, 23(3): 1–4.

Chambers, R. (ed.). (1970). *The Volta resettlement experience*. New York: Praeger.

Chazan, N. (1992). Liberalisation, governance and political space in Ghana. In Bratton & Hyden (eds.), *Governance and politics of Ghana*. Boulder, CO: Lynne Reinner Publishers.

Commins, P. (1979). *Cooperation and community development in the west of Ireland*. Dublin: Fifth International Seminar on Marginal Regions.

Conyers, D. (1982). *Introduction to social planning in the Third World*. New York: Wiley and Sons.

Copperrider & Srivasta (eds.). (1990). *Appreciative management and leadership*. San Francisco: Jossey-Bass.

Cornia, G.A., & Helleiner, G.K. (eds). (1994). *From adjustment to development: Conflict, controversy, convergence, consensus?* New York: St. Martin Press.

Cornia, G.A., Jolly, R., & Stewart, F. (eds.). (1987). *Adjustment with a human face. Vol 1: Protecting the vulnerable and promoting growth*. Oxford: Clarendon Press.

– (1988). *Adjustment with a human face. Vol. 2: Ten country case studies.* Oxford: Clarendon Press.

Dadson, J.A. (1973). Farm size and the modernization of agriculture in Ghana. In I.M. Ofori (ed.), *Factors of agricultural growth in West Africa.* Accra: Legon Press.

Damida, Pierre-Claver. (1991). Government and economic development. *Africa Forum,* 1(1).

Dawson, J.M. (1992). Non-profits need their own perestroika to be effective in today's changing world. *African Link,* 2(2).

Donkor, K., & Lea, J.P. (1980). Self-reliance and African building materials industry: Cautionary tale from Ghana. *African Urban Quarterly,* 1(2).

Ewusi, Kodwo. (1987). *Planning for the neglected rural poor in Ghana.* Legon, Ghana: University of Ghana, ISSER.

Falconer, J. (1990). The major significance of minor forest products in West Africa. *Appropriate Technology,* 3.

Food & Agricultural Organization. (1989). *Community forestry rapid appraisal.* Rome: FAO.

Franzel, S., & Crawford, E. (1987). Comparing formal and informal survey techniques for farming systems research: A case study from Kenya. *Agricultural Administration,* 27: 13–33.

Government of Ghana. (1972). *Outline of government economic policy.* Accra: Ghana Publishing Corporation.

– (1978). *Primary health care strategy for Ghana.* Ministry of Health.

– (1983). *Economic recovery programme 1984–1986, Vol 2.* Accra-Tema, Ghana: Ghana Publishing Corporation.

– (1993). *Rural communities in Ghana.* Accra: Ghana Statistical Service Commercial Associates Limited.

Hansen, E., & Ninsen, K. (eds.). (1989). *The state development and politics in Ghana.* London: CODESRIA Books Series.

Harrison, P. (1983). *The Third World tomorrow: A battle from the battle front in the War Against Poverty.* Reading: Cox and Wyman Ltd.

Hay, M., & Stichter, S. (eds.). (1984). *African women south of the Sahara.* London: Longmans.

Herbst, J. (1990). The structural adjustment of politics in Africa. *World Development,* 18(7): 949–58.

Hill, P. (1986). *Development economics on trial.* London: Tavistock Publishers.

Hirschmann, D. (1991). Women and political participation in Africa: Broadening the scope for research. *World Development,* 19(12): 679–94.

Hossie, L. (1991, December 14). New voices of Africa. *The Globe and Mail,* Toronto. D1, D4.

Hutchful, E. (1991, May). Shades of meaning: The struggle to define democracy in Ghana. Paper presented at the annual conference of the Canadian African Studies Association, York University, Toronto, Canada.

– (1992, February). The international dimensions of democratization processes in Africa. Paper presented at the CODESRIA Conference, Democratization Processes in Africa: Problems and Prospects.

Jefferies, R. (1992). Urban attitudes towards the economic recovery programme and government in Ghana. *African Affairs*, 92, 207–26.

Johnstone, P. (1993). *Operation world*. Grand Rapids, MI: Zondervan Publishing House.

Koenig, D. (1986). Research for rural development: Experiences of an anthropologist in rural Mali. In M.M. Horowitz and M. Painter (eds.), *Anthropology and rural development in West Africa*. Boulder, CO: Westview.

Leach, E.R. (1967). An anthropologist's reflections on a social survey. In D.G. Longmans & P.C.W. Gutkind (eds.), *Anthropologists in the field*. The Netherlands: Van Gorcum-Assen Netherland.

Lindblom, C.E. (1977). *Politics and markets*. New York: Basic Books.

Mushi, S. (1981). Community development in Tanzania. In Ronald Dure and Zoe Mass (eds.), *Community development*. London/Paris: Croom Helm, UNESCO.

Nkrumah, K. (1962). *Africa needs her farmers*. Accra: Government Printer.

Ofori, I.M. (1973). *Factors of agricultural growth in West Africa*. Accra: Legon Press.

Pettie, L.R. (1981). *Thinking about development*. New York: Plenum Press.

Robertson, C. (1974). *Social and economic change in twentieth century Accra: Ga women*. Doctoral dissertation, University of Wisconsin.

Salmen, L. (1987). *Listen to the people: Participation-observers evaluation of development projects*. New York: Oxford University Press.

Sautoy, P. (1960). *Community development in Ghana*. London: Oxford University Press.

Sheperd, G.S. (1971). *Marketing farm products economic research* (No.18). Legon: University of Ghana.

Sklar, R.L., & Whitaker, C.S. (eds.). (1990). *African politics and problems in development*. Boulder and London: Lynne Rienner Publishers.

Stokes, B. (1981). *Global housing prospects: The resource constraints*. Washington, DC: Worldwatch Institute.

Part VII

Bangladesh

Co-ordinated by PROFULLA SARKER

Bangladesh

1. INTRODUCTION
Profulla Sarker

Bangladesh has an area of only 148,393 square kilometres with a population of about 125 million, making it one of the most densely populated countries in the world (870 persons per sq. km). The population is culturally and ethnically homogeneous as a result of twenty-five centuries of integration between the local Bengalis and migrants from central Asia. There are some small minorities, however, the Hindus and Urdus being the most significant. Bangladesh is primarily Islamic, with Buddhist and Christian minorities.

The country is made up of a fertile alluvial plain where rice, tea, and jute are grown. The land, crisscrossed by seven major rivers and over 200 minor ones, is home to vast rain forests and swamps. The economy is based primarily on the land, with agriculture employing the majority of the country's people. The average landholding is 0.11 hectare (Mahtab, 1992, p. 50). Although about 85 percent of the people live in rural areas, less than 40 percent own cultivable land. Because of the laws of inheritance and traditional systems of farm management, small farms are being fragmented into scattered plots.

Bangladesh remains a very poor country in spite of numerous development plans and programs, with a per capita income of US$210 and GDP growth of 4.1 percent annually. Only about 26 percent of its people are literate. The country's labour force stands at 52.2 million; 65 percent are employed in agriculture, 16 percent in industry, and 19 percent in services. An estimated 30 percent are unemployed (Government of Bangladesh, 1994).

The major development challenge facing the country is the reduction of poverty. About 60 percent of the urban and 57 percent of the rural people live below the poverty level. Less than 5 percent of Bangladeshis consume enough food (World Bank, 1985, p. 4). Malnutrition is acute, especially among children. The infant mortality rate is 90 per 1,000 live births, one of the highest in the world, and life expectancy is only 56 years for males and 54 years for females.

Rapid urbanization has created another set of problems. Rural poverty is almost a 'normal' feature of the social fabric; urban poverty and the rapid growth of slums and squatter settlements are newer phenomena and even more destabilizing. Although Bangladesh is still predominantly rural, unregulated urbanization has added a new dimension to its demographic explosion.

Thus, the situation of Bangladesh is characterized by poverty, unemployment, overpopulation, illiteracy, malnutrition, a high incidence of morbidity and mortality, and poor housing and sanitation. The forest and crop areas are shrinking yearly, posing a serious threat to the ecology and to the security of food supplies. On top of this, natural disasters like floods, drought, tornadoes, and storms frequently cause extensive damage to crops, lives, and property.

Many government and nongovernmental organizations are working closely with the people to alleviate poverty in Bangladesh. Community development in Bangladesh is supported and practised by government organizations (GOs), such as the Department of Social Services, the Co-operative Department, the Bangladesh Rural Development Board, and the Directorate of Youth and Women's Affairs, as well as by many NGOs such as the Bangladesh Rural Advancement Committee, Grameen Bank, CARITAS, and Proshika. These efforts encourage the people in local communities across the country to participate in the task of enriching their socio-economic and cultural life.

The urban and rural élites include wealthy businessmen, high-level officials, military officers, politicians, and large landowners, who control Bangladeshi society at both the national and the local level. The great majority of landless peasants and wage labourers are illiterate and have little or no means to defend their interests, even under a democratic system. Many of the rural élites are powerful rather than rich. Patron–client relationships are still strong, and the poor fall back on these in times of need and distress (Jansen, 1987).

For community development (CD) to be effective, government must commit itself to it in a spirit of democracy. Politics in Bangladesh has been characterized by leadership crises, poorly organized political parties, extreme factionalism, and coups and countercoups led by ambitious military officers. The resulting political instability has increased the suffering of the people and hampered their efforts to achieve self-reliance through development activities.

Even so, the government of Bangladesh has taken a number of measures to improve conditions for its people. According to the fourth of the five-year plans (1990-5), the poor are to be included in development efforts as 'creative and productive citizens' rather than as liabilities. The plan has three main objectives: to spur economic growth, to alleviate poverty, and to create employment opportunities. The employment and income concerns of the poor have been brought to the very centre of overall development policy and planning (United Nations Development Program, 1992). Government organizations are emphasizing a participatory approach that involves the poor in development programs, enlarges their choices and opportunities, and provides for their participation in the decisions that affect their lives (UNDP, 1990). The NGOs have developed various participatory approaches that involve target groups in the process of identifying problems and designing and implementing solutions to them.

In other words, the GOs and NGOs are emphasizing the optimum utilization of community resources, which are 'freed up' by mobilizing local people in community affairs and welfare. The case studies in the following section indicate how people in different communities have been mobilized through these programs: the Nandanpur Farmers' Co-operative Society, the Family Development and Mothers' Centres of the Social Services Department, the Shishapara Group Development Project of CARITAS, and the Slum Improvement Project of UNICEF. The section on supportive institutions discusses the resources provided by various institutions for CD-related programs. The section after that gives an outline of the trends in education and training in the country, with specific reference to CD. Then the research activities conducted in CD-related programs in Bangladesh are described and analysed. The final section discusses developments in CD theory and policy trends in Bangladesh.

2. CURRENT PRACTICE
A. Nandanpur Farmers' Co-operative Society:
The 'Two-Tier' Co-operative System
Taimur Rahman

Through experiments and action research initiated in the early 1960s by the Bangladesh Academy for Rural Development (BARD) in Comilla, a number of interrelated models for rural development evolved (Mannan, 1987, pp. 27–35). One of the models was a two-tier co-operative system for helping small and marginal farmers. This case study describes this model's basic features, as well as its limitations in dealing with rural poverty.

In the early 1970s the two-tier co-operative system, called the *Comilla Model*, was adopted by the government when it launched the Integrated Rural Development Program (IRDP) as part of its new development policy. This program was implemented by the Bangladesh Rural Development Board (BRDB). Despite its various limitations, it continues to be the government's major approach to rural development (Mannan, 1989, pp. 45–7; BRDB, 1993).

In the Comilla Model, a number of village-level co-operative societies (KSSs) are federated at the *thana* (subdistrict) level into a central co-operative association (TCCA). Each KSS has a managing committee consisting of a chairman, a manager, a model farmer, and selected members. The role of the manager is to maintain links with the TCCA and other relevant *thana*-level government agencies. The model farmer is expected to serve as the extension agent and to attend weekly training sessions at the TCCA in order to acquire and disseminate knowledge about improved agricultural techniques and other related aspects of socio-economic development. Members of the KSS are required to attend weekly meetings to discuss management issues, and to hear from the manager what he has learned at the TCCA (Mannan, 1987, pp. 33–4).

EVOLUTION OF THE CO-OPERATIVE SOCIETY (KSS) IN NANDANPUR

Nandanpur village is located near the Dhaka-Rajshahi highway, about 25 kilometres from the regional capital, Rajshahi. The village was established about 200 years ago on the banks of the Sundar river (now stagnant). Some of the lands are high, while others are marshy and are cultivable only during the winter season. This was a food-deficit area before the IRDP program was introduced. The farmers had no other source of income. Up until the late 1970s, most of the people lived in thatched houses. They had to drink pond water and often fell ill with cholera, typhoid, dysentery, and water-related diseases. Sanitary and drainage facilities were absent. There was no collective effort to deal with these problems, and the government provided little help.

In the mid-1970s the farmers of Western Nandanpur decided to form a co-operative society to solve their socio-economic problems on a self-help basis. The society was originally set up for these purposes:

- To accumulate funds by mobilizing resources.
- To improve skills in modern methods of mechanized cultivation.
- To develop local leadership.
- To create opportunities for paid employment.

In 1978 this society became a registered co-operative (KSS), affiliated with the TCCA of Puthia for financial and other supports.

OBJECTIVES

The main objectives of Nandanpur (Paschim) KSS as specified in its constitution are these:

- To procure loans for its members.
- To purchase and distribute resources for members.
- To help members to avoid extravagant expenditures, and to develop habits of saving.
- To help control and eliminate contagious and other diseases.
- To help members educate their children.
- To help members produce and sell agricultural goods.
- To undertake works of rural development – for example, to bring fallow lands under cultivation, to create employment opportunities, and to help the distressed.
- To encourage and arrange joint cultivation.
- To encourage self-reliance.

ORGANIZATION AND MEMBERSHIP

The area the KSS serves is a part of Nandanpur village and is free from urban influence. It has 194 families with 998 persons. Of the families, 60 (about 31 percent) are farmers, 30 are fishermen, 75 are labourers, 15 are businessmen, and 14 do salaried work. Among the 60 farmer families, 40 family heads are members of the KSS. The managing committee operates under democratic principles. Members over the age of 21, having membership for twelve months or more, are entitled to vote in

TABLE 7.1
Age, Sex Distribution, and Education of Members of Nandanpur KSS
(Village Level Co-operative Society), 1993

Age	Sex			Level of education			
	M	F	Total	Illiterate	Primary	Secondary	Higher secondary and above
18–29	1	1	2	–	1	1	–
30–39	12	0	12	1	6	4	1
40–49	12	0	12	3	7	–	2
50–59	6	0	6	2	4	–	–
60 and above	7	1	8	3	4	1	–
Total	38	2	40	9	22	6	3

elections of the managing committee. Elections are held every three years. A member may continue on the managing committee for not more than three consecutive terms. The manager discharges the day-to-day affairs of the KSS. All major decisions of the society are taken after discussion by the managing committee and with the sanction of the members in the weekly meeting. A profile of the members of the KSS on the basis of age, sex, and education is provided in Table 7.1.

Under the current social structure of the country, males are the principal breadwinners of the family. This is reflected in the predominantly male membership of the managing committee, which focuses on economic development. The members are family heads, and most are middle-aged and older. Only one male and one female member are under thirty years of age. Most of the members have not studied beyond the primary level. Most have no strong political affiliation; however, this does not affect the growth or functioning of the society. The 20 percent of the members who have a secondary-level education make a significant contribution to the smooth running of the society.

A profile of the members of managing committee according to educational qualifications and land held is provided in Table 7.2. Members are elected to the managing committee not on the basis of educational attainment but on the basis of wealth and of land held under irrigation in the deep tubewell area.

Members of the KSS may be classified on the basis of the land they hold. The members who have comparatively less land usually have less formal education (see Table 7.3).

TABLE 7.2
Education and Land Held of Members of the Managing Committee, Nandapur KSS, 1993

Position	Educational qualification	Land held (in acres)
Chairman	B.A., B.Ed.	6.66
Vice-chairman	Primary	4.00
Manager	Higher secondary	4.00
Model farmer (1)	Primary	5.00
Model farmer (2)	Primary	3.66
Director	Primary	2.66

TABLE 7.3
Education and Land Held of Members of Nandapur KSS, 1993

Land held (in acres)	Number	Educational Achievement			
		Illiterate	Primary	Secondary	Higher secondary
Marginal (less than one acre)	5	1	4	–	–
Small (1.00–2.49)	20	6	14	–	–
Medium (2.50–7.45)	12	1	3	5	3
Large (7.50 and above)	3	1	1	1	–
Total	40	9	22	6	3

ACTIVITIES AND ACHIEVEMENTS

The society stresses capital accumulation through thrift savings and the purchase of shares. At the initial stage, the KSS borrows money from the TCCA; through loans, this money is disbursed to members so that they can improve (i.e., mechanize) their methods of cultivation. After repaying the entire amount of the loan to the TCCA, with interest, the society stops further borrowing from the TCCA and begins to advance loans to its members from its own fund. Because loans are available from their society as and when necessary, the members can avoid going to moneylenders, who charge exorbitant rates of interest. This has increased their confidence in their *own* organization. The capital accumu-

TABLE 7.4
Position of Capital Formation of Nandapur KSS, June 1993

Number of members	Amount of share (Tk)	Thrift savings (Tk)	Total capital (Tk)	Average	National average
40	5,830	75,901	81,731	2,043	14.88

lated by the society's members through shares and savings is shown in Table 7.4.

By utilizing mechanized cultivation and high-yielding seed varieties (which are supplied by the society), members have increased their yields by 5 to 6 *maunds* per acre (one *maund* equals about 37.8 kilograms). Members, including marginal and small farmers, have learned how to produce vegetables, winter crops, and fruits on their fallow land and in their home yards, and this has erased the deficit of foodstuffs. During an interview, the members of the society asserted that they are now producing different crops and vegetables throughout the year and that seasonal unemployment has ended. With financial assistance from the society, they are producing papaw, potatoes, bringals, cabbage, gourd, cauliflower, beans, garlic, onions, turmeric, and green chilies. This production occurs during the off-season, when there is no cultivation of such main crops as paddy, rice, wheat, and jute. The seasonal vegetables and spices they produce meet their domestic needs, and the surplus is sold for cash.

The members have achieved significant socio-economic improvements through the society. Table 7.5 shows the total land owned and the count of semi-pucca houses (mud wall with tin shed) belonging to members at the time of admission to the society in 1978 and at the time of the field work for the case study in June 1993. The average landholding per family had increased to 2.58 acres by 1993, from 1.4 acres in 1978.

It was reported that the members now employ local labourers in both joint and individual farms. With the increased amount of agricultural activity, employment opportunities have increased and unemployment has been substantially reduced.

The members of the society meet every Saturday evening to discuss various subjects, such as modern methods of cultivating different crops, vegetables, and fruits, tree planting, health, sanitation, and family planning; and to decide on new programs for the society. The society has

TABLE 7.5
A Comparison of the Land and the Houses of the Members of Nandapur KSS, 1993

Number of members of the society	Average land held (in acres)		Pucca or semi-pucca of the members			
			1978		1993	
	1978	1993	Thatched	Tin shed	Thatched	Tin shed
40	1.43	2.58	42	12	15	115

engaged in pisciculture (fish farming) by leasing two tanks, and has also purchased an orchard. It operates irrigation schemes through a deep tubewell and provides members with the means to cultivate high-yielding varieties of crops. So far, the society has accumulated a net profit of Tk 159,868 ($3,997 U.S.) – an average of Tk 3,997 per member – from its joint enterprises.

ROLE OF THE SOCIETY IN THE VILLAGE

The co-operative society also attends to the welfare of other inhabitants of the village. It provides functional education to nonmembers in the fields of health, sanitation, disease prevention and other aspects of social and community life. It also arbitrates simple social and family disputes in its weekly meetings.

The society encourages *all* villagers of Nandanpur to vaccinate children and pregnant mothers and to practise family planning. The manager and the model farmer of the society, on the basis of the knowledge gained from relevant experts through their training at the TCCA, educate the members and nonmembers of the village. As a result, most of the people have become free from superstitions related to family planning, health, and disease. Religious ceremonies such as *jumma* prayers are observed collectively in the village. Members take an active part in community activities such as marriages, burials, treatment of the sick, and so on. They also organize local games and sports. The society keeps in its office a television set for all inhabitants of the village. Thus, it does much to preserve social harmony and strengthen the sense of community participation.

CONSTRAINTS AND PROSPECTS

The two-tier co-operative system provides guidelines for organizing and operating co-operative societies in Bangladesh. The Comilla Model includes three other components – viz., the Thana Training Development Centre (TTDC), the Rural Works Program (RWP), and the Thana Irrigation Program (TIP). However, it is felt that the four components have not been properly co-ordinated in an integrated strategy of rural development. From its inception, the Nandanpur Co-operative Society did not have comprehensive assistance from different government agencies. Lack of an adequate road between the village and the *thana* headquarters hinders regular interaction between the society and the TCCA. The TCCA, because of its supervisory and advisory weaknesses, could not extend the required support for the development of the society. What the society has achieved so far is a result of its own collective efforts. Any development project, if it is to succeed, must enjoy the initiative and participation of the people. This was evident in the performance of the Nandanpur Farmers' Co-operative Society. But adequate guidance and appropriate supports – especially continuous training in various aspects of production technology and social improvements – are also essential for the underdeveloped rural areas of Bangladesh.

Although increased agricultural production has greatly reduced the village's food deficit, the society's members are engaged in small business ventures only in a disorganized way. The need to create employment opportunities for the ever-increasing numbers of young people is seen as a priority. Permanent jobs are more likely to be created once the dairy and poultry farms are developed, pisciculture is improved, cultivation of fruits and vegetables is expanded, and credit for marketing local agricultural goods is easier to arrange.

This question emerges: To what extent is this approach consistent with the concept of BRDB? The Comilla Model was based on the concept of integrated rural development and was designed to bring *all* villagers, irrespective of occupation and resources, under a village co-operative society. The BRDB system incorporated only one aspect of the model and emphasized farmers' co-operatives and faster agricultural development. Clearly, the two-tier BRDB co-operatives have deviated somewhat from the philosophy of the Comilla Model. More recently, the BRDB has expanded its coverage to area development projects (including the construction of rural infrastructure), and a number of schemes to bring landless men and women into separate co-operatives (BRDB, 1993).

B. Mohanpur Rural Mothers' Centres: A Multidimensional Approach to Family Planning and Education for Rural Women
Abdul Halim

The Rural Social Service (RSS) program of the Department of Social Services (DSS) was initiated in 1974, with the goal of extending social services to rural areas, where about 85 percent of Bangladeshis live. The RSS uses a multidimensional CD approach. Its specific aim is to improve the socio-economic conditions of those deprived groups who had been left out of earlier developmental programs (Mia et al., 1985; Ali, 1986; Akbar & Mustafa, 1988).

Rural Mothers' Centres (MCs), widely known as *matrikendras*, constitute a special project for poor village women. Initiated by the DSS, they have been introduced with the assistance of the World Bank in eighty *thanas* across Bangladesh. The case study of the MCs presented here is limited to Mohanpur *thana*, a subdistrict of Rajshahi. The data for this study were gained through field visits, discussions with the local officer (TSSO) and other field personnel, and an examination of relevant reports and documents.

In Mohanpur, the MCs were started in 1992. Within two years, sixty-four such centres had been developed in forty-one villages. An MC consists of an association of mothers of reproductive age, and may include some unmarried young women as associate members. The MCs, through a range of income-generating and social development projects, provide an opportunity for the rural poor and distressed women to rise above their poverty and achieve responsible motherhood. The MCs have these specific objectives:

- To help members become aware of the importance and advantages of a small family; to motivate them to adopt family planning; and to provide them with contraceptives.
- To arrange skills training and credit for the members and assist them in undertaking income-generating activities.
- To organize education in health, nutrition, and sanitation, in maternal and child care, and in other areas of social development.

IMPLEMENTATION PROCEDURES

The first step in project development was to undertake a household survey in forty-one villages to collect data on age, women of reproductive age, single-parent families, and divorced and separated women;

along with data on landholding, income, occupation, employment, health status, and access to facilities. These socio-economic data were then utilized to identify segments of the population to be included in RSS programs. The households were classified into three categories:

- Category A: *extremely poor* – families having an annual per capita income of less than Tk 2,330 (US$58).
- Category B: *poor* – families having an annual per capita income of Tk 2,331 to 3,400 (US$58 to 85).
- Category C: *well off* – families having an annual per capita income of more than Tk 3,400.

The families of the MCs in Mohanpur are drawn largely from Category A households. A few Category B families are included because of their keen interest in the program.

MOBILIZATION PROCESS

The *thana*'s social service office (TSSO) arranges for the Union Parishad chairman and members to meet with women and prominent inhabitants of the village to encourage interest in forming an MC. Special attempts are made to see that women from extremely poor families attend. In this way the TSSO enlists the community's support and full co-operation in accepting the idea of an MC. Once the decision is made to establish an MC, an executive committee is formed consisting of a chairperson, vice-chairperson, secretary, assistant secretary, and seven members. The executive committee is responsible for keeping records, acquiring equipment, and finding a suitable place to hold meetings. The secretary calls all meetings, opens bank accounts in the name of the MC, and operates the account jointly with the local union social worker (USW) employed by the government's Department of Social Services. It is her duty to see that each member contributes Tk 5 each month as personal savings.

The total membership of the sixty-four MCs in Mohanpur is 3,388, with an average membership of fifty-seven mothers. From the social service office, each MC receives a fixed amount for a revolving fund for advancing loans to its members. In their meetings, MC members make decisions about income-generating schemes and loan applications. The membership of each MC thus assumes responsibility for the repayment of the loans.

The secretary plays the key role in running the MC. Essentially, the MCs function as local democratic organizations for this largely neglected segment of the rural population, in that they provide a forum for discussing and disseminating information received from the *thana* headquarters.

RESOURCES

The funds are distributed through the TSSO to the sixty-four MCs of Mohanpur. Between July 1992 and December 1993, Tk 435,200 were invested in various projects undertaken by the MC members. The loans are repaid by instalments, along with an annual service charge of 15 percent. The loans and the service charges are then deposited in separate bank accounts. The service charges eventually become the capital of the MC concerned. When the accumulated service charges become equal to the revolving funds given to the MC, the original capital is reinvested in a new MC. In addition, each MC member saves Tk 5 per month, which is deposited. The total savings become the capital of the MCs concerned. By December 1993, the MCs in Mohanpur had saved a total of Tk 187,117 – about 43 percent of the total investment (see Table 7.6). When a reasonable amount of savings is accumulated, it is distributed again as loans to be repaid, with a service charge. The MCs of Mohanpur have already started advancing loans from their own savings.

Thus, there exists a built-in system to help MC members attain self-reliance. The amount of credit repaid by borrowers, along with service charges, is redistributed to new applicants. Similarly, personal savings are distributed and redistributed among members as loans to augment the government's investment. This innovative system of capital forma-

TABLE 7.6
Capital Accumulation and Loan Operation of Mothers' Centres of Mohanpur, July 1992–December 1993

Number of MCs	Number of members	Total savings (Tk)	Amount disbursed (Tk)		Percentage of loan realized	
			Govt. fund	Saving	Govt. fund	Saving
64	3,388	187,117	435,200	100,700	98	68

TABLE 7.7
Distribution of Loans for Mothers' Centres' Income-generating Activities in Mohanpur,
July 1992–December 1993

	Revolving fund		Own savings	
I-G activity	Loans (Tk)	Loanees	Loans (Tk)	Loanees
Petty trade and business	105,600	140	18,200	26
Poultry raising	121,700	164	34,900	47
Goat raising	202,000	264	46,800	63
Cattle rearing	5,200	7	800	8
Bamboo works	700	1		
Total	435,200	576	100,700	144

tion through government investments and personal savings is called *a
'revolving fund system.'* The average size of loans from revolving funds
and savings was Tk 756 and Tk 735 respectively. By the end of 1993 the
MCs in Mohanpur had extended loans to 21 percent of their members
(see Table 7.7).

Both MCs and the Grameen Bank (GB) finance the rural poor. While
MCs extend financing to poor women of reproductive age, the GB advances loans to the poor of both genders. Loans from the GB are larger
than those from an MC. Also, loans from the GB are distributed through
small groups of five members each; MCs extend their smaller loans to
larger groups. The GB operates through small groups and through centres around which eight such groups are federated. The GB functions as
a specialized financial institution rather than a social service agency; for
this reason, it charges a higher rate of interest than MCs (Fugelsang &
Chandler, 1987; Hossain, 1988).

PROGRAM CONTENT

Besides loans and skills training, MCs provide programs in child care
and adult literacy. Activities related to health and sanitation include
vaccination programs, the construction of sanitary latrines, and the sink-
ing of tubewells. MCs are also involved in forestry.

One of the primary objectives of the MCs is to encourage fertile couples to practise family planning. By the end of 1993, 358 mothers had
accepted methods of contraception on a permanent basis and another

2,662 had adopted temporary methods. About 89 percent of the members had adopted family planning practices, compared to the national average of around 45 percent.

ADMINISTRATION OF THE PROGRAM

Mothers' centres are part of the government-promoted Rural Social Services (RSS) program. At the *thana* level, the social service officer is assisted by a few field supervisors and trade instructors, who work at the village level. This officer is responsible for program implementation; to this end, he or she secures the co-operation of other local GOs and NGOs and serves as the link between the MCs and the program's district and national offices. The executive committee of each MC works under the guidance of the officer. The success of an MC largely depends on the professional competence and personal efficiency of its social service officer.

CONCLUSIONS

The MC programs in Mohanpur have several limitations. Their funding is inadequate, considering the number of MC members. The small loans invested in different projects do not yield enough income to raise members above the poverty line. The RSS program, including its MCs, faces competition from NGOs that are engaged in implementing similar programs in the locality. The skills training received by MC members does not sufficiently prepare them to take up viable income-generating activities. Most members are compelled to enter into traditional activities, which are less remunerative. For this reason, mothers do not feel encouraged to take out loans from the MCs. MC members have limited knowledge with respect to what to produce and how to market their products.

Despite these limitations, the MCs in Mohanpur have achieved significant success in organizing poor mothers and involving them in raising capital, utilizing loans, and taking part in income-generating activities. Also, many of the mothers have been motivated to accept and practise family planning. Behind all these achievements lurks the question as to whether the small profits generated through the MCs are sufficient to liberate rural women and their families from the shackles of poverty, tradition, and oppression that have relegated them to a subordinate position in both economic and social life.

C. The Shishapara Landless Group: An International NGO Multipurpose Development Initiative
Paul Rozario and Shorowar E-Kamal

CARITAS is one of the leading international NGOs in Bangladesh and operates programs in 2,411 villages spread over thirty *thanas* in twenty districts (Aziz et al., 1992). It is a multipurpose development organization with ten major programs divided into twenty-nine smaller ones. The primary emphasis is on alleviating poverty by organizing groups, arranging credit, creating employment, and encouraging savings.

CARITAS ACTIVITIES

In 1979, CARITAS initiated a pilot project called Development Extension Education Services (DEEDS), with the goal of empowering the rural poor (i.e., the landless and other marginalized people) through the formation of groups of 15 to 30 members. In recognition that the poor face many problems, an integrated multipurpose approach to alleviating poverty was followed. The plan was to promote awareness through nonformal education and to support income-generating activities of group members through personal savings and loans. For arranging credit, a revolving fund system was used. By the end of 1989, CARITAS through the DEEDS project had organized 4,117 groups across Bangladesh, with 131,387 members, who together had accumulated a total savings of Tk 13,497,260 (Tk 3,278 per group, or Tk 103 per member).

Based on this experience, CARITAS implemented an expanded scheme in 1989, called the Integrated Plan for Rural Poverty Alleviation and Employment Creation. In addition to the above, this five-year plan provides programs for literacy and adult education, health and sanitation, family planning, tree planting, agricultural development, fisheries and horticulture, and low-cost housing (Aziz et al., 1992, pp. 23–30). The midterm evaluation of this plan found that during the first two years of its operation, from 1989 to 1991, no less than 7,543 groups consisting of 148,763 members had been organized. The incomes of the main and subsidiary occupational groups had increased by about 60 percent for male and 44 percent for female members (Aziz et al., 1992, pp. 40–1). This may be considered a significant achievement.

CONCRETE STEPS IN THE CARITAS APPROACH

CARITAS's activities involve a series of steps:

- A baseline survey of the proposed program site is conducted, to identify the target population and to assess its socio-economic condition.
- During the site selection and baseline survey, field workers of CARITAS seek support from village leaders in mobilizing the target population and organizing it into informal groups.
- Priority is given to the formation of groups among the landless.
- Plans and activities are arrived at through discussions between CARITAS workers and group members.
- Provision is made for continuous training with the goal of promoting awareness, group cohesion, and leadership.
- Even though each group has a small executive committee, all important decisions are taken in group meetings.
- Groups also make periodic evaluations of their income-generating activities.
- Each member is expected to attend weekly group meetings and to deposit savings for capital accumulation.
- Each group has a representative on the *thana*'s 'apex' body, which functions as a general council for social development and combines anywhere from 200 to 300 groups.
- CARITAS advances loans to groups, to be repaid in instalments under a revolving fund system.

SHISHAPARA LANDLESS GROUP

Shishapara is a village about 6 kilometres from Rajshahi city. In that village, CARITAS, under its DEEDS project, organized a landless group of agricultural workers, who eventually become self-reliant through fish cultivation and the operation of a small hatchery.

At first, there was much resistance to the efforts by CARITAS to form a local group, but with the active support of local members of the Union Council, the Shishapara Landless Group was formed on 12 January 1986. Its activities were limited to holding weekly meetings and collecting savings.

Eight years later, in January 1994, the group had increased to twenty-seven members, with a strong managing committee of five members headed by a chairman. With the capital accumulated, the members started to undertake some income-generating activities, jointly and individually. In 1986 the members leased a local pond for fish farming. Having little experience in this activity, they failed to make any profit. The following year the group obtained a lease on 1.18 acres of cultivable land, from which the members were able to make a net profit of

Tk 3,690. In 1988 they were granted a lease on 1.5 acres of low land and re-excavated a pond there. In that one season the members made a net profit of no less than Tk 15,800 through fish farming. Between 1989 and 1991 the group, with assistance and support from CARITAS, re-excavated another seven ponds for fish cultivation. By using a more scientific and systematic approach, the group was able to realize larger profits. By 1994, the group was managing eleven ponds, most of which belonged to its members.

Through loans and supports from CARITAS, the Shishapara group set up a small hatchery for supplying fish fry (newly hatched fish) to seventy ponds owned by the various landless groups affiliated with the Paba Thana Apex, a people's organization at the subdistrict level under CARITAS's supervision. The Shishapara group is a member of this organization. The hatchery cost Tk 260,000 to install. An instructor was appointed to train group members to operate the hatchery, and a committee of three members was established to look after its affairs. Production started in April 1991. By January 1993 the group had repaid the entire loan. It now owns the hatchery.

GROUP ACTIVITIES

The group has been holding regular meetings since its inception. By January 1994, 240 weekly meetings and five annual meetings had been held to discuss and resolve matters related to the group's activities. These meetings serve to develop group solidarity and are also an opportunity for training. At the annual meetings, called general meetings, yearly accounts are discussed, activities are evaluated, plans for the next year are formulated, and profits are distributed.

Members deposit a minimum saving of one taka (Tk) per week. The savings are kept in the local bank. Loans at 12 percent interest per year are issued to members for income-generating activities. The total savings in January 1994 stood at Tk 16,495. The members had made a net profit of Tk 62,578 out of a revolving fund of Tk 24,900 combining the CARITAS investment and their own savings.

The group began by cultivating fish in eleven ponds covering about 5.61 acres of land. Seven of these ponds belonged to the group, the other four were under a ten-year lease. On 15 January 1993, the group took ownership of the hatchery after repaying the loans for its installation. The group has purchased 2.17 acres of land out of the income from the hatchery and the ponds. In 1993 it made a profit of Tk 228,000 from the hatchery. The average monthly income of the members rose from

Tk 615 in 1986 to Tk 1,307 as of January 1993. Besides participating in the hatchery's operations, sixteen of the group's members, with assistance in the form of loans from the group funds and from CARITAS, have undertaken income-generating schemes involving cow fattening, milk cows, land leasing, small farming, rice husking, goat raising, and poultry and duck raising.

The group is also involved in many social activities: addressing social injustices, obtaining fair wages for landless labourers, maintaining peace, ensuring women's rights, and the 'giving in marriage' of girls without dowry.

CONCLUSION

Following the success of the men's co-operative, a women's group was formed in Shishapara village. The women's group now owns four fish farming ponds and is moving toward self-reliance. The two Shishapara co-operatives of landless men and women can serve as a model for other poor people in the area and elsewhere in Bangladesh. Many visitors from abroad have come to observe directly the workings of CARITAS's approach to alleviating poverty.

D. Urban Community Development: Two Case Studies

Since the mid-1950s, the Department of Social Services of the government of Bangladesh has been operating urban community development (UCD) projects in low-income neighbourhoods and slum areas. Each project was intended to mobilize and pool local and government resources to organize programs and activities to address local needs and problems (Ali, 1986, pp. 31–46). The original approach was to work through local groups, resource persons, and leaders, who were represented in a co-ordinating body known as the project council. The Project Councils were registered as voluntary agencies to be eligible for government grants-in-aid. Each UCD project was staffed by two social welfare organizers (one male and one female) and between three and five neighbourhood workers (at least one of whom was a female). This staffing pattern was based on the idea that male and female staff would work *separately* with male and female residents' groups in the project area (Ali, 1986, pp. 31–33).

The UCD projects emphasized community cohesion, self-help, local initiative, and co-operation between the government and the people. Community organization methods were used to develop local initiatives. Each project was preceded by a community survey that had the active support and participation of local groups and leaders. The survey was intended to create community awareness, identify local needs and problems, and explore ways to initiate programs and activities on an aided self-help basis (Ahmed, 1981).

As the Project Councils were dominated by local élites, voluntary contributions were insignificant (Ali, 1986, p. 37) and the grants from government were very small. Programs in the area operated mainly through local voluntary agencies; the activities promoted were in the fields of education (night schools, adult literacy centres, libraries); health and sanitation (maternal and child health and family-planning clinics, health education, cleaning campaigns); and skills training in different trades and vocations (Ali, 1986, pp. 33–41). The UCD projects organized mothers' clubs in order to involve women from poor families in vocational training and to promote health care, family planning, and child welfare.

By the 1960s the Department of Social Services was shifting its emphasis away from local mobilization and toward the provision of direct services to the poor in order to 'demonstrate the tangible results' of these projects (Ahmed, 1981). This shift in policy was made possible by UNICEF assistance in the form of tools and equipment for the following: vocational training cum production centres; mothers' and children's health clinics; night schools and adult literacy centres; and youth clubs. Vocational training, especially for the women, was consistent with the 'felt needs' of the residents of low-income neighbourhoods and slum areas, but the incomes from production centres were very small, and only a few could use the skills acquired for self-employment without start-up assistance in the form of loans and materials (Ali, 1986, pp. 41–2). UNICEF's assistance ended in 1968.

The second five-year plan (1980–5) recommended an integrated and comprehensive approach that took the family as the unit for helping the urban poor (Government of Bangladesh, 1980, pp. 396–7). But this shift in emphasis had not been objectively evaluated and resulted in not enough funds being provided for UCD projects. In 1984, by administrative decision, the UCD program was renamed the Municipal Social Services program, and its staffing was reduced, so that each project now had only one social welfare organizer and three neighbourhood workers. These projects are now called urban social service projects. There are now forty-three of these in different cities and towns. The renaming did not change the general features of these projects. In 1982 the Department of Social Services and UNICEF jointly initiated community-based projects for the urban poor in fourteen of the UCD projects in the four metropolitan cities of Dhaka, Chittagong, Khulna, and Rajshahi. This new program was expected to deliver an integrated package of services and facilities to slum dwellers, who would be actively involved in the operation of those services. Although UNICEF ended much of its support by 1985, the financial assistance it had provided in the form of revolving funds remained, to be used with those projects for a new program known as the Family Development Program (FDP). The FDP seeks to involve women from slums in socio-economic activities in order to raise their standard of living. In the following section, 'Community Development with Women in Urban Slums,' Mohammad Sadeque describes the performance of the FDP in improving the standard of living of slum dwellers through women's organizations in a slum of Rajshahi city.

The inevitable consequence of urbanization in Bangladesh is the growth of slums and squatter settlements (Hossain, 1989; Islam & Haq, 1990). The increase in urban population is mainly a result of in-migration of the rural poor. It was estimated that between 1974 and 1982, the number of urban poor in Bangladesh had increased from 5.6 million to 6.4 million (66% of the urban population), and the number of hard-core poor from 2 million to 3 million (44%) (World Bank, 1989). The proportion of the hard-core poor (i.e., those with a per capita daily intake of 1,805 calories) continued to increase during the 1980s (Task Force, 1990). This was confirmed in a recent survey by the Institute of Bangladesh Studies (Rahman & Sen, 1993).

The slums and squatter settlements of Bangladesh are characterized by extreme poverty, congestion, and overcrowding, and by generally unsanitary and unhygienic conditions. The slum dwellers have little access to basic municipal services and facilities (Islam & Mahbub, 1988; Siddiqui, Qadir, Alamgir, & Huq, 1990). As already noted, the government-supported UCD projects, even with UNICEF assistance, could not address the multifaceted needs of the ever-increasing numbers of slum dwellers. A number of NGOs are operating diverse programs in urban slums and for slum dwellers (Pathfinder, 1991; Underprivileged Children's Educational Programs – UCEP, 1991). In the section 'Slum Improvement Project of Rajshahi City,' Munshi Asadur Rahman describes the operation of the UNICEF-supported Slum Improvement Project (SIP) in Rajshahi city and shows how it has improved the capacity of the city corporation to provide some basic facilities to slum dwellers.

CASE STUDY I:

FAMILY DEVELOPMENT PROGRAMS WITH WOMEN IN URBAN SLUMS
Mohammed Sadaque

The UCD project in Rajshahi was introduced in 1961. At first, it followed the traditional CD approach. A Project Council co-ordinated and supported its activities, which until recently involved training poor women in sewing, knitting, and embroidery, and supporting affiliated agencies. In 1986 the UCD project in Rajshahi began implementing a UNICEF-supported FDP in five slum areas. This case study describes the performance of an FDP in one of those slums.

STRATEGIES OF FDP

The strategies that are used in implementing an FDP include the following: selecting slum areas; identifying the target households; providing loans for income-generating activities; and arranging other services such as skills training, education in health and sanitation, and immunization, literacy, and cultural programs. The FDP's activities are undertaken through organized women's groups.

FDP IN MALDAH COLONY

In a slum called Maldah Colony, FDP was initiated in 1987. This colony was set up by the government in 1962 for migrants from the neighbouring district of Maldah of West Bengal, India. Except for shelter, the migrant families had received little assistance. Over the years, population increases and economic distress have reduced the area to a slum with severe economic, social, and environmental problems that denied the inhabitants of any hope for a decent life.

The FDP began by conducting a baseline survey to identify the target households. The survey found that, of the 386 households, about two-thirds were living in 'extreme poverty' (Category A, with an income of below Tk 2,300), about one-third were 'poor' (Category B, with an income of between Tk 2,300 and 3,400), and only 1 percent were above the poverty line (i.e., Tk 3,400).

MOBILIZING THE WOMEN FOR THE FDP

The households in extreme poverty were eligible to be included in the FDP. However, the people of Maldah Colony, a depressed slum, were apathetic and sceptical about the notion of improving their living conditions through organized community activity. At first, female UCD officers tried to encourage the poor women from target households to form their own work groups. However, there was a great deal of resistance to getting women involved in economic activities outside the home. The UCD officer and her staff had to make door-to-door visits and hold group discussions. Finally, they decided to hold a community meeting with the local ward commissioner and other leaders and a representative from UNICEF to gain support for the FDP in Maldah Colony. By June 1993, eighteen women's work groups that included about 80 percent of the women from target households had been organized in the colony.

Each work group held weekly meetings, during which the members learned about the art of co-operative action. These work groups were kept small – at around twenty members – to facilitate closer interaction. The meetings enabled members to become aware of their roles and responsibilities in group activities, and also familiarized the members with the plan and procedures of the FDP. The worker had to provide much advice and guidance, especially during the early stages. A number of program issues were addressed at these meetings – for example, seeking approval for income-earning schemes, deciding on loan disbursement, collecting personal savings, and promoting school enrolment, vaccination, and family planning.

PROJECT COMMITTEE

The project committee for Maldah Colony is made up of the leaders of all work groups and has a rotating chairperson. At the beginning of the financial year, the committee draws up action plans for the whole project. Monthly meetings are used to review the progress of action plans, to identify constraints, and to decide on appropriate action.

INCOME-EARNING ACTIVITIES

The most important activity of the FDP is the promoting of income-earning activities through a supervised revolving fund. The official records of the project show that by the end of 1993, 661 income-earning schemes of eighteen work groups had been supported by loans from the revolving fund. Most of the income-earning activities were related to small trades and businesses, which yielded a regular flow of income and helped repay the loans.

The FDP's loan operations compare favourably with those of the Grameen Bank, though the FDP operates in urban slums and the GB in rural areas. The two organizations also differ with regard to group size, interest rates, and mode of repayment. GB's borrower groups consist of only five members, and pay an interest of more than 20 percent per year, and must repay in weekly instalments. By comparison, the work groups under the FDP have twenty members each, and pay a 10 percent service charge, and can repay in monthly instalments. Other program features of these two loan operations are similar.

PERSONAL SAVINGS

The FDP encourages regular savings by its participants. All eighteen work groups in Maldah Colony have responded well in this regard. The total accumulated savings reached Tk 275,000 in January 1994. With the consent of group members, personal savings may be used to meet emergencies and for special purposes such as marriage and medical treatment.

SOCIAL DEVELOPMENT

The FDP also encourages its beneficiaries to send their children to school. Those who are unable to take advantage of regular schools are encouraged to attend adult education centres operated by the UCD project. The groups provide a forum for GOs and NGOs to offer education in health and sanitation, promote family planning, and initiate vaccination campaigns. The city corporation has provided residents with several tubewells, a number of sanitary latrines, and garbage bins, which are maintained by members of the work groups, who co-operate in improving the drainage system of the area.

Despite the gains made by the FDP program in Maldah Colony, its people continue to live in unhygienic conditions and face a daily struggle for survival. The resources are not adequate to deal with the enormous problems that slum dwellers confront.

CASE STUDY II:
SLUM IMPROVEMENT PROJECT IN RAJSHAHI CITY
Munshi Asadur Rahman

UNICEF, in co-operation with the Local Government Engineering Bureau, initiated the Slum Improvement Project (SIP) during the period 1985–8. By June 1994, it was operating in sixteen municipalities and four city co-operatives. Operational control of the SIP lies with the local municipal authorities. The broad aim of the project is to improve the capacity of municipal authorities to work with the urban poor living in slums, to provide those poor with some of the basic facilities, and to assist in improving their living standards and environmental conditions.

SIP IN RAJSHAHI CITY

Rajshahi city is the northwestern divisional headquarters of Bangladesh. It is one of the major urban centres of the country. In 1993 the city had an estimated population of 520,000 and counted fifteen slums. The SIP covered an area of eight slums with a combined population of 16,573, comprising 2,348 families. The program focused exclusively on women in selected slums.

OBJECTIVES OF THE PROJECT

The main objectives of the SIP in Rajshahi city are these:

- To organize women into groups.
- To provide loans to women through their groups for income-generating activities.
- To arrange leadership training for group leaders.
- To train selected women as community health workers in order to provide primary health care services to slum dwellers.
- To teach women how to read, write, and keep simple accounts.
- To improve the physical infrastructure in the project area by installing tubewells and sanitary latrines, constructing internal roads and drainage systems, and installing access lights.

ORGANIZATIONAL STRUCTURE AND MANAGEMENT

The SIP in Rajshahi city has a Project Implementation Committee (PIC) that oversees its operations and progress. The funds for the project are channelled through the committee. The chairman and project manager jointly handle the funds. The PIC, which meets once every two months, consists of nine members, with the city's mayor as chairman and representatives from different departments and agencies.

Each of the selected slums has a subcommittee with one chairperson and one vice-chairperson; both are elected by the beneficiaries. The member-secretary of the subcommittee is a SIP staff member (community organizer). These subcommittees, which are responsible for implementing the project, meet once a month.

There are 109 groups in the eight slums. Each group consists of between ten and twenty-five 'like-minded' women and meets once a week. They solve community problems, encourage savings, and distribute loans for income-generating activities. Their leaders, secretaries, and community health workers (CHWs) are elected by the group. The community organizers (COs) monitor and supervise their activities.

ACHIEVEMENT OF THE PROJECT

CD activities within the project area included organizing of 2,348 slum families into 109 groups, and the groups into project subcommittees. Two COs and thirty-seven CHWs assisted groups and subcommittees.

Installation of tubewells and streetlights, construction of sanitary latrines, and provision of dust bins, garbage drains, and internal roads are considered to be essential elements of physical development. The targets of the project in this regard included one latrine for each family and one tubewell for every ten families. There were twenty-seven tubewells in the area when the project started. By June 1994 the tubewell coverage amounted to one for every thirty families – still far below the project target. Similarly, while the SIP's target was one sanitary latrine per family, coverage has been limited to one per four families. According to a municipal report, 35 percent of the city's families had sanitary latrines, 60 percent had closed pits, and 5 percent had open pits.

Regarding other physical facilities such as streetlights, dust bins, drains, and internal roads, progress has been significant. The target for streetlights was one for every forty families, for dust bins one for every hundred families, for drains 2 metres per family, and for roads 3 metres per family. Progress made by June 1994 was one streetlight per 138 families, one dust bin per 234 families, 1.5 metres of drain per family, and 2 metres of internal roads per family. Project results are shown below:

Item	Number installed
Tubewells	49
Streetlights	17
Latrines	560
Dust bins	10
Drains (metres)	3,456
Internal roads (metres)	4,607

Primary health care is provided through the activities of COs and CHWs. It includes health education for group members, immunization for women of 15 to 49 years and for children under one year, Vitamin A for children under five years, and the supply of some essential drugs and growth-monitoring services for children. The project also provides family planning services to couples. Through these services, 997 couples have been persuaded to use permanent or temporary family planning methods, a proportion far greater than in the city's general population.

Immunization coverage in the slum areas is significant. A total of 885 mothers and 1,059 children have been immunized against the six 'child killer' diseases (diphtheria, poliomyelitis, pertussis, tuberculosis, measles, and tetanus).

The providing of credit through women's groups for income-generating projects is a vital component of the SIP, as it enables group members to increase their family incomes and employment opportunities. As of mid-1994, 627 families have been given loans amounting to Tk 1,228,000. They have accumulated savings of Tk 392,820, deposited in the project account.

CONCLUSION

The SIP in the slums of Rajshahi city has brought significant changes for the inhabitants. In the words of one participant:

We never thought of having a pucca drain, a narrow pucca road, streetlights, sanitary latrines, tubewells, and dustbins, or of receiving credit from a formal source. But to our utter surprise, SIP has brought all these facilities and services to our doorsteps. We now have access to a bank, to City Corporation officials and to some other government officials. We are now better off than before. We are grateful to SIP.

3. SUPPORTIVE INSTITUTIONS
Nurul Islam

The primary goal of CD in Bangladesh, currently, is poverty alleviation through participation. To this end, GOs and NGOs are engaged in a wide variety of programs and activities (Mannan, 1989, pp. 44–71). A significant number of institutions provide support to these organizations, helping them to implement and expand their programs. These supportive institutions include multilateral organizations (e.g., UNICEF and the World Bank), domestic and international NGOs (e.g., CARITAS and Enfants du Monde), foreign government aid agencies (e.g., USAID and Canada's CIDA), other external funding organizations (e.g., foundations), training and research institutions, and government departments. Institutional support for CD takes various forms: the funding of entire programs, the supplying of equipment and other materials, the providing of technical advice and services, and the sharing of training and research facilities.

Development activities in Bangladesh, whether operated by GOs or NGOs, depend heavily on foreign assistance. In most cases the type of program and the scale of operation are determined by the donors. New programs are initiated, and old ones discontinued, according to the availability of external assistance. The proliferation of NGOs in Bangladesh during the 1980s was largely the result of the availability of foreign funds from diverse sources.

URBAN COMMUNITY DEVELOPMENT (UCD)

The UCD program was initiated by the Bangladeshi government with the advice and technical assistance of the United Nations. Up to the mid-1960s, the UN continued to support the UCD program by assigning advisers to the project. Training in modern social work arose from the need for trained personnel, mainly for UCD projects. In the beginning this training was short-term, nondegree, on-the-job training; later, two-year postgraduate programs were developed at two universities.

The kind of material and financial assistance provided to UCD by UNICEF differed notably between 1960–8 and 1982–8. In the first phase, UNICEF supplied sewing, knitting, and embroidery machines, typewriters, and carpentry tool-boxes for production and vocational training centres, games and sports equipment for youth clubs, school accessories for night schools and adult literacy centres, equipment for some of the maternal and child health clinics, and motorcycles and bicycles for the project staff (Ali, 1986, pp. 31–46). During the period 1982–8, UNICEF provided financial assistance to fourteen community-based projects for the urban poor in four metropolitan cities: Dhakka, Chittagong, Khulna, and Rajshahi. Most of the assistance was for promoting income-earning activities by women from extremely poor households.

The activities of the UCD projects are also supported locally by voluntary agencies, which are represented on the project councils that oversee the activities of each project; and by local municipalities, which provide occasional assistance.

RURAL COMMUNITY DEVELOPMENT (RCD)

RCD activities began in the early 1950s with assistance from the ICA (now USAID). Although the program was terminated in 1959, the national training academy continued to function, having evolved into the now well-known Bangladesh Academy for Rural Development (BARD) in Comilla. An international exchange of scholars was established through links between BARD and Michigan State University. This exchange promoted co-operative research and experiments, out of which emerged the Comilla Model of RCD (described in the Nandanpur Co-operative Society case study). The Bangladesh Rural Development Board (BRDB) is the government's most extensive RCD program. It currently operates thirteen rural development-cum-poverty-alleviation programs, all of which are supported by aid agencies of different donor countries such as Norway, Sweden, Canada, and Japan, and by international organizations such as the UNDP and the World Bank. Most of the donors have provided experts to promote and monitor their own programs (BRDB, 1993).

A growing problem faced by the Bangladesh government is how to continue experimental or pilot programs, which by nature are of short-term duration. The government does not have sufficient resources to provide the staff required to integrate such pilot projects into ongoing programs.

A second rural development program that uses a participatory approach is the Rural Social Service (RSS) program operated by the Department of Social Services. The RSS program was initiated in 1974 as a series of experimental projects in nineteen *thanas*. A Geneva-based NGO, Enfants du Monde (EDM), began supporting the program components that were relevant to family and child welfare. At present, EDM supports rural family and child welfare projects in forty-six *thanas*. The major purposes of these projects are similar to those of the mothers' centres (described in the Mohanpur case study): to educate the poor in the areas of health, sanitation, nutrition, immunization, and family planning, and to provide skills training for income-generating activities. EDM assigns one field co-ordinator to each of its rural projects to monitor the implementation of its programs.

In the early 1970s, the World Bank, another UN-affiliated organization, began providing financial support for Mothers' Centres in forty of the RSS projects. This support continues to be used to increase income-generating activities and to educate mothers in family planning, health, sanitation, nutrition, backyard gardening, and so on.

In addition to its work in urban areas, UNICEF has been supporting rural development since the 1980s, through family development programs (FDPs) in 540 villages, involving fifty-four RSS projects. By the end of 1992, 58,437 women from extremely poor families had been organized into 2,569 groups for skills training and loan assistance for income-generating activities. The emphasis of FDPs is on improving maternal and child health. In addition, FDPs promote backyard gardening, immunization, training of traditional midwives, and training of village women as community health workers.

National and regional academies of the Department of Social Services provide support in the form of on-the-job training. They also organize refresher courses for the officers who are responsible for local training activities in the development programs.

4. EDUCATION AND TRAINING
M. Solaiman and Tahamin Banu

A wide variety of programs have been undertaken by GOs and NGOs to address the multifaceted problems of urban and rural poverty. These programs require personnel with skills in organizing and social mobilization to motivate the poor and assist them in their socio-economic advancement. The personnel required to implement these programs are generally recruited from among the graduates of different educational programs in the social sciences. Also, many of the operating organizations have their own in-service training units.

Education and training programs related to CD in Bangladesh are provided by various agencies including universities, GOs, and NGOs. This section discusses nine such institutions and organizations and briefly outlines their training methods, curricula, and relationships with community practice. These are the nine institutions:

1. University of Dhaka (Department of Sociology and Institute of Social Welfare and Research)
2. University of Rajshahi (Department of Sociology and Social Work)
3. Bangladesh Academy for Rural Development (BARD), Comilla
4. Co-operative College, Comilla
5. Youth Training Centre, Dhaka
6. Training Centre of the Women's Affairs Directorate, Dhaka
7. Training Centres of the Bangladesh Rural Development Board (BRDB), Dhaka

8. Training and Resource Centre (TARC) of the Bangladesh Rural Advancement Committee (BRAC), a national NGO
9. Training school of CARITAS, an international NGO

TYPES OF COURSES

Courses offered at the universities by sociology, social welfare, and social work departments focus on theoretical knowledge, with supervised practice learning at both undergraduate and graduate levels. In GO and NGO training centres the emphasis is on practical experience and training.

The sociology departments provide a general study of rural development along with courses on theory, research, and social statistics. Courses on community organization and community development, in both rural and urban areas, are offered in the social welfare and social work departments, which also offer field courses through which students gain practical experience. Lecture courses are offered to larger groups, and tutorials to smaller ones. Students of sociology at the undergraduate level are required to prepare a research monograph in addition to tutorial assignments and term papers. At the graduate level, students of social welfare and social work may be required to submit theses.

The Bangladesh Academy for Rural Development (BARD) and the Co-operative College, both government-level institutes, train the officers who have been recruited to implement specific development programs. This training is both preparatory and ongoing. The same institutes offer refresher courses and organize seminars and conferences. The officers, in turn, train field-level workers in departmental training centres located at the district and subdistrict levels. In the training process, both BARD and the Co-operative College utilize lectures, case studies, group discussions, role play, and brainstorming.

The Co-operative College trains officers and field-level functionaries in the organization and management of co-operatives, co-operative law, accounting, auditing, and so on. Some of these trainees are posted to zonal institutes, which have been established to provide instruction to the members of co-operatives. There are eight such institutes.

To facilitate self-development among participants, the training centres of the Youth and Women's Affairs directorates offer courses in skills such as sewing, secretarial work, computer operation, carpentry, and livestock and poultry rearing. CARITAS training centres offer vocational courses in welding, plumbing, carpentry, pump operation, and the like.

A 'learning by doing' method involving practical demonstration is applied in most of these skill-training courses.

The BRDB's three institutes – one specifically for women – train field functionaries, called 'inspectors,' and the leaders of co-operatives. Members of the co-operatives receive training at regular intervals at the 450 *thana* training and development centres (TTDCs). They are trained in the following subjects: organization and management of co-operative institutions, leadership development, capital formation, credit operation, bookkeeping, farming methods, irrigation technology and management, local-level planning, fish farming, and livestock and poultry rearing. The BRDB training centres make use of lectures, group discussions, and field visits. *Thana*-level training courses operated by the BRDB at the TTDCs and other training units offer lectures as well as practical demonstrations.

The Bangladesh Rural Advancement Committee (BRAC) operates training and resource centres (TARCs) outside Dhakka that offer courses in human development and management and in occupational skills development. The human development and management programs are designed to develop social awareness but also include training in leadership, rural development, and project planning and management. The programs in occupational skills training have the goal of increasing the capacity of the poor and include courses on agriculture, pisciculture, poultry, animal husbandry, and sericulture, and the relevant technologies. The training programs operate with the active participation of the trainees, which encourages participants to think, analyse, reflect, and act on their own behalf (BRAC, 1993, pp. 45–47). BRAC uses lectures, group discussions, brainstorming, and role play in the training of its development workers.

NGOs working for the socio-economic advancement of the poor have developed a 'target group approach' aimed at giving the poor a stronger organizational base from which to build self-reliance. The target groups are members of the growing landless class, which comprises more than half the rural population (Chowdhury, 1986). This approach places a strong emphasis on formal and nonformal training – specifically, the 'conscientization' of the poor. Inspired by the work of Paulo Freire, this development approach seeks to effect change not only through programs but through 'liberating education,' whereby the poor are made aware of the external causes of their condition, including exploitation and social injustice (Chowdhury, 1986). Group solidarity, group cohesion, and leadership development are central themes. Since these training courses are usually aimed at the poor and other disadvantaged people, issues such as increasing production, generating income, and creating employment receive high priority.

Courses offered by NGOs to develop awareness and leadership at the grass roots level are mainly of short duration, from three to fifteen days. Training for some occupations – sewing, pump machine operation, typing, secretarial work, and so on – may last for up to six months. At the universities, degrees are awarded to students of sociology, social welfare, and social work after up to four years of study (three years at undergraduate and one year at graduate level).

CONCLUSION

A review of the course content at selected institutions reveals that the courses available vary as to how much they emphasize theory over practice, or vice versa. The theory courses and some practice courses offered at universities to students of social welfare and social work establish a foundation for a professional career in the development field.

Courses offered at the BARD and co-operative college, and at the BRDB training centres, build on the theoretical base provided to graduates by university programs. They focus on specialized training aimed at preparing students to become managers of CD programs in the areas of rural development, local-level planning, organization and management of institutions, participatory development, and project management. Later, as managers, these trainees will in turn plan and organize practice and skills training courses for the beneficiary groups, especially in such areas as income generation and employment creation.

5. RESEARCH
Ali Akbar

Research activities relevant to CD in Bangladesh may be placed in two categories: macro and micro socio-economic studies that provide an understanding of the changing context of CD practice and contribute to the evolution of approaches and strategies for working with and for the poor; and internal and external studies, reviews, and evaluations of programs or program components. These research activities are undertaken by individual researchers and academics, by universities and research institutions, by consulting firms, and by organizations engaged in program implementation. Most of the major operating organizations such as the BRDB, BRAC, EDM, and the Grameen Bank have their own research and monitoring units, which are staffed by professionals and experts.

FINDINGS OF SOCIO-ECONOMIC STUDIES

Since the 1970s a large number of empirical micro studies and macro analyses have attempted to examine and assess the nature, trends, and dimensions of rural and urban poverty (Ahmed & Hossain, 1984; Mannan, 1989; Muqtada, 1986; Rahman & Sen, 1993) and to describe the survival patterns and vulnerability of the poor (Siddiqui, 1982, pp. 355–68; Sadeque, 1990). Several village studies have concentrated on issues of social stratification and local power structures and their implications for the local people in terms of poverty and inequality. These studies also considered appropriate development strategies aimed at overcoming the adverse effects of the exploitative social structure (Arens & Bueden, 1977; Bertocci, 1979; Jahangir, 1982; Jansen, 1987, 1991; Rahman, 1986a). Some of the studies have focused on the condition and status of women, children, and other disadvantaged groups (Begum, 1988; Chen, 1986; Chowdhury, 1986; Shah, 1986; UCEP, 1991; UNICEF, 1993). A significant number of empirical studies have examined the consequences of rapid population growth, urbanization, and growth of urban poverty (Hossain, 1989; Islam & Haq, 1990; Islam & Mahbub, 1988; Mizanuddin, 1993; Siddiqui et al., 1990).

A critical review of the findings and conclusions of these studies indicates that development strategies have more or less bypassed the poor and other disadvantaged groups. There are considerable income and power disparities (GOB, 1985; Islam & Khan, 1986; Sarker, 1992; World Bank, 1989). Often the rural élite, by virtue of their dominance in landholding and other related economic activities, control the village institutions (Jansen, 1991) and direct and misappropriate the flow of external resources through their links with officials and politicians (BRAC, 1980, 1983; GOB, 1985; Jahangir, 1982; Jansen, 1987).

Demographic studies point out that the persistence of mass poverty must be understood in the context of (a) the increasing pressure that the growing population is placing on limited land, and (b) a relatively stagnant economy. Some of these studies reveal that the landless and the near-landless, having uncertain or less than subsistence incomes, have been forced to take up self-employment in various nonformal sectors (GOB, 1985, pp. 101–12; Hossain, 1984). Studies on urban poverty indicate that the increase in urban population has been mainly due to in-migration of the rural poor, who have had to create their own means of income and find shelter in slums and squatter settlements (Islam & Mahbub, 1988). All of these studies conclude that the proximate cause of poverty in Bangladesh is the high incidence of underemployment (Hossain, 1984).

Most rural studies state that to stem the rise in inequality and impoverishment, development policies and programs should be designed and implemented specifically for the poorest segments of the population, and that the poor need *class-based* organizations so that they can gain control over their destiny, protect their rights, and improve their socio-economic condition (Arens & Bueden, 1977; BRAC, 1980, 1983; Economic and Social Commission for Asia and the Pacific, 1992, pp. 10–12; Hartman & Boyce, 1979; Jansen, 1987; Muqtada, 1986; Rahman, 1990). These conclusions are consistent with the experiences of many operating agencies (Alauddin, 1983; BRAC, 1980; Chen, 1986; Chowdhury, 1993; Khan, 1991; Lovell, 1992; Novib, 1993; UST, 1993). There is, however, a divergence of views among the analysts about whether the rural power structure is monolithic and stable, and whether there is any class consciousness among the poor (Bertocci, 1979; Jansen, 1991; Mizanuddin, 1993; Rahman, 1986b, 1987). Some point out that rural factionalism and occupational fragmentation (reflected in various forms of patron–client and kinship relationships) tend to constrain the emergence of class consciousness (Bertocci, 1979; Jansen, 1987; Rahman, 1986a, 1987). The poor are not a clearly defined homogeneous group; they differ in terms of income, wealth, and influence (Mannan, 1989, pp. 27–32).

RESEARCH RELATED TO GOVERNMENT PROGRAMS

All government programs relevant to CD in Bangladesh are target-group oriented and emphasize the active involvement of the participants. The government operates diverse programs of poverty alleviation through a number of departments (BRDB, 1993; DECA, 1992; Mannan, 1989, pp. 120–7; Wood, 1984). These programs have several components and cover a number of categories of the poor – small and marginal farmers, the landless and other occupational groups, unemployed youths, women, destitutes, and so on. The research activities of government programs involve internal monitoring, compilation of annual reports, periodical reviews by the Planning Commission, monitoring by consultants assigned by donors to operating organizations, and occasional external evaluation of programs or program components as required by donors (BRDB, 1993; Enfants du Monde, 1993). In addition, micro and macro analyses of government policies and programs are conducted by researchers and academics (Akbar & Mustafa, 1988; Ali, 1986; Akbar, 1992; Sarker, 1992).

Program duplication is a concern. Records indicate that similar programs, albeit with different components and emphases, are being implemented by various government departments. There is no attempt to synthesize these experiences to arrive at a uniform policy that would result in more efficient and effective programs (Akbar, 1991a; Khan, 1991). Furthermore, political instability and frequent changes in government hinder continuity and commitment in the development of public policy (Mannan, 1987, pp. 120–7).

These studies and reviews have reported the successes, near-successes, and limitations of government programs for poverty alleviation. They indicate that government programs have reached and organized a sizable proportion of different categories of the poor. They have provided functional education in primary health care, sanitation, family planning, and homestead utilization. Savings accumulated by the poor have been impressive. Supervised credit and skills training have helped expand family enterprises; these have also provided opportunities for better utilization of underused family labour, engaged a large number of women in income-earning activities, and promoted various forms of nonfarm employment and income-earning opportunities in the rural economy, which is insufficiently diversified (Akbar & Mustafa, 1988; Ali, 1986; Begum, 1988; BRDB, 1993; Development Consulting Association, 1992; Mia et al., 1985; Momen & Hye, 1983).

But it is also pointed out that government efforts have failed to establish substantive community organizations among the poor, and that some of these organizations continue to be dominated by the rural élite and are not being used for collective efforts. Since the government has not allocated adequate resources, its efforts may end up making the poor less poor but no more self-reliant.

No program, however well conceived, can produce the desired results without a dedicated field staff and appropriate structure. In Bangladesh, as a result of continuous political and social instability, there has been an erosion of moral values. Corruption and malpractice have increased, and the confidence of the people in the government has declined. It is not surprising that the government has failed in its efforts to mobilize and inspire the masses.

RESEARCH RELATED TO PROGRAMS AND STRATEGIES OF NGOS

NGOs have played an important role in alleviating poverty in Bangladesh (Task Force, 1990). In 1991, 460 NGOs supported by agencies in international co-operation were operating various programs aimed at the socio-economic advancement of the poor through institution building, resource mobilization, employment creation, income generation, and human resource development (Alauddin, 1985; Fugelsang & Chandler, 1987; Lovell, 1992; Rahman, 1986c). Despite significant differences in program emphasis, there seems to be a convergence in NGO approaches to alleviating poverty (Aziz et al., 1992; Akbar, 1991a; Chen, 1986; Chowdhury, 1993; Novib, 1993).

There is a growing consensus among researchers and program organizers that the expansion of productive employment should be the most important component in strategies to alleviate poverty (Hossain, 1988; Muqtada, 1986; Rahman & Sen, 1993; UST, 1993). In this, the emphasis should be on creating nonfarm self-employment through skills training, supervised credit, and improved access to productive assets (Ahmad, 1983; Ali, 1986; CDS, 1993; Getubig, 1992; Khan, 1991; Proshika, 1989; Smillie, 1992). A review of the records of major NGOs indicates that the income-generating activities promoted by them are similar. On average, about three-quarters of the participants are women (Hossain, 1988).

At the same time, NGOs are criticized for perpetuating subsistence activities and dependency (Akbar, 1991a; Government of Bangladesh, 1985, pp. 209–45), and for operating as money-lenders (Akbar, 1991a; van Schendel, 1988). Some analysts, however, have pointed out that the NGOs have shown that the poor can profitably use credit and repay it promptly, and can accumulate small savings, work hard, and improvise for their survival (Getubig, 1992). At the same time, however, the declining involvement of the men and young people, the failure of collective enterprises, and diminishing returns from successive loans indicate the limitations of employment creation and income generation activities.

Although the emphasis is on a participatory approach, actual participation is limited to receiving benefits offered under conditions set by implementing organizations (Getubig, 1992). It was pointed out that most NGOs have failed to build a client-controlled institutional base (Akbar, 1991); that participation of target groups is sought to implement predetermined strategies (Getubig, 1992; Momen & Hye, 1983; Rahman,

1986b); and that most NGOs are more concerned about the *sustainability* of their credit programs (Fugelsang & Chandler, 1987; Hossain, 1988; Lovell, 1992; Novib, 1993; Proshika, 1989; Unnayan Shahajogi Team, 1993). It has been suggested that the NGOs' efforts should be evaluated in terms of far-reaching social gains rather than more modest achievements in promoting economic self-reliance (Begum, 1988; Rahman, 1987; Shah, 1986; Shehabuddin, 1991).

ISSUES RELATING TO RESEARCH METHODOLOGIES

A significant proportion of research in the field of rural development is carried out by academics and professionals at home and from abroad. The topics they choose, and their methodologies and analyses, though applied in nature, are in most cases not applicable for immediate use by program planners. These studies are often undertaken as part of the requirements for an academic degree or to prepare professional papers and are usually influenced by the terms of funding. Academic researchers, who are insulated from operational issues and have no lasting commitment to programs and organizations, are frequently blamed for being too critical – too eager to find faults rather than strengths (Chambers, 1983; Chen, 1986).

This view, however, fails to appreciate that the critical attitudes of academic researchers have led to useful insights into the shortcomings of program strategies, and to constructive suggestions for improving the effectiveness and efficiency of ongoing policies and programs. Similarly, academic researchers have continued to advocate decentralization, suggesting the need for community action and participatory approaches to development (Rahman, Aminul, 1990; Rahman, Anisur, 1990; Sarker, 1992). A significant contribution is made by researchers who work with operating agencies to penetrate remote areas and who adopt anthropological case study methods for in-depth analysis, examining what is wrong, what works, and what does not (Chambers, 1983; Chen, 1986; Getubig, 1992; Richter, 1988; Shehabuddin, 1991; Smillie, 1992).

Program reviews undertaken by donors or outside experts or visitors are another type of research. These are based on field visits, analyses of records, and participation in workshops and staff meetings. Some of the reviews are concerned primarily with performance evaluation, while others focus on the lessons learned. However methodologically weak, these reviews are considered very important for continued external assistance and support, and for publicizing organizational activities. Often, donor agencies employ consultants for external evaluations of the programs they support.

Most operating organizations start with formal or informal surveys of selected program sites in order to identify target groups and to establish baseline data. Such surveys adopt a Triple-A approach – a process of assessment, analysis, and action, followed by reassessment, further analysis, and more focused action (UNICEF, 1990). The baseline data obtained from initial surveys are not always reliable for future comparison (Akbar & Mustafa, 1988).

Unlike government organizations (which must follow rigid rules), most NGOs are able to take on the role of learning organizations, undertaking a more responsive, inductive process. In this way research is integrated into the program strategies (Fugelsang & Chandler, 1987). Thus, even though they have their own research and evaluation units, they feel that conventional research by itself would seldom be adequate to find solutions to practical issues in designing field programs or in evaluating their impact (Chen, 1986; EDM, 1993; Novib, 1993, pp. 35–7). More emphasis is placed on 'disciplined observation, guided interviews, and informal panels over surveys ... informal interpretation over statistical analysis ... intermediate outcomes as a basis for rapid adaptation over detailed assessment of *final* outcomes' (Novib, 1993, p. 35). BRAC, for example, has developed its own research perspective, skills, and staff in order to train field staff to listen, observe, and learn (Chen, 1986, p. 260). Similarly, the Grameen Bank trains its field staff to observe and record, and to share their experiences with fellow practitioners in staff meetings and workshops (Fugelsang & Chandler, 1987).

NEW TRENDS IN CD RESEARCH

Most evaluative studies emphasize problem analysis, examining the efficacy of implementation procedures and assessment of program outcomes. Such studies usually recommend more training, better supervision, and additional resources, but ignore the importance of the need for the affected persons to participate in the evaluation process. Some of the NGOs therefore prefer 'focus group' discussions and staff workshops to formal evaluation.

Recently, the participating rural appraisal method (PRA) has become more widely used. This method is deemed more systematic and insightful than the rapid rural appraisal method (Anyanwu, 1988; Novib, 1993). This methodological innovation has emerged out of the program experiences of NGOs and has demonstrated that poor people, even if illiterate, are creative and capable of investigating and assessing their own situation, with or without outside animators. PRA therefore is consistent with the participatory approach used in rural development and poverty alleviation in Bangladesh.

6. THEORY AND POLICY TRENDS
Ali Akbar

Though its essence may be always the same, there is no universally accepted theory of community development. The goals, priorities, and theoretical framework of CD differ from country to country, and change over time in the same country. In the context of Bangladesh, CD theory may be described as an approach based on a set of assumptions about people's capacity for self-development and the value of promoting involvement of the population or target group in development activities at the grass roots level. These assumptions are based on a changing ideology of development, on analysis of socio-economic conditions, and on trends and syntheses of program experiences.

EVOLUTION OF THE CONCEPT AND PRACTICE OF CD

The concept and practice of CD in Bangladesh has significantly changed in recent years. The primary goal of CD has been to improve the standard of living of the impoverished masses through a participatory approach. There is no single approach to alleviating poverty, as can be seen in the following brief overview of the various efforts that have led to the present formulations of CD in Bangladesh.

- In the early 1950s the government introduced CD in order to mobilize local communities (villages and urban neighbourhoods), to deal with local needs and problems on the basis of aided self-help. The approach emphasized the value of consensus and co-operation but played down the existence of inequalities and conflicting interests. Such a top-down approach also overemphasized the capacity for self-help in impoverished communities, and failed to establish a suitable institutional framework that would involve the poor and other disadvantaged populations (Ali, 1986, pp. 112–13, Mannan, 1987, pp. 23–6).

- The Integrated Rural Development Program (IRDP) was introduced by government in the 1970s. The lion's share of benefits from this two-tier co-operative system went to large landowners, widening inequalities and increasing rather than decreasing poverty (GOB, 1985, pp. 212–39, Jones, 1977; Karim, 1991; Mannan, 1989). It became apparent that in an unequal society confronted with mass poverty, a co-operative approach to alleviating poverty is not appropriate. To give priority to the needs of the poor, the government, relying on diverse forms of funding, initiated multidimensional area development projects and formed special co-operatives for those rural men and women who were lacking assets (BRDB, 1993). While co-operatives provided a means to obtain credit and encourage savings, little emphasis was placed on training for human resource development (Khan, 1991, pp. 184–92; Wood, 1984).
- From the mid-1970s onward, the Department of Social Services (DSS) had been operating a target group oriented rural social service (RSS) program for the poor (Ali, 1986). Until recently it did not organize its clients into groups; rather, it took a welfare-based approach (Akbar & Mustafa, 1988). But as with the IRDP, donors persuaded the DSS to develop a theoretical framework and promote the formation of viable organizations among the poor (DECA, 1992; EDM, 1993).
- The urban community development (UCD) projects initiated by the DSS in the mid-1950s used a community organization approach to mobilize local groups and deal with local needs. The process-oriented approach failed to show tangible results. UCD projects now use target group oriented approaches in low-income neighbourhoods and slums, and often focus on *individual* clients (Ali, 1986, pp. 31–57; Ahmed, 1981; Rahman, 1980).
- In the 1990s the new, democratic government pledged that it would implement 'pro-poor' development strategies by developing organizations of the poor with appropriate national support. The prime minister declared that her government had adopted a participatory development model to ensure the participation of the people in efforts to alleviate poverty, control population growth, increase literacy, and address special issues such as the role of women and the conservation of the environment. Through access to education, health, and credit facilities, the poor would be empowered, and thus be more productive and creative *(Bangladesh Observer, Dhaka, July 23, 1993)*. It is doubtful to what extent the government will be able to

implement these policies. Doing so would mean restructuring entire social institutions, introducing administrative reforms (which would require political support), and reallocating resources in a way that is commensurate with the new thrusts of development. The deeply rooted social institutions, powerful bureaucratic vested interests, and long standing, relatively ineffective programs, with their vast networks of field operations, constitute formidable obstacles to any government in a country where political consensus is absent and democratic traditions and practices have yet to find roots in society.

- Since the late 1970s, NGOs have begun to multiply and emerge as a dominant force in the development field, with innovative ideas and diverse strategies for poverty alleviation (Akbar, 1991a; Alauddin, 1985; Mannan, 1989, pp. 60–71). Government programs were hindered by constant pauses at the end of each five year plan and at each change in regime; thus, even while the number of poor people continued to rise, they did not participate as expected in such programs (Mannan, 1989, pp. 44–60; Novib, 1993, p. 31). In contrast, the NGOs, by constantly readjusting their approaches, have evolved several internationally acclaimed models and strategies for alleviating poverty (Akbar, 1991a; Chen, 1986; Fugelsang & Chandler, 1992; Proshika, 1989; Rahman, 1986c; UST, 1993; World Bank, 1990). At the behest of donors, some of these innovative ideas developed by NGOs have been adopted by different government departments, as is apparent in their more recent programs.

NATURE OF CD ACTIVITIES IN BANGLADESH

The traditional concept of CD, which focuses on the community as a spatial unit and as a local population with shared interests, has been discarded by GOs and NGOs alike in favour of a more participatory approach that is based on target groups and that aims to alleviate poverty in both rural and urban areas of Bangladesh (Akbar, 1991a; Khan, 1991; Mannan, 1989, pp. 44–71). While these organizations differ in emphasis, ideology, and specific program content, they generally share the following goals:

- To build institutions by organizing the poor into formal and informal groups.
- To create employment and generate income by encouraging savings, distributing loans and providing skill training.

- To empower the poor through motivation, conscientization, and the development of group solidarity through collective action.

These organizations also promote health and sanitation, literacy and nonformal education, family planning, and tree planting. Whether they are dealing with multi- or uni-dimensional programs, all organizations have come to realize that the participation and involvement of their clientele is of central importance (Akbar, 1991b; Askew, 1991; Pathfinder, 1991; Richter, 1988; UCEP, 1991; UNICEF, 1991).

CD THEORY AND STRATEGIES OF NGOS IN BANGLADESH

Strategies for alleviating poverty through a participatory approach have been developed by NGOs, with some notable successes. The government, as mentioned above, has borrowed these ideas and concepts for many of its programs. When discussing theory and strategies relevant to CD in Bangladesh, we will mainly be referring to those in use by NGOs.

There exists a widely held opinion that the proximate causes of mass poverty and inequality in Bangladesh are widespread unemployment and underemployment (GOB, 1985, pp. 101–6; Hossain, 1988; Muqtada, 1986; Rahman & Sen, 1993). Most of the NGOs, however, believe that poverty 'stems from injustices in the social, economic and political systems of power' (Proshika, 1989). They operate on the assumption that since a radical restructuring of power relations in Bangladesh is not feasible, a more pragmatic approach is needed that aims at a gradual empowerment of the poor and that induces social change by working from the grass roots level up.

The major activities of this approach involve organizing the poor, creating awareness, fostering group solidarity, improving capabilities, and promoting income-generating projects through savings, skills training, and loans. It is expected that the formation of groups will introduce a new factor in social relations between the poor and the élites, increasing the overall bargaining power of the poor, reducing their dependency, and enabling them to take collective action against local injustice and exploitation. Furthermore, it is assumed that the inevitable conflicts and confrontations with the power structure and other vested interest groups will be capable of resolution within the context of the law (BRAC, 1993; CDS, 1993; Chen, 1986; Chowdhury, 1993; Khan, 1991; Lovell, 1992; Novib, 1993; Proshika, 1989; Rahman, 1986c; Shehabuddin, 1991; UST, 1993).

The implementation of the approach involves the use of several recognized strategies and steps:

- The employment of social animators to reach, motivate, and organize the poor into small, homogeneous groups, which in turn are federated into 'apex' bodies or regional councils.
- The advancement of continuous nonformal and functional education aimed at raising the level of critical awareness among the poor about the exploitative social milieu; and at encouraging the people to use their collective strength in safeguarding their rights and preventing exploitation, abuse, and unjust practices.
- The development of group discipline and self-confidence through weekly meetings, accumulation of savings, joint economic activities, and other forms of collective action.
- The promotion of income-generating activities through loans to groups, use of personal savings, skills training, and access to and utilization of other productive resources for economic self-reliance.

Some of the NGOs, like Proshika, ASA, and Nijera Kari, emphasize human resource development as a precondition to the material development of those among the poor who struggle for survival below subsistence level and who are deprived of education and other essentials. They give priority to mobilization and self-development on the assumption that severe economic deprivation for extended periods of time destroys self-confidence, creativity, and skills (Chowdhury, 1993; Proshika, 1989; Rahman, 1986c).

The Grameen Bank gives priority in its credit operations to those poor who are organized into groups and who are working toward economic self-reliance through income-generating activities and regular savings. The creation of a viable and sustainable credit scheme for the rural poor is important but is not enough by itself. It is now recognized that credit inputs should be part of a combination of measures to overcome the multifaceted problems faced by the poor (IFAD, 1993). Hence, the Grameen Bank also includes programs for the empowerment and self-development of its clients. These programs are based on the bank's '16 principles' (Shehabuddin, 1991).

BRAC, besides offering credit programs, gives special attention to organizing and awareness-building (BRAC, 1993; Chen, 1986; Lovell, 1992; Novib, 1993). There is a growing consensus, however, among GOs and NGOs that the crucial factor in empowering the poor in an extremely impoverished country like Bangladesh is economic self-reliance through employment creation and income generation.

All organizations give priority to disadvantaged women, who are subject to gender discrimination and are denied or deprived of access to facilities, services, and information for their self-development. From a strategic perspective, women's involvement in development projects is seen as important to alleviate poverty and as essential to improve their capacity for self-development and autonomy (Begum, 1988; Chen, 1986; Shah, 1986; Shehabuddin, 1991; UST, 1993; World Bank, 1990).

THEORY AND REALITY

In the participatory approach to poverty alleviation, the emphasis is on developing client-controlled organizations so that the poor can assess their own situation, identify their own needs, and decide on appropriate action. But the organizations, in fact, are usually not developed and run by the poor.

The poor are not an undifferentiated class. It is the poorest of the poor – and disadvantaged women in particular – who have become the main focus of NGO programs. Other categories of the poor, such as small and marginal farmers, underemployed males, and unemployed young people, are mostly underrepresented in their programs.

The idea that the poor are unaware of oppressive social structures may not be true, but it is obvious that they lack the power necessary to overcome the effects of inequality (Jahangir, 1984). There is also little evidence of class solidarity among the poor. It appears that the underprivileged learn to accept the unpleasant reality that it may be more sensible to offer loyalty to the élite so as to enjoy their protection and have access to resources (Jansen, 1987). Thus, even when the poor form separate organizations, they tend to remain subordinate to the village system of power relations. Recent evidence, however, seems to indicate that a breakdown is occurring in these traditional patron–client relationships (Jansen, 1991). Insufficient information is available about the use of collective action against local injustices and exploitation, and about the nature of the influence the organized groups exert on local politics and established power structures, so it is questionable whether NGOs – themselves dependent on external funding – can promote large-scale organized action from the grass roots level. Nevertheless, groups are formed not only to empower their members to deal with social justice issues but also to administer credit, encourage savings, and ensure repayments (Novib, 1993).

Usually, there is very little opposition to the presence of NGOs; they are tolerated as long as they are not perceived as a threat to vested interest groups. A recent example of such a perceived threat was when religious fundamentalists reacted violently to NGO activities aimed at women's empowerment and secular education. Generally, an NGO's effectiveness depends greatly on the nature of the community, the community's leadership, the relative position of the poor, and the extent of support from the local administration.

The involvement of clients is central to the participatory approach. In reality, however, such involvement is sought only at the point where a predetermined plan of action is being implemented at the local level, at which time animators are used to persuade clients to follow the rules and disciplines set down at the top. Thus, while there may be some discretion within local projects, there is little real decentralization in decision making, particularly when programs are controlled and supervised by staff (Chen, 1986; Getubig, 1992; Hossain, 1988; Novib, 1993). The question is whether informal groups that are made up of the poorest of the poor can survive without continuous support, supervision, and discipline, and without a set of rules pertaining to the running of weekly meetings and the practice of regular savings and loan repayments.

Income-generating activities are considered crucial to alleviating poverty and promoting self-reliance. NGOs, therefore, have invested a large part of their energies and resources in creating and supporting self-employment opportunities, especially in the nonformal sector (Mannan, 1989). In spite of such initiatives, productivity and income levels remain low in the target groups.

The direct benefits of such programs (in terms of incomes and employment) are not large; even so, the number of participants keeps rising, in part because of a lack of alternatives, especially for women. Also, when women who had never been engaged in income-earning activities use credit successfully, their standing in the household and in society is improved (Shehabuddin, 1991). NGOs have usually not set concrete goals spelling out what proportion of the target population is to be raised above the poverty line or to be made self-reliant; for this reason they are often criticized for perpetuating dependency and subsistence living on a day-to-day basis.

In conclusion, NGOs have demonstrated through their CD programs that the poor are creditworthy, and able to use and repay loans with interest. Thus, they have justified their initial investment in such projects.

But it is not clear yet whether the various approaches of different organizations do in fact lead to real empowerment of the poor, and bring about effective change from below.

Contributors

Ali Akbar
Professor, Department of Social Work, University of Rajshahi, with Master's and doctoral degrees in Social Welfare, Brandeis University, Boston, U.S.A.; his field of specialization is community development and research.

Tahamin Banu
Deputy director (training), Bangladesh Academy for Rural Development, Comilla; holds a Master's degree in sociology from the University of Dhakka; her field of interest is women and development.

Abdul Halim
Professor, Department of Social Work, University of Rajshahi; received two Master's degrees from the universities of Dhakka and Western Australia; his field of specialization is social legislation.

Nurul Islam
Professor, Department of Social Work, University of Rajshahi; holds Master's in Social Welfare, University of Dhakka, and a Master's in Social Work, University of Queensland, Australia; his field of specialization is community development.

Shorowar E-Kamal
Officer, regional office of CARITAS, Rajshahi; holds a Master's degree in sociology, University of Rajshahi.

Asadur Rahman
Program officer, UNICEF, Bangladesh; received his Master's in philosophy and demography from the University of Dhakka; he worked for various international development agencies in different capacities; his field of interest is community development.

Taimur Rahman
Assistant registrar of the co-operative department of the government of Bangladesh; obtained his LL.B. degree from the University of Rajshahi; and was conferred a national Co-operative Award for his extraordinary contribution to social services.

Paul Rozario
Director, regional office of CARITAS, Rajshahi; has a Master's degree in history, and a diploma in social leadership from Francis Xavier University, Antigonish, Nova Scotia, Canada.

Mohammed Sadeque
Professor, Department of Social Work, University of Rajshahi; with two Master's degrees from the University of Dhakka, Panjab (Lahore), and Minnesota, U.S.A., and a doctoral degree from the University of Rajshahi; his field of interest is social development.

Solaiman
Director (Admin), Bangladesh Academy for Rural Development, Comilla; with a Master's in sociology, University of Dhakka, and a doctoral degree from Japan; his field of interest is rural development.

Co-ordinator

Profulla C. Sarker
Professor, Department of Social Work, University of Rajshahi, received his Master's in social work from the University of Rajshahi and his doctoral degree in cultural anthropology from the University of Ranchi, India; known as an authoritative researcher of village life, having published up to fifty research articles on the subject; author of *Ideas and Trends in Rural Society of Bangladesh*, and *Social Structure and Fertility Behaviour in Bangladesh*, and co-author of *Beliefs and Fertility in Bangladesh* (with Clarence Kaloney and Aiz); member of the editorial board of four professional journals and a local consultant to UNICEF, Bangladesh.

References

Ahmad, Razia S. (1983). *Financing the rural poor: Obstacles and realities*. Dhakka: The University Press Limited.

Ahmed, Shahera. (1981). *Urban community development program in Bangladesh*. Dhakka: Department of Social Services, Government of Bangladesh.

Ahmed & Hossain. (1984). *Rural poverty alleviation in Bangladesh: Experiences and policies*. Rome: FAO.

Akanda & Islam (eds.). (1991). *Rural poverty and development strategies*. Rajshahi University, Institute of Bangladesh Studies.

Akbar, Ali. (1985). Community participation and involvement in family planning in Bangladesh. *Eastern Sociology*, 5: 49–64.

– (1991a). An overview of poverty alleviation strategies. In Akanda and Islam (eds.), *Rural poverty and development strategies*. Rajshahi University, Institute of Bangladesh Studies. 145–64.

– (1991b, June). *A study on the efficacy of social work in UCEP General Schools*. Dhakka: Underprivileged Children's Educational Programs.

– (1992, June). *Case studies of Adarsha Grams Project in Northern Zone: The Adarsha Gram Project*. Government of Bangladesh, Ministry of Land.

Akbar & Mustafa. (1988). Poverty alleviation: A study of the efficacy of rural social service projects in Shibganj. *The Journal of the Institute of Bangladesh Studies*, 11: 173–87.

Alauddin, M. (1985, July). *Combating rural poverty: Approaches and experiences of NGOs*. Savar, Dhakka: Village Education Resource Centre.

Ali, Mohammad. (1986). *The poor want to exist: International Union for Child Welfare*. Dhakka: Enfants du Monde (EDM).

Anyanwu, C.N. (1988). The technique of participatory research in community development. *Community Development Journal*, 23(1): 11–15.

Arens & Buedeu. (1977). *Jhagrapur: Poor peasants and women in a village in Bangladesh*. Birmingham, UK: Third World Publications.

Askew, Ian. (1991). Helping people to be involved in family planning. *People*, 18(2): 3–5.

Aziz et al. (1992, May). *Mid-term evaluation on CARITAS integrated plan for rural poverty alleviation and employment creation*. Comilla: Bangladesh Academy for Rural Development.

Bangladesh Observer. (1993, July 23). Dhakka.

Bangladesh Rural Advancement Committee. (1980). *NET: Power structure in ten villages*. Dhakka: BRAC.

– (1983, June). *Who gets what and why: Resource allocation in Bangladesh village*. Dhakka: BRAC Prokashana.

– (1993, June 30). *BRAC Report 1992*. Dhakka: BRAC Prokashana.

Bangladesh Rural Development Board. (1993, June). *Annual report: (1991–92)*. Dhakka: BRDB.

Beck, Tony. (1989). Survival strategies and power amongst the poorest in a West Bengal village. *IDS Bulletin*, 20(2): 23–32.

Begum, Nazmir Nur. (1988). *Pay or purdah: Women and income earning in rural Bangladesh*. Dhakka: Bangladesh Agricultural Research Council.

Bertocci, Peter J. (1979). Structural fragmentation and peasant classes in Bangladesh. *The Journal of Social Studies*, 5: 43–60.

Centre for Development Studies. (1993, June). *The 1992–93 annual report*. Dhakka: CDS.

Chambers, Robert. (1983). *Rural development: Putting the last first*. London: Longman.

Chen, M.A. (1986). *A quiet revolution: Women in transition in rural Bangladesh*. Dhakka: BRAC Prokashana.

Chetley, Andrew. (1993). *Going to scale: BRAC experience, 1972–92*. Canada: Aga Khan Foundation, and the Netherlands: NOVIB.

Chowdhury, N. (1986). Re-evaluation of women's work in Bangladesh. *The Bangladesh Journal of Agricultural Economics*, 11(1): 1–28.

Chowdhury, S.H. (1993, June). Around the year 1993. *Annual Report of the Association for Social Advancement*. Dhakka: ASA.

Development Consulting Association. (1992, June). *An evaluation of the expanded rural social service project 1987–92*. Dhakka: DECA.

Economic and Social Commission for the Asia and the Pacific. (1992). *Agricultural success cases for rural poverty alleviation*. United Nations, NY: ESCAP.

Enfants du Monde. (1993, July). *Internal evaluation of rural family and child welfare projects*. Dhakka: EDM.

Fugelsang & Chandler (1987). *Participation process – What can we learn from the Grameen Bank?* Oslo: Ministry of Development Co-operation.

Getubig, I.P. (1992). Replication and scaling up of credit programs for the poor women. *Grameen Dialogue* (9–10): 6–8, 4–9.

Government of Bangladesh (1980). *The second five year plan (1980–85)*. Dhakka: The Planning Commission.

– (1985). *The third five year plan (1985–90)*. Dhakka: The Planning Commission.

– (1990). *The fourth five year plan (1990–95)*. Dhakka: The Planning Commission.

– (1993). *Statistical yearbook (1992)*. Dhakka: Bangladesh Bureau of Statistics.

– (1994). *Progress towards the achievement of the goals for the 1990s*. Dhakka: Bangladesh Bureau of Statistics.

Hartman & Boyce. (1979). *Needless hunger: Voices from a Bangladesh village*. Washington, DC: International Food Policy Research Institute.

Hossain, Gazi Zahid. (1989). *Patterns of migration: Push and pull factors analysis*. Master's thesis, Institute of Bangladesh Studies, Rajshahi University.

Hossain, Mahbub. (1984). *Credit for the rural poor: The Grameen Bank in Bangladesh*. Dhakka: Bangladesh Institute of Development Studies.

– (1988). *Credit for alleviation of rural poverty: Grameen Bank in Bangladesh*. Washington, DC: International Food Policy Research Institute.

IFAD. (1993, July 23). Credit solutions are not simple. *Bangladesh Observer*, Dhakka.

Islam & Haq. (1990). *Population and migration characteristics in Khulna City*. Dhakka: Dhakka University, Centre for Urban Studies.

Islam & Khan. (1986). Income inequality, poverty and socio-economic development in Bangladesh: An empirical investigation. *Bangladesh Development Studies*, 14(2).

Islam & Mahbub. (1988). *Slums and squatters in Dhakka City*. Dhakka: Dhakka University, Centre for Urban Studies.

Jahangir, B.K. (1982). *Rural society, power structure and class practices*. Dhakka: Dhakka University, Centre for Social Studies.

Jansen, Erik G. (1987). *Rural Bangladesh: Competition for scarce resources*. Dhakka: The University Press Limited.

– (1991). *Process of polarization and breaking up of patron-client relationships in rural Bangladesh*. In Akanda & Islam (eds.), 41–5.

Jha, Satish C. (1987). Rural development in Asia: Issues and perspectives. *Asian Development Review*, 5(1): 83–99.

Jones, Steve. (1977). An evaluation of rural development programs in Bangladesh. *Journal of Social Studies*, 6: 51–92.

Karim, Zehadul. (1991). The Comilla co-operative approach: Its problems and prospects for a comprehensive agrarian development in Bangladesh. *Asian Profile*, 19(5): 447–54.

Khan, Tanvir Ahmed. (1991). Comparison of Grameen Bank initiative with other government and non-government organizations towards rural poverty in Bangladesh. In Akanda & Islam (eds.). pp. 171–202.

Lovell, Catherine. (1992). *Breaking the cycle of poverty: The BRAC strategy*. Hartford, CT: Kumurian Press.

Mahtab. (1992). Population and agricultural land: Towards a sustainable food production system in Bangladesh. *AMBIO: A Journal of Human Environment*, 21(1): 50–5.

Mannan, M.A. (1987, December). *Rural development: A study for inter-country comparative analysis in the SAARC member countries*. Bogra, Bangladesh: Rural Development Academy.

– (1989). *Rural poverty in Bangladesh and its alleviation: An assessment of selected programs*. Ph.D. thesis, Institute of Bangladesh Studies, Rajshahi University.

Mia et al. (1985). *Rural social services in Bangladesh: An impact study*. Dhakka: Dhakka University, Institute of Social Welfare and Research.

Mizanuddin, Mohammad. (1993). The nature of political organization and class position in the Bastee-Dwellers of Dhakka City. *The Journal of the Institute of Bangladesh Studies*, 26: 111–32.

Momen & Hye. (1983). *A study of the impact of income-generating activities among the poor rural women of Bangladesh*. Dhakka: Dhakka University, Institute of Social Welfare and Research.

Momin, M.A. (1992). *Rural poverty and agrarian structure in Bangladesh*. New Delhi: Vikas Publishing House.

Muqtada, M. (1986). Poverty and inequality: Trends and causes. In Islam & Muqtada (eds.), *Bangladesh: Selected issues in employment and development.* New Delhi: International Labour Organisation. 41–60.

Pathfinder. (1991, August). *Sustainability of family planning NGOs in Bangladesh.* Workshop report: Pathfinder International. Dhakka.

Proshika. (1989). *Annual activity report (1988).* Dhakka: Proshika Manobik Unnayan Kendra.

Rahman, Aminul. (1990). *Politics of rural local self-government.* Dhakka: The University Press Limited.

Rahman, Anisur (1990). The case of the Third World: People's self-development. *Community Development Journal,* 25(4): 307–14.

Rahman, Atiq. (1986a). *Peasants and classes: A study in differentiation in Bangladesh.* Dhakka: The University Press Limited.

– (1986b). Poverty alleviation and the most disadvantaged groups in Bangladesh agriculture. *Journal of Bangladesh Development Studies,* 14(1): 29–85.

– (1987, August). *Impact of Grameen Bank intervention on rural power structure.* Evaluation Report No. 31. Dhakka: Bangladesh Institute of Development Studies.

Rahman, Habibur. (1980). *Evaluation of urban community development program in Bangladesh.* Dhakka: Social Science Research Council, Ministry of Planning.

Rahman, R.S. (1986). *A praxis in participatory rural development: Proshika with prisoners of poverty.* Dhakka: Proshika Manobik Unnayan Kendra.

Rahman & Sen. (1993, April). *A time of hope, a time of despair: Findings on household-level changes in rural poverty (1990–92).* Dhakka: Bangladesh Institute of Development Studies.

Richter, Heider. (1988). An evaluation study of a health education program for rural women in Bangladesh. *Community Development Journal,* 2(1): 51–5.

Sadeque, Mohammad. (1990). *Survival pattern of the rural poor.* New Delhi: Northern Book Centre.

Sarker, Abu Elias. (1992). Who benefits? An empirical investigation of Upazila decentralization in Bangladesh. *The Journal of Social Studies,* 55: 1–19.

Shah, Madhuri (ed.). (1986). *Without women, no development: Selected case studies from Asia of non-formal education programs.* London: Commonwealth Secretariat.

Shehabuddin, Elora. (1991). The social impact of the Grameen Bank. *Grameen Dialogue,* 7–8, 5–6, 6–9.

Siddiqui, Kamal. (1982). *The political economy of rural poverty in Bangladesh.* Dhakka: National Institute of Local Government.

Siddiqui, K., Qadir, S.R., Alamgir, S., & Hug, S. (1990). *Social formation in Dhakka City.* Dhakka: The University Press Limited.

Smillie, I. (1992). *BRAC at 20*. Dhakka: BRAC Prokashana.

Task Force. (1990). *Report on Bangladesh development strategy for the (1990s)*. Vol. II. Dhakka: The University Press Limited.

Underprivileged Children's Educational Programs. (1991). Working and street children in urban areas of Bangladesh: Policy and program intervention. Proceedings of the Seminar-cum-Workshop, organized by UCEP. Dhakka: UCEP.

United Nations Development Program. (1992). *Human resources development: Intersectoral coordination issues*. New York: UNDP.

– (1994). *Human development report*. New Delhi: Oxford University Press.

United Nations Children's Fund. (1990). *Food and health care*. New York: UNICEF House.

– (1993). *Situation analysis of children and women in Bangladesh (1992)*. Dhakka: UNICEF.

Unnayan Shahajogi Team. (1993). *Towards women's empowerment: The (1992) annual report*. Dhakka: UST.

van Schendel, W. (1988). Ghorar Dim – rural development in Bangladesh. *The Journal of Social Studies*, 39: 59–81.

Wood, G.D. (1984). *A study of government approaches towards the rural poor in Bangladesh*. Dhakka: Nordic Donors.

World Bank. (1985). *Bangladesh food and nutrition sector review*. Report No. 49, 74–BD. Dhakka.

– (1989). *Promoting higher growth and human development*, Vol. II. Dhakka: World Bank.

– (1990). *Strategies for enhancing the role of women in economic development in Bangladesh: A World Bank country study*. Washington, DC.

– (1990). *Bangladesh: Managing the adjustment process – An appraisal*. Dhakka: World Bank.

Zaman, Wasim Alimuz. (1984). *Public participation in development and public health programs in Bangladesh*. New York: University Press of America, Inc.

Part VIII

Chile

TERESA QUIRÓZ MARTIN and
DIEGO PALMA RODRIGUEZ

Chile

1. INTRODUCTION

Chile, flanked by the Andes Mountains to the east and the Pacific Ocean to the west, is a narrow strip of land 3,500 kilometres long and 402 kilometres at its widest point. It is inhabited by approximately 14 million people, close to 4.5 million of whom reside in the capital region of Santiago.

Chile has a centralized government; however, in 1974 a decentralization process was begun that transferred centralized functions to the regions and municipalities. This process continues today.

THE ECONOMY

The Chilean economy suffered two profound setbacks in the last twenty years, with -8% growth in the GNP during 1975–6 and -16 percent in 1982–3; during this time, the country went through a process of modernization and major restructuring. Its budget was balanced, which led to a drop in inflation from 142.3 percent in 1985 to 12 percent in 1993. The rate of investment rose from 12.9 percent of GNP in 1983 to 25 percent in 1993. The economy was opened up, and production of trade goods was stimulated and diversified. The total value of exports rose from US$1,100 million in 1970 to US$8,310 million in 1990. The Chilean economy has grown consistently since 1986, and in the past five years has maintained a growth rate of 5 percent per year.

Although the state long ago introduced social policies, such as compulsory insurance for workers in 1924, in many cases benefits have gone only to salaried workers. This has excluded many of the poor.

Between 1973 and 1989 the military government of Augusto Pinochet reduced the budget for social services. Technology was introduced to the system, so that the administration and provision of assistance became mechanized. The government stopped subsidizing jobs and channelled funds into needier sectors. Thus, while progress was steadily maintained in the area of human development, poverty increased as social expenditures decreased between 1973 and 1989.

As indicated by social welfare indicators, Chile has one of the highest standards of living among Latin American countries: an infant mortality rate of 16 per thousand; an expected lifespan of 68 years for males and 75 years for females; an illiteracy rate in absolute terms of 5.2 percent; an average of 7.5 years of formal education per inhabitant; and, finally, running potable water in 98 percent of houses and adequate sanitation in another 80.8 percent. For these reasons, the UNDP has assigned Chile a rating of 36 on the Human Development Indicators Scale – the highest in the region. However, these indicators, and what they mean in terms of the social reality for Chileans, are misleading.

POVERTY IN CHILE

Poverty is extensive and cuts deeply into Chilean society. A family is deemed to be living in poverty when its total income is insufficient to acquire the most basic necessities of life. In the 1970s and 1980s, as a direct result of free market policies and the withdrawal of compensation by the state, wealth became concentrated in fewer hands. In 1978 the wealthiest 20 percent of the population appropriated 44.5 percent of the national product; by 1990, the same sector had increased its share to 54.6 percent. In 1978 the poorest 40 percent of the population shared 19 percent of the national product; by 1990 that share had dropped to 12.6 percent.

As a result of this reallocation of resources, the number of families living in poverty rose from 28.5 percent in 1970 to 41.2 percent in 1990. Between 1990 and 1994, national expenditures on social services increased. A policy of increasing salaries beyond the rate of inflation (agreed upon by employers and workers) was also implemented, and this led to a decrease in the number of people below the poverty line, from 41.2 percent to 35 percent. Another indicator of the plight of the poor is calorie consumption: among the poorest 40 percent of society, daily calories consumed fell from 2,019 calories in 1970 to 1,629 in 1990.

POLITICAL CONTEXT

In 1829, eight years after achieving independence from Spain, Chile established its own Constitution. Until 1973, Chile enjoyed a democratic tradition, a tradition that had been interrupted only twice in its history – in 1891 and again between 1925 and 1932.

In 1970 a coalition headed by the Communist and Socialist parties was elected to govern. Three candidates had participated in the election, and the president-elect, Salvador Allende, had won with only 36 percent of the vote. The social and economic changes that the Allende government sought to institute became intolerable for the majority of Chileans, many of whom united in opposing and hindering government initiatives. In 1973 there was a military coup that resulted in the death of Allende and a dictatorship that would last seventeen years.

In 1988 a plebiscite was held in which most Chileans rejected the military's proposal that it continue in power for a further eight years. This opened the way for a return to democracy, and general elections were held the following year. Since 1989 the country has been governed by a coalition called Consensus for Democracy, which includes the Christian Democrats as well as supporters of Allende. The Christian Democrats, who formed the opposition to Allende's government of 1970–3, are the largest party in the country.

CD AND LOCAL DEVELOPMENT

In the early 1960s, a particular model of CD – one that originated in the countries of the North – was promoted throughout Latin America under the auspices of the Alliance for Progress. The Kennedy administration implemented this plan in the region to counteract the influence of the Cuban revolution.

The Alliance for Progress initiative created two unfavourable conditions for the practice of CD in Chile. At first, CD was perceived as part of U.S. policy toward Latin America: thus, in the 1960s much of Chilean society opposed the idea on principle. Then later, when Lyndon Johnson cancelled the Alliance strategy in 1966, CD as a field of professional practice was seen as tainted by the Alliance plan.

Historically, then, CD-related policies have been negatively viewed in Chile. Even so, churches, university groups, rural assistance programs, natural disaster teams, and some government programs have continued to carry out various forms of community work. But many of these

efforts have lacked a systematic method of practice that promotes continuity and growth.

The context for development has changed quite radically since the
1960s. During the dictatorship of Pinochet, the government, which was
uninterested in the fate of the poor, applied structural adjustment policies. This led social activists to group together in NGOs on the fringe of
the state. Inspired and sustained by the work and writings of Paulo
Freire, these activists supported local groups that had organized for
survival and self-sufficiency. While providing technical assistance to
these groups, the activists also encouraged solidarity at the local level
and political responsibility in terms of the broader society.

Since popular education was carried out in isolation from the traditions of CD, practitioners had to learn from painful experience many of
the principles, strategies, techniques, and lessons that CD practitioners
had long ago learned and discovered. For example, popular education
workers had to learn how to determine and assess local needs and
resources; how to work pedagogically with people to address the shift
in emphasis from short-term to long-term needs; and how to negotiate
the shift in priorities from small-scale, concrete (i.e., local) issues to
larger-scale community planning. This method of working with communities was practised throughout the 1980s but was not identified as
CD. Rather, in the second half of that decade it was identified as 'local
development' and viewed as a viable method and practice for working
with communities on development issues.

If we look closely at the work of the popular educators, we can make
three points relating to the particular circumstances in which community work was being undertaken. First, education is a powerful means
of working with people to find solutions to material situations. Very
often, NGOs lacked the resources to carry out solutions. Even so, community education provided an opportunity to build solidarity and encourage collective responsibility among local people. Second, although
community practice was often carried out on a trial-and-error basis,
great care was taken to apply a clear methodology in work with small
groups. Third, neighbourhood organizations were emphasized, and help
from the state was virtually nonexistent – which should surprise no one
in the circumstances.

Chile's return to a democratic system at the beginning of the 1990s
resulted in local development being given a high priority on the government's agenda. Local development is now viewed as a viable option, and joint initiatives are being undertaken by local organizations

and local governments. This challenge demands that we critically analyse not only the history of development in the 1980s, but also the roles
and performances of the principal actors, who until this point in time
had been acting separately. This new encounter between society and the
state occurring at the local level has narrowed the distance between the
traditions of CD and what we call local development.

2. DECENTRALIZATION AND LOCAL DEVELOPMENT IN CHILE: CONCEPTS AND ISSUES

DECENTRALIZATION AND LOCAL DEVELOPMENT AS A PROPOSAL FOR DEVELOPMENT IN CHILE

The concepts of decentralization and local development are very fash-
ionable these days. The public, which has accepted these ideas quite
spontaneously without much critical analysis, understands them as positive initiatives and steps toward a desirable future. Three factors have
created this boom in popularity.

One of these factors involves a crisis in the 'totalizing paradigms,'
that is, in the basic foundations of modern thought that have shaped
our ways of understanding particular situations and procedures. These
paradigms, grounded in rational thought, have organized and controlled the different fields of human endeavour to an ever-increasing degree. Thus, 'modern civilization' has continued to believe that history is
creeping along the road to progress.

Independently of the debates on the definitions of rationality, the
power of the paradigms of modernity to explain reality is being seriously questioned today. Reality now appears to be too complex to be
understood on the basis of the general ideas espoused by these paradigms. This crisis has put into doubt totalitarian arguments and led
to a shift toward the opposite pole. Common sense dictates that anything
'small' is to be valued, and anything 'small' will always be 'beautiful,' according to the title of one of Schumacher's works (1973). Concern is now focused on the ways in which human development can be
stimulated.

Another factor contributing to the popularity of decentralization and
local development concerns the exhaustion of development schemes
that centred on the state as a business enterprise or supervisor. Those
schemes had been the driving force behind the growth of Latin American economies since the 1950s (ECLAC, 1985), but by 1980 they appeared

to have lost all validity. This crisis of faith in the power of central government to develop viable economic policies has effectively paved the way for alternative development plans and proposals. Local dynamics are now part of these alternative plans.

Third, decentralization and local development have benefited from the success of the neoliberal offensive. For us in Latin America, neoliberalism refers not only to economic practices based on the primacy of the free market but also to the philosophy that supports those directions. A key point in the neoliberal argument pertains to the theory of a 'minimal state.' An efficient economy and an effective society both depend greatly on the largest possible transfer of initiative and responsibility to the private sector. This general attitude lends itself well to all types of privatization; in the context of local development, it results in decentralization and in the transfer of development initiatives to various and different bodies in each locality.

Of the three factors contributing to the popularity of local development and decentralization, the main one is neoliberalism. Since the decline in centralized and planned economies, neoliberalism has been perceived by Latin Americans as the only viable approach for constructing a modern society. Consequently, neoliberal thought is the dominant of the three factors outlined here, and utilizes the other two to reinforce its argument (Hopenhayn, 1989).[1] It is important to point out that the neoliberal proposition is championed as if a causal relationship existed between decentralization and local development. According to neoliberal propaganda, decentralization measures automatically lead to local development.

At this stage in our discussion, three important questions emerge. We will address them in the remainder of this article.

In Latin America during the 1960s, CD practice coincided with the implementation of the Alliance for Progress development plan. This particular practice of CD was heavily criticized and consequently set aside. We pose the following question: Is the current idea of local development a revival of the previous practice of CD? If so, what are the

1 See M. Hopenhayn (1989), who notes how the postmodern proposition in Latin
   America has developed characteristics that differ from those in the original European
   version. In Latin America the interaction of economic and political debate has led to
   postmodernism being defined not as an internal movement of modernity as such, but
   rather as an ideological option that reinforces through culture the legitimacy of those
   theories that favour market policies. Enthusiasm for diversity now turns out to be
   elation for a market policy that alone can guarantee such diversity.

specific circumstances that led to its rejection then, and what are the conditions that favour its acceptance now? If the current approach is not simply a revival, what are the features that distinguish the two approaches from each other?

Another question of theoretical importance remains: Why does decentralization – a technical process directly related to a reordering of space – have social and political repercussions, given that such repercussions involve relations and processes of a different kind? In other words, what is the relationship between decentralization and local development? Does one provide the conditions for the other, and if not, then what relationship exists between the two?

Lastly, questions must be asked about the appropriate relationship between local development and national initiatives. Is local development a new strategy that replaces earlier ones? Is national development perceived today as the sum of multiple efforts at the local level? Or is local development proposed *in addition to* national development? If it is, then how will responsibilities and tasks be allocated? What will the relationship of national development be to local development efforts, and how will these parallel processes mesh with each other?

The following section will tackle these three areas of concern by focusing on three main points: local development as an ambiguous, incomplete proposal for development; local development as a concept susceptible to different political directions; and the relationship of local development to various currently contested concepts.

THE AMBIGUITY OF THE CONCEPT OF LOCAL DEVELOPMENT

In accordance with present trends, some scholars of local development have pointed out that the definition of local development varies greatly with the theoretical and political arguments in which it is employed (Coraggio, 1991). By alerting us to the false logic of neoliberalism, these authors wish to demonstrate that not all decentralization initiatives pursue or attain local development. Such admonitions distinguish between growth and development. The difference between the two is often conceived in terms of the attention given to human development from a holistic perspective. Thus, *growth* refers to the quantity or rate of increase in goods and services, while *development* in its strictest sense refers to quality and encompasses human growth and development (Demo, 1986). Therefore, when we talk about an increase of 5 percent in the GNP, we are talking about growth. On the other hand, when we consider the environmental impact of a hydroelectric plant on an entire region, we are discussing development, which encompasses a regard for the quality of life.

When local development and decentralization are situated within these two discourses, their meanings will vary according to the particular discourse. For example, decentralization is understood and promoted as a healthy mechanism through which the bureaucratic apparatus can effectively channel the benefits of growth to address identified local needs. Suggestions abound that the increase in Chile's national product has led to the well-being of its citizenry. However, many people have not reaped the benefits of this growth because it has been centred in certain regions and districts and has favoured specific social sectors. In this situation, then, local development and decentralization are proposed as initiatives that will create growth in places where people have not yet reaped its benefits.

This idea of decentralization presents itself as a step ahead of neoliberalism because it recognizes that the 'trickle-down effect' does not occur naturally. Therefore, specific measures must be taken to ensure that growth is distributed throughout society. This type of decentralization has very often been accompanied by forms of community organizing that call for participation. This has served to confuse decentralization with an approach that we will address later. In the situation under discussion, people are organized primarily in terms of those tasks which are required to achieve bureaucratic efficiency in the decentralization process.

In the context of the Alliance for Progress, CD was applied and promoted in Latin America in precisely this manner. A typical case involved the construction of houses. The ministries decided where construction would take place as well as the designs and materials to be used. Civil servants managed the projects and administered the finances; families became involved only when the houses were ready for occupation. Obviously, in this case we are talking about growth and a policy for maximizing the efficiency of resources at a local level.

There are, however, other approaches to decentralization. Communities and local organizations can be viewed not merely as executors of decisions handed down from above, but as genuine partners in determining how proposed policies will be implemented. Through consultation, grass roots organizations can respond to and fill in the general outlines of proposed policies. Priorities can be identified and proposals advanced. In this way, policies are shaped and defined through constructive dialogue and the exercise of collective initiative and responsibility. In this approach, social policies do not reflect the paternalistic gestures of a welfare state; rather, they are an opportunity for people to organize and transform their own reality. The state can respond to the needs of the people by providing material and technical resources rather than a welfare apparatus.

Although the specific outcomes of these approaches may be very similar, we view the latter approach, given certain conditions, as the more efficient. The fundamental difference between these approaches to decentralization lies in the potential of the latter to foster responsibility and initiative among those who will reap the benefits of their efforts. Local development demands more than material achievements: it must facilitate the development of those who participate. In the efficiency-oriented approach to decentralization, human growth and development does not constitute a goal.

Sergio Boissier, an expert at the Economic Commission for Latin America and the Caribbean (ECLAC), has written an article aptly titled 'The Social Construction of the Region' (CLAEH, 1989). In it he addresses the difficulties and limitations that all locally centred proposals face when they encounter a shortage of socially involved actors who clearly identify with their community. In an earlier study of the region of Valparaíso, the same author stated that 'the problem is that this region is not a region as such. The container has been defined but not its contents. The boundaries have been defined and an incomplete administrative structure has been imposed upon the territory that has no counterpart in society or in the regional community' (EURE, 1985). This approach to decentralization and local development, as pointed out by Boissier, is bereft of regard for the development of those people who are to be responsible for the construction of their own society. Such an approach attempts to administer a scheme of CD without addressing the political and educational components that are pivotal in local development.

THE POLITICS OF LOCAL DEVELOPMENT

As we have pointed out, the meaning of the term 'decentralization' depends on the political context in which it is applied. The Chilean experience reveals that decentralization has been conceptualized in three ways.

First, the military viewed decentralization primarily as a means to achieve more control over the regions of the country. The long arm of authority was to reach the farthest corners of the nation. A centralized authority was decentralized through a pyramidal chain of civil servants that deprived communities of any local command. Second, some democratic governments seeking greater efficiency and effectiveness in policy implementation have attempted to decentralize the operations of socially sensitive programs to respond better to the differences in local realities. Third, there were during the crisis years of the 1980s (and there still are) responsible local actions by popular organizations carried out with the support of NGOs. The challenge is to build a more efficient administration that serves as a framework for fostering human development. Practices that encourage people to participate in the social construction of their daily lives are what we term, in its strictest sense, local development.

Our purpose in distinguishing among different approaches to decentralization and local development is to point out that the general proposals for local development put forward in the last decade have the potential to benefit the popular sectors. However, local development that will truly benefit these sectors will not be achieved without a struggle against those of other political persuasions who seek to strengthen other sectors of society. Thus, determining the direction decentralization and local development will take is a question not only of political manoeuvring but also of proper technical control.

The Relationship between Material Reality and Collective Participation in Local Development

We do not wish to suggest that the differing approaches to local development are mutually exclusive, so that acceptance of one approach rules out the others. Some authors, when pointing out the weaknesses of one approach, fall into the trap of asserting the mutual exclusivity of the various approaches. For example, Carlos De Mattos, an economist at ECLA, emphasizes that proposals for localization cannot be viewed simplistically as realistic options for growth when economic processes are increasingly tied to international combines and when 'localization' represents only one moment in a global process. De Mattos concludes that local development is a myth. In economic terms, his analysis is valid; however, he completely excludes consideration of the socio-political dimensions of local development.

Assertions of mutual exclusivity are also evident when local practices are proposed strictly as educational experiences in which material achievements are accorded little importance. For example, a housing committee may be considered a valid entity because of its role in encouraging community participation and social awareness, even when little emphasis is placed on whether the work of the committee actually provides participants with material solutions to the lack of housing.

At this point, let us assume that all three approaches to local development that we have outlined above contain some disjunctive and contradictory dimensions. This disjunction is most notable in the decentralization model that was carried out under the dictatorship, under which decentralization was intended to increase repressive rule. Such a model excludes any possibility of sharing power with organized groups of citizens. However, an efficiency-oriented model of decentralization need not always exclude endeavours that seek to share power with organized groups at the local level. In reality, local development as an approach and in practice can embody both dimensions: the transformation of material reality and the development of citizens. When these two dimensions are conceived as mutually exclusive, the potential of local development remains undeveloped.

Human Development and the Transformation of Material Reality
Local development calls for changes and improvements in the material conditions that affect the quality of life. Here we are specifically concerned with local development proposals that deal not with growth per se in terms of the quantity of things, but rather with the urgent material needs of people.

What characterizes local development as a unique approach is the struggle of groups of people to define and develop strategies to enhance their quality of life. These groups build on their experience and concrete needs to organize and strengthen themselves as individuals and as a group. In this approach, the state or municipality organizes the different initiatives and commitments, and grants material and technical resources; however, it should never replace self-determination and responsibility.

When we consider that local development calls for changes in the material conditions of people's lives, local development appears very similar – in both its intention and effects – to development as it was carried out under the Alliance for Progress plan; which was a well-intentioned effort to channel the benefits of national growth to under-developed localities.[2] When we consider that local development is a way of facilitating struggles for self-determination, it is clear that the policies to be adopted must seek to stimulate the participation and development of local communities.

To the extent that both of these dimensions contribute to the overall process of development, local development must not only include but go beyond effectiveness and technical efficiency. Thus, it combines both dimensions insofar as it places effectiveness at the service of strengthening the local people. These two dimensions do not constitute separate alternatives because they are not mutually exclusive processes. Our proposal concerning local development differs emphatically from those proposed because it views efficiency not as an end in itself, but as a means of developing the potential of the local people to define and address their needs.

3. TOWARD A LOCAL DEVELOPMENT POLICY IN CHILE: ENABLING AND HINDERING FACTORS

At this time, we cannot say whether local development constitutes a priority in Chilean internal politics; however, it is the centre of much debate. Certain sectors assume ownership of the issue, while others see local development as the preferred scale on which development should take place. This may be because they think of it in terms of the necessary reform of the state apparatus, or possibly in terms of the effectiveness of social policies. In more humanistic terms, local development is viewed as an environment in which people can develop their capabilities as social actors. Even so, relatively few policies in specified areas reflect what we have identified as local development.

A number of diverse questions and contradictions emerge from our assessment of the current state of local development:

- Why would a dictatorship stimulate decentralization when it had no intention whatsoever of promoting active participation in any area?

---

2 As a result of the point made by de Mattos, theorists of local development do not propose to limit development to the self-sufficiency efforts undertaken by any individual community. All stress that local development can only be conceived in the context of linking local processes and measures to the global situation. For examples, see J. Gajardo (1988) and also J. Arocena (1987).

- Why have democratic governments, who profess to distance them-selves from an authoritarian system and seek reasonable ways of doing so, not made substantial progress on this issue?
- Given that some of the factors essential to local development already exist (i.e. financial and administrative decentralization, and local organizations), why have they remained separate and failed to engage in a real way?

These questions will be addressed in the following discussion of three central points: the dictatorship and the process of administrative decen-tralization; socio-economic policy with regard to strengthening popular collectives following the crisis in Latin America; and the limits to the initiatives of democratic governments in local development.

A HISTORICAL PERSPECTIVE

According to the historian Mario Góngora, 'the state [in Chile] is the mother of nationality: the nation would not exist without the State, which has shaped it through the nineteenth and twentieth centuries' (1988, p. 13). This thesis, emphatically stated, has been the subject of much debate. Nevertheless, it highlights a factor that all studies see as central: the importance of the centralized state in Chilean society.

After independence from Spain in 1821, all calls for regional self-government were quickly silenced, at first by the propertied aristocra-cies of the south, and later by the powerful mining companies of the north. By 1850 a strong central government had taken root, based on a constitution. This process did not occur in other South American coun-tries, where either federal systems were introduced, or regional leaders rose up against the central government, thereby creating an instability that lasted well into the twentieth century.

During the period of the parliamentary system (1891–1925), a law of self-governing municipalities was passed that sought to strengthen the town councils, politically and administratively. But this movement dis-integrated when the parliamentary system fell into disrepute. This sys-tem was managed by an agricultural aristocracy that was incapable of understanding or offering solutions to the problems posed by emerging social groups. Through the first quarter of this century, these groups (i.e., the middle class and the nitrate workers) struggled for a share of the wealth the nation was producing.

During the 1940s, development everywhere in South America involved making long-term investments in infrastructure (i.e., building roads, dams, and industry in general). This approach reinforced the power of the state in the economy and in society. At this stage the state acted as manager of the economy and as guardian of social welfare.

During the period of Christian Democratic government (1964–70), the National Planning Office regrouped the twenty-four provinces into regions. This policy, which was intended to create specific areas for growth, did not become law and resulted only in a decentralization of some public services. Interestingly, this initiative, which was similar to other regionalization schemes carried out in later years, emphasized the role of the central state as an agent for development.

Until the military coup in 1973, there had been a steady trend toward greater centralization of decision-making and public spending. This trend permeated successive governments of very different ideologies. The town councils, those administrative units representing local identity – were gradually shorn of any real function. In the larger municipalities the mayor was nominated by the central government. By the mid-1960s, most municipal posts were honorary positions awarded to prominent local people, who assumed the minimum routine tasks of approving new construction, improving the appearance of the town, and offering local entertainment. To finance these functions, municipalities were permitted to charge for various permits and to hand down petty fines.

It should be pointed out, however, that until 1973, municipalities did act like self-governing entities even if their powers and resources were negligible. With no hierarchical connection to central government, the municipal authorities were elected by local citizens. These elections were an important political exercise in the national way of life.

DECENTRALIZATION UNDER THE DICTATORSHIP: 1973–89

Following the military coup of 1973, a process, new to Chile, was begun to shift certain functions from the central administration to the regions and municipalities.[3] The junta did not propose a simple change in government but rather a complete remodelling of the relationship between the state and society. From the very beginning, decentralization was seen as pivotal to this new relationship. In the Declaration of Principles of the Government of Chile, published in March 1974, it was declared

3 For an account of regionalization in Chile as conceptualized by the military government, see the Corporation for Administrative Reform (1976).

that 'the essential point of the new establishment is the decentralization of power.'

This statement – unusual coming from an autocratic government that never hesitated to use violence to impose its will – must be considered in the context of the Declaration as a whole. In that text, a distinction is made between political and social power: 'political' power refers to the power to decide matters of general interest for the nation, whereas 'social power' refers to 'the power for intermediate bodies of society to legitimately develop themselves in order to fulfil their own specific objectives.' The Declaration states that decentralization does not pertain to political power; accordingly, 'social power' is not power as such (remember Max Weber's classic definition), and moreover, social power had never been centralized.

The Declaration asserts that the way to enhance the power of society is to depoliticize all intermediate bodies between man and the state; the task of these organizations does not include determining the global concepts of society.[4] What the Declaration effectively proclaims is the total separation between civil and political society. Political society thus refers solely to government, because the legislative body as well as all political parties have been dissolved. Thus, political power defines and decides what each organization in society should undertake, and also assigns areas of action for all intermediate bodies.

On 12 July 1974 the military government passed Law 573, the Statute for Government and Interior Administration of the State. It had been prepared by the National Commission for Administrative Reform, an *ad hoc* organization created in December 1973.[5] The nation was divided into thirteen regions, each comprising a number of provinces. The provinces were again subdivided into municipalities for the purpose of local administration. Each region's government and administration was assigned to a regional governor, who was considered 'the immediate and natural agent of the President of the Republic and an exclusive and trustworthy servant.' A Regional Council for Development (COREDE) was created in each region, as well as a Secretariat for Regional Planning. Regional ministerial offices were also created, with each office representing a ministry of the central government.

4 For an analysis from the government's point of view, see J. Fernandez (1981). For a critical view of the process, see E. Morales (1987) and J. Borja et al. (1987).
5 See Corporation for Administrative Reform (1976) in the references section.

At the provincial level, authority was assigned to the provincial governor, who was nominated by the president of the republic and was subordinate to the regional governor. The provincial governor was assisted by a Legal Advisory Committee, which he governed and appointed. At the municipal level there was a town council, 'whose paramount authority is the Mayor, nominated by the Supreme Chief of the Nation after hearing advice from the Regional Governor.'

What we wish to underline here is the verticality of this system of government – a system that functions from top to bottom. One analyst commented that regionalization permits the highest authority in the land to have at his disposal a pyramidal organization that makes his presence and actions felt throughout the entire nation (Canessa, 1979).[6] Decentralization in Chile has been characterized as a simple deconcentration of functions, directed toward the effective and efficient practice of ruling. The established structure could control all discordant opinion and initiative by reaching into the farthest corners of the nation.

With respect to municipal organization, the mayor could rely on two organizations: the Council for Municipal Development (CODECO), composed of directors of local services and representatives of municipal organizations; and the municipal Office for Planning and Co-operation, part of the national system of planning. CODECO comprised eight to twenty members, with equal representation from the Union of Neighbourhood Assemblies, the Union of Motherhood Centres and other organizations of the municipality, important economic organizations in the area, and the heads of municipal services. All were nominated by the regional governor.

The new Constitution of 1980 reformulated the pertinent clause in Law 573 to read 'representatives of organizations of a local and functional character and of those activities relevant to the municipality, with the exception of guilds and trade unions.' By including 'those activities relevant to the municipality,' it opened the door for private enterprises to join CODECO. Because guilds and trade unions were prohibited, workers' organizations were excluded. Beginning in the early days of the military government, the former heads of all neighbourhood assem-

---

6 Pinochet himself endorsed this perception when he reminded the nation that 'the regional governors are, as established by law, representatives of the President of the Republic in their respective regions, and not, as some seem to think, representatives of the regions before the President of the Republic.' Cited in Corporation for Administrative Reform (1976).

blies and motherhood centres were replaced by nominees of the new local authorities.

In accordance with the policy of reducing the responsibilities of the state and transferring them to the private sector, some public services that had been administered by the ministries were transferred to the municipalities. On 12 July 1980, some education and health services were transferred to the municipalities, the purported goal being greater administrative efficiency and local control, and increased responsiveness to local needs. Other parts of the health and education services, including homes for disadvantaged children, were auctioned off to private firms.

With respect to education, the 1982 decree added: '[The transfer] will allow an improvement in the income of academic staff who will be able to choose those municipalities which are more in line with their own interests and aspirations.' This statement expressed too much confidence in the fairness of the free market system. Dispersed into small groups, teachers had to accept conditions that were imposed upon them; their situation had deteriorated. Until recently, a permanent demand of the teaching profession was a restoration of their status as civil servants of the ministry.

THE SOCIO-ECONOMIC CONTEXT AND THE EMERGENCE OF POPULAR ORGANIZATIONS

Here, we will consider three factors: the socio-economic processes in Latin America during the world crisis; particular characteristics of impoverishment in Chile; and the emergence of local collectives.

The Crisis in Latin America

The general contraction of the economic system affected Latin America most notably in the 1980s. Between 1950 and 1980, production in Latin America increased steadily by 2.8 percent per inhabitant. After 1980, the trend reversed violently. By the end of the 1980s, the level of production per capita was similar to that achieved in 1970 (Economic Commission for Latin America, 1990).[7] Faced with this, all countries eventually instituted policies similar to those recommended by the International

---

7 The accumulated variation in total regional production (excluding Cuba) during the period 1980 to 1989 was 8.9 percent. For a detailed study of this situation and its effects, see the Economic Commission for Latin America (1990).

Monetary Fund: a cutback in public spending to reduce the national debt; deregulation of the labour market; privatization of state-owned companies; and the promotion of activities that would foster competitiveness in the global market.

In most cases it was the workers who suffered the most from economic adjustment: for example, salaries fell in real value, unemployment rose, and the government cut expenditures for social programs. The Regional Program for Employment in Latin America and the Caribbean (Regional Program for Employment, 1988), which is the regional office of the International Labour Organization, pointed out that 'the cost of the adjustment was borne by the workforce, whose participation in earnings shrank by 4 percentage points; at the same time, the greater part of capital in earnings meant in practice an excessive increase (9%) in consumption by capitalists, at the expense of a reduction (6%) in consumption by the workers (ibid., 1988).

In the contracting economy, the rich were able to improve their situation while the poor, the middle class, and wage earners became poorer. CEPAL (Comisión Económica para América Latina) comments: 'In the period between 1960 and 1980 poverty in Latin America decreased from 50% of the total population to 33%, but by 1989 had risen again to 41%' (1989). Governments, heeding the neoliberal policies of the IMF, failed to consider the plight of their own people. The poor in Latin America had to use their own initiative, resources, and ingenuity to hold on to the bare minimum.

In response to these social and material conditions, popular groups formed and proliferated throughout the region. At the local level, these groups struggled to hold back the trends that threatened their daily lives and to defend quality-of-life matters they considered critical. Collective assemblies formed 'people's kitchens,' where poor families could obtain nutritious food at low cost; health committees, which confronted the deterioration in official services; housing committees, which sought sites (sometimes illegal) to build homes; educational groups, for young people; and Christian-based communities, which rallied to defend human rights.

These popular organizations shared the experience of confronting and meeting common needs. Expression of these experiences varied with local circumstances. Such groups have been studied under the term 'new social movements.' The use of the word *new* is debatable, because the struggle for survival, education, and spiritual fulfilment has led to the creation of social movements since at least the Middle Ages. It is only in the second half of this century that these movements have shifted to the field of production. Perhaps what should be considered *new* is that more women and young people are joining these organizations and moving into public view.

What is really novel, however, is that these groups are completely independent of the state. This suggests a relationship between civil and political society – something previously unheard of in Latin America. Since their birth on this continent, social movements have tended to relate to the state in either an aggressive or an amicable manner. In the period 1930 to 1980, the political response to that relationship was influenced to some degree by forms of persuasion that in Latin America have been called 'populist' (Weffort, 1978).[8]

Given this dominant trend, which continued until the third quarter of this century, the popular organizations of the 1980s are novel because they generate ideas and have the capacity to put them into practice. In differing from the populist model, they go beyond the status of beneficiaries and become partners in development *with* the state. These organizations sow the seeds that enable local development policies to be implemented.

Because this partnership will not develop automatically, it is important to note the advances along these lines that have taken place over the past two decades.

Popular organizations have been supported by NGOs which have operated under the rubric of international co-operation. It is important to note here that NGOs have accumulated significant knowledge about the methodology of intervention, pedagogical practices, the sociology and psychology of organizations, and epistemological thought. This knowledge has not always been acquired in an organized fashion; even so, it must be used to strengthen the relationship between popular organizations and the state in matters of local development.

The socio-economic processes in Latin America have certain general dimensions that can be highlighted over and above those of individual

8 The populist model may be a leader (e.g., Perón, Vargas, Velasco, Cárdenas, Haya de la Torre); an official party; an official system of organizations that are controlled by the party and extend their influence and control to different sectors of the economy and society; or an ideology that includes the promotion of the leader and an anti-oligarchic, nationalistic, and modernizing discourse. Populism operates as a pact of mutual loyalty between the leader, his party, and the people. Through an official organization, the former offers to improve the quality of popular life; in return, the latter give their trust and support to him. Concerning 'popularism,' see Weffort (1978).

countries. Thus, the context for our analysis of the situation in Chile encompasses a range of critical elements: the world crisis, IMF policies, the impoverishment of the poor, and the development of organizations with a popular base. Keeping these parameters in mind, we will now explore the situation in Chile, in particular the crisis of impoverishment, and the response of popular organizations to this crisis.

Impoverishment in Chile

In Chile, guidelines for a market economy began to be applied in 1975. The ministers involved, the most influential of whom were ex-alumni of the University of Chicago and disciples of Milton Friedman, firmly believed in the need to devise an economy based on the forces of supply and demand. Other areas of society were to yield to that dynamic; the state was not to intervene in business or society, except minimally, in the sense of maintaining law, order, and property rights.

The military government perceived many people and activities as suspicious. Consequently, maintaining minimum law and order involved a permanent and massive violation of human rights. Thus, the Chilean state was able to push through a radically neoliberal economic policy without losing control of society. Paradoxically, given the social consequences of the economic policy, the oppressed could not have gained ground without the strong military control of society.

Before 1975, steps were taken to control inflation. The national debt was reduced by decreasing public expenditures on social activities deemed outside the productive sphere. Steps were also taken to expand the Chilean economy into the global market. Import taxes were reduced, and those political elements which interfered with the smooth operation of the economy were eliminated: for example, the entire system of popular protest was either dissolved or incapacitated; and labour laws were modified substantially, particularly in relation to minimum salaries, collective bargaining, and job security.

In these circumstances, Chile was unprepared – economically as well as socially – for the crisis of the 1980s. Between 1982 and 1983 the national product fell by 16 percent (the greatest contraction in Latin America). In 1983, almost 30 percent of the economically active population were unemployed (the official figure was 20.7 percent). In response, the government initiated a program for minimum employment (PEM) and another for heads of households (POJH) – programs that absorbed up to 8.8 percent of real unemployment. Both programs exacted hard physical labour, almost always outdoors, without equipment or proper tools, and paid 40 percent less than the lowest wages in business firms.

Faced with this economic situation, the government insisted on cutbacks to social spending that served as indirect salaries to the poor. The poor now had to pay for social services that had once been provided free of charge. An official document of the Ministry of Planning stated:

During the 1980's public spending on health reduced its share of the total in public spending. Whereas in the period 1970 to 1980, the part of public spending on health represented 15%, it went down to a little over 7% between 1980 and 1990 ... On a closer analysis of public spending on health as a proportion of the GNP, one can see a gradual decline over the decade, so from 3.56% of the GNP in 1982, we arrive at 2.3% in 1990. (Ministry of Planning, 1993)

The government took a similar approach to education (Corvalán, 1990).[9]

As a result of these policies, the less fortunate sectors of society carried the burden of the crisis. The increasing concentration of revenue and consumption is reflected in Table 8.1 (Lechner, 1990).

Local Organizing in Response to the Crisis
Since the market economy has gained momentum in Chile, organizations for mutual aid and the defence of quality of life have multiplied. Urban neighbourhoods in Chile had been marked by the absence of community traditions – traditions found, for example, among urban neighbourhoods in Peru. Given this absence, the swift response by the people

TABLE 8.1
Santiago: Consumer Distribution per Homes
(in percentages over the total)

Quintile	1969	1978	1988
I	7.6	5.2	4.4
II	11.8	9.3	8.2
III	15.6	13.6	12.6
IV	20.6	21.0	20.0
V	44.5	51.0	54.9
	100.00	100.00	100.00

9 See Corvalán (1990). In the case of housing, the method of direct benefits, operating through the ministry, was changed to a system of monetary benefits in order to resolve the problem through the private sector. This change makes it difficult to compare data.

was most likely influenced by previous experiences of organizing. Previous community organizing efforts to improve quality of life had been promoted by governments between 1964 and 1973 (Campero, 1988).[10]

Christian-based communities, or organizations supported by the churches, established community kitchens, food-purchasing co-operatives, health and housing committees, workshops and small firms, and neighbourhood day care for children. Churches were able to offer some protection from the dictatorship. By the beginning of the 1980s, such initiatives began to be supported, economically and technically, by NGOs. Consequently, popular organizations increased in number and improved in quality (Razeto, 1984; Razeto, 1990; Hardy, 1988; Scholnik & Teitelboim, 1988).

The Economy of Work Program (PET), an NGO specifically interested in popular organizations, surveyed this trend and concluded that by the beginning of the 1990s, one out of every four families in the popular sectors was directly involved in a popular economic organization.

The best assessments demonstrate that these popular organizations are an efficient way to address survival needs. Although they may never function as self-governing economic systems disengaged from the dominant one, they have proved themselves capable of dealing with inequities in the distribution of goods and services – inequities that have been introduced by the dominant system. Thousands of families have been able to improve their incomes by joining workshops, collective bakeries, or community laundries; others have been able to reduce consumer costs by sharing in community kitchens, health committees, and community day care for children.

Popular organizations enable people to improve their quality of life, but only in terms of their most basic needs. Without technical and material assistance, these groups do not appear to be capable of rising above the threshold of subsistence. Technical and material assistance thus emerges as a necessary condition for raising people any higher. However, organizations must discover ways to make a substantial impact on the larger social dynamic without losing focus on their area of competency. Also, productive organizations must expand into those areas where there is a real demand for their products. When the product is made for community consumption, organizations must unite to carry out any necessary development programs.

10 This is the central theme of Guillermo Campero's excellent work on popular organizations in Chile (1988: 11).

In addition to economic effects, popular organizations have important socio-political effects. They situate impoverished groups such as women and the unemployed in the public view. As a result, collective situations such as feeding and child care – traditionally considered of a private nature and resolved in the private sector – constitute material for discussion and rethinking. Popular organizations create situations where people can develop new practices and ways of responding. This adds new dimensions to their existence.

From the thousands of testimonies we have received from participants over the years, one woman's words are particularly expressive:

I think that the workshops provide a very positive experience because the women, apart from learning, gain experience in other areas as well ... in the beginning I stuttered when trying to speak, but I no longer have this problem. A friend, who is now a good saleswoman, told me that for some time when she was offering goods for sale, her heart would pound ... 'surely someone will be rude to me,' she thought; now she feels very confident when she is selling. (Angelo, 1987, p. 71)

DEMOCRACY AND LOCAL DEVELOPMENT INITIATIVES SINCE 1990

We have been arguing that the military government refrained from implementing a policy of local development because dialogue with the local communities about their proposals for development would have gone against the political aims of the dictatorship. However, collective proposals that did emerge at the local level led to the formation of popular organizations. They achieved a certain amount of technical expertise and, by the end of the 1980s, could be considered as potential material for local development plans.

However, decentralization motivated by administrative and geopolitical concerns cannot possibly stimulate the participation of the people. Consequently, local groups operated at a subsistence level while government, enshrined in an economic ideology, ignored their fate.

All of this raises key questions regarding the current climate for local development in Chile. The democratic sectors that fought against the dictatorship denounced the vertical and exclusive exercise of power. Why, then, once they became government, did they not act with determination to unite decentralization and local organization? Is it that perhaps democratic government does not require the participation of the people in order to function properly? Is participation then to be considered a disposable adornment, something foreign to the nature of democracy? Or, as is so often the case in Latin America, is it possible that democracy as carried out in Chile is a form of 'legality' that shapes the rights of individuals as citizens to elect authorities, but does not touch the relationship between the state and its citizens? Does this relationship remain unaltered, vertical, and exclusive, a confirmation of the political tradition, whatever political party is in power? In grappling with these questions, we must face others of a more specific nature. These relate to both the reality and the possibilities of local development, and must be situated in the larger context of democratic rule in Chile.

Democracy in Chile

The peculiarities of democracy in Chile are difficult to understand for an outsider. Particularly hard to understand is how the present democracy not only retains and honours its previous dictator as commander-in-chief of the army, but also respects the laws and institutions that the dictatorship imposed on the nation. Whether or not we agree with the current situation, we can neither understand nor judge it unless we situate it in a proper context.

Opposition to the dictatorship in Chile was eliminated in 1973 – all opponents were dead, disappeared, arrested, tortured, or exiled. Opposition to the dictatorship did not reappear until 1984. From 1984 to 1986, this opposition tried to overthrow the dictatorship by mobilizing those citizens who were disappointed with the economic failures of the military government and fed up with autocracy and state-sponsored violence. The street mobilizations, the 'protest days', did not topple the dictatorship; even so, these efforts marked the beginning of the transition to democracy in Chile.

Democratic government did not arise from the defeat of the dictatorship but rather from a political agreement that opened the door for a plebiscite and, eventually, elections. This agreement, and the events that followed it, left unscathed the armed forces and the power of those groups which supported Pinochet. In the plebiscite and elections, groups that supported Pinochet were favoured consistently by 40 percent of voters.

The coalition that forms the government today has demonstrated that its priority is governing the nation, not stimulating new projects. This coalition brought together very diverse forces that only united for the first time when they opposed the military government. After the coalition agreed to govern, cracks began to appear in it when it came to establishing and carrying out policies. The main task was to determine how to govern the nation. After what Chileans had experienced for twenty years, a very heightened sensitivity to precisely this problem was bound to exist.

Democracy after 1990

The elected, democratic government took control in 1990 and began to tackle a set of very contradictory tasks.

First, it set out to maintain economic growth by stimulating capital investment while controlling inflation. In following this course, the state absolved itself from any responsibility for improving the welfare of the people. After 1986 the economy, directed by less orthodox policies than the ones applied between 1975 and 1982, had begun to grow and inflation had begun to fall. In 1988 the Right warned Chileans through its electoral propaganda that any triumph of the opposition would lead to another economic failure.

The democratic government has been fairly clever and efficient in overcoming economic difficulties. Between 1991 and 1994, the national product grew more quickly than in previous years, at an average annual rate above 5 percent. Inflation has fallen from 16 to 12 percent, in spite of a tax increase to cover social services. Also, wages have increased annually above the rate of inflation.

Social stability and the democratic climate have managed to attract increasing levels of investment. Even more important, the opposition on the Right generally accepts that the problem of poverty must be addressed and agrees with the means being used. In general terms, the policy of the coalition government is to attack poverty, but only in ways that do not hamper economic growth.

Second, the government set out to exclude the armed forces from direct participation in politics. Their participation conflicts with the need to restore the human rights that were lost during the military government. Democracy has proved itself less effective in dealing with this point than in stimulating economic growth. Every time the armed forces have found themselves at odds with the government, they have spoken out and the government has backed down. For this reason, many analysts have labelled democracy in Chile 'guided democracy.'

When the Rettig Report, verifying more than 3,000 human rights violations in Chile, was made public, President Patricio Aylwin acknowledged that Chileans can only hope for 'justice in the measure that is possible under the circumstances.' Nevertheless, many conditions that prevented civil society from acting against the arbitrariness of the armed forces have changed for the better since 1990. Through legal channels, things can now be done that would have been impossible before the return of democracy. Yet advances in this area have been slower and less significant than Chile's democrats would have liked.

Third, democracy has permitted greater citizen participation in political life, even though the state retains control over social demands and expectations. This situation seems to contain contradictions.

During the presidential campaign of 1989, the Right warned that if a coalition government came to power, the expectations of popular sectors would rise beyond all reason. The new government would be overcome by citizen actions that would lead to chaos.

The democratic government responded to this fear by treating social organizations prudently, and by maintaining and implementing policies in the traditional way. It operates as though Chileans have given their representatives a monopoly on making decisions. The government acts as if it will be judged only on whether it fulfils its mandate before the next election.

Whether or not the government has responded to social demands, this traditional style of leadership has not met the expectations of popular organizations regarding public participation. In the 1980s the capacity, experience, and maturity of these organizations had grown significantly. However, government policies were established without consulting the pertinent groups. Under democracy, popular programs in the areas of health, day care, and education, although respected, have not been accepted as the basis for new social policies. Rather, the government has incorporated these programs into its policies only in limited cases.

The government's lack of interest in promoting public participation has resulted in the disillusionment of many sectors of society that had actively opposed the dictatorship – particularly young people. It has also fostered apathy toward politics, and in some cases encouraged the kind of fringe politics that existed under the dictatorship. Senior representatives of the governing coalition acknowledge this situation. This relates to the question we posed at the beginning: Is the present democracy only a formal, legal democracy that permits citizens to elect authorities but fails to change the nature of the relationship between the authorities and citizens? We can respond to this question in the following way.

First, the state in Chile respects civil rights. This, in our opinion, represents an advance over the situation of the previous decade. Second, since 1990 people have struggled using legitimate means to strengthen and extend the democratic process. This struggle has been fraught with difficulties because particular sectors of society also using legitimate means work against that aspiration, very often with an advantage over those who want to strengthen democratic procedures. Third, the search for a more dynamic democracy will be obstructed when those in the legal and institutional framework – in other words, those in formal democracy – take a narrow, legalistic stance. We believe that this is not the situation in Chile.

The Particular Context for Local Development in Chile

As a result of the advances made by the democratic government, political decision-making and resources have intersected with the goals of popular organizations at certain moments and in certain circumstances. For example, since 1993 municipal authorities have been chosen by popular vote rather than presidential decree. As a result, many municipalities now promote programs that take the community into account. With the participation of the communities, the Ministry of Health has implemented a primary health care program based on local groups.

The Ministry of Planning has created a new department called the Solidarity and Social Initiative Fund (FOSIS). Many of its civil servants have worked in NGOs. FOSIS does not implement programs directly; rather, it administers funds to tenders, which compete for the proposals presented by communities.

At this point we want to emphasize that policies for local development do not exist. In other words, there are no policies designed to address the socio-economic needs of specific localities and that depend on communities themselves for implementation and monitoring. Chile lacks an approach to development that establishes a distinct relationship based on dialogue between the state and civil society.

We can summarize our discussion of local development policies in the following ways. The situation in Chile is ambiguous. Although democracy in Chile proclaims equity and participation, the state promotes a free market economy that benefits particular sectors and marginalizes the 40 percent of the population that, in 1990, lived in poverty. Although public participation is pursued to the degree possible, Chile does not have an official policy on local development that would merge the initiatives of local organizations with state policies and resources. Although specific programs in some state entities have promoted local development, Chile has not yet developed a public policy regarding local development, which is implemented, *when* it is implemented, on a sectoral basis.

4. LOCAL DEVELOPMENT PROGRAMS: THREE CASE ILLUSTRATIONS

We will now examine three specific cases: the Solidarity and Social Initiative Fund (Ministry of Planning); the Workshops for Local Integration (Ministry of Education); and the Area for Basic Primary Health Care (Ministry of Health). Each of these cases will be discussed briefly, with a focus on how they promote participation. Following this, we will select testimonies from participants in each program in order to highlight the achievements and difficulties encountered in the program design.

THE SOLIDARITY AND SOCIAL INITIATIVE FUND – FOSIS

FOSIS was created in 1990 shortly after the coalition government was formed. Latin American governments have increasingly adopted FOSIS programs to address poverty. However, the particularities of the Chilean experience are worth pointing out. These peculiarities are based on the fact that FOSIS was created as a palliative for the social effects of structural adjustment programs (*World Bank Review*, 1991).[11] Since structural adjustment in Chile had already taken place when FOSIS was created, the goal of the fund was to attack structural poverty.[12]

An official fund document asserts that FOSIS was conceived on the initiative of the democratic government, created to carry out an additional and complimentary contribution to public and private works that have as their objective the social integration of the poorest sectors and

11 The entire volume of the *World Bank Review*, 5(2) (1991) is dedicated to this issue. The best-conceptualized and most efficient fund for counteracting these effects operated in Costa Rica. For discussion of this case, see Sainz and Menjivar (1991).

12 As we have indicated, although the democratic government did not make the elimination of poverty a priority, it was concerned about it. It has allowed basic wages to rise faster than inflation; it has channelled more funds to social spending; and it has extensively promoted a national training plan for youth. According to official figures and measured by (debatable) indicators, the poverty index has fallen from its initial level by one-third.

an improvement in their living and working conditions (FOSIS, 1992). From the beginning, the characteristics of the fund have been clear.

First, the fund, as a decentralized entity responsible to the Ministry of Planning and Co-operation (MIDEPLAN), seeks to act in a nonsectoral manner. This is difficult because the ministries of Labour, Health, Education, and Housing have continued to act in a sectoral way. FOSIS is headed by a council appointed by the president of Chile, on which both the state and social bodies are represented. Second, FOSIS as an entity does not implement programs directly. Like other programs created since 1990, it was developed in an atmosphere of political opinion in favour of reduced state intervention. Rather than intervening directly, the fund concentrates on developing policy and distributing resources to other public and private organizations, which in turn assess needs and design and execute specific programs.

Third, the goals of FOSIS are to eradicate extreme poverty and reduce unemployment, with special focus on underprivileged youths and the rural poor. Fourth, FOSIS encourages people to participate in identifying and resolving their own problems. In philosophy and method, FOSIS funding thus contributes to communities' own efforts (de la Maza, 1993).

The fourth characteristic merits further discussion because it speaks to the task of orienting local development. The executive director of FOSIS states, in the institution's manual:

We wish to offer this Manual to all those who are working with the aim of overcoming the conditions of poverty that exist today in Chile; to all those who believe that poverty has to be met with the effort and participation of the affected parties, counting upon the support of other sectors of society; to all those who consider that it is more important to open up opportunities, to support initiatives, to generate capabilities, to improve education and the acquisition of skills at a local level than to hand out solutions and answers conceived, executed and managed by external forces. (FOSIS, 1993, p. 3)

The theme of this passage is reinforced throughout the manual by the use of the concept of 'promotion,' which refers to actions based on three interrelated objectives: to find solutions to a material problem that the community itself has identified; to work collaboratively with different public and private entities; and to resolve the problem using methods and processes that educate and strengthen the community (FOSIS, 1993, pp. 7–18).

FOSIS operates in five realms: assisting small businesses; strengthening the efforts of rural workers and aboriginal peoples; supporting youth; developing poor districts; and promoting CD initiatives. An essential part of the FOSIS process is the stimulating of creative social policies. This is achieved through open national competitions that solicit proposals from communities, some of which receive advice from NGOs. This process is vastly different from the way other ministries operate, which is through tenders for already defined projects.

PROGRAM FOR THE IMPROVEMENT OF QUALITY AND FAIRNESS IN EDUCATION – MECE

The government implemented an educational policy through its Program for the improvement of Quality and Fairness in Education (MECE).

MECE is designed to improve the quality of education, especially education for the poor. To the degree that education influences performance and achievement, all children should receive similar educational opportunities at each educational level. MECE has been directed mainly toward those sectors for whom education is uncertain and precarious. In this sense, the program has been narrowly but progressively applied. A brief diagnosis of the crisis in the educational system will place MECE in the appropriate context and illuminate its objectives and directions.

The program claims that unsatisfactory educational experiences, evidenced by failing grades and high dropout rates in primary school, are the result of a combination of factors: the scant attention paid in course content to social realities and organization; poor teaching methods; a lack of incentives for teachers; poor-quality study environments at school and at home; and a shortage of teaching materials.

The priorities of the program are as follows: to improve basic language and mathematics skills at the elementary level; to enhance children's ability to apply the knowledge they acquire to their daily lives (in other words, to ensure that knowledge in the classroom is created from everyday experience); and to support teacher and pupil initiatives that invigorate participation in meeting the educational needs of the group. The program attempts to address the difficulties that arise when uniform and identical lessons are given to groups of students with a range of socio-economic and cultural backgrounds.

In contrast to traditional teaching, MECE encourages teachers to set their own lessons and establish independently their pupils' educational goals. The teacher acts as an intermediary between the daily lives of his or her pupils on the one hand, and universal knowledge on the other. To move beyond merely reproducing school texts:

means the need to revision [sic] the relationship between teacher and pupil, between school and community, establishing continuity between the education received at school and the pupil's progress on a day to day basis in the use of knowledge, between methodology and the practice of abilities and skills in daily life. (Miguel, Sepulveda, & Williamson, 1994)

MECE calls the above 'participation'; in other words, education in the classroom seeks to incorporate extracurricular experiences and community needs and perspectives into children's learning processes. Because teachers play a key role in this process, the program concentrates on stimulating new training strategies and providing teaching assistance through specialized workshops (Ministry of Education – MINEDUC, 1990).[13]

In March 1992 the Ministry of Education approved a proposal on preschool education presented by the Interdisciplinary Program for the Investigation of Education (PIIE), an NGO whose experience, professionalism, and prestige is renowned in Chile. The ministry was anxious to fund PIIE, since it had had previous successes in the field of preschool education. Funds were available from the World Bank for unconventional programs, particularly those dealing with preschool issues. Also, PIIE's proposal for local development was compatible with the government's intention to 'retool' the decentralization plans formulated under the dictatorship. However, this direction is made explicit in MECE.

The official brochure prepared by the PIIE team states that its workshops are designed for those involved in community programs for young children: teachers, teachers' assistants, mothers, young people, professionals, technicians, promoters, and leaders. Workshops organize participants into groups at the local level. After their educational needs are assessed, they receive training in the methodology of working with adults, families, and communities; group dynamics; local development and culture; child development; participatory diagnostic research; and

13 'More than methods based on problem solving, the practical ability to perceive, define and formulate problems will be stimulated by means of observation and the analysis of situations as they arise. Problems that cannot be detected and perceived by the teachers do not have an easy educational solution' (1990).

the planning and management of projects. Workshops have been carried out in 95 percent of all municipalities in the country; this figure includes 120 Workshops for Local Integration at a National Level (TILNAs), in which 4,000 people have received training as educational agents.

The TILNA groups have been trained to research and assess local needs and possibilities in relation to work with children. Each TILNA group develops a project; at the end of 1994, all of those developed were presented for approval and funding. Each needs assessment by a TILNA group centres on the strengths of the community rather than its weaknesses – an approach the PIIE team considers critical to the program. PIIE hopes that the TILNA groups will become advocates for children at the local level.

The TILNA approach tries to promote local development by moving from 'perceived needs' to 'real needs'. Analysis of real concerns can reveal how a particular issue is intimately related to structural and global situations. Local resources can thus be reorganized accordingly. The PIIE–TILNA team expressed this idea as follows: 'The workshops are designed to stimulate substantial changes in participants. In contrast with other training programs that are centred around content (knowledge and abilities), the emphasis of TILNA is on cultural transformation.' The challenge materializes in the teachers: they develop self-determination, leadership, critical thought, and a respect for social reality. They arrive with a marked institutional mentality and identity, which they must learn to enlarge. The idea is to generate a collectivity that will integrate its concerns about the well-being of children at the local level.

BASIC PRIMARY HEALTH CARE PROGRAM, MINISTRY OF HEALTH

Under the dictatorship, decentralization transferred to the municipalities the responsibility for specific services, including 90 percent of the centres for primary health care. This meant that primary health care was separated from health services, which continued to depend on the ministry. Several operational problems arose from this. First, after municipalities became responsible for primary health care, the decision-making process became politicized. Second, the funding mechanism for primary health care services favoured case treatment rather than prevention. Third, the funds allotted to municipalities were insufficient to meet the needs of health care centres in poor neighbourhoods, which did not receive any income for services rendered. Fourth, the morale of the staff plummeted because their salaries deteriorated and they received no supplements or other benefits such as training.

The government sought not only to address these operational problems but also to develop a set of primary health care strategies. The Department of Basic Primary Health Care, officially incorporated into the Ministry of Health, set out to develop a program, which was then folded into the global policies and strategies of the ministry (MINESAL, 1991, p. 26).[14]

Viewed in this light, community participation operates in the context and framework designed and decided upon by the ministry. In cooperation with health authorities, the department is responsible for establishing the goals, strategies, and procedures to be followed. There is no mention of popular organizations. In fact, the ministry has not recognized the role of health committees and appears unconcerned about strengthening them. As previously noted, these committees had been formed during the dictatorship. Rather than strengthening these committees, new groups were formed and trained according to the interests of the officials of the ministerial project.

The four units of the Department of Basic Primary Health Care are these: Assessment and Improvement of the Quality of APS; Support for Management; Studies; and Social Participation. The Social Participation unit is divided into two sub-units: one of these strengthens ties between the ministry and NGOs, and the other tackles community work. The former sub-unit, as described in the objectives prepared by the ministry, 'offers technical and financial support for NGOs to carry out specific projects of Basic Primary Health Care in conjunction with agreements with the Health Services' (MINESAL, 1991, p. 43). The activities of this sub-unit have been reduced to reviewing and selecting annual projects. In 1991, seventy-one projects were approved; US$2 million was provided for them. Interestingly, these projects are prepared and presented by NGOs, not communities. The recognized beneficiaries of these projects 'are concentrated in certain age groups, regardless of whether they belong to a grassroots organization or not' (MINESAL, 1991, p. 44).

14 In contrast to the two programs previously discussed, where ideas emanated from civil servants as well as NGOs, this program is managed by medical doctors with official experience. Civil servants trained outside the ministry are found only at lower levels of the program (MINESAL, 1991: 26).

Although seventy-one projects from NGOs were approved in 1991, the community work sub-unit did not even refer to community work in its Annual Report. But during the same period, the management unit, which provides management training to departmental teams, carried out numerous activities. Ministerial priorities clearly do not include community work.

In May 1990 in Santiago, a workshop on basic primary health care trained eighteen teachers, who then carried out twenty-nine workshops that trained 640 new 'promoters' at twenty-six centres. Subsequently, these new promoters conducted 507 workshops at primary health care centres throughout the country. In all, 11,000 participants were trained (MINESAL, 1991, p. 36).

In summary, participation as practised in this program does not engage popular organizations; rather, people are encouraged to support civil servants acting on behalf of the ministry.

5. THE REALITY OF LOCAL DEVELOPMENT: ANALYSIS AND DISCUSSION OF CASE EXAMPLES

To what degree do government policies create the necessary conditions for stimulating local development? Our evaluation of these policies will address this question rather than the technical components or other aspects of these policies. We wish to situate our assessment of the strengths and weaknesses of each initiative in the context of local development. With respect to the three programs discussed above, we interviewed civil servants responsible for the program as well as participants. In the case of FOSIS and TILNA, we interviewed NGO teams; in the case of the Basic Primary Health Care program, we interviewed twelve social workers at local health care centres. Two social workers were selected by their colleagues in each of the six districts of the metropolitan area defined by the ministry.

FOSIS

At FOSIS we interviewed the heads of the Program for Small Businesses and the Program for the Promotion and Development of Poor Districts as well as four NGO teams who worked with organized community groups. These groups prepared the proposal, executed the project, and often evaluated it, with FOSIS support. It is fascinating to examine the conditions that have to be created and the possibilities that must be opened up in order for local development to occur.

Based on the ideas proposed by FOSIS, local processes have been activated since the program was introduced in 1990. The foundation of local development is the work of local groups who receive the support of NGOs. Popular groups have collaborated with other public and private actors in developing an initiative that is tailor-made for the needs and concerns of the community. With financial and technical support, their efforts have come to fruition.

Clearly, social policies focus not only on the product and on the material effectiveness of the project, but also on education and human development. A new relationship is created between the state and civil society – one that moves away from the traditional relationship that organizations and their leadership had been accustomed to maintaining with the public apparatus. At first glance, this may seem to be a tenuous attainment involving only a few limited projects. However, that the state is engaged in listening to and believing in the people and their capacity to find solutions to their needs constitutes both a challenge for organizations and an important step toward greater participation.

Generally, FOSIS has respected local processes. The greatest difficulties with NGOs relate to lack of bureaucratic 'style' in meeting deadlines and requirements and completing reports. However, since the majority of civil servants in the FOSIS team have previous NGO experience, they have confidence in the capacity and commitment of these organizations; thus, they are more able to accept these differing work styles. Other situations contrast with the Chilean experience, however. A report on a conference in Bolivia for members of NGOs and civil servants revealed that the basic impediment to working together was mutual distrust.

Not one NGO team voiced concern about the degree of control FOSIS exercised in the field. Other difficulties existed outside the metropolitan area, where FOSIS managers are young people fresh out of university who are interested solely in quantitative results rather than field-work. In another situation, a southern NGO team opposed the local representative of FOSIS, who quickly travelled to Santiago and expressed his point of view to the civil servants at the FOSIS head office.

In general, however, FOSIS understands that each project involves a learning process. Education is a necessary component in the development and consolidation of the responsibility assumed by popular groups.

The two civil servants whom we interviewed asserted that 'the NGOs know how to work with the people.'

Gonzalo de la Maza, a Chilean scholar on the issue, reaches a conclusion similar to ours:

With respect to the second great objective of social participation, it can be stated that FOSIS has maintained a special concern for this issue, principally by means of support programs in poor areas. At this stage there is a very wide global agreement between the Fund and the NGOs because the generation of capabilities of the community itself is held in high esteem. It is a well focused program with an integrated strategy. (de la Maza, 1993)

FOSIS has communicated this concern about community participation to NGOs even though FOSIS itself had to learn and incorporate the concept of social participation. This has been a source of irritation to the NGOs, but not to the local people. A civil servant of FOSIS explained the pressure to adhere to external demands: 'What happens is that we have to answer to the Ministry and to the Comptroller, that the funds are being applied to those projects for which they were approved; we must use the channels of public administration.' Regarding the same point, an NGO team commented, 'It's annoying, because we are not accustomed to it, but, once you learn the rules they use, there is no problem. We can respond to that and continue to stimulate qualitative processes in people.'

Progress has been made on both sides. For example, in the beginning the application forms were much more complicated than they are now. During the first year of operation, FOSIS did not allocate all its funds, but this has now improved. The relationship between FOSIS and NGOs has matured since FOSIS has become more than a funding source for projects. Given these difficulties and points of friction – including some we shall mention later – a fruitful relationship remains to be developed.

However, these difficulties and points of friction should not be blamed on the nature of the state apparatus. Greater in-depth study of this issue would reveal at least two achievements that relate to this point. First, an institutional procedure has been adopted that permits a group of civil servants to allocate substantial funding (approximately US$13 million over three years), to be administered by the beneficiaries at the local level. Second, these funds have been successfully allocated and distributed in an open and honest manner.

On the other hand, the ways in which FOSIS pursues its goals have caused certain difficulties. This calls for changes in methodology that will contribute to local development. A difficulty consistently raised by NGOs concerns the one-year completion deadline for projects, after which FOSIS supports projects in other areas of the country. NGOs point out that although the work to be undertaken can be scheduled within a year, educational and organizational processes proceed at a much slower pace. When a project finishes and the NGOs leave, these processes are left hanging, without closure. This is a grave problem that arises consistently in all relations between NGOs and state institutions. FOSIS has tried to be more flexible by extending the monitoring phase of projects in which NGOs maintain contact and by providing extended regional workshops that complement the projects after they officially end.

Second, FOSIS, the NGOs, and the local communities are limited in the degree to which they can attack the roots of poverty. This is particularly evident when their initiatives are viewed in the context of an overall strategy for economic and social development. The concentrations of wealth and poverty that necessarily accompany any economic model highlight the urgent need for a combined economic and social policy.[15] However, any hopes that such a policy may be formed are rather exaggerated at this stage.

Third, in order to overcome the above difficulties and facilitate more flexible and effective local development processes, municipalities must prepare a strategy or plan for CD. This plan should be developed with community participation and incorporate the perceptions and initiatives of different sectors of the community. At the same time, initiatives at the local level should be accepted as legitimate by the entire community. A plan for CD would be able to integrate multiple initiatives and efforts into a dynamic and complex overall process. It would solicit and co-ordinate contributions and sources of external support – such as NGOs – that by necessity are transient. Such a plan should utilize a multisectoral approach at the local level.

At the same time, a comprehensive plan for CD should encourage collaboration among NGOs operating in the same municipality, albeit with different specializations and foci. One municipal civil servant work-

15 'Economic growth creates new problems related to the restructuring of very important areas of the economy such as coal mining and traditional agriculture. The feasibility of a policy with social objectives in these sectors will always be in direct relationship to its capacity to influence the types of restructuring, a question that up to now appears outside the scope of entities like FOSIS' (FOSIS, 1993: 15–16).

ing with community organizations south of Santiago made the following comment about NGOs: 'Following the election of the democratic government, we wanted to start talking with the people. We approached NGOs for a diagnosis of the Municipality, but they had never completed one. They had been working here for 10 to 15 years but had never got together to make a community diagnosis; each one was blinkered in his/her own little world.'

Fourth, in spite of FOSIS's good intentions and NGOs' efforts, a serious problem exists in relation to the co-ordinators for local development (CDLs), another actor in these programs. The CDLs tend to take the place of and act as substitutes for popular organizations. This is because CDLs permit the influx of external resources, while popular organizations and neighbourhood groups lack any funding other than that which they raise from their own members. These members reside in the poorest municipalities.

In many cases the CDLs have brought together people who are not traditional leaders in the community. Most often, these people are unprepared in terms of skills and leadership abilities. Even when CDL members have these skills, the issue of continuity and the accumulation of experience re-emerges. It is important that the community rather than external elements be the initiator and developer of initiatives. A development strategy is needed that helps communities make sense of and deal with external influences.

MECE

In relation to MECE and TILNA preschool education projects undertaken by PIIE, we interviewed a civil servant from the Ministry of Education and held a collective interview with the PIIE team. After a change in direction, which we will address shortly, we interviewed a member of this team and the head of the team separately.

The collective interview communicated that the relationship with the ministry appeared very promising. The authorities were impressed with the idea of implementing a preschool education programs at the local level. The use of a multidisciplinary team would ensure that the educational approach encompassed a multiplicity of contextual variables. This perspective coincided with the goal of the MECE program, which was to provide 'an education referring to the particularities of daily life outside school' while simultaneously promoting local development. Interviews with civil servants in the ministry confirmed this finding.

The difficulties that have surfaced in this particular relationship between the central and the local mirror those that have arisen in the other programs analysed here. Two different traditions and modes of working coincide: a functional bureaucratic approach and an approach that encourages heterogeneous, locally based initiatives. The distance between the two perspectives is amplified by mutual ignorance and prejudice: 'It is like being in a country with a different language.' This obstacle was difficult to overcome during the presentation of the project to the ministry, whose support for the proposal was critical. However, given that the perspectives of the ministry and PIIE initially coincided, it was anticipated that differences in 'style' could be overcome. In fact, learning from each other and confronting mutual prejudice forms an integral part of establishing new relationships between the state and civil society.[16]

At the beginning of 1994, both parties were optimistic; however, significant changes occurred. At the end of 1994, the 120 TILNA groups from various parts of the country were to present projects based on a participatory needs assessment. These proposals for working with children at the local level were to be financed by MECE in 1995. However, the ministry announced that funds for these projects had dried up. Instead, MECE would select and contract the best of those 'promoters' trained in the Workshops for Integration at a National Level. The ministry intends to take charge of TILNA, perhaps because FOSIS has demonstrated its ability to administer programs in different localities. PIIE will be excluded from following up TILNA projects but will remain an 'adviser.'

Beyond the ways in which this abrupt change directly affects PIIE, what is clear to PIIE is that the nature of the TILNA project has changed dramatically. TILNA was originally conceived of as an alternative to preschool education that emerged from the community. Institutions were

16 The middle ranks of the ministry are fearful and feel threatened. For technicians who are out of date or who were in the previous government, the greatest security lies in control of routines. This tension directly affects the program because the middle ranks maintain very vertical and functional relationships with those agents of education in the settlements. In these conditions, time is wasted in establishing and maintaining relations with civil servants and normal channels. The PIIE team estimates that the percentage of time spent in maintaining good relations with the promoters is very high, but that effort is absolutely necessary for the program to function properly. If time were not invested in this way, the promoters would be crushed by the state apparatus. (From the interview with the PIIE team.)

to provide technical and financial support to community initiatives. Once TILNA is incorporated as part of the regular program of the Ministry of Education, the most competent 'promoters' trained by TILNA will become civil servants. The energy expended by the people will be subordinated to official plans.

This abrupt deviation in the direction of the TILNA program poignantly illustrates the principal concern of this article: What are the necessary preconditions for local development, and how can these considerations assist in the development of clear policies on local development?

Given this abrupt change, the initial concurrence between MECE and the TILNA proposals now appears suspect. MECE is an important, progressive program of considerable importance to the ministry. Like FOSIS, MECE was conceived during the dictatorship, not by civil servants of the ministry but by workers from NGOs. MECE advocates a critical approach to education: the valuation of knowledge as a product of daily life as well as the expectation that formal education should build on that practical knowledge. Thus, the dialogue that exists between popular knowledge or everyday experiences and universal knowledge[17] forms the core of the TILNA proposals and the MECE program.

However, although MECE is advanced epistemologically concerning education, it does not explicate the relationship that must exist between preschool education and local development. For example, PIIE's proposals for preschool education in terms of local development coincide with MECE's, in that both organizations desire to promote a nontraditional, 'democratic' form of education that differs significantly from the authoritarian educational model that was followed during the dictatorship. Information from the interview with the PIIE team suggests that circumstances surrounding the democratic triumph strengthened the links between PIIE and MECE. For example, TILNA, which had successfully operated as a demonstration project during the period 1987–9, formed part of the plans of the coalition government. The Ministry of Education probably adopted the project because of political connections between the minister and PIIE, and because of the World Bank's interest in funding progressive preschool education.

Despite agreement on the desirability of progressive education, however, a fundamental difference in perspectives emerged after two years of collaboration. PIIE was committed to local development and viewed

17 This point is based on the innovative work of Paulo Freire and his successors. See Balbín (1988), Giroux (1983), and Sohr (1987).

multidisciplinary teams as a way to embrace different points of view. The local people as well as technicians and professionals could all contribute to solutions to community needs. On the other hand, the ministry continues to work in a sectoral manner, concentrating on fulfilling its responsibilities to the school system. These divergent perspectives make one wonder why the ministry accepted the TILNA proposal in the first place, when such divergences existed. According to PIIE, the TILNA project was accepted from the moment it was first presented to the ministry. It would appear that the factors favouring its acceptance at that time were not considered as valid in 1994.

The goal of the TILNA preschool education program was to train local communities in the theory and practice of education. For the ministry, community participation is expedient because it reduces program costs. In our analysis, the major difference between this program and the FOSIS program relates to the capacity to stimulate local development. Working from an intersectoral and multidimensional perspective, FOSIS understands that each problem encountered in a particular locality – for example, health or housing needs – forms part of a much more complex system of needs. The projects stimulated by FOSIS are varied precisely because each problem serves as an entrance for local development to address this complex system of needs.

Local development is much more difficult to facilitate when public and private institutions approach problems with a sectoral outlook. Institutions may collaborate with each other, but their efforts will most likely be piecemeal unless they strive to meet common objectives. Local development clearly advances in situations where an energetic force succeeds in uniting different contributions under one common goal. Where that does not happen, the future of local development is uncertain.

BASIC PRIMARY HEALTH CARE PROGRAM

The sectoral vision that limits the potential of MECE for promoting local development appears even more extreme in the case of the Basic Primary Health Care Program of the Ministry of Health. As previously stated, the process of transferring local services to municipal jurisdiction under the guidelines of the democratic government demands community participation. However, once participation is operationalized, the focus shifts to training civil servants to motivate, organize, and guide the participatory process. Thus, the nucleus of the Basic Primary

Health Care Program is the civil servants themselves. This manifestation of a sectoral outlook is evidenced in the following statement: 'Now we are going to work with the people.'

One significant detail illuminates this sectoral stance. Both FOSIS and MECE were conceived by NGO personnel. The design and direction of the Basic Primary Health Care Program resides in the hands of physicians who, for ideological reasons, did not co-operate with the dictatorship. Although they are now working with the democratic government and agree to 'working with the community,' their professional training and experience has been in the area of health care, not in community work. Social workers, on the other hand, because of their training and experience, tend to listen to and respect the needs and concerns of the local people. It is interesting that since the 1960s, social work as a profession in Chile has emphatically rejected traditional ways of exercising its professional duties.

Because social workers constitute a special group among civil servants, the idea emerged of researching their perspective and experience in relation to the meaning of 'working with the community' in the Basic Primary Health Care Program. With the support of the Guild (the governing body for social workers in the Santiago Area), social workers chose two representatives from each of the six regions of the Metropolitan Area. All participants were women.

All participants agreed that working with the local people through different centres was the most productive strategy for preventive care; that the system of health 'promoters' who were trained and supervised by the respective centres was effective in helping mothers and children stay healthy without continually resorting to the centres; and, finally, that the focus on community participation enabled the people to address environmental health problems (garbage disposal and sewage, sanitary conditions in markets and stalls, the management of contaminated waters) – problems that the centres could only have dealt with on a limited basis.

However, the social workers noted that 'bottlenecks' to community participation existed at four levels:

First, the central apparatus of the state was viewed as a significant impediment. State reform should not to be understood as a reduction of the state in all areas, nor should decentralization be viewed as a simple transfer of functions. Theorists in this area note that reform involves not only decreasing the size of the state apparatus but making it more efficient so that it can carry out those tasks which are indispensable to society as a whole (Portantiero, 1989; Lechner, 1993; O'Donnell, 1993).

Any development of policies designed to promote local development requires a rethinking of the role of the central state. The bureaucracy must function in an open way and collect, organize and prioritize all initiatives, responsibilities, and resources for development that exist at the local level. At the same time, it should be capable of resolving the imbalances that exist among departments and managers in the different regions and localities.

To the extent that this reform in the central state apparatus does not transpire, initiatives for local development will remain hampered by rigidity in administrative practices; by decision-making processes that engage in duplicity or are detached from the people; and by inadequate resources to support solid ideas. Meanwhile, successful experiences of local development that focus on local abilities and resources will stand out as exceptions. Unless substantial change occurs, local development initiatives will continue to be faced with unrealistic deadlines, will continue to depend on the ministry for resources, transfers, guidelines, and directives.

Second, the municipalities themselves require urgent reform if they are to respond effectively to the needs of local development.

Municipalities have a responsibility to encourage community participation in the development and implementation of local policies. This means making effective participation a central component of the process, and improving the ways in which decisions are made. It is informative to point out that the best example of local development in Latin America is Villa El Salvador, a self-sustaining community on the southern edge of Lima. There the municipality handed over a series of functions it normally would have carried out itself to CUAVES, the neighbourhood organization.

If municipal reform is not forthcoming, what we call local development will most likely consist of a handful of initiatives created exclusively by grass roots organizations. As heroic as these initiatives are, and as demonstrative of people's knowledge and capabilities, they are likely to address local problems with limited scope and efficiency.

A third impediment to local development has to do with professional staff who must learn to function within a new set of conditions. In authoritarian as well as in self-declared non-authoritarian systems, professional employees may be accustomed to working in a hierarchy where policies and decisions are imposed on those below. These professionals cannot be expected, from one day to the next, to work productively with a community.

The social workers interviewed saw this particular obstacle as requiring immediate action. In particular, staff feel insecure about their ability to work with people who lack technical and professional training. Other factors mentioned were the loss of 'status' associated with horizontal, equal relationships with consumers of service; and staff objections to working outside normal hours, since community groups are normally available only in the evenings and on weekends. Also, the training programs offered by the Central Department for Basic Primary Health Care are considered good but insufficient. Training should include field work; some social workers hoped that they could carry out this work, with centre staff and additional resources.

Finally, more often than we care to admit, difficulties arise from the local people themselves. Evidence suggests that many consumers view the state and the municipality mainly as providers of services and benefits. They do not necessarily see the value of self-determination and local development initiatives. The oligarchic state, populist governments, and the different types of welfare state have failed to encourage self-reliance. Subordination has been so internalized that it now may be part of our culture. (Some analysts have even wanted to link this to our Iberian heritage.)

However, it is also true that many segments of our society do not form part of this culture of subordination. In fact, one of the least expected effects of neoliberalism has been that grass roots organizations, faced with an ever-retreating state, have multiplied all over Latin America. They have very powerfully defended their right to a decent quality of life.

Perhaps this obstacle to development is the easiest to confront, especially when sectors of society that are willing to actively take up the challenge can demonstrate to others the feasibility and benefits of local development.

6. CONCLUSION

We now want to highlight the general issues in relation to possible directions for local development in Chile.

LOCAL DEVELOPMENT POLICY IN CHILE

Our initial suspicion has been confirmed: in Chile, a decisive policy favouring local development does not exist. Rather, the democratic government has made a firm commitment to enlarge the arenas for citizen participation at the programmatic level. This has allowed progress to be made in special cases. An alternative hypothesis would suggest that participation is encouraged for purposes of legitimization – that the goal is to change not policies but rather the consciousness of the people. We believe that the experience of FOSIS and similar programs such as SERNAM (the National Office for Women) raises doubts about this hypothesis.

Although the 'new' commitment to participation is expressed in the 'general objectives' of different institutions and programs, in many cases it has not been translated into concrete political action. What steps must be taken to transform this commitment into concrete practice? Unfortunately, the stages in this process are neither straightforward nor mechanical. However, if this process is not carried out on a motivational and technical level, democratic willpower will prove insufficient to encourage community participation and local development.

THE DECENTRALIZATION PROCESS

The decentralization of decision-making and of state administrative functions is a necessary prerequisite to local development. There are a myriad of arguments both for and against decentralization as a way of promoting flexible problem-solving processes. However, decentralization alone is not enough. If other aspects of development are neglected, local policy and decision making will continue to be undertaken by central authorities, and community participation will be viewed in terms of efficiency and expediency.

Our research has demonstrated the importance of an intersectoral approach. When decentralization occurs within one sector's boundaries, technical elements tend to prevail and the experiences of grass roots organizations or NGOs are recognized only insofar as they remain merely functional and under the control of specialists. In relation to this point, the major difference between the FOSIS program, and the MECE and Basic Primary Health Care programs lies in FOSIS's 'holistic' view of the community. Although FOSIS projects deal with concrete necessities, the local people determine which specific needs will be addressed; grass roots organizations are strengthened for their own sake and viewed as valuable to the process.

FUTURE DIRECTIONS FOR LOCAL DEVELOPMENT

A comprehensive plan for CD is the most appropriate instrument for stimulating an intersectoral approach. This plan must be understood by executive powers as a concrete proposal; it must also be backed up with real technical and political support. Under these conditions, a plan for CD would facilitate and co-ordinate a range of organizations, contributions, supports, and specific initiatives that enrich and benefit each other. The goal is to put an end to co-ordination efforts of the kind that result in superficial, circumscribed, and often parallel contributions to local development.

In order to become a reality, the CD plan must evolve from a very clear consensus among all institutions and organizations involved in promoting CD – grass roots and labour organizations, NGOs, the central bureaucracy, and so on. Other conditions, although perhaps not necessary to this process, may facilitate it: the co-ordination of NGOs at the local level, and possibly the construction of a 'people's movement' consisting of neighbours, citizens, and grass roots groups. This movement is not intended to absorb or dissolve grass roots organizations but rather to complement their efforts in working with other local development actors.

This comprehensive plan for CD should not be designed only in the technical offices of the municipality, nor should it be the product of the municipal government in power. Such a plan can only be considered legitimate when it is the result of a participatory process. Because of a lack of space, we are unable to explore the experiences of those municipalities which have elaborated and proposed a development plan. This is a topic for further development. We suspect that once again we will encounter civil servants who are incapable of working in a participatory process. This again raises the issue of staff training for this particular work. A change from sectoral development to local development represents a qualitative rather than a superficial change. Other more predictable and obvious problems – for example, the differences in style between the state bureaucracy and civil society – are gradually being resolved through experience and the resolve to work together. The problem now is not that differences exist but rather that a process must be developed to deal with differences.

DEMOCRACY AND LOCAL DEVELOPMENT

We can now at least partially answer some questions that very much concern Latin America. Should democracy as a political system favour local development? Does Latin American democracy favour local development? And finally, can local development be stimulated by a democratic system?

Regarding the last question, in many South American countries the answer seems to be no. This has been pointed out to us every time we have raised this issue with other Latin American scholars.[18] Other works have distinguished between democracy and democratization, and between the legal–political system and the possibilities and opportunities for development and advancement that the system offers its citizens (Palma, 1993). Democracy as a system does not always open the doors to democratization as a process of broadening and deepening democracy.

Our conclusion is that this bond between system and process is found in Chile, with difficulty, and that local development, while not necessarily a consequence of Chilean democracy, is probably a hope that can – and must – be pursued.

Co-ordinators and Authors

Theresa Quiróz Martin

Appointed as senior professor at Arcis University in 1995, after five years directing the women's program and serving as vice-president of the national NGO for adult education, Canelo de Nos. She was director of the Catholic University of Chile School of Social Work before the 1973 military coup. From 1973 until her return to Chile in 1989, she worked in many countries of South and Central America as professor, and served as academic co-ordinator and director of the Centre of Latin American Social Work (CELATS) in Lima, Peru. She has a degree in social work and received her graduate degree in rural sociology from the Latin American Faculty of Social Sciences.

Diego Palma Rodriguez

Principal researcher for the Latin American Council of Adult Education (CEAAL) from 1989 to 1995, and professor at the University of Chile Centre of Public Policy Analysis and ARCIS University. During his exile from Chile, he served as the director of the Latin American Master's program in social planning at the National University of Honduras; as researcher in Costa Rica and with DESCO in Lima, Peru; and as visiting professor at many universities across Latin America. He obtained his graduate degree in sociology from the Latin American Faculty of Social Sciences.

18 This issue has been dealt with in detail by the Argentinian political expert, Guillermo O'Donnell (1993). O'Donnell deals with the limits of what he calls 'emerging democracies,' which are transitional systems arising out of recent dictatorships.

References

Angelo, G. (1987) . *Women are essential*. Santiago: CEM. 71.

Arocena, J. (1987). Local development – slogan or challenge? In *Notebooks of CLAEH*. No. 49. Montevideo: CLAEH.

Balbín, J. (1988). *The dialogue of knowledge: A search in popular language*. Bogotá: CINEP.

Borja, J., et al. (1987). *The decentralization of the state, social movement and local management*. Santiago: FLASCO.

Campero, G. (1988). *Between survival and politics*. Santiago: ILET.

Canessa, J. (1979). *A geopolitical vision of Chilean regionalization*. Santiago.

CLAEH (1989). *Notebooks of CLAEH*. No. 49. Montevideo: CLAEH.

Comisión Económica para America Latina – CEPAL. (1989). *The dynamics of social deterioration in Latin America and the Caribbean in the eighties*. LC/G 1557. San Jose: CEPAL/ECLA.

Corporation for Administrative Reform. (1976). *Chile heading towards a new destiny – its complete administrative reform and the process of regionalization*. Santiago: CONARA.

Corragio, J.L. (1991). *The two trends of decentralization in Latin America in context and education*. Brazil: UFC Editions.

Corvalán, A.M. (ed.). (1990). *The funding of education in times of austerity*. Santiago: UNESCO–ORLALC.

De la Maza, G. (ed.). (1993). *The non-government sector and the funds for social investment*. Santiago: ECO.

Demo, P. (1986). *Participation and conquest*. Brazil: UFC Editions.

Economic Commission for Latin America and the Caribbean. (1985). The crisis in Latin America: Its assessment and perspectives. *Studies and Reviews of ECLAC*. No. 46. Santiago.

– (1990). *Preliminary balance of Latin American economy*. Santiago: ECLAC.

EURE (1985). *The Catholic University of Chile*. No. 33/34. Santiago.

Fernandez, J. (1981). *The legal system of the municipal administration*. Santiago: Edit. Jurídica.

FOSIS – Solidarity and Social Initiatives Fund. (1992). *Investing with the people*. August.

– (1993). *Promoting local development*. Santiago: Department of Social Programmes. 3.

Gajardo, J. (1988). Local development. In Osorio & Weinstein (eds.), *The force of the rainbow*. Santiago: CEAAL.

Giroux, H. (1983). *Theory and resistance in education: A pedagogy for the opposition*. South Hadley, Mass: Bergin and Garvey. (With foreword by P. Freire.)

Góngora, M. (1988). *Historic essay about the notion of the state in Chile during the 19th and 20th centuries.* Santiago: Editorial Universitaria. 13.

Hardy, C. (1988). *Organize to survive: Urban poverty and popular organization.* Santiago: PET.

Hopenhayn, M. (1989). *The postmodern debate and the cultural dimension of development (a descriptive outline).* Santiago: ILPES.

Lechner, N. (1990). *In search of the lost community.* Working Document. Santiago: FLASCO. 11.

– (1993). *Notes on the transformation in the Latin American state.* Working Document. Estudios Politicos No. 28. Santiago: FLACSO.

Ministry of Education – MINEDUC. (1990). *Program for the improvement of quality and fairness in education.* Santiago: MINEDUC.

Ministry of Health - MINESAL. (1991). *Annual Report 1990/1991.* Santiago: MINESAL, Department for Basic Primary Health Care.

Ministry of Planning and Co-operation. (1993) *Mideplan.* Santiago.

Morales, E. (1987). *Public policies in a local framework.* Santiago: FLACSO.

O'Donnell, G. (1993). State democratization and citizenship. *Nueva Sociedad,* No. 128. Caracas, Venezuela.

Palma, D. (1993). *The construction of Prometheus.* Lima: Ed. Tarea. Chap. 1.

Pérez Sainz, J., & Menjivar, R. (1991). *Urban informality in Central America: Between accumulation and subsistence.* Caracas, Venezuela: Edit. Nueva Sociedad.

Portantiero, J.C. (1989). The multiple transformation in the Latin American state. In *Nueva Sociedad,* No. 104. Caracas, Venezuela.

Razeto, L. (1984). *The economy of solidarity and democratic markets.* Santiago: PET.

– (1990). *Popular economic organizations.* Santiago: PET.

Regional Program for Employment in Latin America and the Caribbean – PREALC (1988). *The social debt: What is it and how is it paid?* Santiago: PREALC. 24.

Sainz, J., & Menjivar, R. (1991). *Urban informality in Central America: Between accumulation and subsistence.* Caracas, Venezuela: Edit. Nueva Sociedad.

San Miguel, J., Sepúlveda, G., & Williamson, G. (1994). The MECE basic rural program. In *La Piragua,* CEAAL, No. 8. Santiago.

Scholnik, M., & Teitelboim, B. (1988). *Poverty and unemployment in poor settlements: The other face of the neoliberal model.* Santiago: PET.

Schumacher, E.F. (1973). *Small is beautiful: Economics as if people mattered.* London: Blond & Briggs.

Sohr, L. (1987). *Critical teaching and everyday life.* Chicago: University of Chicago Press.

Weffort, F. (1978). *Popularism in Chilean homes.* Santiago: Mideplan. 55, 166.

Wildenmeersch, L. (1985). Social formation, interaction and communication in the learning process. *The education of adults as a process*. Buenos Aires: Editorial Humanitas.

World Bank Review (1991), 5(2).

Part IX

Comparisons and Conclusions: An International Framework for Practice in the Twenty-first Century

HUBERT CAMPFENS

Comparisons and Conclusions

OVERVIEW

As pointed out in several of the country studies (Ghana, Bangladesh, and Israel), the classical model of CD and community work emphasized self-help projects in rural villages, drawing on the traditional communal or mutual aid forms of societal organization; adult literacy and education; extension campaigns in health and disease control; agriculture, land resettlement, and housing programs; local institution building and leadership development; and co-operation. In all of these, external entities provided support in the form of expertise and resources. This model of modernization and social mobilization was devised by Western planners and instituted in primarily agricultural societies of the Third World within the socio-political context of highly centralized, paternalistic, and state-managed settings.

CD gradually found its way into the industrialized societies of the West and into urban centres, where it adapted to a different reality. In the developed Western societies, community organization and (later) social planning were the dominant fields of professional practice in community work, operating within the context of political pluralism and an expanding welfare state. The main concern was with systems of service delivery; the focus was on needs identification and assessment, citizen and client participation, interorganizational and intergroup relations, social integration, and other such functions. CD practice, also known as grass roots or locality development, was perceived as a mere corrective to the societal guidance or social reform orientation of social planners moved by 'technical reason.' For a brief period during the 1960s and early 1970s, community workers adopted radical social action and conflict strategies in the tradition of the oppositional movements to address issues related to the imbalance in power between the 'haves' and the 'have nots.'

The shift in theory and practice focus in recent years, and in the organizational framework within which CD is carried out, has been quite dramatic, as is evident from the country studies presented in this book. I will now highlight this shift using an expanded typology based on a review of cases that are representative of a broadening field of practice. As was pointed out in the introduction, and confirmed in varying degrees by the country studies, much of this shift is a result of radical changes to the world order, which have had their counterpart in changes in the economic, political, and social order of each society. Concretely, these changes consist of the following:

- Strong trends toward decentralization and localism, especially in matters related to social development.
- A push for a reduced welfare state in most Northern countries, and the promotion of self-reliance and self-help based on the assumption that it will counter dependency and foster enterprise.
- A growing involvement of the voluntary sector in both Northern and Third World countries.
- The emergence of new grass roots based social movements and their organizations.
- A change in the composition of local communities, with an increase in cultural diversity as a result of rural–urban migration and major population movements (of immigrants, refugees, and migrant workers) across cultural boundaries.

These new political and social phenomena are redirecting the functions and roles of CD practitioners.

To these trends should be added another factor: the disastrous impact of the structural adjustment policies (SAPs) on the poor in Third World nations. This impact is highlighted in the study from Chile, a country that is often upheld in international circles as a 'success story' in economic development. While it may be trite, it must be repeated here that according to study after study, the rich in the world are getting richer and the poor are becoming poorer, with all the accompanying problems (International Association of Schools of Social Work – IASSW, 1992). This is not merely a Third World problem; it is also true for the United States, where an 'underclass' is developing rapidly, and for all other countries of the North. (See Table 9.1, and the section 'Contrasts in Context.')

Each of the trends mentioned above has a major influence on which problems are addressed, the level of intervention, and the dynamics of practice. While poverty alleviation and prevention remains a top priority of CD practice, as reported by all six country studies, new priorities have emerged that twenty years ago were either not on the agenda or received scant attention, and that call for community-level as well as state-level and institutional initiatives. These include such problems and issues as the following:

- The devastating threat of AIDS, as well as the drug epidemic, crime, and vandalism.
- The heightened awareness of the importance of the environment and its relationship to the quality of life (see the Dutch case).
- The rise in interethnic group tensions in multicultural neighbourhoods. This requires conflict resolution strategies (see the Israeli case on peace and welfare) and effective approaches to social integration (see the Canadian refugee case and the Israeli illustration of community work in an ultra-Orthodox neighbourhood).
- A shift in CD practice that, besides the traditional emphasis on locality development and functional community work, includes a focus on population groups (i.e., 'categorical' community work) and 'people development.' This is illustrated well by the cases on the elderly (from the Netherlands), on single-parent women (Canada), and on various women's development projects (Ghana and Bangladesh).
- The increased interest in community economic development (CED) as an alternative or complementary model to macroeconomic development that addresses both economic and social issues at the local level (see the income-generating and rural shelter projects from Ghana, the various cases from Bangladesh on co-operativism, and the nonprofit housing society case from Canada).

Despite these different trends and changing priorities, we find that the social values and principles that underlie CD practice (see Part II – Introduction) have not changed much since the earlier days of CD, with perhaps a few notable exceptions mentioned already in Part II. Mobilizing and nurturing communities remains the central purpose of CD – albeit with a more discriminating understanding of 'community' in terms of social structure and scope. Social integration, leadership development, local or group initiative-taking, and the promotion of a more participatory democracy, continue to be the essence of CD. What *has* changed in CD practice is that concern has increased for social justice and human rights. This change has moved CD away from its narrow focus on localities and group development and toward the larger sociopolitical sphere of society. The most significant changes are apparent less in the central values and ideas than in the practice and strategic approaches to CD.

The aim of this book has been to compare experiences of CD – to seek out common themes that will contribute to the development of a practice-based theory that is helpful to professionals in community work, to program planners, and to policy-makers. In this undertaking we started from the premise that CD practice needs to be placed in a national and international context that acknowledges the following:

- The new forces at work at the global level.
- The vast differences in political systems and policy practices of governments.
- Differing economic conditions and social inequalities.
- The social and ethno-cultural composition of different populations.
- Differences in relations between the state and civil society.

Each of these factors was recognized as exercising a considerable influence on the degree to which CD will be supported and can be practised with any measure of effectiveness.

There cannot be one simple theoretical framework, technical solution, or formula that can be applied universally, although theoreticians and policy-makers often look for one. Social scientists and theoreticians may wish it were otherwise, but the reality of our rapidly changing societies and communities is that 'knowledge' as it relates to CD must be fluid, nonbounded, particularistic, experimental, and subjective if it is to respond to the complex and sometimes chaotic situations encountered in communities across the globe. As pointed out by Harvey Stalwick in his Canadian study 'CD is a delightfully misshapen square peg in the neat round hole of positivism and other variations of scientism.' However, there may be value in searching for some common strategic approaches to local development, or for a general methodology of intervention in CD, provided the results of such a search are applied thoughtfully and take into account numerous differences in the political, economic, social, and cultural context.

Previous attempts to find universal models and apply them to sharply different contexts have had disastrous results. The best examples of this relate to the Euro-centred doctrines, such as Rostow's stages of economic development (see Part I – Introduction); and to North American models that tried to capture in theory the complexities and dynamics of community practice – for example, Rothman's three models of community organization practice (i.e., locality development, social planning, and social action). This framework gained such popularity in educational centres and fields of practice in many parts of the world (and is still so popular) that it has obstructed attempts to have CD break loose from its singular association with the locality development model. This, in spite of Rothman's later revisions to the three models (1987, 1995).

In a recent publication (Bingham & Mier, 1993), the contributing authors discussed no less than fifty theories of local economic development from the perspective of the various social sciences. The editors then proposed some seven metaphors for local practice – local economic development as problem-solving, as running a business, as building a growth machine, as preserving nature and place, as exerting leadership, and as a quest for social justice – to situate those theories and show their application to CD practice.

In contrast, the attempt in this book has been to construct a framework theory that is useful for policy development, program planning, and CD practice; that is grounded in contemporary economic, political, and local realities; and that takes into account differences between cultures and systems. The central importance of *context* will become quite clear when we review and compare the country studies. Let us do this now. Then we will discuss the apparent shift in the concepts and practice of CD, and critically assess some of the common themes that have emerged in this book.

CONTRASTS IN CONTEXT

The differences in national contexts are highlighted in Table 9.1, which provides some qualitative and quantitative measures of a variety of variables.

North–South/Rich–Poor
The first contrast we must point out is the one between the countries of the North (Canada, the Netherlands, and Israel) and those of the South (especially Ghana and Bangladesh), particularly regarding per capita

TABLE 9.1
Comparative Indicators of Participating Countries (including the U.S.A.)

Country	Canada	The Nether-lands	Israel	Chile	Ghana	Bangla-desh	U.S.A.
Population in millions ('94)**	28	15.4	5.67	14	17	125.2	260.5
Density per sq. km. ('94)**	3	412	273	18.5	71.3	869	27.8
Annual pop. growth ('91–'94)**	1.3%	.6%	2.9%	1.5%	2.9%	2.4%	1%
Urban-(rural) percentage**	77%	89%	91%	86%	33%	16%	75%
GNP/capita ('92)*	20,710	20,480	13,220	2,730	450	220	23,240
Actual survival rate (U5MR[1]) ('80s)*	8	8	12	20	170	133	11
Performance gap[2]*	+1	+2	+1	+18	-37	+41	-3
Malnutrition (mid- '80s)[3]	—	—	—	3%	27%	66%	1 in 8 hungry
Performance gap*	—	—	—	+11	-1	-33	—
Immunization measles '91	85%	94%	86%	93%	39%	53%	77%
Primary educ.[4] ('88–'90)*	96%	94%	94%	75%	74%	47%	96%
Adult literacy ('90)** – male	97%	95%	95%	94%	70%	47%	95%
– female	99%	95%	95%	93%	51%	22%	95%
Family pl. TFR[5] ('91)*	1.8	1.7	2.9	2.7	6.1	4.8	2
Women MMR[6] ('91)*	5	10	3	67	1000	600	8
Pop. access to safe water ('85–'90)**	97%	100%	98%	89%	57%	81%	100%

TABLE 9.1 *(continued)*

Country	Canada	The Netherlands	Israel	Chile	Ghana	Bangladesh	U.S.A.
Aid disbursed as % of GNP ('91)* **	0.5%	0.9%	—	—	—	—	0.2%
In billion $U.S.	2.6b.	2.52b.	—	—	—	—	11.26b.
Official dev't aid[7] received as % of GNP ('91)* **	—	—	1.75b.	120 mill	724 mill	1.64b.	—
	—	—	3%	.3%	10%	7%	—
Received/cap	—	—	$353	$9	$47	$15	—
External debt in $billion**	—	—	26.3 ('87)	19.4 ('92)	4.3 ('92)	13.2 ('92)	—
Debt service as % of export	—	—	25%	21%	27%	17%	—
debt/capita			$5,839	$1,424	$271	$115	
Armed forces ('93)**	78,100	105,134	176,000	91,800	6,850	107,000	1,729,000
Ethnocultural**	88% European descent, 0.3–0.5% Aboriginal; increasingly multicultural; with Third World immigrants and refugees (11%)	Most of Dutch/ Germanic origin with some minorities from former colonies and immigrant workers totalling 5%	Mostly Jewish immigrants from all over the world, plus Palestinian, Druz, and Bedouin minorities	Culturally mixed population between natives and European immigrants since 16th century; and small native communities	Six main ethnic groups with Akan(44%) and Ewe(13%) as the dominant groups	Ethnically and culturally homogeneous, some small minorities (Urdu and natives)	Most of European descent; and immigrants from all over the world; 1% aboriginal; 11% of African, and 10% of Latin American origin.
Religion	R.C. predominates, followed by Protestants, some Muslims	R.C., Protestant and others (Muslim)	mainly Jewish	mainly Roman Catholics (R.C.)	Christian 50%, Muslim 13%, traditional 32%	Muslim 83%, Hindu 16%	Protestant majority, many R.C.,5m Jews, Muslim minority
Human Dev't Index[8]	.983	.976	.95	.878	.311	.186	.976

*Data obtained from UNICEF (1993). *The Progress of Nations.* New York: UNICEF.
**Estimate obtained from Instituto del Tercer Mundo. *The World: A Third World Guide 95/96: Facts, Figures, Opinions.* Montevideo, Uruguay.

1 U5MR – under 5 mortality rate per thousand live births, as the composite indicator of children's well-being providing both a quantitative measure of death but also the quality of life (statistics are based on mid-80s figures) reflecting in this one statistic income, education of parents, prevalence of malnutrition and disease, availability of clean water, efficacy of health services, status of women and their health.

2 Performance gap – the gap between U5MR and the level that could be expected for the country's GNP per capita.

3 Malnutrition – caused as much by frequency of illness and lack of information as by a lack of food, stunting the mental and physical growth of children and sapping the economic and social development of children.

4 Primary Education – measures the percentage of children reaching grade 5.

5 TFR – total fertility rate in average number of births per women.

6 MMR – maternal mortality rate reflects the strength of health services, generally measures as deaths related to pregnancy and childbirth per 100,000 births.

7 Official development aid – less than 10% is allocated directly to meeting the most obvious needs of the poorest people, i.e., primary health care, primary education, clean water, safe sanitation, and family planning. There is limited aid to create jobs and incomes to have families meet needs by own efforts.

8 Human development index (HDI) – is a combination of three indicators: life expectancy at birth, adult literacy and standard of living measured in per capita GNP adjusted to reflect earning power. The index does not take into account environmental degradation. The HDI adjusted for gender, race and income distribution disparities places especially the USA and also Canada, well below the Netherlands, Scandinavian countries and Japan. The almost perfect scores in adult literacy for some countries included here does not account for very limited literacy skills in everyday reading tasks of millions of people.

Source: The 93/94 Third World Guide, edited by Instituto del Tercer Mundo, Montevideo, Uruguay, p. 70.

GNP and human development as measured by the HDI. For Ghana and Bangladesh, the difference is staggering, and indicates the extent to which the magnitude of poverty and the lack of resources set the policy priorities of national government and determine local CD practices. If we also factor in population, population density, and annual population growth in Bangladesh, we see not only the all-pervasiveness of poverty in that country but the obstacles to achieving any semblance of social development.

CD practice on the 'ground level,' in a country where advances in national economic development are outstripped by population growth and a shrinking land base, can best be understood as a rearguard action. Practitioners are involved in perpetual crisis interventions; they are experimenting with any number of approaches that perhaps make little sense in theoretical terms but nevertheless respond to people's immediate concerns for survival.

In the Bangladesh study, what stands out (besides the complexity of that country's situation) is the target-group, multidimensional approach to alleviating poverty. This approach was devised by the NGOs in the 1980s and adopted later by various state agencies. It combines collective or group-based employment and income-generating schemes with social development activities relating to family planning, primary health care education, literacy training, and immunization. The conscientization approach is often used to empower target groups and bring about structural changes. Such an integrated approach, which is based on a holistic notion of poverty and human development, if it is to succeed, must involve fundamental reforms in public and social administration. The Dutch, under far more favourable socio-economic conditions, are in the midst of such reforms, as reported in their study.

Urban/Rural
A second contrast noted by a glance at Table 9.1 is in the proportion of the population that resides in urban centres as opposed to rural areas. As can be observed, the three Northern countries, and also Chile, are heavily urbanized. Even Canada, which has a very low overall population density, has a largely urban-based population – more so even than the United States. Consequently, much of CD practice in those countries takes place in urban settings; community workers, in working with deprived neighbourhoods and groups, have tended to focus on issues related more to ensuring equitable access to public services and power, and to promoting client and citizen participation.

Ghana and Bangladesh, in contrast, are largely rural and agricultural societies; the traditional state-administered programs of CD focus on promoting community self-help and self-reliance as part of a general plan for rural development. With a strong trend toward rural-urban migration in these two countries, urban CD is now taking on greater significance and dealing with other problems besides poverty. Our findings suggest that the differences between rural and urban CD in both Southern and Northern countries are less pronounced today than they were forty or even twenty years ago. Rural CD is moving away from a locality-focused, communitywide, village development approach, and toward a more integrated regional approach that emphasizes target groups.

Ethnocultural and Religious Heterogeneity/Homogeneity
A third factor in national approaches to CD relates to the ethno-cultural and religious make-up of populations. Israel in particular is a strongly heterogeneous society, and is continuing to receive a disproportionate number of immigrants from diverse cultures across the world. Community workers in that country have played an important role in promoting integration at the community level, with the goal of fostering a civic culture and positive social relations between groups.

Ghana, too, is strongly heterogeneous. Like so many other African nations, it is experiencing unprecedented intertribal tensions, with chieftaincy rivalries draining the limited financial resources available and diverting attention from immediate community and human needs, and from the problems of deprivation and inequity that are often the real causes of discontent and conflict. Clearly, for countries like Ghana, intergroup conflict resolution and mediation strategies need to become an integral part of those CD programs which target education, health care, and housing issues.

For Western countries including Canada and the Netherlands, interethnic tensions with racist overtones have been rising in recent years, particularly in urban centres, as those societies become increasingly multicultural. Racism has always been a part of Canadian history, particularly in relation to aboriginal people; however, it was not until the 1970s, when large numbers of immigrants and refugees from the Third World entered Canada and economic realities began to change, that ethnic tension became more overt and widespread. In the Netherlands in recent years, the arrival of former colonials and migrant workers has resulted in similar tensions.

Unlike Israel, Canada and the Netherlands in their integration policies did not until recently place much emphasis on community work as a means of bringing about integration at any level. The governments and major institutions in these two countries have focused mainly on helping individual newcomers integrate themselves into the various sectors of society (through employment, education, health, and housing programs and so on). Policies for achieving group integration at the societal and local levels, acknowledging differences in cultural identity and practice, have been largely neglected. Nevertheless, as illustrated in the Canadian case on refugees, innovative programs are now being carried out, especially by NGOs, and these incorporate CD approaches.

In Chile and Bangladesh, which in terms of culture and religion are more homogeneous, intergroup relations have not yet become a serious

concern, although the existence of native communities in both countries and a large Hindu minority in Bangladesh have produced some
frictions.

Centralization/Decentralization
A fourth and final contrast to be noted here relates to the issue of
decentralization. Of the six countries, only Canada, perhaps because of
its huge land mass, has always been a federal state. It has a long history
of periphery-versus-centre challenges based on socio-political forces such
as regionalism and biculturalism. Even so, the federal state has continued to play a dominant role in Canadian society by providing top-
down programs. As a result of the diminishing capacity of the federal
and provincial governments to deal with the new economic realities –
including rising unemployment, increasing poverty, and soaring debt
problems – there has been a demand for a devolution of powers to
regions and local communities.

There is a notable change in the local initiatives being taken. Increasingly, local authorities, nonprofit NGOs, the business sector, and community organizations are working together through partnership councils. These groups recognize that local communities must develop their
own resources and skills to address not only local economic and employment needs but also the needs of children, young people, the elderly, young families, and others.

High levels of community spirit, or 'social capital,' figure greatly in
this new, bottom-up approach to effecting change at the neighbourhood
or regional level. The social capital referred to here includes not only
service clubs, schools, chambers of commerce, social agencies, and local
fund-raising campaigns (all of which remind us of the long tradition of
voluntarism in Canada), but also grass roots organizations representing
the deprived and excluded, in which community workers are active as
facilitators and resource people. What we see here is a revival of the
locality development model of CD, albeit in a different shape, with
diverse actors (including the state) being drawn into new horizontal
and co-operative partnership arrangements.

Similar developments are occurring in the Netherlands and Chile.
Both countries have long had strong central government. In the Netherlands, which is such a small country, population pressures have always
made urban and rural planning a priority, with much of the policy-
making and execution done by municipalities. In this, CD has played
an integral part. In contrast, the welfare state remained highly central-

ized until the late 1970s, when criticism began to grow about the cost and sustainability of welfare state programs, and deep concern began to be felt about the spread of individualism in Dutch society and the loss of such traditions as mutual solidarity, civic participation, and community building. All of these had been considered necessary for retaining a stable, socially coherent, and humane society. These concerns, together with the changes in the economic climate, led the Dutch state not only to decentralize much of its power to local authorities but also to privatize parts of its social welfare and development systems. It should be emphasized, however, that the state remained actively involved through policies that encouraged administrative and social renewal. These policies were aimed at revitalizing local communities, at fostering citizen participation, and at encouraging the economically and socially excluded (as organized groups) to get involved in improving their living conditions. This has led to a strong resurgence of interest in CD and in the training of community workers, as discussed in the Dutch study.

As for Chile, there had always been a strong tendency toward centralization in decision making and in the administration of public funds. This held right up to the military coup of 1973. But there had also always been a strong tradition of democracy, with elections representing an important political exercise in the national and local way of life. This democratic tradition was rudely interrupted by a seventeen-year authoritarian regime that focused on macro-economic development, structural adjustment, and the complete dismantling of the welfare state without regard to any impact on the poor.

Augusto Pinochet, the Chilean dictator, instituted a policy of decentralization that drew clear boundaries between political and social power. Political power was reserved only for the state, which could thus extend its long reach into the farthest corners of society. Civil society was only permitted to engage in a form of social power; social development responsibilities were relegated to the local governments, but there was no accompanying transfer of resources from the state so that people could address their basic human needs in their own communities. Because of the unique political circumstances of Chile, the authors of that country study decided to focus on an analysis of the possibilities and realities of local development (used interchangeably with community development) in the context of the emphasis on decentralization, which continued even after democracy returned in 1990. This analysis, based as it is on extensive research and a discussion of various initiatives in local development, makes the Chilean study of particular relevance to other countries with a dictatorial and authoritarian history; but it is also relevant to those more democratic nations which are undergoing structural adjustment, and this includes the developed countries of the North.

Regarding Israel: community work (as opposed to community development) has always been a special feature of that country, especially in the field of social welfare. Its practitioners have been employed by local municipalities and supported (i.e., paid and provided with resources) by the central government. However, because of the country's security and economic problems and its need to integrate very large groups of immigrants, community workers have had to function in an environment that favours a strong centralized state and leadership. In this context, attempts to bring about greater decentralization and localism – to reinforce voluntarism, an active civil society, and community development – have often been frustrated. Yet, as indicated in the Israeli study, there are changes at work that have led to increased local power and opportunities for community work to realize some of its objectives, including those specifically related to community development.

Ghana, which has a unitary form of government, has been implementing CD programs longer than almost any other country, with substantial support from the central government and donor agencies. However, it was not until January 1993 that a new democratic constitution was introduced aimed at promoting local governance and thereby also reinforcing voluntarism, citizen participation, and local initiatives in economic and social development. This change promises an expansion in CD.

In Bangladesh, the state has supported co-operative developments and CD programs carried out by various institutes and government agencies as well as by donor agencies working through local NGOs. However, while the country has a strong communitarian tradition of mutual aid (which is also part of the practice of Islam), it lacks a democratic culture and political system that encourages grass roots initiatives and control. Consequently, most development programs arise from the centre and then seek local participation.

This comparison of countries has highlighted the importance of tailoring CD to individual countries. CD practice must reflect local needs and the economic, political, and cultural realities of the country where it is carried out.

SHIFTS IN CONCEPT AND PRACTICE

The changes in macro-context, and the differences between countries in structure, trends, and priorities, have given rise to a greater diversity of approaches to CD and of organizing, planning, and development practices among community workers. This becomes clear when we review the cases included in this study. These cases also tell of the enormous potential that exists for people everywhere in the world to benefit from community development. For purposes of comparison, the editor has systematically reviewed these cases and highlighted their main features. He has summarized his findings in concept form (see Appendix) so that a typology of approaches to CD can be formulated as well.

Before this typology is presented, some recent trends are worth noting in the following matters: what 'actor' in the system takes the initiative and gives it legitimacy; what population group, community problem, or issue serves as the target of the community action taken; and what organizing strategies are utilized in achieving CD.

The Initiators of Development
Traditionally it was the state – through a national, provincial or municipal agency, or through one of society's major institutions – that initiated the action, and then sought local or community participation in the tradition of 'societal guidance.'

In contrast, 'autonomous' grass roots groups are now 'spontaneously' emerging to engage in community action. Following in the tradition of the oppositional movements, these groups express themselves through mutual aid, seeking support in free association; through a disengagement from the state and the rest of society (as seen in ultra-Orthodox communities); or through confrontation with the state and vested interest groups in the context of perceived class, racial, ethnic, or gender oppression.

Another category of initiating actors are the NGOs representing the ideology of voluntarism. While these have played an important role in nations characterized by political pluralism, they have also become important actors in Third World settings.

A variation on these voluntary sector initiatives is the new phenomenon of collectives, as illustrated by the community workers' collectives in Quebec, which are committed to conscientization and politicization practice; and in Israel, which are promoting peace and welfare in multiethnic communities.

The most widespread of the newer practices involves organizations whose members are linked in horizontal rather than vertical relationships. This trend reflects how the ideology-driven policy agendas of governments have led to a major restructuring of relations between the state and civil society, and to new expectations that the needs of communities and groups must be met by sectors other than the state.

Targets of Community Action and Organizing Strategies
The initiatives undertaken by CD are aimed at a broad range of targets, from population groups and rural and urban communities to the public at large.

The Bangladesh study illustrates how both state agencies and NGOs have opted for more direct interventions in their attempts to alleviate poverty in rural areas. In this they have relied on group development and the formation of co-operatives. This new orientation departed from the Swanirvar Movement, launched in 1975, which favoured a government-sponsored, communitywide approach to development. It had become evident that the locality or village based approach, adopted earlier as a strategy for employment generation for the rural poor, in fact favoured the rural élite and failed to reach landless, poor women, unemployed young people, and small farmers.

Another state initiative supported by international NGOs that has targeted designated groups is the Ghana Rural Shelter Project, which provides school dropouts and illiterate young people with skills training and employment opportunities in housing construction, and which relies on the formation of community self-help groups and production-oriented co-operatives. As well, poor women in Ghana, Bangladesh, and elsewhere are targeted for income-generating projects and brought together into groups and co-operatives.

From a different perspective, a number of single-parent women in Vancouver, Canada, having been excluded from the general opportunities and benefits enjoyed by most Canadians, targeted their own conditions of poverty and took collective action. They adopted a self-managing community economic development strategy that in time decreased their reliance on and vulnerability to the economic interests operating in the larger society.

Some governments and NGOs target vulnerable groups and apply community-based strategies as a preventive measure. One such example is the Canadian case 'Onward Willow,' which targets young children and their parents who are considered at risk and who reside in socio-economically disadvantaged neighbourhoods.

A similar example is the Flesseman project in Amsterdam. The neighbourhood in question has a high concentration of elderly who favour independent living over institutional care. The interesting feature here is the degree to which the elderly, through a neighbourhood foundation, participate in decision-making about facilities, services, standards, and management.

The concerns of ethno-cultural minorities are often addressed by NGOs. A special example is the Canadian case dealing with victims of torture, who constitute an 'invisible population' within Toronto's large immigrant communities. It is noteworthy here that the strategy adopted in this case did not target just refugees. Through consciousness raising, partnership developments, and public education, service professionals, social agencies, and community groups were encouraged to change their usual way of relating to refugees and to take a nonmedical, social approach to integration.

The Dutch integrative approach to alleviating poverty is both unique and highly innovative. Besides targeting the structurally unemployed in economically depressed neighbourhoods and regions facing plant closures and modernization, it also targets the state, which tends to compartmentalize the various official sectors and to bureaucratize relations between ordinary citizens, professionals, and officials. The project adopts a multidimensional, multipartnership approach known as 'social renewal,' which mobilizes the unemployed through grass roots organizations.

What is clear from the above examples is that CD practice is moving away from a singular preoccupation with the local community, and toward a strategy that incorporates multiple targets. This is particularly true of programs that aim at poverty alleviation or social integration. In some instances, however, the 'community as a locality' is the proper target for development initiatives, as illustrated by the slum improvement project in Rajshahi, Bangladesh, which focused on physical infrastructure. Yet this project also emphasized getting women involved in activities to improve their living standards.

The Israeli case on community work in an ultra-Orthodox neighbourhood of Jerusalem is another illustration of a neighbourhood being specifically targeted. Again, women played a significant role in this process; it was they who built bridges of understanding between genders within the neighbourhood, and between the neighbourhood and the municipality.

A final example of an effective locality-targeted approach to CD is provided by the Dutch study that focused on the vulnerability of neighbourhoods as 'livable environments.' Here, the underlying tension was between the neighbourhood and the local authorities. Concerns included sanitation, hygiene, traffic, the management of green spaces, the contamination of the environment, and security issues related to crime, drugs, and vandalism. In the community work that was carried out, the different organizational models that emerged, all of them involving local residents, were particularly noteworthy.

Typology of Approaches to CD
The typology presented here, not to be equated with 'models,' focuses only on the 'dominant' concept apparent in each of the approaches taken in practice, viewed from the perspective of CD:

- The *continuum* concept of CD, which aims at achieving human development through group, community, and international development. This includes the advancement of human rights.
- The *group or co-operative* concept, which is aimed at individual, social, and economic development in the tradition of mutual aid, social support, and social action.
- The territorially bounded *locality* concept, which views the local community as a physical, economic, social, and political unit in its own right. Here the concern is with the quality of life and the optimum involvement and participation of individuals and organizational members in community affairs.
- The *structural-functional* concept, in which CD forms part of a larger policy framework that focuses on the various partners in development, – that is, state agencies, institutions, NGOs, the voluntary sector, the business sector, and the target group or community as presumed beneficiary.
- The *categorical* concept, in which CD forms part of a larger policy framework that aims to alleviate or prevent a social problem (e.g., poverty) that disproportionately affects certain groups or communities, which have found themselves economically, socially, or politically excluded from the benefits, resources, or opportunities offered by society.
- The *self-management* concept, in which CD takes a bottom-up, empowering approach to the development of communities or groups.

- The *social learning or educational* concept of CD, which brings together professional experts, with their 'universal knowledge,' and the local residents, with their 'popular knowledge' and 'lived experience.'
- The *intergroup* concept of CD, which focuses on mutual understanding, conflict resolution, and social integration.

This typology demonstrates clearly the diverse approaches that can be taken to CD and how each approach can complement the others, thereby contributing to a just and socially integrated society. It separates CD from its singular concern with 'locality development' by placing its practice on a continuum of levels of intervention that link micro-level (the empowerment of individuals and groups) with mezo-level (neighbourhood and municipality) and macro-level (national and international) development.

COMMON THEMES

The following section will identify and assess some of the common themes that are relevant to CD as they are reflected in the social movements of recent years and in the innovative public or institutional policies reported on in this study.

A Proactive Policy on Nurturing Associative Communities
There have been strong ideological forces at work, spearheaded by the neoconservative position, that would have the local community and the voluntary sector assume primary responsibility for the care and support of people in need, with a minimal role for the state. These forces are trying to recover certain traditional values (central also to CD), including mutual aid, self-help and self-reliance, social support through informal networks and civic solidarity, local initiatives, and self-determination. This position was most strongly pursued during the Reagan and Thatcher years, and projected itself onto the international sphere through IMF structural adjustment policies imposed on Third World countries.

Societies without such values and practices at the personal and interpersonal level would surely disintegrate; however, that is not a sufficient rationale for states to remove themselves from the sphere of social welfare and social development, especially in an age of profound economic and social transformation. To counter the modern forces of individualism, secularization, materialism, and anomie, there must more than ever be proactive policies that nurture communities through association, local community building, and social integration. To suggest that one can revert to the solidarity and mutual aid traditions of the extended family, village, parish, and neighbourhood – which for many centuries served as the bedrock for human welfare and support in the absence of the welfare state – ignores the fact that these traditions had deep cultural and religious roots that are disappearing rapidly in the developed nations of the North and even in the Third World, where structural adjustments are taking place.

The Limits of Self-reliance and the Role of the State

A second development is that of the neoliberal position, which reinforces neoconservatism. It calls for an unfettered market that heeds its own forces of demand and supply, and for a state that no longer sets norms, oversees macro-economic development, or regulates the market. It especially rejects the notion that the state should embody the value of mutual solidarity, through which wealth is redistributed through income assistance and social services. Like the neoconservatives, neoliberals consider social welfare and social development to be the responsibility of local communities and social organizations, and the philanthropic sector – not of the business sector and the state.

This position was pushed to its extreme in Chile from 1973 to 1989. There the state, under control of a military regime, concerned itself primarily with revitalizing the business and economic sector. In the process, it cut itself loose from the social sector; instead, policies of privatization, decentralization, and reliance on local development initiatives were to take care of people's needs in education, health, housing, employment, and income. The result was disastrous, with millions of people being driven into poverty. As the state busied itself promoting the free market, local organizations for mutual aid began to emerge, with some economic and technical support from churches and international NGOs. The best assessment of the Chilean experience is that these popular organizations, forced into self-reliance, found 'efficient' ways of addressing survival needs and of dealing with some of the inequities introduced by the dominant system. However, it should be emphasized that without appropriate social policies and substantial assistance and support from the state, these popular organizations were not able to help people to rise above poverty and address quality of life issues.

The People Development Focus

A third concept relevant to CD that has gained momentum in recent years is the 'people development' focus. It acknowledges that the classical 'locality development' and 'communitywide participation' models of CD – whether applied to villages, urban neighbourhoods, or regions – have a limited capacity to address the personal needs of the more vulnerable or excluded members of society. These people and supportive institutions are becoming aware that in order to advance their own welfare and to protect their own interests, beliefs, and lifestyles in a social and cultural environment that is becoming increasingly diverse, they must come together as groups and form relations with the larger society through circles of solidarity.

Case after case shows how, through associative activity for mutual aid or dissent, and through learning to act in the economic, social, and political spheres, participants become connected to the community, regain a sense of self, undergo a change in their life situation, and become personally transformed. Thus, the people development model in CD work departs from the locality development model in two essential ways. First, in development activities, it concerns itself as much with individuals as with the community, relying on group development, leadership training, popular education, and consciousness raising. Secondly, 'community' is sought and strengthened in places provided for conviviality – in co-operatives, collectives, grass roots organizations, and circles of solidarity, as well as in committed relationships in which the participants share common interests. These interests may coincide at times with those of the local community (i.e., the village, neighbourhood, or municipality) when the concern relates to the community as a livable environment (see the Dutch case on 'CD and the Environment.') But frequently, interests extend beyond the locality, particularly when the issues involve social justice and economic fairness.

Program Integration (Multidimensionality)
and Organizational Partnerships

A fourth development of significance to CD and community work relates to state and institutional initiatives in search of greater program integration and new organizational partnerships involving the community and voluntary sectors. These initiatives are a response to a number of social forces pursuing very different agendas. For the community movements active in the West during the 1970s and 1980s, which pitted organized communities against the state, the goal was clearly not to do away with the welfare state, but rather to reform program delivery methods so they were more community-based, integrated, and multidimensional. This political force cut across the racial, ethnic, and income lines of traditional interest groups. For the neoconservatives and neoliberals the goals were to find less expensive community alternatives in caring for the sick, the elderly, delinquent youths, and others; to make greater use of the voluntary sector; and to draw more on business principles in the management of programs (i.e., to make them more cost-effective).

The new challenge for program planners is how to overcome the nineteenth-century view that the state and its bureaucracy, the civic and voluntary sectors, the business sector, and the community are separate entities. In such a scheme of things, the various players pursue their respective interests at cross-purposes to each other, with the community as loser.

An additional challenge to CD is to overcome the boundaries erected during this century through the processes of specialization among the disciplines and professions. While specialization has undoubtedly resulted in deeper knowledge, technological progress, and methodological perfection, it also has led to a technological patchwork in the matter of the day-to-day needs and problems experienced by people in their communities. Not surprisingly, in the move toward community-directed approaches to development – as found in such sectors as community health, primary prevention, community economic development, and participatory action research – the resistance tends to come from those same disciplines and professions which see their interests as tied to classical models of inquiry and to the existing institutional frameworks with their specialized services.

With the goal of encouraging social innovations that would cut across sectoral lines, organizational interests, and professional specializations, the Dutch in the early 1990s introduced a state policy called Social Renewal, which embraces different assumptions about the role of the welfare state and community work in the emerging post-industrial, postmodern, multicultural society. The issue for the policy's supporters is how to reconnect in a meaningful way the economic, social, and political domains with the kind of social and organizational structures that can address the social needs of people today. Among the priorities identified are employment, income, and training; environmental quality; and social and cultural practices.

Besides reforming the state bureaucracy to make it more 'connected' with other sectors of society, Social Renewal is actively seeking the organized participation of the marginalized and excluded in matters of selecting, supervising, and implementing programs. As the Dutch anti-poverty case shows, the policy involves starting from a given local problem or need as it is perceived by those who directly experience it. It rejects preconceived solutions, and programs that seek community participation as a means to service institutional ends.

For the community worker, these institutional initiatives involve an expanded field of action:

- At the grassroots level it means nurturing a sense of community among those excluded from the economic, social, and political spheres and encouraging them to form grass roots organizations to articulate common interests and participate in development planning through collaboration and negotiation as organized groups.
- At the organizational level it means working toward intersectoral, horizontally functioning partnerships in which people's organizations come to play an equal part.

Such approaches may be more realistic in the Western countries, with their liberal democracies and strong traditions of voluntarism and community activism. They would be more difficult to follow where a centralized state system is entrenched, to the detriment of people's lives at the community level; and where strong traditions of religion, paternalism, and patronage resist any change that is perceived as undermining the established order. The latter would certainly be the case for Bangladesh, and also for Ghana and Chile, particularly in the rural regions.

Popular and Community Participation

Participation is the sine qua non of CD. Without it, policies and programs that aim at people development, poverty alleviation, local development, community health, and social integration of the marginalized and excluded are likely to meet with little success. This is confirmed by increasing numbers of international studies, including this one, that point to the importance of participation in development and also explain the growing interest in participatory planning and development (Bhatnagar & Williams, 1992).

It should be noted, however, that development programs which see popular participation mainly as a cost-saving device (and there are many of them) are bound to fail unless other benefits, that are *perceived* as benefits by community participants, are aimed for and incorporated into participatory program planning. The Ghana case that evaluated income-generating projects, and focused on the perceptions of the participating women, provides an excellent illustration of this point and supports other studies on the subject (Finsterbusch, Van, & Warren, 1989; David, 1993). High on the list of 'real' benefits are increased spending power, new or better social and community services and facilities, and the acquisition of technology that reduces the drudgery of work and allows more time for social relations and recreational activities. At the more intangible level, participants must feel themselves empowered through their involvement in decision-making, and their increased awareness and exercise of their rights and responsibilities, as well as through skills learning, group solidarity, and community or group self-management.

For participation to be effective as a central value of CD, a number of additional factors must be in play, as pointed out and discussed by the six country studies. These include:

- An open and democratic environment.
- A decentralized policy with greater emphasis on local initiatives.
- Reform in public administration.
- Democratization of professional experts and officials.
- Formation of self-managing organizations of the poor and excluded.
- Training for community activism and leadership.
- Involvement of NGOs.
- Creation of collective decision-making structures at various levels that extend from the micro to the meso and macro levels and link participatory activities with policy frameworks.

The degree to which popular participation can be actively promoted among disadvantaged and excluded groups, especially as a strategy for socio-political and cultural development (i.e., not simply economic development), will vary depending on the government in power, the nature of democracy, and cultural traditions. This was highlighted particularly well in the Chilean study, but it also can be observed in the Bangladeshi and Israeli studies, in relation to the issue of empowerment of women in an environment of religious fundamentalism.

The need for decentralized policies and administrative reforms to permit increased community participation in decision-making has been addressed. What must be added here is that initiatives undertaken by state agencies that aim to improve the quality of life of people and that at the same time aim to strengthen CD should acknowledge the presence, knowledge, and experience of existing autonomous community organizations. To this end, such popular organizations could be designated as the funding channels for community or social development projects. Such action would not only show respect for local processes but also strengthen the capabilities of the community, as illustrated by the Canadian case 'Onward Willow.'

Too often, however, co-ordination committees for local development are set up with structures and procedures imposed by state agencies. This pushes aside existing grass roots organizations and undermines CD (see the Chilean case study on primary health care). To reverse this tendency, state officials and professional experts must learn to form horizontal partnerships with the community and consumers groups, and to abandon the traditional, top-down processes that characterize so many bureaucratic organizations. This calls for special training programs, which should include field work, as suggested by the authors of the Chilean study. The Canadian study on refugees is an excellent example of how relations between professionals and refugees can be transformed.

The adoption of participatory research by professionals would go one step further by applying the democratization process to science itself rather than just to officials and professionals. This form of research departs from conventional social science by bridging the distance between institutional researchers and community groups and by aiming for shared ownership of the research process. Both the Ghana and the Canadian studies in their respective research sections provided some detailed examples.

But institutional officials and professionals are not the only ones who require reorientation within the changed relationship between the state and civil society. With the renewed emphasis on community self-reliance and popular participation, people at the community level need to learn how to end their subordination to state programs, and turn toward community activism and self-managing ventures. The Israelis, through the Service for Community Work unit of the National Ministry of Labour and Social Affairs, have established local schools for training local activists (see case study). They target those who are or who wish to become active in neighbourhood committees, parent councils, community centres, social clubs, voluntary organizations (NGOs), and local branches of political parties. In a country characterized by a powerful state and centralist tendencies, these local schools have become an effective mechanism for building local leadership and an active civic society.

In Ghana, leadership training has always been an integral part also of CD, though this training now requires retooling to address contemporary economic and social realities. A different training model is provided in Quebec, where professional community workers, in partnership with neighbourhood leaders, train for pedagogical strategies based on conscientization and politicization models of practice.

NGOs, as organizational vehicles in the field of development, have become a vital and often indispensable force in promoting popular participation among the poor. This is very much apparent in Third World countries, as noted in all three country studies from the South. Development NGOs have considerable knowledge and experience in working with popular organizations. They provide appropriate educational and technical assistance in support of CD and collective self-help activities, thereby enriching participation (see the Chilean study). This ability of NGOs to reach out more effectively than state agencies to the grass roots through innovative projects has been recognized by by foreign aid ministries of the developed countries of the North, which support such efforts through partial funding. It has also been recognized by the state governments of host countries, many of which have adopted successful NGO initiatives in their own development programs (see the Bangladesh study). In this sense, NGOs are important intermediaries between communities in need and funders interested in practice innovations.

However, to increase the economic and social impact of participatory and CD activities, development NGOs need to move beyond the local communities and merge their own efforts with those of others. Furthermore, to achieve sustainable development, grass roots organizations, supported by NGOs, must work toward linking their development activities to the larger policy frameworks and resource bases of government. As Edwards and Hulme (1992) noted in their study of NGOs, the state is the ultimate arbiter and determinant of the wider political and policy changes on which sustainable development depends. In this sense, NGOs could serve well as mediating institutions between the community and the state in the context of the emerging economic and social order. The case on the elderly from Amsterdam is a good example of how local innovations can lead to national changes in policy when community workers are mindful of the significance of the results of their work.

The Social Justice Agenda and Human Rights

Social justice issues were once pursued mainly through social activist strategies, separate from any locality development agenda. More recent practice in CD incorporates a strategy that views disadvantage in terms of class differentiation, and of differences based on gender, race, ethnicity, religion, age grouping, or sexual orientation. Such an analysis has resulted in a more 'group development' focused form of practice, which is usually initiated at the local level and eventually extends to the regional, national, and sometimes international levels through participation in such social movements as human and civil rights, feminism, ecology, and so on. Such initiatives are often supported by NGOs in their role as educationors and advocates.

This additional dimension of CD practice is very much apparent in the cases from Canada on victims of torture, single-parent housing, and conscientization training. In the same vein, the Israeli study reported on successful cases where a community worker employed by the National Association of Social Workers helped local steering committees in distressed neighbourhoods to organize themselves into a national coalition to block government attempts to reduce the funds available for these neighbourhoods. The same community worker also assisted in setting up a national body of health service consumers that demanded certain amendments to the national health insurance act. The use of professional community workers by international, national, and regional NGOs, while still the exception rather than the norm, appears to be on the increase. The strategies followed in such cases link grass roots organizations addressing local development issues with broad-based human and civil rights movements through coalition-building and federated structures.

A social justice agenda is more difficult to pursue in poor agricultural societies. Having assessed the theory and reality of CD activity in Bangladesh, and having conducted extensive research and a literature review on the subject of power, Ali Akbar notes that the idea that the poor are unaware of oppressive social structures may not be true; however, whether they are aware or not, they lack the power to overcome the effects of inequality. There is also little evidence of class solidarity among the poor. It appears that the underprivileged learn to accept the unpleasant reality that it may be more pragmatic to offer loyalty to the élite so as to enjoy their protection and have access to resources. Thus, even when the poor form separate organizations, they tend to remain subordinate to the village system of power relations. Recent evidence, however, seems to indicate that a breakdown is occurring in those traditional patron/client relationships.

It is questionable whether NGOs that are dependent on external funding can promote large-scale organized action from the grass roots level. NGOs, especially international NGOs active in development work, will be tolerated as long as they are not perceived as a threat to vested interest groups. The Chilean study also reports how the state, during the military regime, prevented people's organizations and sponsoring NGOs from engaging in social actions focusing on social justice and human rights, by reserving political power for state agencies only.

The social justice agenda is closely related to the international debate about individual rights versus collective rights, principally of the poor. Western developed nations, with their liberal cultures, have tended to emphasize the civic and political rights of the individual, which are enshrined in the UN Charter and viewed as synonymous with democracy; advocates of the poor in Third World countries place greater emphasis on the enforcement of socio-economic rights, which are also backed up by international treaties. Yet NGOs active in international co-operation charge that the IMF ignores these socio-economic rights when it imposes structural adjustment programs (SAPs), which cut food subsidies, health, and education at a severe cost to the poor. The North's penchant for equating SAPs with democracy and human rights is even more insulting in cases where Southern governments clamp down on dissent in order to force people into new economic straightjackets (New Internationalist, 1993).

The issue of socio-economic rights is gaining increased attention as well from human rights activists and community workers in developed Northern countries as more and more people find themselves excluded economically, socially, and politically as a result of economic restructuring, a shrinking welfare state, and a hardening in the position of the public vis-à-vis welfare recipients, refugees, immigrants, and migrant workers.

Global Networking and the Emergence of a 'Worldwide Civil Society'
There is deep concern among thoughtful people across the world about the globalization of forces that undermine mutuality and solidarity among people at all levels: in their natural habitat, in work places, in their activities as citizens, and so on. To counter such forces and prepare adequately for practice in the twenty-first century, CD practitioners must adopt global networking strategies and techniques in their

professional activities to strike new partnerships in international social development and link the local with the global, and the global with the local (Campfens, 1996).

Specifically, new action strategies include the linking of grass roots organizations, NGOs, human rights activists, and development workers in both rich and poor countries, North and South, through the use of Internet, fascimile, teleconferencing, and other such electronic devices (in addition to the more traditional face-to-face working groups). Such electronic links allow an immediate mutual exchange of information and support for joint action related to development and human rights. International caucus groups of women, human rights activists, and international NGOs have already made effective use of these new devices and techniques to develop common action plans, and function as a counterbalance to the IMF, the World Bank, the World Trade Organization, multinational corporations, and other such global organizations.

The challenge for the new CD is to forge circles of mutuality and solidarity around the globe that will lead to the emergence of an active 'worldwide civil society,' and reinforce development and human rights work done at the local, regional and national levels.

CONCLUSION

As pointed out at the start of this part, changing economic, social, and political realities are redirecting the functions and roles of CD practitioners. These differ significantly, however, for each country because of the large variations in conditions and needs of diverse population groups. This is quite evident when we compare, for instance, the Netherlands and Bangladesh. The Netherlands is a highly developed welfare state with an advanced industrial economy and a large urban-based population that is becoming increasingly multicultural; Bangladesh, in contrast, is resource scarce, has a rural-based population that is in essence culturally homogeneous, and operates an economy that is mainly agricultural. From a theoretical perspective, this calls for the development of quite different 'action theories' which must consider the distinct needs and problems of the people of those countries. Each country study has considered this point and provides a critical and new theoretical perspective relevant to CD practice.

At the same time, the comparative analysis found in this book, besides highlighting the obvious contrasts, has identified a range of approaches to CD, along with common elements that together serve as the basis for developing a synthetic 'framework theory.' This framework is strongly grounded in an increased awareness of the new realities of practice that are facing each country as a result of the structural changes at the global and national levels.

The 'framework theory' that has emerged from this comparison of country studies is summarized here in broad outline as a conclusion to the research effort. It consists of three parts: context, approaches to CD, and common themes.

'FRAMEWORK THEORY' OUTLINE FOR POLICY DEVELOPMENT, PROGRAM PLANNING, AND CD PRACTICE

I. Contextual Factors
1. Global Environment: A Growing Interconnecting World
- The move from East–West ideological rivalry to a new reality of North–South and domestic inequalities.
- The rise of international capitalism, speculative money markets, and multinational corporations; and heightened competition for export markets.
- The dominant role of UN-affiliated institutions (such as the IMF, the World Bank, and the WTO) in shaping global economic realities.
- Breakthroughs in communications technology: facsimile transmission, the Internet.
- An increase in social turbulence, human rights abuses, and mass movements: refugees, migrant workers, immigrants.
- Population growth, primarily in the Third World.

2. National and Regional Characteristics
- Urban or rural; rural-urban migrations; urban issues.
- Ethno-cultural/religious homogeneity or heterogeneity.
- State of the economy: underdeveloped or developed (welfare state).
- Relations between state and civil society.
- Democratic environment: multiparty, single-party, dictatorial.
- Centralization, or decentralization with emphasis on local initiatives and control.

- Population groups excluded from economic, social, and political life.

II. Emerging Themes in CD Practice
- Nurturing associative communities and mobilizing circles of solidarity.
- Self-reliance, and the role of NGOs and the state.
- The people-development focus.
- The group and organizational expressions of popular and community participation.
- The social justice agenda and human rights.
- Global networking and a worldwide civil society.

III. Approaches to CD
- The 'continuum' approach to practice extending from the micro to the mezo and macro levels, including global networking.
- 'Group' or 'cooperative' development for mutual aid and social action.
- 'Locality' development, concerned with the quality of life in terms of community economic development, and with the live-ability of the physical and neighbourhood environment, and so on.
- 'Structural-functional' community work, working toward the development of relevant policy frameworks, and focusing on organizational structures, partnerships, and program integration.
- 'Categorical' focused CD, aimed at emancipation and self-reliance and at the alleviation and prevention of social problems; targeting particularly the economically, socially, and politically excluded and marginal population groups.
- The formation of 'self-managing' empowering organizations of the poor and excluded.
- The 'social learning' training workshops for experts and local activists.
- The 'intergroup' social integration approach relying on mutual understanding and conflict resolution measures.

References

Bhatnagar, B., & Williams, A. (eds.). (1992). *Partnership development and the World Bank: Potential and directions for change.* Washington, DC: World Bank.

Bingham, R., & Mier, R. (eds.). (1993). *Theories of local economic development: Perspective from across the disciplines.* London, U.K., and Newbury Park, CA: Sage.

Campfens, H. (1996). Partnerships in international social development. Evolution in practice and concept: A critical perspective. *International Social Work,* 39(2). April.

David, G. (1993). Strategies for grassroots human development. *Social Development Issues,* 12(2): 1–13.

Edwards, M., & Hulme, D. (eds.). (1992). *Making a difference: NGOs and development in a changing world.* London: Earthscan Publications.

Finsterbusch, K., Van, W., & Warren, A. (1989). Beneficiary participation in development projects: Empirical tests of popular theories. *Economic Development and Cultural Change,* 37(3): 573–93.

Instituto del Tercer Mundo (1995). *The world: A Third World guide 1995/96.* Montevideo: Uruguay.

International Association of Schools of Social Work. (1992). *New reality of poverty and struggle for social transformation.* Plenary papers and abstracts of the 25th International Congress of Schools of Social Work, Lima, Peru. Vienna: International Association of Schools of Social Work.

The New Internationalist (1993). New Light on Human Rights. *The New Internationalist,* No. 244 (June).

Rothman, J. (1987). Models of community organization and macro practice perspectives. In F. Cox, J. Erlich, J. Rothman, & J. Tropman (eds.), *Strategies of community organization.* Itasca, IL: Peacock Publishing (4th ed.).

– (1995). Approaches to community intervention. In J. Rothman, J. Erlich, & J. Tropman (eds.), *Strategies of community intervention.* Itasca, IL: Peacock Publishing.

UNICEF (1994). *The state of the world's children.* New York: United Nations Children's Fund.

Appendix:
Highlights of Cases Compared

Canada

1. Transforming relations between refugee groups, professionals, and the larger community.
    - An NGO centre serving torture victims as an invisible population in an ethnically and racially diverse community.
    - Creating a self-help, nonmedical model of integrated community services on a continuum from mental health to resettlement services and social integration.
    - Involving traditional grass roots work and leadership development training.
    - Focusing on empowerment of refugees as a high risk group through consciousness raising and mutual support groups; and linkage building between formal and informal resources through community networks, community education, and advocacy coalitions.
    - Participation in new social movements at the local level through a gendered view of community partnerships (women supporting women), and at the more global level through the human rights movement.
    - Extending the community concept from treatment to group, community, and international development – a continuity model of CD.

2. Single-parent women and community economic development
    - Women in poverty adopting an economic development strategy in which safe, affordable housing becomes the organizing tool for group and community development.

- Becoming self-reliant and self-empowered as women in housing design, property management, and ownership of a nonprofit housing society.
- Relating the personal to the political, leading to social action.
- Achieving social integration by linking up to the broader community through membership and participation in organizations.
- Decreasing dependency and vulnerability to economic interests in the larger society as a strategy for poverty alleviation.
- A 'bottom up' self-managing model of development through the formation of an independent community organization.

3. Kindling community capacity
   - A state-supported community-based prevention project focusing on children (0–8) residing in socio-economically disadvantaged neighbourhoods.
   - Mobilization of a community-based organization to develop and implement a locally relevant prevention program with the active participation of residents, community service providers, and state agencies.
   - A locality development model involving the creation of local organizational structures for collective action; adult education that integrates adults' life and community experience into a learning model of reciprocity; social support; and skills development in social competence.

4. The training and practice of conscientization in community work
   - Formation of a professional community workers' collective committed to the conscientization and politicization model in training and practice.
   - Collaboration between the professional collective and neighbourhood leaders in training for pedagogical strategies.
   - Liberation practice involving mutual education to bridge the social and cultural distance between the professional and the excluded (marginalized).
   - Ethical commitment to and belief in the dialectical analysis of existing social conditions as a practice requirement.
   - Application of conscientization to literacy, women's, health, public housing, mental health, immigration, and refugee issues.

The Netherlands

5. The antipoverty 'European Community' action program – the Dutch integrative approach.
   - Three project areas affected by de-industrialization and structural adjustment trends with activities aimed at the economic and social integration of excluded persons based on three basic principles: active participation of the 'excluded' in the selection, supervision and implementation of program activities through community based self-organization of potential beneficiaries; partnership in poverty alleviation between the social and business sectors and between professional and self-organizations seeking new, more horizontal collaborative forms of co-operation; and a multidimensional conception of poverty countering compartmentalization of the various official sectors in their delivery of service, and bureaucratization in relations between ordinary citizens, professionals, and officials.
   - The centrality in development planning of such factors as differences in local contexts; participatory planning in poverty alleviation starting out from a given problem in a local setting and not from a given solution or institutionally devised program; and the multidisciplinary and multisectoral approach, requiring institutional reform.
   - A functional model of community work not bounded by neighbourhood limits.

6. Environmentally focused CD
   - Three illustrations of community strategies advocating the interests of a neighbourhood in relation to the environment vis-à-vis the municipality.
   - Community work aimed at the formation of locally based residents' groups in the self-management of green spaces; neighbourhood councils, with resident and municipal representation, drawing up neighbourhood plans for liveability; and neighbourhood-based corporations to carry out projects involving recycling, repairs, trades, and local employment, carried out in partnership with the municipality.

- Key concepts include the liveability or quality of the environment regarding the building environment, poverty, green spaces, crime, transportation, and security; resident participation; and nurturing joint responsibility in the maintenance and management of the neighbourhood environment between the community and local government.
- A territorial model of community work focusing on the neighbourhood and its interests.

7. Flesseman neighbourhood services for the elderly
   - An inner city neighbourhood of Amsterdam with a high concentration of elderly, protected from redevelopment.
   - Formation of a neighbourhood foundation as a legal entity with representation of the elderly community to contract with public and private sector organization.
   - Reform in public financing shifting from institutional care to neighbourhood-based independent living, with support services in health, social support, mutual aid, home repairs, and professional advice in dealing with local authorities and health insurance companies.
   - Participation of the elderly in decision-making regarding essential services, location of facilities, and quality control in service delivery and management.
   - Community worker as facilitator, adviser and advocate to the elderly.
   - A categorical model of community work focusing on the elderly community and its interests.

Israel

8. Pioneering community work in a Jewish ultra-Orthodox neighbourhood
   - An attempt to open up a self-contained neighbourhood to the external world in a nonthreatening way
   - A pluralistic form of social integration.
   - Focusing on optimum participation and leadership development, especially among women, through the use of dialogue and program planning – a form of empowerment.
   - Building bridges of understanding and co-operation between men and women within the community and between the neighbourhood and municipality.

- Turning inherent conflicts into beneficial courses of action. This includes allocating resources from the city to the neighbourhood to meet various essential needs.
- In an ultra-Orthodox community, the legitimacy of the community worker is a key dimension of practice.

9. A community demonstration project for peace and welfare
   - The founding of a professional community social workers' collective (Ossim Shalom) committed to promoting welfare and peace in local communities.
   - A preventive, community-based approach to counter potential outbreaks of racial violence in low-income multiethnic neighbourhoods.
   - Formation of an intergroup steering committee of neighbourhood leaders, who serve as catalysts.
   - Leadership training workshops in conflict resolution, involving consciousness raising that focuses on the sources of fear and stereotyping, the building of trust, and working toward collaboration.
   - Partnership development involving the public sector, the voluntary sector, and the organized community (steering committee) to address unjust distribution in resources and services.
   - An intergroup conflict resolution model of CD.

10. Training local activists
    - A program initiative of the Service for Community Work (SCW) unit of the national Ministry of Labor and Social Affairs in collaboration with local authorities, to establish local schools for training citizens.
    - Targeting those who are or who wish to become active in grass roots groups and organizations such as neighbourhood committees, parent councils, community centres, social clubs, local voluntary organizations, and local branches of political parties.
    - Formation of a representative local steering committee responsible for adjusting the general curriculum to the unique circumstances, needs, and expectations of the local community; and for running the program, with actual training carried out by eight institutions.
    - Making use of various formal and informal teaching and learning techniques.

- Research on program impact indicates significant independence in functioning of local activists following graduation, in spite of intensive central-government involvement in the program's design.
- Considered an effective mechanism in building local leadership and an active civil society in a country characterized by a strong centralized state.

Ghana

11. Integrated community centres for employable skills (ICCES):
   A rural shelter project
   - A state-initiated community-based program of seventy centres aimed at reversing dependence on imported construction materials and fostering a greater use of local building resources.
   - Targeting school dropouts and illiterate youths for skills training, and creating employment in housing construction and building crafts.
   - Forming community self-help groups and production-oriented co-operatives in rural areas with input of start-up capital, skills training, tools, and expertise from government and NGOs as collaborative partners.
   - Centres are controlled by local ICCES managers together with town and village development committees, with government field-extension officers providing consulting services.

12. Income generating projects (IGPs) in southern Ghana:
   Women's perceptions
   - A state initiative with international NGO support, targeting low-income women and their development.
   - The production activities of women – related to agriculture, crafts, manufacturing, and fisheries – serve as organizing tools for individual improvement in health and welfare, for empowerment, and for group, community, and economic development.
   - Research findings show the following: improved technology reducing drudgery, saving time and improving women's health; empowerment of women through knowledge of rights and responsibilities, group solidarity, economic independence and community management; group solidarity as a central factor in fostering empowerment, giving common identity, settling

disputes, providing social support and mutual aid, and offering a forum to discuss women's problems; significant contribution to goods, services and development projects in the community; and limited potential of IGPs for increasing women's purchasing power in the absence of state projects to improve marketing, transportation, credit, taxes, resource inputs, and repayment periods.
- A group development model resulting in individual, social, economic, and community development.

Bangladesh

13. Nandanpur farmers' co-operative society:
   A two-tier co-operative system
   - Part of a major state policy on integrated rural development (Comilla model) introduced in the early 1970s aimed at assisting farmers in agricultural production.
   - Co-operative societies organized at the primary village level, with active participation of regular farmers; federated at the subdistrict level as a central co-operative association providing training and resource inputs from different state agencies.
   - An updated scheme brings landless men and women and small farmers into separate co-ops. (The original Comilla model was designed to bring all villagers into a cooperative society regardless of their of resources and status.)
   - Activities include leadership development, loan procurement for investment in agricultural production, encouraging accumulation of savings, providing opportunities for employment, and undertaking works of rural development.
   - Co-op service extension is provided to the village community in health education, family planning, sanitation, prevention of diseases, and arbitration of family and social disputes. Social harmony and community participation is encouraged.
   - A structurally imposed, self-reliant co-op model of local economic and social development with input of external resources.

14. Mohanpur rural mothers' centre
   - Part of a state-administered and World Bank–funded social service program.

- Targeting primarily the 'extremely poor' village mothers, who are organized into associations that provide a forum for discussion and training, and a channel for dissemination of information and essential resources.
- The regional social service officer, as community worker, mobilizes support of the community leadership for a Mothers' Centre, and secures co-operation of other state agencies and NGOs.
- Activities include arranging skills training and credit for income-generating ventures; and organizing education efforts in family planning, health, education, sanitation, maternal and child care, and related areas of social development, with the assistance of trade instructors and supervisors.
- A women's model of group development, education, and integrated service delivery for poverty alleviation.

15. The Shishapara landless group
    - Part of an 'integrated plan of rural poverty alleviation and employment creation' among the landless by a leading international NGO (CARITAS), introduced in 1989 and expanding on an earlier pilot project initiated in 1979.
    - Formation of separate co-operative groups for men and women, federated at the subdistrict level (along with 200–300 groups) into a general council for social development.
    - The plan integrates nonformal education for increased awareness, with emphasis placed on income-earning schemes and programs for personal and social development.
    - Frequent group meetings to develop solidarity and opportunities for skills training, to encourage savings for capital accumulation, and to decide on profit distribution and planning programs in partnership with CARITAS.
    - Group participation in promoting such social justice issues as fair wages for landless labourers and women's rights.
    - A co-op model aimed at achieving self-reliance.

16. Family development program for women in urban slums
    - A municipality-administered 'integrated social service' program, assisted by revolving funds from UNICEF, that works through a community-based project committee which draws up yearly action plans.

- Targets urban households in extreme poverty, which are organized into work groups that provide a forum for learning and a channel for resources and services from state and municipal agencies and NGOs.
- Action strategy involves selecting of slum areas, identifying target households, forming groups, which then have representation on the project committee, providing loans for income-earning activities, and arranging delivery of a range of social services.
- Experience indicates that support of the community leadership is required in forming work groups of extremely poor women, who are difficult to mobilize.
- Similar to the mother's centre program.

17. Slum improvement project in Rajshahi City
   - A UNICEF initiative, in partnership with the municipality, to work with slum dwellers (primarily women) to improve the physical infrastructure (tubewells, latrines, drains, internal roads, streetlights, dust bins) and living standards (through income-generating activities and social development programs).
   - A basically top-down organizational structure headed by the mayor, with a project implementation committee on which are represented different city departments and women from eight slums. Project is organized into 109 groups of ten to fifteen members, who in turn form project subcommittees assisted by community organizers and health workers.
   - A community model combining environmental and people-oriented development.

Chile

18. Solidarity and social initiatives fund (FOSIS)
   - A state fund used as a tool by many Latin American governments to address the social effects of structural adjustment policies, or structurally caused poverty as is the case in Chile.
   - Targeting extreme poverty, with special emphasis on underprivileged youth and poor rural areas, with the objective of improving livelihood, working conditions, and social integration.

- Funding creative proposals that integrate actions of different public agencies and NGOs at a decentralized level and aim to strengthen development capabilities of the community through direct participation in local co-ordinating committees of those to whom the program is directed.
- A local-community development model targeting the poor and their integration.

19. Program for the improvement of quality and fairness in education (MECE)
    - A state initiated educational policy.
    - Targeting children of the poorer sectors of the population.
    - Addressing content taught in relation to the local social realities of poor children, deficiencies in teaching methodology, and the poor quality of study areas (home and school).
    - Use of specialized teacher workshops that organize teachers and assistant teachers of infants, mothers, the young, professionals, technicians, promoters, and local leaders into groups at the local level for training in the methodology of working with adults, families, and community; local culture, group dynamics, and local development; the reality of infancy, participative diagnosis, planning, and project management.
    - A second set of workshops for local integration at the national level for training in local diagnosis and project elaboration.
    - A community-based educational model that mediates between universal knowledge and popular knowledge and that comes from the lived experience of daily life with children at the local level, thus promoting a heterogeneity of locally based initiatives in child education.

20. Area for basic primary health attention, Ministry of Health
    - A state initiated and controlled project, based on a policy of decentralization, intersectoral participation of state services and executive actions of the community; aimed at improving the quality of life of the population.
    - Establishment of a 'unit for social participation' to strengthen ties between the ministry and NGOs (evidently of ministerial priority) and to support community work (largely neglected).
    - Use of a national workshop that trained a strategic group of 18 basic primary health teachers, who in turn trained 680 new

monitors in 29 regional workshops, and so on, reaching eventually a total of 11,000 local operatives.

- The strategy included the formation of new local health groups in line with the state project, bypassing existing local health committees and grass roots organizations with their rich experience and knowledge of local conditions and resources.